Vamps, Virgins and Victims

A new series of books from Casssell's Sexual Politics list, Women on Women *provides a forum for lesbian, bisexual and heterosexual women to explore and debate contemporary issues and to develop strategies for the advancement of feminist culture and politics into the next century.*

COMMISSIONING:

Roz Hopkins
Liz Gibbs
Christina Ruse

Vamps, Virgins and Victims

How Can Women Fight AIDS?

Robin Gorna

Foreword by Jonathan Mann

CASSELL

For a catalogue of related titles in our Sexual Politics/Global
Issues list, please write to us at the address below.

Cassell
Wellington House
125 Strand
London WC2R 0BB

215 Park Avenue South
New York
NY 10003

First published 1996

British Library Cataloguing-in-Publication Data
A catalogue record for this book is available from the British Library.

ISBN: 0-304-32807-3 (hardback)
      0-304-32809-X (paperback)

Cover: based on 'Women on Women' series design by Spark Ceresa.

Typeset by Keystroke, Jacaranda Lodge, Wolverhampton
Printed and bound in Great Britain by Biddles, Guildford and
King's Lynn

Contents

For
Kate Thomson
and
Dean X Johnson

Foreword

Those who know Robin Gorna will surely not be surprised by this book – by its concentrated energy, its gently argumentative way of getting at the facts and its activist passion. Fortunately, Ms Gorna has all these qualities in abundance, for a book about women and AIDS is inevitably more: it is necessarily also about health and society. And a book about women and AIDS must inevitably challenge – for the vulnerability of women to AIDS is determined by, and embedded within, a societal status quo which must no longer be allowed to escape its responsibility.

A long path has led from victim blaming to recognizing the societal dimensions of vulnerability to AIDS – and, by extension, to other health problems such as cancer, heart disease, injuries and violence. Societies work very hard to prevent people from seeing through the veil of myth, fantasy and propaganda which is used to hide the realities of health and disease. For example, the simple fact that the rich live longer and healthier lives than the poor is so easily ignored; society distracts us to consider instead the individual misfortunes and tragedies occurring to poor people. Similarly, societies work hard to conceal the connection between discrimination – towards women, or homosexuals, or adolescents – and vulnerability to many causes of preventable illness, disability and premature death, including AIDS.

Through struggles against AIDS, for women's health, and for health for all, we can now perceive the underlying societal factors which determine health status. Those whose human rights and dignity are respected within each society live healthier lives, for they are able to make and carry out those free and informed choices which are vital for the health of individuals and societies. In contrast, those who, even before any health problem such as AIDS emerges, are marginalized, stigmatized and discriminated against will bear the burden of illness, disability and premature death. The struggle for health and the struggle for human rights and dignity are now understood to be inextricably linked.

Thus, AIDS has sounded the clarion call or, if you prefer, the alarm. Once discovered, brought to the light of day, understood and acted upon, the health impacts of social injustice, discrimination and violation of human rights and dignity can no longer be denied or ignored. Once individual misfortunes are converted into an awareness of injustice, the process of societal change becomes imperative, if not inevitable.

Ms Gorna merits high praise for undertaking the tremendous challenge of this subject and for focusing her discussion on one society – the United Kingdom. It is far easier to speak clearly about somewhere else and to identify someone else's problems than to direct the spotlight upon one's own society, history and culture. It is also easier to criticize than to propose ways forward. Ms Gorna does both, for only if we can identify, and uproot, the profound and pervasive discrimination against women in our own society can we truly deliver a message of hope and confidence to others.

In the end, this well-informed, passionate book is about hope and confidence: in our ability to analyse and respond, in our capacity to promote and protect human rights and dignity. It also expresses hope and confidence about our world, in each other and, ultimately, in ourselves.

Jonathan M. Mann, MD, MPH
François-Xavier Bagnoud Professor of Health and
Human Rights and Professor of Epidemiology and International
Health, Harvard School of Public Health, Boston

Preface

In September 1986, when I became a volunteer with the Terrence Higgins Trust (THT), a total of twelve women and three girls in the UK had been diagnosed with AIDS. I volunteered because I cared about the impact AIDS was having on gay men, not from any sense of the effects it could have on women. My initial involvement in AIDS work was in fighting a disease that affected other people. I suspect that this is true for most women involved in early AIDS work. I remain firmly committed to combating the devastation AIDS has on the lives of gay men and their communities – and, some ten years on, my activism has developed additional dimensions as the AIDS crisis has evolved.

Throughout this book I use the term 'AIDS' liberally, both to refer to the Acquired Immune Deficiency Syndrome and also to the complicated social reality this medical condition has come to represent. Many of my colleagues in the AIDS industry[1] would use 'HIV/AIDS', but I find the term 'AIDS' more useful as it incorporates the total societal construct that leads to fear and discrimination, in a way that references to the virus do not. I use the term 'HIV' when I am referring specifically to the Human Immunodeficiency Virus.

The scope of this book is huge. I have frequently wondered why I was so foolish as to consider all the ways in which women are impacted by AIDS – I would be astonished if anyone wrote a tome on 'Men and AIDS'. The scope is at least restricted to women in the industrialized world, and principally those living in the UK. Compared to women in the developing world, and to men in Britain, there are relatively small numbers of women with HIV or AIDS in the UK. However, this is one of the reasons why the impact AIDS is having on women requires analysis. The situation facing women in developing countries[2] and in the USA[3] have been well documented, yet the interactions with poverty, race and scale are remarkably different. By focusing on the situations elsewhere, it is easy to avoid the painful complexities of the issues women face in respect of AIDS in the UK.

Responses to AIDS and HIV, and the people experiencing these medical conditions, have been underpinned by prejudice and discrimination. Overwhelmingly, the discrimination is rooted in fear and hatred of the populations most affected by this life-threatening condition, principally gay men. In the early 1980s, AIDS was often described as a 'gay plague', but towards the end of that decade there was a mainstreaming of the condition. Commentators shifted their focus to 'heterosexual AIDS' and AIDS workers promoted notions of HIV as an 'equal opportunities virus'. From 1992 there has been a backlash against approaches which conceal the excessive impact AIDS and HIV continue to have on gay men. These responses, known as 're-gaying', are shifting the resourcing of AIDS work and public perceptions of the epidemic, but how do they impact on understanding about the increasing effects of HIV on women?

In Chapter 1 I look at some of the different ways in which AIDS is conceptualized, and how the linking of AIDS and women affects public understandings of the epidemic. Deconstructing phrases which have been used to normalize AIDS shows that they conceal more than they reveal. Normalising discourses pump out images of a safe and sexless epidemic. The simplistic generalizations deny the complex and uneven ways in which AIDS challenges women's lives. Instead of making visible the marginalization of women living with HIV (and vulnerable to acquiring the virus), these notions create an image of a bland egalitarian epidemic.

Most popular understanding of AIDS has been mediated by the press, television and radio broadcasts. In Chapter 2 I examine some of the most common media representations of women and AIDS. Women are frequently used by the media in order to hetero-sexualize AIDS, but there are also stories where women take centre stage. On these occasions, the discourses range between stodgy victimologies of infantilized women, through stories of selfless madonnas abandoning all for their offspring, to priests' fantasies of vampish, lewd women avenging society through their diseased bodies.[4] The ways in which the epidemic is conceptualized and represented are not troubling only for women living with the virus, or profoundly affected by it. The linking of women and AIDS tends to buy into pre-existing prejudices about women, and intensifies fears of women's sexuality. It is just as damaging for other women seeking to protect their sexual health and express their sexuality.

The sensationalism of many media accounts of women and AIDS, and the preference of journalists for interviewing women rather than men, creates an imbalanced picture of how AIDS and HIV are increasing among women. In Chapter 3, I review the epidemiology to consider what is known about the numbers of women acquiring the virus. During 1994, for example, 188 women and 23 girls were newly diagnosed with AIDS. More than fifteen times as many women had developed the condition in those twelve months as had *ever* developed it at the time when I became a THT volunteer. Reviewing the figures does not simply reveal the mammoth growth in women infected with HIV, but also shows how much is concealed in the ways these figures are reported. Simple considerations, like a woman's sexual orientation, are not recorded, and the disproportionate impact of HIV and AIDS on women from Africa is hard to glean from the statistics.

The reality of women's lives is invisible in epidemiological reports, and the medical realities for women living with HIV and AIDS tend to be equally concealed in clinical descriptions of the condition. In Chapter 4, I look at what is known about the different impacts HIV disease has on women's bodies. In particular this highlights the many questions which remain unanswered or unasked, and which need to be advocated by treatment activists. In the US, treatment activism has been a key component of communities' responses to the AIDS crisis, yet this is something which receives far less attention in the UK and the rest of Europe. This is due to cultural and socio-economic differences (in the US patients are purchasers of their healthcare), and also to the stages of the epidemic (it is older in the States, and consequently there are far larger numbers of people who have become ill).

The European AIDS Treatment Group (EATG) is the first structure to develop treatment activism in Europe, and I have been a part of it since the first meeting in 1991. Initially I became involved as a funder because I was on secondment to the European

Commission (EC). During that time I was required to attend numerous conferences, and had numerous opportunities to stare blankly at scientific data and slowly begin to understand. My last EC project was a European meeting of self-help groups, where I spent my time with a small group of HIV-positive women. I was shocked by how little these women knew about what was happening to their bodies, or felt able to enter into dialogue with their doctors, or access information. As we talked the women encouraged me to become involved in treatment activism, and when I left the EC I joined EATG. Immediately after I left the EC I went to work for the 1992 International AIDS Conference. This gave me opportunities to develop my activism around women and AIDS, and I was extremely fortunate to learn from leading academics and researchers who guided me, both individually and by their elegant conference presentations, through the science: psychosocial, epidemiological, clinical and basic. They empowered me to trust that, although I stopped biology at the age of thirteen, I could understand research data – and ultimately present in this book a layperson's understanding of science. (Most of the scientific detail has been checked by scientists, but any crass simplifications or faults remain my own.)

Like Chapter 4, Chapters 6 and 7 are scientifically based. In Chapter 6 I review the evidence that exists for how a woman can acquire HIV. The rules of HIV transmission can be reduced to three modes of infection: penetrative sexual intercourse, shared drugs-injecting equipment, and from a mother to her baby. However, there are significant debates about the precise mechanisms by which transmission happens, especially from sex – for example, whether HIV enters through the cervix only, or also the vaginal wall. Chapter 7 looks at HIV transmission in the other direction, that is, from an HIV-infected woman. As well as examining what is known about women's infectivity to men in sex (and finding that it is lower than in the opposite direction), I pull together current thinking about how a woman can transmit HIV to her child and how this can be reduced from the already low rate of one in seven.

Part of my personal motivation to research the scientific facts of HIV transmission has been the debate about whether women can acquire HIV from sex with an HIV-infected woman.

My reading of the science suggests that this is highly unlikely, and only on the bounds of possibility if sex toys are shared without being cleaned. However, this debate has never focused on the scientific facts, but has a more complex agenda. I discuss the heat generated by this element of lesbian responses to AIDS, and my perceptions of why they have arisen, in Chapter 10.

In Chapter 5, I look at some of the psychosocial impacts on women affected by the AIDS crisis. In this book I am not solely concerned with the effects AIDS has on the lives of women who are living with HIV in their bodies, although they retain a central focus. After reviewing some of the non-clinical ways HIV-positive women are affected – for example, because of the isolation which most experience – I look at the greater numbers of women who are profoundly impacted by AIDS. This includes the lovers of people living with HIV, and the lesbian, bisexual and heterosexual women who care, as relatives, informal and formal carers, as well as workers in the field. As a member of the massed ranks, I am keen that these women's untold histories are made more visible, and to explore the diversity of ways in which women carers are affected by AIDS, including how this impacts on their sexualities.

Many factors affect a woman's ability to avoid HIV. Since nearly all HIV-infected women acquired the virus from sex with men, the ways in which women's sexualities are understood and promoted are of major importance, and some of these elements are considered in Chapter 8. Understanding women's sexuality entails considering the economics of risk, ranging from the financial dependence many women experience in marriage, to the extremes of poverty which lead women to exchange sex for goods. Commercial sex work does not need to be a risk in itself, and prostitute women may have much to teach others about their commitment to safer sex. By contrast, sexual violence is a major threat for women, and rape, abuse and coercive sex are rendered more terrorizing by the fact that they can facilitate HIV transmission. As well as addressing the neglect of sexual violence, it is also essential to promote women's sexual pleasure and enhance the opportunities women have to explore their unique sexual desires. It is from a position of strength that women are most likely to be able to choose safer behaviour and avoid HIV.

Chapter 9 looks at the ways in which safer sex can be promoted and how women can be supported to avoid acquiring HIV. This looks at the paucity of technologies available to women to prevent HIV transmission. Research into the role of diaphragms has never been undertaken adequately, and, although efforts to develop a microbicide are under way, it will be many years before a reliable female-controlled HIV-prevention technology is available. Although the only technologies currently available are either worn by men (the male condom) or require male consent (the female condom), safer sex is essential for many women. This chapter also considers the best mechanisms for promoting healthy sexual behaviour, and in particular how empowerment models can provide a holistic approach.

Finally, the book ends with an activist agenda of steps women can take to fight the AIDS crisis. There is much that individual women can do to confront the harms caused by HIV and AIDS, to protect their own health, to support women living with the virus, and to promote a fairer understanding of the epidemic's effects.

Notes

1. The phrase 'AIDS industry' has extensive negative connotations, but it is useful shorthand to describe those workers dedicated to preventing HIV and developing services for people living with HIV. The numbers of people undertaking this work have grown swiftly since I became involved in 1986, and this is (mostly) a good thing. What is problematic is not necessarily the size of the industry, but that co-ordination and a shared direction are often lacking.

2. M. Berer, with S. Ray, *Women and HIV/AIDS: An International Resource Book*, Pandora, London, 1993.

3. For example, G. Corea, *The Invisible Epidemic: The Story of Women and AIDS*, HarperPerennial, New York, 1992; The ACT UP NY Women & AIDS Book Group, *Women, AIDS and Activism*, South End Press, Boston, 1990.

4. In September 1995, Father Michael Kennedy told his parishioners in Dungarvan, Southern Ireland, that an 'angel of death' had visited their town, bent on revenge sex. He claimed she had sex with eighty men in a couple of months and had infected at least five of them with HIV. The medical authorities were not aware of any increase in infections. Father Kennedy later withdrew his assertion, but it was too late to stop many in the press using this 'mythical vamp' for their own purposes.

Acknowledgements

My deepening awareness of the issues women face in respect of AIDS dates back to 1989 when I undertook some work with Sue O'Sullivan. She formed my thinking about sex more than it is decent to record, and also introduced me to the links between existing feminist arguments and what was happening with AIDS. The same year I met Kate Thomson, and she continually inspires me and teaches me about the needs of HIV-positive women. Their insights have threaded through the generalist AIDS work I have undertaken since then, and informed my growing understanding of the personal effects of AIDS on my life. When I was invited to write a book about AIDS, it was inevitable I should want to look at a feminist dimension. I would never have tried to write this without the faith placed in me by Joanna Moriarty, and I thank her for the initial generous support in suggesting this and clarifying my thinking. I am very grateful to Steve Cook and Cassell for taking the book so eagerly when I had to leave Sheldon.

This book has not been written in the cloister of academia, but in the midst of my AIDS activism. I have taken far longer than I wanted, because of the demands of living with the daily horror of this epidemic. However, I have been very fortunate in being simultaneously invited to carry out work that has informed and matured my understanding of the issues. Positively Women asked me to analyse all the data from their research into seventy-five HIV-positive women and compile the report *Women Like Us*. Although other research has observed the needs of HIV-positive women, this was the first piece of research generated and controlled by HIV-positive women themselves. I also compiled the leaflet on symptoms and treatments which is published by Positively Women and THT. I am grateful to the *National AIDS Manual* who invited me to research and write much of their material on women; to Gordon Nary at the *Journal of the International Association of Physicians*

in AIDS Care, who sent me to document many clinical conferences; and the International Community of Women living with HIV
and AIDS, whose European project I helped to co-ordinate. Thanks
also to Rita O'Brien and Cath Jackson who employed me to
research sex education in schools, and to compile guidance on
AIDS for the Health Visitors' Association. When the manuscript
was in the home run, I returned to the Terrence Higgins Trust, and
I am grateful to all my colleagues for their immense support and
forebearance in the end stages of this project.

Throughout this project, Keith Alcorn has been a constant
source of inspiration and support. He talked through the science
repeatedly, fed me references and read, reread, and commented on
many chapters. I am also indebted to Dr Mike Bailey, Frances
Williams, Dr Lucia Grun, Barbara James, Kate Thomson, Debbie
Vowles, Ruth Parry, Suzanne Rose and Kelly Hunter, whose
insights improved the chapters they read. Helen Sandler was ruth-
less in cutting through my verbosity and I am grateful for her skill.
The faults remain my responsibility, and they would be far worse
without all of their guidance.

Della Hirons, librarian at THT, is notorious for her
dazzling efficiency and exhaustive knowledge, and I am indebted
to her for responding to my unreasonable requests with grace,
good humour and reams of photocopied papers. I am also grateful to Kristina Bird and Sara Thomas, at the National HIV
Prevention Information Service, who provided source material and
repeatedly helped me to think through and digest the information.
I have debated the issues extensively with Edward King and Simon
Watney, and their continued support has been essential.

The new game of book-writing landed me in two crises,
through which I was gently coaxed by the wise counsel of Richard
Kirker, Rowan Williams, Jane Havell and Sara Maitland; I am
immensely grateful to them. My thanks also to Caroline Armstrong,
Nermin Bindal, Ethan Maynard, Joe Mills and Chitra Ramgoolam,
who have been bedrocks of support for this and the rest of my life.

I have benefited from the help of many people who have
informed my ability to write this book, by providing me with
ideas, material, or simply offering their insight and encouragement.
Thanks to Dr Frans van den Boom, Father David Campbell, David

Corkery (an unsung hero of this epidemic), Katie Deverell, Professor Anke Ehrhardt, Dr Karin Galil, Sue George, Dr Diana Gibb, Professor Nobby Gilmore, Dr Kate Hankins, Dr Frank Johnstone, Dr Jayne Kavanagh, Sylvia Kelcher, Holly Ladd, Frankie Lynch, Neil McKenna, Professor Jonathan Mann, Ruth Morgan-Thomas, Kate O'Neill, Dr Jurgen Poppinger, Richard Rector, Dr Lorraine Sherr, Alison Thomas, Rachel Thomson, Peter Weatherburn and Tony Whitehead.

All of my friends have shown extraordinary patience with my interminable book crises, and I thank them for their generosity, in particular Monik Charette, Jonathan Cooper, Maurice, Marina and Margot Forsythe, Virginia Gorna, Steve Haines, Harriet Hill, Ky Hoyle, Dean X Johnson, Lenny Johnson, Mary, Pete, Harriet and Phoebe Kaspar, Helen Mountfield, Chris Murgatroyd, Jamie Taylor, Kate Thomson, Sophie Walters, Robert Warden, Paul Wiley, Dr Jay Wilkinson. And thanks Vicki and Mike.

Since I started to write, many friends and colleagues have died, and I am bored and enraged by the monotony of loss. My world is less without David O'Donnell, Johan Westenberg, Jim Wilson, Nathalie Dagron, and Stephen Anderson, Benn Brown, Charmain Duff, Tomas Fabregas, Jan Haan, Michael Howard, Arne Husdal, Bil McManus, Simon Mansfield, John Mordaunt, Jim Myer, Eddie Peters, Will Pressley, Michael Sharp and Jonathan Varker-Littlewood.

List of Abbreviations

ACT UP   The Aids Coalition To Unleash Power
AIDS   Acquired Immune Deficiency Syndrome
AJPH   *American Journal of Public Health*
ASO   AIDS Service Organization
BMJ   *British Medical Journal*
CDC   Centers for Disease Control and Prevention (USA)
CDR   *Communicable Disease Report*
CDSC   Communicable Disease Surveillance Centre (UK)
CIN   cervical intraepithelial neoplasia
ECS   European Collaborative Study
ESG   European Study Group on Heterosexual Transmission
          of HIV
GMFA   Gay Men Fighting AIDS
GMHC   Gay Men's Health Crisis
GP   *General Practitioner*
GUM   genito-urinary medicine
HEA   Health Education Authority
HIV   Human Immunodeficiency Virus
HPV   Human Papilloma Virus
IDU   injecting drug-user
J.AIDS *Journal of Acquired Immune Deficiency Syndromes*
JAMA   *Journal of the American Medical Association*
MMWR   *Morbidity and Mortality Weekly Reports*
N9   Nonoxynol 9
NEJM   *New England Journal of Medicine*
PCP   *Pneumocystis carinii pneumonia*
PCR   polymerase chain reaction
PHLS   Public Health Laboratory Service
PID   pelvic inflammatory disease
STD   sexually transmitted disease
THT   Terrence Higgins Trust
WHO   World Health Organization

Chapter one

A Queer Disease

'Heterosexual AIDS' did not shift the equation AIDS=
Queer; rather, these heterosexuals were counted as queer
because they got AIDS.

Cindy Patton[1]

AIDS began among gay men – at least in the UK and the
USA – and it is bizarre not to look at the current impact of AIDS
on every population within this context. In the context of
AIDS, links between women and gay men are rarely made, except
perhaps to say that talking about gay men and AIDS makes women
invisible.[2] Women have a lot in common with gay men – not
least that many get fucked by men. In mainstream society, the
sexualities of both are either ignored, or perceived as a rampant,
uncontrollable force. A lot of straight men seem to be so afraid
that they exclude women and gay men from decision-making,
policy-making and images of 'normality'. The realities of their lives
often go unheard, and when they speak out about their needs they
are ignored or accused of 'special pleading'. These are just a
few of the reasons why women – like gay men – are vulnerable to
HIV (the virus which can cause AIDS[3]). In the UK gay men (and
bisexual and other 'men who have sex with men'[4]) continue to
have the greatest vulnerability to HIV, since they are far more
likely than women to be fucked by an HIV-infected[5] man.
Although people with haemophilia[6] and injecting drug users have
also been badly affected, new infections are now extremely rare
among people with haemophilia and declining among drug users.
Currently, after gay men and bisexual men, the group in society
which is most vulnerable to HIV is women who have sex with men.

2 : *Vamps, Virgins and Victims*

Self-evidently, there are many things women don't have in common with gay men, and one of them is the way (as a group) women have been affected by the AIDS crisis. It is estimated that up to 25 per cent of gay men in British cities have HIV;[7] it will be a long time before a quarter of all women have HIV – and probably this will never happen. Yet, the potential for sharp increases in HIV infection among women is real and under way. At local, national and global levels the absolute numbers, percentages and rates of increase of women with HIV and AIDS have grown steeply since AIDS was first identified. For example, between June 1993 and June 1994 there was a 10 per cent increase in the number of male AIDS cases, but a 37 per cent increase in cases in females.[8] When absolute numbers are small, percentages are easily distorted and it is important to be wary about misinterpreting such statistics.[9] Even so, this 37 per cent increase does demonstrate an important, growing epidemic among women – a growing epidemic seen throughout the world.[10] These statistics refer to AIDS cases, and since on average it takes ten years for a person infected with HIV to develop symptoms of AIDS, it suggests that in the early 1980s (say between 1983 and 1984) there was a 37 per cent increase in HIV infections among women. There is no accurate data about the current rate of HIV increase among women, but in the UK HIV could be increasing at least 15 per cent faster than among men.[11]

Caution is essential when considering such statistics, yet it is rarely applied. HIV continues to be a major health concern for the first groups infected, and it still disproportionately affects gay men and bisexual men. The fact of increasing HIV infections among women does not mean that somehow the epidemic has lifted up and moved on to different populations, leaving behind those first affected. With infectious diseases there is always a clustering effect, and so it is with HIV and AIDS. This rarely happens with other life-threatening diseases, such as cancer, unless they are linked to environmental factors (like a local nuclear processing plant). The social and geographical scattering of most life-threatening conditions means that multiple loss and grief will be rare, whereas this is not the case for AIDS. In the initial phases of the AIDS epidemic the cases are necessarily connected, because HIV is transmitted intimately from one person to another. The continued clustering of HIV and AIDS is inevitable in this early history of the disease, as is the increasing move away from these clusters. You would be hard-pressed to see that reality in most of the UK public health and media presentations of the epidemic which wilfully encourage a vision of respectable 'heterosexual AIDS'.

The heterosexual AIDS terminology obscures important differences in the way HIV affects heterosexual women and heterosexual men. It is used as a catch-all phrase to encompass the impact of HIV on all women, and all men who are not noticeably tainted with an aura of homosexuality. The construct of heterosexuality in this context is extremely unhelpful since it postulates an unreal identification with sexual orientation for the majority of the population whose sexual object choice has never been in doubt. The swing towards a heterosexual AIDS discourse has clear political roots, which become most evident in the light of the other constructions that emphasize everything but the queer epidemic. Indeed, since the beginning of public-information campaigns about AIDS in the UK, the central public health message has been 'AIDS Is Everyone's Issue', which slips into the facile phrase 'HIV Is an Equal Opportunities Virus'.

AIDS is not heterosexual, it is not normal, and it has nothing to do with equal opportunities – AIDS is special. The most common representations of AIDS in the UK are fallacious, value-laden fantasies, and so it becomes important to describe the broad elements of this difference, to define the reality of the current epidemic. Since 1992 there has been a surge of energy from gay men demanding that AIDS is understood as a 'gay disease'. So much so that I am just waiting for an activist like Larry Kramer[12] to suggest we reclaim the most-loathed phrase 'gay plague' (the notion of AIDS=plague is gaining ground in New York City). From an epidemiological, and social, perspective it is easy to have sympathy with those who emphasize the gay dimensions of the disease. The vast majority of British people with AIDS and HIV are gay men, and the prevalence of HIV among gay men is far higher than among any other community. But what does calling AIDS a gay disease mean to an HIV-positive woman, or indeed a feminist addressing the realities of AIDS? The HIV-positive woman may be a minority among people with HIV, and within her own community, but she is a growing minority, and one with specific needs and concerns which are frequently rendered invisible. At least the term 'hetero-sexual AIDS' has the advantage of being inclusive of women – but, given its problems, perhaps we could conceive of AIDS as a 'woman's disease'? Perhaps, but frankly neither the numbers nor the rationale are there. For me, the only catch-all is to see AIDS as a 'queer disease' – an inadequate description, but it goes some way towards capturing the complexity, strangeness and non-conformity of AIDS reality.

Patton also detects that there is a 'queer paradigm' central to the representation of AIDS. She describes how 'the insistence that AIDS is somehow a mark of perversion transforms infected persons into "queers", regardless of their exposure route'.[13] AIDS is a queer disease because it affects queers and it is queer, in the sense of not normal. AIDS has always suffered the moral repro-bation of the right. It is an unacceptable disease, the disease that has no name, the disease that is miraculously transformed in obituaries to 'a long-standing illness', or on death certificates to 'pneumonia'. AIDS is a disease of the margins, infecting and affect-ing people who are denied their humanity by society at large, whose concerns and lifestyles are dismissed as 'perverted' or 'extreme' and who are not afforded the respect given to the white, middle-class, able-bodied, heterosexual male minority. Those who have been infected with HIV, but who live outside the queer world of the margins, who are not poor, who are not black, who never shot drugs (or knew anyone who did), who are not lesbian, gay or bisexual (and never knew anyone who was), these people become queer when they acquire HIV or AIDS. AIDS is queer because stigma sticks.

The notion of AIDS as a queer disease is terminology that will offend some people with HIV or AIDS, and be welcomed by others. There is no terminology that will be welcomed by all: how many are offended by the description 'heterosexual AIDS'? Perhaps there is no need to find such a definition – after all, why define what is not definitive? Perhaps people will, as Susan Sontag desires, come to appreciate the pure fact of illness and cease to invest it with higher meaning. Yet for so long as they do, AIDS needs to be contextualized – and if activists don't do so, our detractors and the media will do it for us. Notions of equal AIDS and heterosexual AIDS promote a constant confusion between what is happening and what could develop, between actuality and potential. Potentially, people from all walks of life will acquire HIV – actually the bulk of UK cases of HIV and AIDS are among gay and bisexual men, drug-using women and men, women and men from Africa, and their sexual partners. 'AIDS is not randomly distributed', state Black American feminists Gasch and Fullilove, 'HIV disease is concentrated in "high-risk" communities.'[14]

Heterosexual AIDS

The principal aim underpinning most discussions of women and AIDS seems to be to prove that Britain is on the brink of a 'heterosexual epidemic'. Is it? In examining the role women play in the 'heterosexual AIDS' discourse it is important to understand that the majority of HIV-positive women in the UK (and world-wide) have acquired the infection through sex with a man, and the vast majority of women with HIV and AIDS are heterosexual in their orientation or identity. A few may identify as lesbian or bisexual, but for women the overwhelming risk of acquiring HIV is posed by sex with an HIV-infected man. It may, therefore, seem logical – even obvious – to discuss women and heterosexuality together in the context of HIV. It may seem that this is the best way to alert women to the risks they face. Sadly, this is rarely the reason for making the 'women-heterosexual' connection. It is not women who are central to this connection, but the safety of notions of heterosexuality. 'Heterosexual AIDS' serves more to obscure women, than to reveal the reality and potential of the crisis facing women; it shifts attention from the complexities of individual women to the bland, massed ranks of heterosexuals.

This concept of a heterosexual AIDS epidemic is curious and confused. 'Heterosexual AIDS' has become a term to describe a range of different things: that heterosexual men and women have AIDS and HIV, that HIV can be transmitted by vaginal inter-course, that AIDS is a mainstream condition. The first two are facts (albeit often manipulated), the latter is not. There are many reasons for talking about 'heterosexual AIDS': some are admirable (to lessen prejudice based on an over-identification between all people in these groups and a stigmatized condition), laudable (to prevent the epidemic getting worse among heterosexual men and women) and reflective of the discriminatory norm (most people with AIDS don't matter and won't attract concern). The question of whether 'heterosexual AIDS' is increasing obsesses public debate about AIDS, but is fundamentally flawed and unhelpful. The whole notion of 'heterosexual AIDS' is a false construction which obscures the multiple and complicated impacts HIV and AIDS have. 'Heterosexual AIDS' responds to society's fantasies of what is normal, of the people whose lives are important and about the ways in which a crisis becomes truly critical. Primarily, 'heterosexual AIDS' has been used to panic heterosexual men. It is not a discourse which serves women with, and vulnerable to, HIV.

The public obsession with 'heterosexual AIDS' peaks every three months when the government releases HIV and AIDS statistics, and journalists squabble over the meaning of these numbers. On the same day newspaper articles can promote sharply differing interpretations of the statistics: '"Hetero" AIDS rise', 'Experts revise threat to heterosexuals in Britain – the AIDS explosion "just won't happen"', 'Heterosexual AIDS cases to rise steadily'.[15] There is something called 'heterosexual AIDS' which appears to matter far more than the impact of AIDS itself, and which has to be charted and analysed closely. Yet as American Sandra Elkin realized back in 1983, 'How foolish – how incredibly foolish – to think that anything could be a "gay" disease or a "heterosexual" disease! The whole concept was outrageously misguided.'[16] The notion that a disease has social and political qualities is manifestly not outrageous, yet the idea that a deficiency has a sexual preference is clearly nonsense. It is nonsense driven by fantasies of normality and acceptability.

• *What is 'heterosexual AIDS'?*

As this term starts to be unpacked there is the first whiff of ideology overpowering epidemiology. Those debates about 'heterosexual AIDS' are not really asking whether *heterosexuals* get AIDS, but whether *nice* heterosexuals get AIDS – the kind of heterosexuals who warrant compassion. Patton comments on early cases:

> None of these people were considered 'real' heterosexuals (even if they were non-homosexuals); the illegal drug or unconventional sex behaviors of drug injectors and bisexual men, and social stereotypes which feminized men with hemophilia and desexualized anyone old enough to receive a transfusion during surgery already marked these people as sexually feminized, unmasculine, not fully heterosexual . . . they became honorary queers.[17]

AIDS is about queers. Whether it be the 'queer paradigm' Patton describes, or the simple fact that a lot of men with HIV and AIDS are queer in the old-fashioned sense of gay or bisexual (i.e., non-heterosexual). Queer can be a useful (and brief) description for the range of people who sexually desire their own sex – some also desire the other sex, others are 'pure' Kinsey 6s. Those who fall into the category 'queer' are diverse: they define as gay, bisexual, straight, queer, dyke, homosexual, lesbian, and in many other ways; some will invoke their 'queerness' only in sex, for others it informs their political and cultural identity.

In the context of AIDS, queer describes far more than those men and women whose sexual desire or practice involves people of the same gender. Queer is this and it is also all those 'others', the women and men who are 'abnormal' by societal standards: the junkies, the whores, the refugees, the haemophiliacs. These are the exceptions to the 'nice' rule, by dictionary standards the 'strange, odd, eccentric; [people] of questionable character, shady, suspect'[18] – queer people are those who don't deserve sympathy. While I do not use the term queer pejoratively, many of the women and men I refer to with this catch-all phrase will be very uncomfortable with it and reject any association with themselves. I am not suggesting that this is how individuals self-define, nor how they should.

Queer becomes important when discussing women and AIDS

since a key function of the heterosexualizing tendencies (which so dog the representation of women and the epidemic) is to promote a fantasy of the normal: normal people having normal sex get this normal disease. The term 'heterosexual AIDS' is manifestly over-laden with values and notions of correct lifestyle which are easy to deconstruct. After all, the term points us to the 'fact' that hetero-sexuals are 'characterized by (*the normal*) attraction to the opposite sex'[19] (my emphasis) – or so the establishment Oxford Concise Dictionary tells us. Yet the battle is not merely the ideological position of 'normality'. The whole concept of a 'heterosexual epidemic' is flawed because it relies on an unnatural framing of sexual identity. The very description of AIDS (and things associated with it) as 'heterosexual' reveals that it truly is homosexual, or queer.

The gay/homosexual community is defined in opposition, and queer identities develop through a need for lesbians, gay men and bisexuals to reach a personal accommodation with their social definition as 'other'. Queers are not what they are supposed to be, and so these identities (lesbian, gay, bisexual, queer) develop in opposition to the universal assumptions of heterosexuality. If AIDS really were 'heterosexual' it would not need to be named as such. 'Heterosexual AIDS' functions just like identity politics: it is defined in opposition.

Since the universal assumption is that AIDS is gay, it becomes necessary to explain that AIDS can be other – yet those who are 'other' in this scenario, the not-gay, may not rally quite so easily to this identity of 'heterosexual'. Many people whose behaviour is heterosexual may not have an internal sense of themselves as 'heterosexual', since they do not have a need of this identity. If pushed to define their sexuality, this is no doubt how many would describe themselves, but the sense of sexual identity rarely arises spontaneously – not, that is, unless it is challenged by others' non-heterosexuality. Indeed, in the development work for The National Survey of Sexual Attitudes and Lifestyles (henceforth referred to as the Sexual Lifestyles survey), researchers discovered that the term 'heterosexual' was unclear to a sizeable number of people;[20] it is highly unlikely that these people were queer. Sexologist John Gagnon writing about the term 'heterosexual community' observes that, 'This misnomer conceals the fact that heterosexuals are not organised into a community based upon their sexuality. Heterosexuality is taken for granted. Men who desire women and most women who desire men do not think of themselves as heterosexuals.'[21] AIDS heralds the consignment of sexualities to disease, for a group of people who have no internal attachment or sense of identity ('the heterosexual community') and it introduces concepts of sexuality for contagion ('heterosexual transmission'), and for sex itself ('heterosexual sex'). All of these heterosexual things are value-laden vague signifiers (signifying nothing).

This leads to the bizarre notion of 'heterosexual sex' which the non-existent 'heterosexual community' is allegedly having. Does this refer to any type of sexual behaviour between men and women? Or is it just intercourse? Or to be more precise, vaginal penetration with a penis? Why would it be necessary to describe sexual behaviour as having a sexual orientation? All becomes clear when the euphemisms emerge: 'heterosexual sex' is also known as 'straight sex'[22] and, most telling, 'normal sex'. For example, a women's magazine (published in early 1989) stated, 'Sixty-one women in the UK have AIDS, but only nine appear to have caught it through "normal" heterosexual sex.'[23] The act of giving sexual activity a sexual identity again reveals that there is an underlying agenda. This is nice, natural sex. It's the least embarrassing type of sex, the one with a potentially procreative excuse.

This notion skips deftly over the fact that 'heterosexual sex' which might transmit HIV includes the anal variety. The practice of anal intercourse by women with men is viewed with so much distaste that it is either ignored or warranted as deserving a fatal result. Wherever HIV-positive heterosexuals are discovered to have had (or worse still, enjoyed) anal sex, their veneer of innocence dissolves. So, for example, the girlfriends of a man who was hounded by the press as an 'AIDS time bomb'[24] had all public sympathy revoked with the discovery that their sex lives included anal fucking. What is particularly odd about this is that anal sex is more frequently practised between women and men than between men.[25] In, for example, the Sexual Lifestyles survey, 12.9 per cent of 9721 women report ever having anal sex with men,[26] whereas 33.7 per cent and 35.4 per cent of the 300 'homosexual' men have (respectively) fucked and been fucked,[27] and the survey estimates the lifetime prevalence of male homosexual experience at 6.1 per cent.[28] The survey has been criticized for underestimating its data on homosexuality, but even taking the highest estimates (as per Kinsey that 10 per cent of men are gay, and assuming they all have anal intercourse – both of which are unlikely, especially the latter) it still means that 10 per cent of the total male population are having anal sex with men, while 13 per cent of the total male population are doing the same with women. The neglect of anal sex as a heterosexual activity has nothing to do with its prevalence and everything to do with its taboo quality. The reality of 'heterosexual' anal sex troubles representations of a nice clean epidemic which can curry public sympathy. Heterosexuals engaging in such taboo behaviour become coded as queers by engaging in activity which is increasingly described, with parallel imprecision, as 'homosexual sex'.

The imprecision of the term 'heterosexual sex' is alarming, and its use widespread. It is not just the dreaded media who use such a simplistic phrase, it is also normalized in the work of AIDS researchers who talk about 'HIV transmission by heterosexual intercourse' or 'Heterosexually acquired AIDS'.[29] It is shocking, and sadly predictable, that even scientists get caught up in this ideological construction. The incessant use of 'heterosexual' as an adjective, where it has such an imprecise meaning, tells far more about the values of the writer than about anything the reader can practically use. Since the 'heterosexual' in 'AIDS', 'epidemic', 'transmission' or 'sex' is rarely appealing to individuals' sense of self, it must be there for some other reason. The prime concern is to move AIDS away from homo to hetero. In a very early review of the politics of AIDS, Canadian feminist Mary Louise Adams, noted that the 'women-can-get-AIDS-too' pieces of journalism in mainstream women's magazines present AIDS as 'a moderately contagious fatal disease slowly making its way from homosexual to heterosexual communities.'[30]

It is the transition from core groups to the 'mainstream' which obsesses most contemporary discussion. 'Heterosexual AIDS' has become code for 'nice heterosexuals' and what magazines tell us when they talk about women and AIDS is that *you* (you nice heterosexual) should be worried about AIDS. The 'nice heterosexual' is really the 'nice girl', and so *Cosmopolitan* screamed on its January 1991 cover 'Meet a girl *like you* who's HIV positive' (my emphasis). Accompanying the article is a photo of a very 'ordinary' young white woman. Denise Hathaway tells her story: she didn't use drugs, was from a nice middle-class background, was serially monogamous and had four steady boyfriends in the last eight years. She explains why she is telling Irma Kurtz her story: 'I feel I have an important role to play in breaking down stereotypes and prejudices,' she says. 'I'm doing it right now, by talking to you and coming out and saying it can happen to anyone. I mean *anyone*' (her emphasis).[31]

There is nothing strange about this statement, which is a standard formula for personal testimony, especially from HIV-positive women, yet it is noteworthy in its relationship to concepts of the queer. Hathaway describes her testimony as 'coming out', the term used by queers to describe revealing their sexual orientation/identity to loved ones (and sometimes themselves). She has clearly been trained by queer culture, even if it is just that element of AIDS organizing among gay men which has influenced self-help groups for HIV-positive women. Hathaway describes her motivation for taking the difficult step of going public with her disease, a step which inevitably involves going public with her sex life, as an HIV awareness exercise and ultimately as a prevention exercise. She is talking at the height of the 'equal opportunities AIDS' campaign,[32] and emphasizes the indiscriminate nature of the epidemic: anyone can get it – normal women – nice girls – you. Perhaps *Cosmopolitan* know that their readership, their 'you', are all young white middle-class women who don't do drugs and have very few sexual partners (although this is hardly consistent with *Cosmopolitan*'s editorial obsession with sexual technique and fulfilment, which assumes that *Cosmo* woman's appetite for sexual experience is as huge as her lust for shopping). It seems more likely that the moral myth of the nice girl is what comes in to play here: whatever the reality of your life, you ought to want to be a nice girl (an assumption which is fundamental to *Cosmo*'s editorial line). Such discourses obscure the fact that for a sexual woman vulnerability to HIV is determined by a complex interaction of biological, societal and economic dimensions. Instead, the vulnerability is coded as linked to a certain moral correctness for which these young women strive. Apparently, *Cosmo* readers can only be expected to identify with someone who fits such an image, whereas honorary, and real, queers with HIV just wouldn't cut it with the readership.

• *A myth?*

The 'heterosexual' signifiers are so imprecise that they almost take on a mythological quality, invested with a value system and higher meaning while simultaneously functioning as apparently straightforward descriptive terms. Shockingly few people question whether 'heterosexual AIDS' is a useful concept, or have tried to deconstruct this strange terminology. With the exception of activists concerned with re-gaying (examined later), the only people to have considered the notion in much depth tend to be conspiracy theorists, principally American journalist Michael Fumento, the Revolutionary Communist Party (RCP) and Marxists like Susil Gupta. Fumento and Gupta claim that 'heterosexual AIDS' is (respectively) a 'myth' or a 'fraud', and the RCP claim that they will expose 'The Truth About the AIDS Panic'.[33] Their theories seem to be advanced in order to promote 'family values' or oppose anti-sex 'moral crusades'. They do not explore the problem with the concept of 'heterosexual AIDS' itself, and while this may not be surprising with moralists like Fumento, it is bizarre that a Marxist should accept so uncritically an ideological construction of the Right.

Fumento gained notoriety as the author of *The Myth of Heterosexual AIDS*, published first in 1990 and revised in 1993.[34] He is regularly hauled on to talk shows where he is showcased as the anti-establishment voice, the one who says 'Crisis? What crisis?' He is vehemently opposed to what he terms the 'AIDS alarmists', and has worked up some neat little conspiracy theories to explain why all these public health officials are promoting condoms.

In the UK it is the RCP which adopts the anti-establishment line but, with some irritating exceptions, their views get little airing. Gupta (the most persistent RCP dissident) and Fumento argue for their different conspiracy theories based on the same core issues. Their arguments get occasional airings in the press, notably the *Sunday Times*.[35] The argument begins by showing that early predictions of the development of AIDS among heterosexuals have not come to pass and highlighting the small increase in cases among women and men who have no connection to gay men or drug use. When it becomes indisputable that some heterosexuals have AIDS, the next line of attack tends to be that 'straight sex' is safe.

Few people in the UK have read Fumento's book, although many have seen excerpts in the *Sunday Times*, or followed its controversy. Fumento could not find a British publisher and claims censorship (the second edition is now available). Certainly, his book caused a storm in the USA. ACT UP (the AIDS Coalition To Unleash Power) did its worst and kept it out of the bookstores or off people's shelves with damning reviews. No wonder they were angry: Fumento's rejection of 'AIDS alarmists' is submerged in a rigidity which despises homosexuality and promiscuity and he has a mealy-mouthed distaste for sexual acts he finds unpleasant. Yet what is so frustrating with *The Myth of Heterosexual AIDS* is that some very good points are lost in Fumento's bigoted diatribe. Albeit from a smug, white, male heterosexual vantage point, he surveys the literature and concludes that 'heterosexual sex' is a poor viral transmitter. Although by no means beyond technical criticism, the evidence he garners is compelling in showing that HIV transmission from women to men is relatively inefficient.

He reviews the epidemiology and shows how most hetero-sexual women and men who have HIV have strong links with 'high-risk groups'. He criticizes generalized HIV prevention messages by drawing up league tables of the number of unprotected fucks a 'promiscuous college student' will need to risk HIV infection (100,000 if she has sex once with ten male partners a year, 10,000 if she fucks with the same man 100 times – or so he claims).[36] Yet what Fumento lacks is any hint of compassion or sense of how his academic arguments translate into the real world. He may well be right about the failure of generalized campaigns, but precisely how does his league table help a student to protect her sexual health any better than an encouragement to use condoms? He clearly has no truck with those deviants who become infected, and his protestations of sympathy for 'this terrible disease' are academic in the extreme. His underlying contempt and anti-sex message seeps through in, for example, his attack on safe(r) sex campaigns where he tells us,

> the moralists are absolutely right when they say condoms can't make sinful sex safe, as in safe for the soul. . . . [T]he foisting of condoms onto children, the effort to accustom teenagers to their use, and treatment of condoms generally that bordered on the ancient Roman worship of phalluses, is difficult to construe as anything less than decadent. One need not be a certified moralist, a conservative, or a Christian to be horrified at what the condomites passed off as responsible behavior in time of crisis.[37]

Curiously, the other main rejection of 'AIDS alarmists' is rooted in an entirely different world view: the RCP rage against the government's AIDS campaign which they claim is a moralizing force to mandate 'family values'. Their conspiracy theorists detect too little decadence. The RCP share Fumento's mistrust about the current direction of the epidemic, although their analysis comes from the dreary, predictable Marxist line. They conclude – from the same basic evidence – that the anti-AIDS message is a Tory plot to curb hedonism which would, unfettered, lead to the overthrow of the government: they wear us down by damping our sexual energy in order to damp our political energy. It is only through class struggle and the uprising of marginalized and oppressed communities, that the crisis will be solved. Gupta goes further. He reaches his conclusions through a process of denial which is extra-ordinary. Not only does he claim that 'there is neither an Aids [*sic*] epidemic in the UK nor in any developed country',[38] he also argues that it is not a problem for gay men.[39] The statistical gymnastics required to reach such a conclusion should alert the reader to be mighty wary of all other truth claims made by such commentators, and allegedly rooted in official statistics.

The basic message with which these conspiracy theorists do battle is that everyone will be massively affected, and that the impact of AIDS will fall evenly across society. This facile prediction of the progress of the AIDS epidemic is clearly wrong and has not come to pass. In their critique of the idea that HIV will spread in the 'heterosexual population', Fumento, Gupta, the RCP *et al.* are reacting against these extreme forecasts – or at least their fantasies that official bodies repeatedly made such forecasts. The earlier predictions of the direction the epidemic was taking were based on remarkably little information. As knowledge about the dynamics of transmission has increased so too the predictions have become more accurate, with real figures fitting closely to the projected curves. The early exaggerations, which have dogged AIDS activists, did not evolve from mass conspiracies, but principally from caution and limited information – and from the media itself. Garfield records how, at the end of 1986, the Chief Medical Officer Sir Donald Acheson estimated that there were 30,000 HIV-infected people in the UK, 'On 9 January [1987] *The Times* believed 40,000 might be infected; on 12 January the *Independent* plumped for 60,000; and within three days *The Times* had increased its estimate to 100,000.'[40]

Curiously, in the 1990s the media has been busy debunking the very same forecasts. The luxury of hindsight is a fine thing, but it is depressing that the so-called dissidents have no appreciation of the horror faced by activists in the early days. A more compassionate review would find groups of gay men gathering information about a terrifying new development, trying to make sense of it and provide information for each other.[41] None of the histories of the early days of AIDS uncovers a cabal of avaricious queens calculating ways to pump money out of the government in order to squash the libido of unsuspecting heterosexuals. Indeed these early efforts tended to be thankless tasks, with the creators of (what is now) safer sex being roundly disliked for their suggestions.[42] Fumento's analysis of alleged conspiracy misses the point. If there is a conspiracy (and this term suggests far more premeditation than is truly the case) then it is not that the public health agencies have conspired to foist a reign of terror on the 'normal' population, but rather they have colluded in the neglect of the health and well-being of the 'abnormal' population.

Despite their conspiratorial fantasies, Fumento and Gupta do draw upon information which is reliable. HIV does not appear to be transmitted as efficiently in unprotected vaginal sex as unprotected anal sex, and most heterosexuals with HIV or AIDS have some connection to established 'risk groups'. But what of this notion of 'myth'? If Fumento means AIDS is a 'myth' at the simplistic level of myth=lie (and he nowhere suggests that he is using the word 'myth' in any but this most obvious sense), then he is utterly wrong. Heterosexuals have had AIDS since the beginning of the epidemic and numbers are increasing, and HIV is transmitted by sex between men and women (sloppily known as 'heterosexual sex').

However 'heterosexual AIDS' could be described as a 'myth' in much the same way that theologians talk about the incarnation and the gospels as mythological. Myths can be rooted in historical fact and then acquire a meaning beyond the event in history. For example, Professor Wiles explains that 'Historical events may contribute to the origin of a myth, and myths may fulfil a function in historical and political life as well as in philosophical and psychological reflection.'[43] The myth exists and has its power because it contains a complex, symbolic and long-lasting meaning which stretches way beyond the historical 'fact'. The 'facts' – of heterosexuals with and transmitting HIV – are only a small part of what is meant by 'heterosexual AIDS'. This phrase has come to signify far more, attaining a political function and shifting philosophical and psychological reflection about the disease. The 'heterosexual AIDS myth' asserts that AIDS does or will affect the 'heterosexual community' in the same way it has impacted the 'gay community'. Since there is no such thing as a 'heterosexual community' (and since few people understand the complex reality described as the 'gay community', or the ways AIDS is affecting it), the 'myth' means: a high percentage of 'normal' people will get AIDS, numbers will rise rapidly and this will happen evenly across the board. Manifestly this is a mythological construction with a political, philosophical and psychological function.

'Heterosexual AIDS' is a myth which increasingly demands to be broken. It obscures the true and varied impacts of the virus by simplistic appeals to the normality of certain types of behaviour and remains distant from the reality of people's lives. It obscures and fails women by assuming that sexuality rather than sex (or gender) is normative to most women's sense of self. While this may well be true for gay or bisexual identified men, it is rarely the case for heterosexually behaving women. All models for fighting AIDS derive, at least initially, from gay men's experience of the epidemic. One key element that simply does not translate is the emphasis on enabling queer men to intensify their sense of self in respect of their sexual object choice(s). Queer men need to rally around a strong sense of their sexuality in order to gain the knowledge, skills and self-esteem to avoid infection. An appeal to women who get fucked by men to rally around their heterosexual identity would not only be comic, but ultimately pointless – it is the fact of oppression of a (queer) sexuality that makes its validation so vital in the struggle against AIDS. Women having sex with men are not oppressed or disapproved of in respect of their sexual object choice (except for lesbians and bisexual women who fuck men), so that it is rarely their orientation *per se* which needs validating and approving in order for them to gain the knowledge, skills and self-esteem to avoid HIV. The heterosexual AIDS myth also fails women by dumping them together with heterosexually identified or behaving men. The risks which HIV poses to men at a biological and social level are different from the risks posed to women; and the ways in which men pose a risk of HIV to women are different from the reverse. Simply put: the principal risks of HIV acquisition faced by a heterosexual-identified man are getting fucked by another man, sharing injecting equipment, or receiving infected blood product. For a woman the principal risk is getting fucked by a man.

This does not mean that men do not acquire HIV from women – of course they do – but the proportion of HIV-infected men who acquired the virus that way (in the UK and USA) is minimal, whereas the overwhelming majority of women became infected from sex with a man. For example, during 1992 there were 47,095 new cases of AIDS reported in the USA: 4.1 per cent of the men attributed their infection to sex with women, and 36.8 per cent of the women said they became infected from sex with men.[44] By September 1994 less than 7.5 per cent of all British men with AIDS claimed to have acquired their infection from sex with a woman (and some of those reports are doubted), whereas 60.5 per cent of

British women with AIDS had become infected from sex with a man.[45]

These facts have important consequences for prevention initiatives which face a major contradiction: the need to engage directly with taboo behaviour to address men, and to address more 'normal', accepted behaviour with women – albeit behaviour which is complicated by multiple socio-economic challenges. These facts are obscured by appeals to heterosexuality as the determinant feature of the epidemic. While it is not true that the UK is on the brink of a 'heterosexual epidemic', the country *is* teetering on the brink of a major public health crisis for many women whose behaviour is heterosexual.

Risky groups or behaviours?

My fundamental concern with the presentation of AIDS as a 'heterosexual epidemic' is that it sustains the invisibility of women. Some will find this an unusual criticism. Indeed they would claim that, since it highlights the effects on people other than gay men and since most women with HIV and AIDS are heterosexual, the framing of AIDS as heterosexual reveals the impacts on women. The argument that women are concealed and rendered invisible is more frequently levelled at the 'risk groups' discourse of AIDS.

Risk groups are a fundamental component of epidemiology, the science which describes the progress of conditions, including infectious diseases such as HIV and AIDS, in populations. In essence epidemiologists are medical detectives. Their role is to unravel patterns in the incidence and prevalence of diseases by seeking out the connections between people with the same, or related, conditions. Their concern is not, necessarily, to address the health of an individual or community, but rather to understand the current patterns and inform about the potential future dynamics of the condition. Epidemics are often described according to their geography, showing the extent of a disease in a particular continent, country or town. Within these locales, it is then important to understand why some people develop the condition and others do not, and this leads epidemiologists to consider biological or lifestyle factors which influence the acquisition or development of the condition. Consequently, they use a tool to define the connections between cases – the term 'risk groups' describes the sub-populations which are most affected.

This terminology came under terrible fire from AIDS activists once its stigmatizing potential became apparent. From the outset the AIDS risk groups were associated with queers. The condition was first named GRID (Gay Related Immune Deficiency) because the only connection among the first people detected with the condition was that they were gay men.[46] As it was described with increasing frequency in other people, so the name shifted to reflect this and it was called AIDS (Acquired Immune Deficiency Syndrome). Apart from AIDS, the risk groups had one major feature in common: they were outside the perceived mainstream, they were the 'other' – queers in the sense of fitting Patton's 'queer paradigm'. Packard and Epstein comment, in respect of TB, that 'like earlier behavioral arguments, physiological models defined the African as essentially different from the European, as the "other", and at the same time placed responsibility for the disease on the victim.'[47] Indeed, for many years in the USA AIDS was described as a disease of the four 'H's: homosexuals, heroin users, Haitians and haemophiliacs.

While risk groups for cervical cancer continue to be named as including women over thirty who have had unprotected sex with multiple partners, and for sickle cell anaemia as being African-Caribbean, it became dangerous to define risk groups for AIDS. The reality of certain marginalized sub-populations (i.e. gay men and bisexual men, drug users, refugees from some African countries) having disproportionate rates of HIV infection has been grossly misused by tabloid papers, as well as so-called 'family' organizations and others who intensify stigmatization and prejudice towards the individuals and communities most affected by the epidemic. Concerns to reduce such prejudice and to clarify the modes of HIV transmission led to the rejection of 'risk groups' terminology, with activists insisting that information should centre on 'risk behaviours' or 'risk activities'.

The notion of risk groups was condemned as an unhelpful, potentially discriminatory concept which obscured the fact that certain acts facilitate transmission. The focus shifted to risky behaviour (unprotected anal or vaginal fucking, sharing injecting equipment, pregnancy and breast-feeding) and to the rules of transmission (HIV is in blood and sexual fluids and needs to enter the bloodstream of another person for infection to occur), and away from the people engaging in this behaviour. At the same time as taking the heat off the risk groups, these developments apparently clarified things well: a heterosexually identified man who occasionally gets semen into his bloodstream through the lining of his rectum could now perceive that he was at risk, even though he had nothing to do with the dreaded gay high-risk group. (Or so the theory went.)

The major reason given for this shift, which in turn has now come under fire, was to reduce stigmatization and prejudice against these already stigmatized groups. This strategy did not work. Despite some apparent gains, all these queers have not suddenly been embraced into a mainstream view of the world. Some more grotesque elements of prejudice may have been avoided, but it is impossible to know if they would have occurred had the notion of 'risk groups' been maintained. The other reason for rejecting the risk group discourse has more validity. As suggested, a man whom an epidemiologist would categorize in, say, the gay risk group would not necessarily so define, and indeed might be alienated by such a definition. The feature uniting the two major risk groups is their tendency to the closet. While many gay men and drug users are not covert about their behaviour, the attitudes of society towards illegal drugs use and homo/bisexuality mean that a significant proportion of people in these risk groups do seek to hide what they are doing from their loved ones, and sometimes even themselves.[48] This poses significant challenges for prevention workers seeking to protect these people and those with whom they have sex. This realization led to a practice, if not a policy, which has been described as 'de-gaying'.

De-gaying, and the backlash, re-gaying,[49] are fundamentally about manipulating the way in which people perceive AIDS. In simplistic terms we can say that de-gaying sought to make AIDS respectable, while re-gaying is seeking to reclaim history and name what is actually happening from the perspective of those directly affected. De-gaying was a complex business with multiple causes and results which are described eloquently in Edward King's book *Safety in Numbers*.[50] By adopting the notion of behaviour, and abandoning the nature of people engaging in that behaviour, the real impacts of the epidemic were concealed and people from sub-populations at heightened risk were not alerted to this fact. Critically, resources for prevention activities were misallocated to communities with far lower HIV vulnerabilities to infection. In one of his more entertaining sections, Fumento likens this approach to using a macho construction worker to promote breast cancer awareness; of course some men do get breast cancer, but the highest-risk group is women over forty who have smoked and have a family history of the disease.[51]

Re-gaying seeks to reorient the discussion about AIDS to reflect the reality of current epidemiology – and it seems to have made a lot of people nervous. King suggests that re-gaying requires that people 'unlearn' the dogmas which the AIDS industry has taught itself[52] – with the constant uncertainty of AIDS, and the sense of incessant attack from 'outside' it is hard for those of us in the 'industry' to accept that we might indeed have got some of it wrong.

Within the context of 're-gaying' there have been moves to reclaim the idea of 'risk groups'. There are many problems intrinsic to the generalized approach, principally that those at highest risk are under-educated, while those at lower risk are encouraged to overestimate their risk – an approach which is counter-productive in the long run. So will reclaiming the term 'risk group' help redress this balance? It is clearly behaviours (not groups) which lead to the transmission of HIV, but the highest risk of HIV transmission still occurs when risky behaviour is practised by or with someone from a sub-population with a high prevalence of HIV. Yet one of the problems with talking about risk groups is that it suggested that people are at risk simply because they belong to that group. Some epidemiologists have started to talk about 'groups with high-risk behaviour' (utter sophistry), and others use the term 'core groups'. 'Core groups' describe the groups most affected by the epidemic, where prevalence is highest and infection established earliest. 'Adjacent' groups comprise individuals in intimate contact with core groups, and 'peripheral' groups are 'on the edge', unlikely to be in contact with core groups, and only marginally vulnerable through their contact with adjacent groups. Alcorn notes that, 'the utility of these terms is that they are at once epidemiological and spatial, allowing us to understand the geographical and social factors in the spread of HIV.'[53] It is a more helpful concept for understanding the overall direction of the epidemic. Since all adjacent groups tend to consist of the female sexual partners of the core groups, it is a helpful way of describing the current and future potential impacts on women.

By reorienting the discussion to core groups, there is a clearer and more honest focus on the key HIV risks. Yet for women there is a major problem with such a focused approach. Men from core groups often have sex with women. Yet these women tend not to identify with the core group or get information from those communities. The vast majority of women who have an enhanced vulnerability to HIV have no internal cohesion, group identity or common network for information flow (with the exception, perhaps, of some women who use drugs or work in the commercial sex industry). In fact, there is no easy way of defining who they are: they are from diverse social classes, age groups, ethnic backgrounds and lifestyles. If a woman does not know the status of her sexual partner, how can she assess risk? The very behaviour which may have placed him at risk, is also so stigmatized that it is often concealed. Many men may not reveal – especially to a new partner – their current or past sexual relationships with men, or their injecting drug use.

This difficulty in reaching female sexual partners may have been enhanced by emphasis on risk groups according to Dr. Helen Rodriquez-Trias, who was concerned that, 'The CDC's creation of "risk groups" . . . helped obscure the evidence from the very beginning that women were being hit in the AIDS epidemic. The effect of delineating "risk groups" – "homosexual males," "IV drug users," "Haitians," "blood recipients," "people with multiple sex partners" – was to totally obscure the heterosexual trans-mission of AIDS (*sic*)'.[54] American Gwen Green tells how she wept at Magic Johnson's HIV diagnosis only to find, two weeks later, that her routine life insurance test was positive. 'I never thought

I was at risk. ... Whenever I'd heard about AIDS on TV or whatever, it just went over my head because I just heard "drugs and homosexuals." No one ever talks about transmission when you just had one partner.'[55] The risks to individual women like Gwen Green are enormous, and it has been argued that women like her can only appreciate them if the notion of 'heterosexual AIDS' is promoted, or messages focus principally on risk behaviours. From another angle the attention paid to 'drugs and homosexuals' has caused confusion with lesbians assuming they are at increased risk (which they are not) simply because they are homosexuals.

Increasing numbers of women are acquiring HIV and women are far more vulnerable than men to HIV transmission in vaginal or anal sex, yet, as I have said, women will frequently not be aware of their male sexual partners' high-risk factors for HIV. A mere glimpse at unplanned pregnancy rates shows that men are notoriously bad at helping to prevent the undesirable consequences of sexual intercourse – and may even need to be scared into taking action. Without perceiving a personal risk, men cannot be relied on to safeguard women's health. Even in the apparently enlightened London gay press, men who behave bisexually are exhorted to use condoms if they have sex with a woman lest *she* infects *him* with HIV.[56] The expectation that men will take responsibility for protecting the women they are fucking seems like a dangerous, distant fantasy. Some have suggested, therefore, that if a heterosexual epidemic is not publicized then heterosexually identified (or behaving) men will not accept that high-risk factors in their lives also pose a risk to the women they have sex with (because only 'others' get HIV). The strategy of publicizing a heterosexual epidemic also encourages women to 'demand' safer sex from their partners, without having to suggest (or even consider) that the men have high-risk factors.

An individual's vulnerability to infection depends upon two factors: whether the other person is HIV-infected and whether safer behaviour is practised. Most health education has focused on encouraging all people to adopt safer behaviour all of the time. Behavioural research indicates that this strategy (which may be laudable in the long term) has immense flaws. The notion of 100 per cent behaviour change 100 per cent of the time has been shown to be unrealistic from research into behaviour modification and maintenance with other potentially health-harming pleasurable activities (e.g. smoking, eating, drinking).[57] In addition, this strategy does not address the most immediate concern, i.e. those people or sub-populations most at risk of infection. As the majority of people do not know their current HIV status, risk assessment may be a useful tool which, in the UK, has been under-promoted in the name of preventing discrimination. Given the (most common) situation of risky sex with a person of unknown HIV status, the HIV rate in the core group to which they belong may be taken as an indicator of the importance of safer sex in this situation. The most obvious examples: if a man has sex with a gay man in New York, or a woman has sex with a bisexual man in San Francisco or a Spanish man who injects drugs, then safer sex is highly advisable.

Many will say that whatever the current epidemiology, the virus can and will spread beyond these groups swiftly so that no con-nection is discernible. Yet after well over a decade of the epidemic, with the accompanying vast quantity of research, the clustering of cases continues. There is a definite hierarchy of risk among groups. In the sexual context, transmission from the insertive partner in anal sex appears to be the most risky activity, followed by transmission from the male in vaginal sex. Transmission from the woman in vaginal sex occurs but is less efficient, as is trans-mission from the receptive anal sex partner. Whilst transmission does occur in all these scenarios, it is important to recognize the relative efficiencies.

For women, there is a major drawback with the focused approach of targeting information to core groups. If prevention messages are focused at gay men and bisexual men, and at injecting drug users, how can messages reach the women who are their sexual partners? There is no easy way of defining who they are – they are from diverse social classes, age groups, ethnic backgrounds and lifestyles. Nearly all information aimed at gay men discusses sex between men exclusively, and most prevention workers reject the idea of including sex with women as it will be distracting or offensive to their target group.[58] Yet if women cannot be reached via the men they are having sex with, how can they be targeted directly? This argument may be the basis for a generalized appeal to behaviour and the exaggeration of a heterosexual epidemic. Yet there are many disadvantages for women. For a start, it uses women to sell an ideology, with a divisiveness which mythologizes women as the innocents. More critically, the fundamental issues for women (such as gender power relationships) are submerged in the generalist discourse. Heterosexual men may not accept that high risk factors in their lives pose a risk (because information does not focus on that behaviour) and women may not be encouraged to focus on the reality of risk factors, and develop skills to negotiate power issues and find ways of protecting themselves in highly vulnerable situations.

Moreover, in the absence of an effective microbicide or other woman-controlled technology, there is nothing a woman herself can do to reduce her risk of acquiring HIV. (A microbicide is a gel or cream that would de-activate sexually transmitted diseases (STDs), including HIV; it is sometimes called a virucide.) The best she can aim for is having the man take preventive action. This is a depressing situation. It is generally unrealistic to expect women to engage in, and sustain, heroic acts of 'forcing' men to use condoms (what force will he use in return?), especially without a more honest appeal to actual risk. What may have seemed plausible when risk groups were dumped in the mid-1980s, when there was often an (unspoken) sense that AIDS would be a short-term problem demanding exceptional measures, no longer works as populations settle down to the long-term realities of the AIDS crisis. In the mid-1990s people are beginning to wonder out loud what happened to the hundreds of heterosexual HIV-positive friends they were promised a decade ago – and as they wonder, they question why they are still being asked to permanently forego latex-free pleasure.

Equal opportunity AIDS?

Simon Watney has noted that 'the rejection of the concept of "risk groups" in favour of "risk behaviors" encouraged the development of a euphemistic, generalised AIDS education that floated the lie that everyone was at *equal* risk of HIV transmission'.[59] Since early on, AIDS workers have put a lot of energy into explaining that AIDS is simply a disease. As Sontag expresses so forcefully,[60] of course diseases are neutral, they are not metaphors, they do not have sexualities, genders or meanings beyond the fact of the condition itself. Curiously, the most effective way many people had to express this meaninglessness of disease was to invoke a metaphor. The notion was born, doubtless in some local authority department, that AIDS is an 'equal opportunities' disease.[61] This became a handy phrase to explain that anyone can become infected, that it is not who you are, but what you do that determines whether you contract HIV. The term swiftly became widespread – even pop goddess Madonna used it on a flyer accompanying her 1989 album *Like a Prayer*. The notion of 'equal opportunities' AIDS came about for good reasons: at the beginning of the epidemic nothing was known about the condition and it was entirely possible that AIDS would affect everyone; discrimination was (and is) central to the general response to the epidemic, and it was believed that, in the same way that equal opportunities policies counter discrimination, this approach would reduce the stigma experienced by gay men.

Sadly the assertion that 'AIDS affects everyone' has become extremely unhelpful. Although it once played an important role, it now obscures more than it explains and has become redundant. By emphasizing the 'equality' of AIDS we fail to address the real needs of HIV-positive women and the ways in which women are affected by the epidemic. AIDS does not affect everyone equally, and it does not affect women in the way it affects gay men. Of course, a woman being fucked up the arse by an HIV-infected man without a condom faces the same risk of acquiring HIV as a man in the same situation; there is no fundamental difference between male and female rectums. Yet current epidemiological data shows that all people do *not* face an equal opportunity of infection.

Despite over a year of high-profile discussions about de- and re-gaying, in the summer of 1994 London Lighthouse ('a centre for people facing the challenge of AIDS') launched a multi-media advertising campaign which exemplified the equal opportunities discourse. There were six adverts. One just relies on text which boldly proclaims: 'We welcome gay, straight, black, white, young, old, cash, cheque or credit card.' Note that, despite the classic equality formula, 'male, female' is not on the list. The other five adverts show photographs of people who are identified in the text as being themselves HIV-positive or family members. The strap line is modified to read, 'Old or young. Him or her. White or black. Straight or gay. AIDS doesn't care. We do. We need you to as well.'[62] Despite the appeal to equal opportunities, the images are telling. They are framed as 'normal' AIDS stories, which Lighthouse deal with on a day-to-day basis. They introduce a smiling elderly couple who have rejected their son with HIV, a man whose family rejected him because he has AIDS, a man who can't bring himself to tell his young daughter he has AIDS, and a woman whose husband beat her, and friends rejected her, when she told them she was HIV-positive.

The sixth image shows a 'happy family' comprising a young man, an older woman and older man, who were surprised that Martin has AIDS because he is sixty-four. By June 1994, 1.6 per cent of all the men who had ever developed AIDS in the UK were aged sixty to sixty-four.[63] Does Martin have haemophilia? Is that woman his wife? Is he gay? And what about these stories of rejection? Could it be that the men are queer? Are they junkies? The ads don't say.

This type of equal opportunities is sexuality-blind and apparently colour-blind. Despite the fact that all of these people are white, and coded as middle-class, the message states that it is an egalitarian disease (but of course all people are not equal in their appeal to potential donors). There is no mention of queers, drugs, refugee status, or any of the other awkward associations which AIDS has. The dishonesty of this approach is manifest in the advert about Martin. It gibes at the fact that he and his family thought AIDS was 'a "young person's" disease'. It is true that AIDS is not *only* a young person's disease, but by June 1994 62.6 per cent of the cumulative total of men who had developed AIDS, and 84.2 per cent of women, were under forty, and only 2.4 per cent of all people who ever had AIDS were over sixty. For the individual sixty-four-year-old with AIDS there is no doubt that the diagnosis is likely to be traumatic – perhaps more so because it is rare – but why is this being presented to the general public as part of the norm?[64]

The uniqueness of individuals' lives and experiences will always create diversity within any situation, yet AIDS, perhaps more than any other illness, has been sold in this unified way: 'AIDS affects everyone', 'We are all living with AIDS', 'All people with AIDS are innocent', 'AIDS doesn't discriminate'. The smoothing out of AIDS to a crass and simplistic unity, or equality, obscures the painful complexities of AIDS reality. These devastating images of normalcy inhibit effective responses by concealing the reality of many people's lives, and that reality is concealed because it is perceived as abnormal and needing to be hidden from the public gaze. This root prejudice is damaging both to the 'others' who are hidden and to the 'general public' which is spared their reality. By muddling messages of anti-discrimination against sub-groups affected by AIDS with general information about AIDS, no one's agenda is met. The real needs for respect and human rights of marginalized individuals and communities are not met by generalized appeals that 'AIDS affects everyone'. The construction of AIDS as an 'equal opportunities' disease is a facile collapsing of a complex situation into an apparently unassailable ideological framework.

A further problem with the 'equal opportunities virus' discourse is that it often slips into a competitive thing. In early 1991, the *Guardian*'s women's page profiled the first woman Chief Executive of THT, Naomi Wayne, who stated that 'AIDS . . . is not a gay or even a male problem.'[65] This implication that AIDS had been transformed into an exclusively straight female disease was made when less than 15 per cent of people with HIV were women, and nearly 9000 gay men were diagnosed HIV-positive. She explained that her reason for this statement was that otherwise 'it will not be taken seriously'. Some might say it was her job to get people to take AIDS seriously whomsoever it was affecting. Wayne's statement was classic of the de-gaying that had befallen THT. Instead of maintaining the organization's description of itself which stated, 'We have our roots in the gay community *and* we serve other communities',[66] Wayne presents what King describes as 'an initially gay organization which had now turned into something else entirely'.[67] She would have been correct if she had told the *Guardian* 'AIDS is not *only* a gay or a male problem' but this comment was not about accuracy. Here women were being manipulated to front someone else's issue, they were set up as a smokescreen to protect detested communities from the public gaze.

The AIDS arena is littered with strange assertions promoted in the interests of acceptance and equality, rather than the epidemic. For example, one activist complains that gay male AIDS activists suggested 'that the concerns of gay women and men were entirely different'.[68] But of course they are! The idea that lesbians and gay men are affected equally by AIDS, or indeed by anything, is a curious misunderstanding of what equality is all about. Why should women and men seek to experience things equally, rather than demand equal access and equal quality in the range of responses to different needs? Equal opportunities policies in the context of AIDS are not the same as equal opportunities in other contexts. The idea that there is some universal formula for securing equality is one of the more misguided and harmful developments, now resulting in the general ridicule of 'political correctness'. To say, for example, that access to child-care should prioritize the needs of black women over those of white gay men would not be racist and homophobic, but rather a policy of ensuring equal access which reflects the general demography of child-care needs. Such a policy would fail to enshrine the principles of equal opportunities if it either refused access to white gay fathers, or prioritized them over black mothers. Equal opportunities should be concerned with reflecting and responding to diversity, not smoothing things out into some crass fantasy of equality as sameness.

As the epidemic progresses, the early claims that 'HIV is an equal opportunities virus' have been shown to be unfounded. Indeed Sontag points out that this constant assertion that AIDS is equal functions in the same way as the discourse which hammers persistently 'It's really heterosexual'. Discussing the AmFAR (American Foundation for AIDS Research) fundraising campaign which proclaimed, 'the AIDS virus is an equal-opportunity destroyer', Sontag comments that 'the phrase subliminally reaffirms what it means to deny: that AIDS is an illness that in this part of the world afflicts minorities, racial and sexual.'[69] Whilst it remains important that the whole population become 'AIDS aware', and of course it is possible for any person to become infected with HIV, it is clear that, as Watney puts it, 'HIV is *not* an "equal opportunity" infection: it has a quite distinctive social profile.'[70]

Attempts to conceal the profile of AIDS can also be detected in policies of 'normalization', which maintain that AIDS is just like any other life threatening disease. In recent years normalizing policies have become extremely common in the AIDS industry, especially in social services and to a lesser degree in health promotion units. HIV specialist services and workers are becoming integrated into generic services; for example, in many boroughs social workers dedicated to the needs of people with HIV are being phased out and all social workers are expected to respond to the needs of people with HIV. In some situations this may be an appropriate service development,[71] yet it is rooted in mis-conceived notions of normal AIDS. AIDS is not normal, it is not like any other illness. It has always created a level of fascination and prurient interest out of proportion with the reality of an infectious condition with a long latency period and complex syndromic manifestation of diseases. Attempts to make AIDS 'normal' before it is a normal part of people's lives and worlds are necessarily doomed. One of the stated motivations of normaliza-tion of the AIDS crisis is to reduce discrimination: the 'general public' cannot be expected to have compassion for people who have AIDS and so they have to be told that AIDS is really 'normal'. The abnormality of gay men, drug users, prostitutes, Africans and all the 'others' who are touched by AIDS is implicit in policies of normalization.

The trend to normalizing has been spearheaded both by people who are prejudiced against people with HIV and by the advocates of people with HIV. Yet forcing normalization must necessarily fail. Things become normal because they *are* normal, not because of a policy statement. In some parts of the world – Kampala, Edinburgh, New York's Greenwich Village, San Francisco's Tenderloin – AIDS really is normal. The proponents of normalization say, look, all of the features of AIDS occur else-where: leukaemia is a life-threatening condition occurring mainly in young people, herpes is an incurable sexually transmitted disease, Hepatitis B is a blood-borne condition, syphilis can be transmitted from a woman to her foetus. All of this is true and offers important lessons to learn from past skills in dealing with situations. The normalizers also say every situation is unique, you shouldn't privilege AIDS over other conditions (as if acknowledging that AIDS is special would mean treating people with other conditions in a worse way). Yet AIDS *is* special because of the extraordinary combination of features. AIDS is special because it is new and fatal (so that a cure is urgent), because it is transmissible and fatal (so it has to be stopped from spreading), because it is queer (why else would some parents claim their son who had AIDS died of leukaemia?). The policies of normalization, which say that AIDS is not special, are terribly misguided.

A disease of 'others'?

• The gay context

Enraged by normalizing tendencies, Michael Callen claimed, 'AIDS IS A GAY DISEASE! There. I said it. And I believe it. If I hear one more time that AIDS is not a gay disease, I shall vomit. AIDS is a gay disease because a lot of gay men get AIDS.'[72] 'Re-gaying', which Callen heralded, falls under the broader banner of 'applied epidemiology',[73] an approach which demands that HIV prevention, policy, care, research and funding should follow the current and immediate future epidemiological trends. There is a rather powerful logic to this. In the 1980s little was known about where the epidemic was going. Well into the second decade of the disease, research has matured and it is a lot easier to detect and predict the broad directions infections are taking. Applied epidemiology provides a more sophisticated framework than re-gaying, since it includes all of the core groups who are (becoming) affected. Yet if the framework is rigorously applied in the UK it brings us swiftly back to 're-gaying', for the simple reason that one high risk group massively outnumbers all the others combined. The problem is that women are effectively locked out of the discourse of 're-gaying', despite the fact that they are the group with the next most important rate of increase.

One of the strongest, and strangest, reactions to re-gaying appeared in the newsletter published by Mainliners. Nicola Field's front-page article 'Take-over bids and monopolies: HIV and the gay community – Gay Men Fighting AIDS: Whose army?'[74] responded to the formation in 1992 of Gay Men Fighting AIDS (GMFA). In seeking to explore the description of AIDS as a gay disease and its impact on women, it is worth dwelling a little on this denunciation from a woman I assume to be a feminist. She complains about 'the dangers of falling in behind such a separatist group', which seems a little bizarre especially when she is writing for Mainliners, an organization dedicated to the needs of one particular community ('an agency working with and for people affected by drugs and HIV'). Most feminists know well the value of separatism in helping to identify the concerns which are specific to a community and then move forward with a clear agenda. Indeed, later on in her article Field acknowledges that 'it's vital that each community affected by HIV can work out its own agenda for the way forward' – something which rarely happens working within coalitions.

A major component of Field's anxiety is apparently her concern about 'gay men's sexism'. Throughout her article she suggests that 'misogynistic gay male supremacy' is behind re-gaying because it indicates that these gay men just don't want to work with women. Most women will be familiar with the reverse accusation when they organize separately. Yet Field is right that some (perhaps most) gay men are sexist, as is evidenced by queer backlashes when lesbians begin to achieve visibility within the mixed community.[75] Indeed, some would say that misogyny is greater among gay men since they can live a separatist life more easily than men who want to have sex with women. The complex interplay between women and gay men deserves greater attention, but the question here is whether AIDS is the right arena for the battle over their sexism. Certainly there are gay men who do not want to work with women, or do anything about women's health. While I would not want to count these men as my close friends, does their misogyny really matter? Complaining about this does seem to reveal a scant appreciation of the devastation AIDS has caused to gay men. O'Sullivan and Parmar point out that, unlike women, 'before the AIDS epidemic, middle-class gay men were not especially subject to life-threatening or out-of-control diseases or conditions.'[76] After fifteen years of building a community, isn't it entirely 'natural' that these men should respond to this new horror by banding together to protect and care for their own? This introspection may indeed reflect a deeper-seated sexism but, in an AIDS context, is it a murderous misogyny? Yes, if it's a gay policy-maker or funder denying that women get HIV; yes, if it's a gay prevention worker who refuses to address the fact that queer men fuck women; but no, not if it is the policy-maker, prevention worker or separatist organization who insists that AIDS continues to be principally a gay disease. In the UK, in the 1990s, it is sophistry to say otherwise.

The most despicable rationale for heterosexualizing AIDS was the belief that gay men's lives and health do not matter. Yet there was another reason, which was that the emphasis on gay men seemed to exclude the realization that anyone else could be affected. There is a certain impasse here: does articulating the fact that gay men are suffering excessively prevent understanding that other people are also suffering? Most pertinently, does revealing the impact of AIDS on gay men conceal the impact on women?

• *Is the future female?*

One option, which would clearly highlight the growing impact on women, would be to describe AIDS as a 'women's disease'. To the extent that women have this disease, it is a women's disease, and since women often want their HIV care and sexual health information from women's health services, these services need to take an active role.[77] Yet in its essence AIDS is not a women's disease since it does not affect something which is only found in women (like a cervix) or which is more vulnerable to disease in females (like a gallbladder). Women and men, of all sexual orientations, have immune systems (the only sub-group which is different here is babies who are born with an immune system which is not fully formed and hence they experience different disease progression from adults). In reviewing why diseases have been inadequately studied in women, an editorial in the *New England Journal of Medicine* identifies three types of women's disease: 'disease that affects women exclusively (such as breast cancer), one that affects women disproportionately (such as gallbladder disease), or one that affects both men and women nearly equally (such as cardiovascular disease).'[78] In the industrialized world, AIDS does not fit under any of these categories since it is a disease which currently affects *men* disproportionately.

The disproportionate impact of AIDS on men is based on historical, not biological, reasons. That history reaches back little more than a decade, and there are clear suggestions that this fact will soon be reversed – indeed, biological factors make it likely. In some parts of sub-Saharan Africa there are now more women with HIV than men, in as high a ratio as 14:10,[79] and one research group suggests that by the year 2000, worldwide, HIV-infected women will outnumber men.[80] However insidiously things seem to be moving in that direction, it would take some pretty serious statistical massage to claim that in the UK AIDS is a women's disease right now.

• *The AIDS competition*

Calling AIDS a woman's disease, a gay disease, a family disease is about responding to social, political and ideological realities. This may be a response which names what is happening (paediatricians describe AIDS as a 'family disease' because they rarely see an HIV-infected child who doesn't have infected family members), which seeks to manipulate the way people imagine the condition ('heterosexual AIDS') or, more usually, all of the above. The panic generated by re-gaying brought into the spotlight a major fear that exists from a grass-roots perspective: if the different impacts among communities are articulated, will they inevitably be drawn into battle with each other? Statements about the diversity of impact can lead to a competitiveness: which community is suffering the most? If one community is suffering acutely does that diminish the suffering of others? Is one disease more important than another? If one disease is 'special' does that negate all others? Still, the existence of separate agencies dedicated to the HIV needs of drug users, the Asian communities, women, black communities, children, people with haemophilia, does not seem to cause the level of anxiety that occurs when gay men articulate their needs. In her article, Field worries at length about GMFA's demand that '60–80 per cent of the jobs should go to gay men or at least those who understand the issues for them',[81] when many of the positions of power are currently occupied by white middle-class gay men. Could re-gaying really be just 'jobs for the gay boys'?

Field articulates the fear that since, as a group, gay men tend not to be impoverished, they will be incapable of responding to the multiple oppressions experienced by other groups which are vulnerable to HIV. On one side this competitiveness buys in to old notions of hierarchies of oppression (that, for example, black women suffer more than white men). It suggests that the most marginalized will necessarily suffer the most, and that the cake of resources should not be divided equally, but rather redress pre-existing oppressive imbalances. In contrast, there is an AIDS-specific hierarchy of suffering, with a competitiveness based upon AIDS' impact. Some communities are suffering (quantitatively) more than others, that is, they have lost a higher percentage of members. This does not mean that the experience will be uniform across a highly affected community,[82] or that an individual from a more impacted community will (qualitatively) experience more distress than one from a lesser impacted community – there may even be an argument that the reaction is in inverse proportion to the level of impact.

The idea that GMFA and the re-gayers have somehow *introduced* these levels of competition into the AIDS movement is ludicrous. There already is a competition – the competition people like Wayne respond to: babies and heterosexuals, women in particular, curry more sympathy; the threat to white, straight, non-drug-using men frees up the public purse; anxiety about poor babies has led to a mushrooming of children's experts organizing family-based care which, in true backlash fashion, pits women against their children. As more is known about pharmaceutical, medical and lifestyle interventions which reduce HIV transmission from a pregnant woman to her foetus/infant, pressure is mounting on women which mirrors the approach of the American Far Right.

It is surely just a matter of time before charges are brought against HIV-infected women for 'foetal neglect' or 'child abuse' if they reject the current preferred intervention to reduce HIV transmission during pregnancy (like AZT). Such charges have already been made against numerous (uninfected) women because of other kinds of 'unacceptable' behaviour during pregnancy.[83]

The spectre of battles between (mythical) foetal rights and adult human rights is a disturbing one for any feminist. Yet the pregnant body is not the only AIDS battleground where children are in the ascendancy: babies buy support. In early 1990 the media was stuffed with reports of Romanian orphanages overwhelmed by hundreds of HIV-infected babies and children – their infections due to unhygienic medical procedures. This high profile 'tragedy' spontaneously loosened many individuals' purse strings (with just a little help from the *Sunday Times*). Moved by the distressing situation (and perhaps sniffing a little easy money) the fundraiser at THT spontaneously set up a 'Romanian Baby Appeal'. This special fund was without precedent and created more than a little controversy at THT – controversy which resulted in the fundraiser's resignation. The appeal was entirely predictable: lots of previously unsupportive people pledged money, with even the Princess of Wales making a private donation to THT. When the fuss was over, and the fundraising team returned to these donors for support with general work, many were abusive and nearly all asked to be removed from THT's fundraising donor base. Comments such as, 'I don't care about junkies and queers' were not uncommon.[84]

It is public opinion and government policies which encourage competition amongst communities and diseases. At the level of public funding, communities' anguished debates about equality simply do not figure. Tory health ministers are not interested in ensuring that all communities' needs are met, or indeed that the most affected communities receive the care they need, but rather that they can politically justify their allocations. In this way women are to some degree lucky: they seem to be normal and acceptable, and might even have babies, so ministers can justify paying attention – but only so long as women really *are* normal and acceptable. Is fitting in to their moral agendas really the 'equality' women seek?

• A queer disease which affects others

A brief romp through AIDS competitiveness suggests that wherever AIDS is linked to one community there is a mini backlash from another community which senses that they are rendered invisible. There is no simple catch-all which expresses the totality and complexity of all of these individuals who are affected by AIDS, and all their communities and affiliations. With a little imagination, however, there is no reason why these different communities should not be addressed separately and in coalition without causing conflict and division.

The tension for women is that they are simultaneously mainstream (the smokescreen that conceals queer AIDS) and the 'other' (not members of the patriarchy). One commentator suggests that AIDS 'consigned those who were already on the periphery to the category of the expendable and further led to the ideological construction of AIDS as emblematic of otherness.'[85] It is this notion of the 'other' which completes and extends the conceptualization of AIDS as queer. This is particularly critical for an understanding of AIDS and women, since the woman is always the 'other'. AIDS is not a women's disease, it is not 'our' disease and yet we get it: a woman cannot recognize the 'other' within herself. Well-meaning men fail to see how they reinforce such distance, for example, leading HIV-prevention workers highlighted the urgency of the changing profile of the epidemic stating, 'in designing prevention programs, we must address *the unique needs* of women' (my emphasis).[86] No less a commentator than the Pope articulated the otherness intrinsic to women saying, 'It is never allowed to deprive a woman of her right to respect and dignity simply because she is not one of us, because she is *other*' (his emphasis).[87] However much the individual woman conceives of herself as 'one of us', she will always be other because the male is the norm. Masculinity is the dominant and defining term in western societies. She is described as posing 'unique' challenges to AIDS policy, the course of disease in her body is examined a decade after the 'normal' male disease course is known, the progress of the epidemic through her sex is submerged to be charted through groupings of sexualities. It is the perpetual role of woman as 'other' which keeps the focus away from women, rather than any rationale that AIDS disproportionately affects men.

AIDS is, Field reminds us, 'a crisis of poverty, homophobia, racism and misogyny'.[88] Yet the ways in which these forms of oppression and prejudice interact with the disease are remarkably different. The existence of AIDS in poor, queer, black and women's communities does not mean that they will automatically form a rainbow coalition or have a united response. It is critically important to make the connections (especially to 'the general public' who tend to be spared this knowledge), but such an analysis cannot replace dealing with the specifics. Attempts to smooth out different communities' needs and impacts into generalized statements like, 'Everyone at risk from HIV infection is being ignored',[89] are fundamentally unhelpful. Surgery patients' minuscule HIV risk is not ignored (as the policies on HIV-infected healthcare workers show), nor are the risks to foetuses (as antenatal screening shows). The bases for ignoring HIV risks are very different. For example, homophobia leads to gay and bisexual HIV risks being ignored; while fundamental to the ignorance of women's HIV risks is institutionalized sexism which suppresses the realities of women's desire and denies the prevalence of coercive sex. Although these issues can be caught together under simple banners of 'oppression' – and they are rooted in a confused, condemnatory attitude towards sex and sexuality – no group is then likely to be addressed adequately, or achieve the aims of having their true HIV risks made visible and consequently minimized.

Learning to live in the long-term with an epidemic, rather than a sudden crisis, makes it essential that diversities are addressed as such. The rhetoric which originated in the early days of panic and poor information no longer has a place, as knowledge improves about the dynamics both of transmission and the future epidemiological profile. AIDS policies rooted in 'applied epidemiology', even 're-gaying', will serve the needs of women far better than the notion of 'heterosexual AIDS'. AIDS is a queer disease which affects others, and because it is queer the condition and people infected are often feared and treated badly. It is only by understanding the dynamics of its 'queerness' that it is possible to uncover the diverse ways in which AIDS affects women, and consequently to develop appropriate responses.

Notes

1. C. Patton, 'AIDS: lessons from the gay community', *Feminist Review*, No. 30, Autumn 1988, p. 109.
2. See, for example, D. Richardson, *Women and the AIDS Crisis*, 2nd edn, Pandora Press, London, 1989, p. 12.
3. Debates about the cause of AIDS are beyond the scope of this book. I work from the assumption that HIV is the prime cause of AIDS, although it seems likely that (as yet unidentified) co-factors are necessary for the development of symptomatic illness.
4. This phrase, often reduced to 'MWHSWM', 'mesmen' or 'msm', is a useful way for policy-makers to define a range of people whose activities may be risky. However, it obscures the identity of these men and as such is unhelpful for targeting interventions. How do you direct work to 'msm'? Has anyone ever met someone who identifies as a 'man who has sex with men'? The term has been criticized by Alcorn, King, Scott, Watney *et al.* See, for example, P. Scott, 'Beginning HIV prevention work with gay and bisexual men', in B. Evans *et al.* (eds), *Healthy Alliances in HIV Prevention*, HEA, London, 1993, and E. King, *Safety in Numbers*, Cassell, London, 1993, pp. 203–5.

   In general I shall refer to 'gay men and bisexual men' or 'queer men', as the lifestyles, relationships with women and experiences of AIDS for men whose identities are in line with their sexual practices will tend to be very different from those of heterosexual-identified men who have sex with men.
5. The phrase 'HIV-infected' is disliked by some women or men who are living with HIV. However, I use it to refer to people who are infected with the virus, irrespective of whether they are aware of the fact. The fact of infection is often more important than an individual's awareness of it (e.g. in the context of transmission), but where women and men know their HIV status this will be described. 'HIV-positive' describes a person who has been tested and found to have HIV, and the term 'woman living with HIV' suggests a degree of self-awareness on her part; these terms will be used as appropriate.
6. Women rarely acquire haemophilia, but they do transmit the gene to their sons. Some women do acquire a milder form of haemophilia (Christmas disease), but very few of them have become HIV-infected, as they receive less blood.
7. S. Tchamorouff, 'Sexually transmitted diseases and HIV infections in homosexual men' (letter), *BMJ*, Vol. 306, January 1993, p. 792.
8. *Communicable Disease Report*, Vol. 4, No. 228, 15 July 1994, p. 131.
9. A 100 per cent increase in cases, when the absolute number is two, means just two more – whereas when the absolute number is 5000 this refers to an additional 5000.

10. For example, WHO state that there are now 12 women with HIV for every 10 men in sub-Saharan Africa (Merson, plenary presentation, X International AIDS Conference, Yokahama, Japan, 7–12 August 1994). The American CDC reports that since 1989 prevalence of HIV among women applying for military service, entering the Job Corps and donating blood remained stable or increased, but prevalence decreased among men in the same categories (Petersen, Abstract 123C, X International AIDS Conference).

11. This is based upon my own rough calculations according to HIV-1 incidence reports for 1991, 1992 and 1993 given in the PHLS AIDS Centre, unpublished quarterly surveillance tables, No. 22, December 1993. The problem with any such calculation is that HIV reports only track people who present voluntarily for testing, not the true HIV incidence.

12. Kramer is the author of numerous hard-hitting plays, books and essays on AIDS. He is a fiery activist not afraid of offending people in the greater interest of urging them on to take action. His essay '1,112 and counting' (*New York Native*, issue 59, 14–27 March 1983) was the activist equivalent of Gottlieb's original report of gay men with PCP. Seeing his play *The Normal Heart* was my personal call to arms.

13. C. Patton, *Inventing AIDS*, Routledge, London, 1990, p. 117.

14. H. Gasch and M. Thompson Fullilove, 'Working with communities of women at risk', in A. Kurth (ed.), *Until the Cure: Caring for Women with HIV*, Yale University Press, 1993, p. 186.

15. *Sun*; *Daily Mail*; *Independent*; all 15 June 1993.

16. G. Corea, *The Invisible Epidemic: The Story of Women and AIDS*, HarperPerennial, New York, 1992, p. 20.

17. Patton, *Inventing AIDS*, p. 117.

18. *The Concise Oxford Dictionary of Current English*, 7th edn, OUP, 1982.

19. *Ibid.*

20. K. Wellings *et al.*, *Sexual Behaviour in Britain: The National Survey of Sexual Attitudes and Lifestyles*, Penguin, Harmondsworth, 1994, p. 18.

21. J. H. Gagnon, 'Disease and desire', in *Living with AIDS*, S. R. Granbard (ed.), MIT Press, Cambridge, MA, 1990, p. 203.

22. Even Lynne Segal used this phrase as the title of her book exploring how feminists can have sex with men – her use may be partially ironic, but it also highlights the normalizing discourse that applies to such acceptable behaviour.

23. J. Cameron, *More*, 11 January 1989, pp. 56–7.

24. Roy Cornes, a man with haemophilia and HIV who died in 1994 at the age of twenty-one, became the focus of tabloid attention and (they claimed) a public health scare, when it became known three of his girlfriends had acquired HIV. Reports differ on whether the women knew of Cornes's HIV status, whether he refused to practise safer sex,

or whether the unprotected sex was mutually agreed. He discovered he was infected as a pre-adolescent, and apparently received very little quality counselling and information about the sexual implications of his HIV diagnosis. No outrage or scare has ever emerged regarding a man infecting three or more men in similar circumstances.

25. I am indebted to Jonathan Mann for pointing this out to me.
26. Wellings, *op. cit.*, p. 151.
27. Based on *ibid.*, Table 5.11, p. 218.
28. *Ibid*, p. 187.
29. Such phrases can be found in nearly every scientific study or review of HIV transmission between men and women. I picked these at random from J. E. Howe *et al.*, 'Contraceptives and HIV', *AIDS*, 1994, Vol. 8, pp. 861–71 and 'Heterosexually acquired AIDS – United States, 1993', *MMWR,* 11 March 1994, Vol. 43, pp. 155–60.
30. M. L. Adams, 'Plagued by the New Right: politics, women and AIDS', in *Herizons*, Vol. 4, No. 6, September 1986, p. 22.
31. Quoted by Irma Kurtz, 'My name is Denise . . . I'm HIV positive', *Cosmopolitan*, January 1991, pp. 68–9.
32. The article was timed to coincide with World AIDS Day 1990, which focused on women to push a heavy message of generalized hetero-sexual danger – see Chapter 2.
33. M. Fitzpatrick and D. Milligan, Junius Publications, London, 1987.
34. M. Fumento, *The Myth of Heterosexual AIDS: How a Tragedy Has Been Distorted by the Media and Partisan Politics*, Basic Books, New York, 1990 and Regnery Gateway, Washington, DC, 1993.
35. In 1990 the *Sunday Times* serialized Fumento's book and subse-quently, under the guidance of editor Andrew Neil, adopted a fierce 'dissident' position on all elements of the AIDS crisis.
36. Fumento, *op. cit.*, p. 65.
37. *Ibid.*, p. 177.
38. S. Gupta, 'The Aids fraud', *Analysis*, Winter 1991–92, p. 26.
39. See King, *op. cit.*, pp. 245–50, for a review of the activities of Gupta and the RCP.
40. S. Garfield, *The End of Innocence: Britain in the Time of AIDS*, Faber & Faber, London, 1994, p. 117.
41. See King, *op. cit.*, Chapters 2 and 3, for details about the development of HIV-prevention information in the early 1980s.
42. David Corkery, personal communication. Most people credit Michael Callen and Richard Berkowitz with 'creating' safer sex in *How to Have Sex in an Epidemic: One Approach*, News From the Front Publications, New York, 1983; see King, *op. cit.*, Chapter 2.
43. M. Wiles, 'Myth in theology', in *The Myth of God Incarnate*, J. Hick (ed.), SCM Press, London, 1977, p. 163.
44. 'Update: Acquired Immunodeficiency Syndrome – United States, 1992', *MMWR*, Vol. 42, No. 28, pp. 548–51.

45. *CDR*, Vol. 4, No. 42, 21 October 1994, Table 1.

46. M. S. Gottlieb *et al.*, 'Pneumocystis carinii pneumonia and mucosal candidiasis in previously healthy homosexual men. Evidence of a new acquired cellular immunodeficiency', *NEJM*, 10 December 1981, 305 (24), pp. 1425–31.

47. R. M. Packard and P. Epstein, 'Medical research on AIDS in Africa: a historical perspective' in E. Fee and D. M. Fox (eds), *AIDS: The Making of a Chronic Disease*, University of California Press, 1992, p. 348.

48. The ability of some men to conceal their sexuality even from themselves is wittily recounted by Julian Clary, who describes a night of sex with a Spanish man who tells him the next morning, 'You gay. Me? No gay . . . I can sleep with a man, but I no gay.' Quoted in 'The food of love', *Guardian, Guide* section, 27 May 1995, p. 98.

49. See, for example, King, *op. cit.*; E. King, M. Rooney and P. Scott, *HIV Prevention and Gay Men*, North West Thames Regional Health Authority, London, 1992.

50. King, *op. cit.*, for example pp. 169–70.

51. Fumento, *op. cit.*, p. 151.

52. King, *op. cit.*, p. xi.

53. Keith Alcorn, personal communication.

54. Corea, *op. cit.*, p. 122.

55. G. Green, in Kurth, *op. cit.*, pp. 144–5.

56. *Boyz* doctor, 'Going straight', *Boyz*, 3 October 1992, p. 22; 'G is for girls', *Boyz*, 1 May 1993, p. 18.

57. F. van den Boom, 'Social impact and response', in *Conference Summary Report: VIII International Conference on AIDS/III World STD Congress, Amsterdam, The Netherlands*, ed. R. Gorna, Harvard AIDS Institute, 1992, p. 34.

58. Numerous personal communications. For example, members of Gay Men Fighting AIDS attended a series of meetings I organized on bisexuality and HIV. They fully accepted that many gay/bisexual/ queer men have sex with women, but would give no assurances that sex with women would ever be discussed in their materials.

59. S. Watney, 'Gay Brits take back the fight', *NYQ*, 30 August 1992, quoted in King, *op. cit.*, p. 267. King has an excellent review of this discussion, pp. 265–8.

60. See S. Sontag, *Illness as Metaphor*, Farrar, Straus and Giroux, New York, 1978; and *AIDS and Its Metaphors*, Farrar, Straus and Giroux, New York, 1988.

61. The first reference I can find to AIDS as an 'equal opportunities' disease is the advertising campaign by Amfar before 1988 – see Sontag, *op. cit.* (1988), p. 82.

62. The list varies in order slightly, but the equality elements are constant.

63. PHLS AIDS Centre, unpublished quarterly surveillance tables, No. 24, June 1994, Table 2.

64. I find this advertising campaign particularly strange because of the huge respect I have for the quality of services provided by London Lighthouse. My friend David O'Donnell spent the last two months of his life in their residential unit. At that time nearly all of the residents were (not surprisingly) under forty, male and gay, some were (ex-)drug users, and a high proportion were not white English.

65. Quoted by S. MacKenzie, 'Rallying to a common cause', *Guardian*, 6 March 1991, and quoted in King, *op. cit.*, p. 214.

66. This was a part of the mission statement defined by THT's Board of Directors during my time on the Board (1988–90).

67. Quoted in King, *op. cit.*, p. 214.

68. N. Field, 'Take-over bids and monopolies: HIV and the gay community – Gay Men Fighting AIDS: whose army?', *Mainliners*, Issue 25/26, August/September 1992, p. 2.

69. Sontag, *op. cit.* (1988), pp. 82f.

70. S. Watney, 'State of emergency' *Gay Times*, April 1991.

71. See *Local Government, AIDS and Gay Men*, NAM, 1994.

72. 'AIDS is a gay disease!', *PWA Coalition Newsline*, 42, March 1989 – quoted in King, *op. cit.*, p. 169. Callen, who died on 27 December 1993, was diagnosed with AIDS in 1982. He was an inspiration for many: a talented musician, creator of the first safer sex guidelines, co-founder of the US People With AIDS Coalition and author of *Surviving AIDS*.

73. See E. King, *FxxxSheet*, GMFA, December 1993.

74. Field, *op. cit.*, pp. 1–3.

75. For example, there was a backlash to the proposal that the 1995 Lesbian and Gay Pride march should be fronted by women with 'Lesbian Visibility' as its theme.

76. S. O'Sullivan and P. Parmar, *Lesbians Talk (Safer) Sex*, Scarlet Press, London, 1992, p. 14.

77. 93.3 per cent of HIV-positive women in London stated that they would like their HIV specialist care to deal also with other women's health problems, including family planning, cervical smears, etc. *Women Like Us: Positively Women's Research into the Needs and Experiences of Women with HIV*, Positively Women, London, 1994, p. 34 (henceforth, *Women Like Us*).

78. M. Angell, 'Caring for women's health – what is the problem?' *NEJM*, Vol. 329, No. 4, pp. 271–2.

79. S. Berkley *et al.*, 'AIDS and HIV infection in Uganda – are more women infected than men?', *AIDS*, 12 (1990), pp. 1237–42; cited in J. M. Mann *et al.* (eds), *AIDS in the World*, Harvard University Press, Cambridge, MA, 1992.

80. Consensus statement of the Center for Strategic and International Studies, 2 August 1994 – cited by G. Nary in *JPAAC*, August 1994, p. 5.

81. P. Scott, *Capital Gay*, 22 May 1992, quoted by Field, *op. cit.*, p. 3.
82. A gay man in NYC who is in his late thirties explained how the younger gay men looked at him with pity, 'like a dinosaur' because so very few of his generation are still alive. Even within a community where the majority of people are HIV-infected it is important to be alert to the subtle, but socially vital, differences of impact. The sole survivor of a friendship circle is likely to experience his grief very differently from a man who has lost two of his friends. What seems to me wrong with King demanding 'respect for the enormous blow that we have suffered as a community, and the courage we have shown in fighting AIDS' (*Capital Gay*, 22 May 1992) is the idea that there is 'a community' or that all gay men have suffered and responded in similar measures. (This woman has lost a lot more friends than many men on the British gay scene.)
83. See S. Faludi, *Backlash: The Undeclared War against Women*, Vintage, London, 1991, pp. 436–91 (pp. 459–73 are frighteningly pertinent).
84. Personal recollections – I was on THT's Board of Directors at this time. A few of these issues are discussed in Garfield, *op. cit.*, pp. 237–8.
85. V. Lewis, 'The Word Made Flesh: AIDS and the Visual Arts', MA dissertation, Royal College of Art, London, 1994, p. 5.
86. P. Lamptey, cited in press release, 'Prevention: is it working?', Abstract PS-02-2, IX International Conference on AIDS, Berlin, 6–11 June 1993.
87. Pope John Paul II, January 1993, in respect of the Bosnian situation. Reported in the *Guardian*, 10 September 1994.
88. Field, *op. cit.*, p. 1.
89. *Ibid.*, p. 3.

Chapter two

Vulnerable Vampires

AIDS seems to foster ominous fantasies about a disease that is a marker of both individual and social vulnerabilities. The virus invades the body; the disease (or, in the newer version, the fear of the disease) is described as invading the whole society.

Susan Sontag[1]

Most books, conferences and training sessions on this topic are imaginatively entitled 'Women and AIDS'.[2] This simple phrase is much (ab)used, yet few seem to notice how troubled the coupling of these two nouns can be.[3] It is an almost aggressive phrasing, where 'women' render AIDS respectable while 'AIDS' queers women. The disease is normalized by its association with the 'fairer sex', but the fairer sex is thrown into a questionable moral light by the mere fact of discussing the disease.

The disease and its representations are negotiated through society, and since society is unequal, pre-existing inequities are highlighted and may be intensified. The oppression of women – and of gay men – and their marginalization from mainstream society, are fundamental components influencing the spread of HIV. Just as homophobia fuels the HIV crisis among gay men and bisexual men, so sexism and gender inequality fuel the HIV crisis among women.

Women are highly vulnerable to acquiring HIV from sex with men, as well as from sharing drug-injecting equipment. At a biological level women are far more vulnerable than men to acquiring HIV from sexual intercourse (see Chapters 6 and 7). But the imbalance between the sexes in terms of HIV risk is just as significantly related to the socio-economic and political imbalances which continue to divide the sexes. Women's lesser power in society, which is often enshrined in unequal financial sexual relationships with men, frequently creates situations of higher HIV vulnerability for women. For example, economic and power inequality may mean that a woman is not able to ensure that safer sex is practised, perhaps because a man rapes her or threatens to withhold money or goods if she insists on a condom. Moreover, there is currently no safer sex mechanism which women can control – the only prevention technologies which are within a woman's control are those which can prevent the acquisition of HIV from unsterile injecting equipment, or lessen transmission of HIV to her child.[4]

In the arena of sex (the route by which over 2000 women in the UK have become infected[5]), the only HIV-prevention technologies are controlled by men. Men wear the standard prophylactic (penile condoms), and high degrees of male compliance are required for the next most efficient technology (the so-called female condoms), while the only other mechanism is rooted in gender-power inequalities (mutual monogamy). This last technique has been over-promoted to women with disastrous effect: many women may keep their side of the bargain while the man does not, and it is estimated that as many as 80 per cent of HIV-infected women worldwide acquired the virus from their one and only sexual partner.[6] While most societies have long-established structures to police and control female sexual behaviour, the same is simply not true for heterosexual men.

Where sexual behaviour is policed, vulnerability to HIV thrives. In his landmark book *Policing Desire*, Simon Watney described how the epidemic among gay men was fuelled by denial and horror of gay sexuality and the prohibition of sexually explicit literature, which could have engaged with the realities of this health crisis for a group assigned to the margins. The policing of women's sexuality promises to have similarly disastrous results, although few feminists have explored the links between the repression of female sexuality and increasing rates of HIV. Mills records that with sex education in schools:

The female body is perceived as a site of passive vulnerability exposed to the danger of rampant male hypersexuality . . . few sex educators dare to promote . . . the pleasure aspect of sex . . . many children are taught about the dangers of AIDS but not about the role of sex in a natural life.[7]

In addressing women's sexuality there is a constant tension between combating the sexual terrorism and violence which oppress women, and making visible women's sexual desire and pleasure. Where the balance is lost between these two elements, women's sexuality remains concealed and denied. Vance maintains that:

Feminism must speak to sexuality as a site of oppression, not only the oppression of male violence, brutality, and coercion which it has already spoken about eloquently and effectively, but also the repression of female desire that comes from ignorance, invisibility, and fear. Feminism must put forward a politics that resists deprivation and supports pleasure. It must understand pleasure as life-affirming, empowering, desirous of human connection and the future.[8]

Representing women and AIDS

The obvious reason for discussing women and AIDS would be to explore the complex interplays between AIDS and women's sexual desire, and to understand the real needs of women living with HIV and AIDS, affected by the AIDS crisis and vulnerable to HIV infection. Yet one of the features of AIDS is that it creates symbols out of human beings, events and behaviour – or women are used as the public face of AIDS, to normalize the epidemic and take the sting out of the horror. AIDS is described as 'a post-modern disease'; graffiti tell us, 'Anal Intercourse = Death Sentence'; it is 'the end of the sexual revolution'; AIDS is symbolic of the destruction of the planet's coping mechanisms; a priest says that in the person with HIV 'I see Christ'.[9] Just as AIDS is rarely described as the medical condition it is, so the woman with HIV is rarely perceived as a person to be cared for, or afforded sympathy for her life-threatening diagnosis. Media images of HIV-positive women are rarely used to enable the public to understand their individual plights, or the general situation of HIV-positive women, their needs and concerns, but rather they are presented as symbols (as will be illustrated). The needs which are allowed expression belong to the pre-existing values of the mainstream, and these do not permit all of women's concerns to be real, to draw sympathy or inspire activism.

The fact that women can be – and are becoming – infected with HIV, has led to an overriding marginalization of the reality of women's lives. Women have become sexy, and simultaneously sexless. For the media, women with HIV are a godsend. Now people will believe that anyone can get AIDS – and journalists go to extraordinary lengths to find the most average looking woman to prove this thesis. The realities of most people with AIDS' lives are papered over with such pieces of AIDS exceptionalism. What is fascinating about this public presentation is that so many of these women are not allowed a sexual persona: she became infected by her bisexual partner/her husband who had sex whilst away on business/her drug using boyfriend. She was passively infected, and now suffers silently on her lonely path to celibate sickness and death. Occasionally, instead, there is the image of the rampant irresponsible whore, wilfully spreading disease. There is rarely a picture of a woman who has a rounded, enjoyable sexual life. And whilst many women may experience difficulties with sex, the problematization of the sexuality of HIV-positive women is out of all proportion.

The first woman with AIDS was reported to the American CDC (Center for Disease Control) in 1981, the year that 'GRID' was identified. By 1983 'Gay Related Immune Deficiency' (GRID) had been renamed AIDS and the UK began to record AIDS statistics which, that September, included the first woman with AIDS. Yet it was not until the end of 1990 that the impacts of AIDS on women were generally presented to the public when the World Health Organization (WHO) named women as the focus of their 'World AIDS Day'. The newspapers took delight in this focus. Partly they were getting used to the idea of 1 December being World AIDS Day (this was the third of these annual events), but it also gave good copy. In Britain, by the time World AIDS Day focused on women, at least 1635 women had tested HIV-positive and 203 had developed AIDS (of whom 99 had died). The self-help organization 'Positively Women' had been operational for three years, reliant primarily on HIV-positive women volunteering. The reason for 'Women and AIDS' as the focus was not because women acquiring HIV was some dramatic new event (whatever the headlines suggested). It was not really about women. Instead, it was about how women fitted into other people's agendas: women could front the queer epidemic and turn it straight. The media focused on the acceptable face of women with AIDS, trivializing the experience of women with HIV who are not mainstream, and undermining any sense of cohesion amongst all people with HIV and AIDS.

Little attention was paid to the real lives of women with HIV who live on the margins of society – drug users, sex workers, prisoners, African refugees, queers – nor to the women whose family, friends or partners have HIV, nor the hundreds of women dedicated to working in the AIDS epidemic. Even more importantly, the complex prevention needs of women were not addressed. For instance, how do women name and explore their sexuality? How can HIV be avoided in the face of sexual abuse or rape? How do you 'make' a man wear a condom? How can women take control of stress and drug use? How do HIV-positive women choose between pregnancy and termination, and get good information and care to make those choices? How are gender power imbalances addressed?

The rationale for World AIDS Day is that the media need a 'hook' for stories. 1 December is now the AIDS hook; and some agencies are so desperate for publicity that the day expands to become 'National AIDS Week' or 'World AIDS Month'. For the AIDS industry, this day is a very mixed blessing. It demands a huge amount of energy, diverted from routine tasks, to promote someone else's idea and to jump to media demands. Sometimes the focus can be used to dovetail with their own aims, but often the themes chosen by WHO are remote from agencies' day-to-day reality of fighting the AIDS crisis. The themes set by WHO are safe, generalized and tend to be based on the assumption that no one is aware of AIDS or doing anything about it.[10] The first theme, in 1988, was 'Global Mobilization' – an appropriate rallying point for a new global initiative. In 1989 an affected group was chosen:

'Youth'. Youth are often perceived as *the* sexually active group, and hence a major target for HIV-prevention activities. This fairly rampant, 'experimenting' bunch is inevitably assumed to be straight – a safe target for global action. In 1990 it was the turn of 'Women'. The motives for this choice were probably good; but many of the ways it was used were not so good. Women became a safe target.

Any hope that WHO had a radical agenda is removed by a quick glance at the themes that followed: 1991, 'A Community Concern'; 1992, 'Sharing the Challenge'; 1993, 'A Time to Act', with 1994 focusing on 'The Family' (how much more 'normal' than that could things get?[11]). In the 1990s WHO abandoned its focus on affected communities. After all, who would they have chosen next? Children? These had been covered with women. Men? Too complex (in a way that women are never assumed to be). Gay men? Not perceived as 'global'[12] and certainly not safe. World AIDS Days of the 1990s have been characterized by bland, irrelevant and sometimes insulting slogans.[13] Being told in 1993 that it's 'Time to Act' is as insulting as being told to 'Wear the [red] ribbon and make a difference'.[14] The overriding aim of World AIDS Day is no longer about global solidarity, but rather about bringing the issue of AIDS close to those who think that it has nothing to do with them: it's a 'them', not an 'us' day.

For marketing any product, women are appealing tools, and so the idea of women as the focus has become ingrained with the image of World AIDS Day. Stories about women and AIDS abound and reach a peak every December. These stories are rarely in women's interests – most use individuals' lives to tell a bigger story. In general these stories are used to infantilize or demonize women, or to heterosexualize AIDS.

The most common tack is heterosexualization – the use of women to prove the existence of a heterosexual AIDS crisis. This genre of reporting is distinct, but sometimes it employs other symbolic roles from infantalized or demonized pictures of women. Infantilization is the de-sexing of women, which can be done in many ways, and is in stark opposition to demonization, where women are portrayed as hypersexual. Demonized women are the whores, sluts and vamps who have too much sex, even enjoy sex, and endanger society through their lasciviousness. The image of the 'junkie' is rarely proffered in the media discourse, since these women are not assumed to have public appeal and their lives are not 'generalizable'. When the image of the 'junkie' appears, the presentation is in the same vein as that of the demonized women, but most of the time any history of drug use is concealed or under-played.

Fundamental to public concern about women and AIDS is anxiety about child-bearing potential and risks to heterosexual men. Women are simply pit stops en route to more vital populations: babies and men. It is not just the media that propagate this approach – they often glean their material from the AIDS industry. Any hope that the focus for health educators is *women's* health is dashed by the Health Education Authority (HEA) AIDS Programme Paper on Women and AIDS which states:

> AIDS in women is important . . . because:
> • the trends in women may be a good marker for follow-ing general trends in *heterosexual transmission*; and,
> • since the majority of childhood AIDS cases are the result of perinatal transmission from the mother, trends in AIDS cases in women may also predict future *trends in AIDS in children* (their emphasis).[15]

Innocent virgins

The symbolic roles of 'infantilization' cover a range of evils: women are trivialized as safe victims for whom the general public can feel sorry, they become martyrish carers, or they are so identified with their (actual or potential) babies that they cease to have any identities of their own. In general these women are asexual.

On a daily basis many women become accustomed to being called 'dear', 'love' and 'girl', being prodded by bus conductors and patronized by shop workers. In the context of AIDS such annoying infantilization runs deeper, stripping women of their adulthood and integrity as human beings, and locating women in childlike roles. Women with, or at risk of, HIV lose all sexual desires (even to the extent of becoming virginal), or are portrayed as the altruistic carer or mother. This de-sexing renders women safe and able to curry public sympathy. In this infantile discourse women have no sexuality: either they lack desire or all of their sexual energy is funnelled into maternity.

Most AIDS Service Organizations (ASOs) are familiar with the journalist who calls up to request (or demand) an HIV-positive woman for the piece she is writing. Frequently the shopping list is specific, like the type of request the Terrence Higgins Trust (THT) is used to receiving for 'a white, non-drug using HIV-positive mother who found out she was positive during her pregnancy'.[16] One of the functions of the Women and AIDS discourse is to make AIDS 'safe'. It provides a mechanism to overcome the general panic engendered by the idea of people actually enjoying sex (an idea which is a necessary component of understanding sexually trans-mitted diseases). The magazine editor who tells the ASO's press officer she 'doesn't want to use a gay man' to illustrate her story on AIDS, usually does want to use a woman (and use she does). She fears that the gay man will not attract compassion, whereas the woman will. This approach is rooted in a trivialization and de-sexing of women, on top of the overt homophobia. A leaflet on *Women and AIDS* produced by Reading Borough Council in 1989 warned women of the risks of acquiring HIV: the list began with ear-piercing and acupuncture and finally got around to sex as the twentieth item of concern. No wonder panics about HIV-infected healthcare workers often rely on images of stodgy, scared women who tell us, 'I'd never thought about AIDS before.' The tabloids exclaim, 'Midwife with AIDS bug has mothers in a panic', 'Hospital mums in AIDS fear', 'AIDS shock for seven mothers'.[17] The stories tell of a male (read 'gay') midwife who helped deliver seven babies when he knew he was HIV-positive – the women are now being offered HIV tests to reassure them that the risk is 'remote'. What about the far more profound 'AIDS shock for mothers' who discover they have HIV during pregnancy? Tabloid journalists could not muster interest in a story about women who are mundanely sexual. Women are vulnerable to HIV when they get fucked, when they conceive, but the emphasis is placed upon the risk (queer) HIV-positive midwives and gynaecologists might pose by assisting with the delivery. These 'midwife mums' are said to face 'an AIDS nightmare'[18] from their blameless action of delivery, which is remote from any act that brought them to a delivery room. The complexity and reality of women's sexuality is submerged beneath the veneer of innocence defiled.

The classic example of innocence defiled is the case of Kimberly Bergalis. Bergalis died as a result of AIDS in 1991 protesting, 'I have done nothing wrong, yet I am being made to suffer like this. My life has been taken away.'[19] She was believed to have acquired HIV from her dentist, David Acer, who died in 1990.[20] Bergalis represents the ultimate fear and horror of what AIDS may become: the virgin whose life is curtailed as a result of the 'dirty' practices of others. Her case caused mass panic in the USA and abroad, fuelled by her impassioned deathbed pleas for routine HIV testing of healthcare workers. Media reports of the patients Acer infected always focus on Bergalis, and other young women such as Sherry Johnson, an eighteen-year-old girl who tested HIV-positive three years after Acer's death. Johnson is reported as weeping, 'Why me? I was looking forward to my life', with her stepmother adding, 'Her dreams and aspirations are already dead.'[21] Such statements could fall from the lips of any young person with HIV or AIDS, but the poignancy is absent without the halo of virginity.

It is not only the tear-jerking comments which draw attention. These pure, young victims (Bergalis and Johnson are most definitely victims[22]) are encouraged to pronounce on any issue and are transformed into experts on infection control measures, public health policy and statistics. Both campaign for universal testing of healthcare workers and Johnson pronounces on how many of Acer's untested patients are HIV-infected. Shortly before her death, Bergalis testified to the US congress, saying, 'Please enact legislation so that no other patient or healthcare provider will have to go through the hell that I have.'[23] The emotional appeal of her testimony is fearsome, and makes great copy, but why should her opinion on these matters be so valued? Women and men infected with HIV by the principal routes of transmission rarely have their opinions on HIV-prevention measures respected in the way that these pure, white, middle-class, young women are deferred to on the question of HIV testing of healthcare workers.

The final irony with these virgins emerged in June 1994 when the American television show *Sixty Minutes* broadcast a 'deathbed interview' with Bergalis. Under oath to lawyers for the insurers settling her case, the video of Bergalis convinced viewers that her protestations of virginity were simply untrue. She admits that her last boyfriend went down on her, and when asked about intercourse with him claims 'it was close to the area, but he never penetrated'. The programme quoted from an investigative document apparently drafted by Harold Jaffe – renowned AIDS epidemiologist at the American CDC. This document reveals that all six of the patients Acer was alleged to have infected in fact had classic risk factors: one man was fucked by a man and had sex with prostitutes, another had sex with a prostitute who has since died as a result of AIDS, one woman had several blood transfusions and an extra-marital affair, another had an HIV-positive boyfriend and Sherry Johnson had sex with at least six men. The document also states that Bergalis's friends were convinced that she had sex with at least one of her boyfriends, probably more. Repeatedly, the document notes that Bergalis '"is concerned that if she tells us her risk, her mother would find out" and that "would have serious negative impact".'[24] The young woman who said she had 'done nothing wrong' needed to remain a virgin in her mother's eyes. In the process, she promoted a lie about HIV transmission which has cost healthcare systems around the world millions of pounds, a lie which intensified the human suffering of HIV-infected healthcare workers who have been demonized and hounded from their jobs.

Bergalis's story was rare and unlikely – and so unlikely that it may well be false. It was seized upon because it exemplified the ultimate fantasy of the innocent victim, and with that, the ultimate fear. The most discomforting feature of AIDS is the central role of sex, and one of the convenient features of talking about women is that the sex can be hidden. Innocence, virginity and infantilization are a central feature of 'the wife'. Bisexual men and punters are imagined as loathsome creatures who bridge the two poles: the innocent wife is connected with the good-time girl or the dirty queer by her man's unbridled enjoyment of his own sexuality. A common theme for dramatic exploitation – as well as featuring in anxious talk shows about the 'AIDS risk' every time prostitution is discussed – is the theme of the innocent wife of a man who uses prostitutes. He is portrayed as making a quick economic exchange to meet his lustful needs and then transporting infection home to his cosy family. And the reality behind this? By 1989, in the USA no AIDS cases had been definitively traced to female prostitution.[25] It is possible for punters to become infected, but the probability is low given the high rates of safer sex practice and low seroprevalence among commercial sex workers, together with relatively low rates of female to male HIV transmission. The issues surrounding bisexuality in men are more complex, yet what is notable is that the bisexual man and his male partners are dehumanized and demonized so as to allow the saintly wife to emerge. Many female partners of bisexual men may indeed be 'wronged' in this way, and acquire HIV infection from this route. Yet such infantile presentations of these wives' realities cast them forever in victimhood, denying these women any power or agency of their own. The women I have met, who have acquired HIV this way, have been feisty fighters and were often well aware of their husbands' sexuality. This is something the media appear incapable of understanding. When bisexual Glasgow surgeon Professor George Browning revealed his HIV status in late 1994 the headlines were predictably hysterical. One newspaper shrieked 'AIDS fear of gay sex surgeon's family' and claimed that his 'shattered wife and children' were undergoing counselling about their HIV risks. Yet buried further on in the article a friend of Browning's wife comments (without the requisite juicy sensationalism), 'She's taking it all in her stride. Her husband was very open about his bisexual lifestyle and she knew all about it.'[26]

Madonnas with child

The infantilization of women underlies the focus on women as mothers. The extraordinary feature of motherhood is that, ever since Mary, it can be imagined as an innocent, virginal condition (so long as the woman is not a single mother 'living off the State'). The intersection of HIV and this 'madonna' image creates heightened anxiety. In all contexts the 'woman as womb' is a familiar symbol. Since HIV can be transmitted during pregnancy, birth and breast-feeding, the womb and its fruits overpower the woman. A newspaper advertisement campaign run in February 1990 by the HEA reproduces the thoughts of two experts. Catherine Peckham, Professor of Paediatric Epidemiology, proclaims: 'As the number of women with HIV increases, this results in more babies being born who are infected. We don't want HIV infection to be a problem in the child population – we must think of the future.' She could be given the benefit of the doubt – after all, kids are her job – but her sentiments are echoed by the Chief Medical Officer, Sir Donald Acheson, who states, 'It may not seem very serious now but if we don't act it could have a disastrous effect on the future of our children and our grandchildren.' As one AIDS activist wrote, 'Isn't the subtext to *both* these statements: "We're not too bothered about the mothers (sluts, junkies, whores, etc.), but oh! their poor innocent babies . . . "'[27]

In the context of AIDS, motherhood is the prime role for women. Newspaper article headlines scream, 'Doctors failing to prevent Aids babies' (because pregnant women are not being tested for HIV) and 'A million children in AIDS nightmare' (which reports that 14 million adults are HIV infected, but relegates all of them to second place after the cherubs).[28] International Conferences are held on 'HIV in Children and Mothers' and the delegates debate whether the title is right: should it be 'Children, Adolescents and Mothers' or 'Children and Families'? No one suggests it might be 'Children and *Women*'.[29] Women are seen as constantly on the verge of conception. This permanent fecundity limits the access women have to clinical trials of promising new treatments and often determines the appeals made to women's health-seeking behaviour. The first phrase on one 'Women and AIDS' leaflet is 'Protect Our Species'.[30] While it may be realistic to appeal to the needs of future generations, this level of denial of current life is startling. Many women are mothers, and of those who are not, many would like to have children, but the focus on fertility is out of all proportion. It is rare for leaflets aimed at men to even make a link with their potential for parenting: why then this excessive focus in respect of female adults?

Mother Teresas

The other group of women who tend to be infantalized and un-sexed are women who are carers. The important role played by many women in caring for people with HIV and AIDS in informal capacities (mothers, sisters, lovers, friends), as AIDS Service Organization (ASO) volunteers or professionals (nurses, doctors, social workers, therapists) is beginning to be recognized. Yet when these women's stories are told, the woman loses her sexuality (unless she is queer, in which case there may be some simple statement about 'solidarity with gay men'). The stories of women whose husbands or lovers are HIV-positive tend to begin with the panic of discovery, the wait for their own test results and the relief that they are negative. There is nothing about the struggle to maintain a sex life, changes to libido and relationships, guilt or bargaining, fear of infection or fatalism. Sex is usually a major concern for a discordant couple (that is, where only one partner is HIV-infected), yet this fades away leaving a virginal carer, devoting herself to her man as if he had any old life-threatening condition. Women carers are perceived as needing help with the psychological and practical burdens of supporting the person with HIV. While this is laudable, there is hardly ever attention paid to how an HIV-negative woman can sustain her status, or any appreciation that she may continue to fuck the person she cares for.

The de-sexualized carer surfaces ever more strongly when she is not a lover of someone with HIV. What happens to the sexuality and sex lives of women surrounded by AIDS as volunteers, doctors, mothers, AIDS activists, sisters, social workers? No one ever asks. Women workers tell each other that sex can become so associated with work and other people's sexualities, as well as with death and illness, that they lose their desire. This is rarely spoken of publicly. Instead, women are left to their 'natural role' of selfless, sexless Mother-Teresa-style devotion.

Where there was no pre-existing sexual relationship, it is assumed that none will develop. Yet stranger things have happened than for a woman carer to become sexually involved with the HIV-positive man for whom she is providing such intimate care (even if he is gay). This is hugely taboo, so where does she get support for safer sex? From her perspective there may be immense struggles around sexuality in the face of death; from the outside it is the charming image of the *pietà*.

The maternal imperative of women is not only visible in the overt presentation of woman as earth mothers and ever-fertile, but also in the trivialization of women as immature, sexless creatures. For nearly six months the display in a THT shopfront window contained a huge reproduction of their leaflet, *HIV and AIDS Information for Women*. In front of the leaflet cover there was a small, cuddly, yellow toy rabbit. Later the bunny was replaced by a soft fabric taxi. Is this highlighting women's lack of access to transport? I don't think so. Doubtless some women like cuddly yellow bunnies – as do some gay men. I'd just love to see the reaction if THT put a reproduction of a gay men's leaflet in the window with the bunny in front.

Madonnas with attitude

When a woman isn't being infantalized, de-sexed or hailed as a madonna, on occasions she becomes a rampant, sexual, Ciccione-style Madonna, a guilty whore, or a dangerous vampire. Women's sexuality is so polarized that she is either without sexual desire or over-brimming with lust. The demonized woman poses such terror to society with her active sexuality that she may even end up terrorizing herself. When she is HIV-infected, the sexual woman may develop an exaggerated sense of responsibility for the virus. So, for example, an HIV-positive Thai woman who was gang-raped refused to press charges against her attackers because 'they were punished enough by exposure to the disease'.[31] Such terrible levels of responsibility are not only self-generated. In Miami, Florida the courts affirmed that HIV-infected women are fundamentally responsible for HIV transmission when they awarded $18 million to the husband of a Brazilian dancer (read 'whore'?) who 'knowingly infected him with Aids before marriage'.[32] There has been no comparable compensation to a woman infected by an HIV-positive man (not even in a rape case[33]) despite the far higher probability and occurrence of male to female transmission.

Outside the context of AIDS, women are frequently punished for expressing their sexuality – for example, in every country which criminalizes prostitution it is the whores not the punters who are penalized for engaging in a mutually consenting act. One of the most common calls to AIDS helplines is from the woman who has had an affair or one night stand and is now convinced she has acquired HIV. The repression of desire is so extreme that the woman who strays from her sexually pure role imagines herself catapulted to the distant extreme of sexual excess – and so deserves the ultimate consequence for such unfeminine wickedness: death. Such extra- ordinary displacement reaches startling levels in a 1993 letter to the *Sun* from a 'married mum' who had a bad case of dermatitis and rubbed 'an erotic male dance troupe['s] . . . oily, sweaty bodies' and asks whether she 'may have put [her] husband and children at risk . . . Do you think I should have an Aids test?' These farcical extremes of what Alcorn called 'Housewives in HIV jockstrap scare'[34] reflect the ways in which women's sexuality is both denied and scandalized. This woman is panicked that she may have brought a fatal condition into her family by unleashing her desire to the perverted levels of watching erotic dancers.

The double standard dictates, classically, that the same sexual frequency transforms men into studs while the women they are having sex with become slags. The death in August 1993 of seventy-five-year-old Anne Cumming gave the press a delicious mixture of AIDS, royalty and an active sexual life which would not retire gracefully into old age. The salacious tabloids did not tarry in preaching sexual morals to the nation: 'Nympho who rocked the Royals: AIDS kills Anne the sexy gran', 'Queen Mum's randy relative dies of AIDS', 'Sex Fan Anne Pays Price of 35-year Orgy'.[35] Not only was Anne Cumming a woman who enjoyed sex, she also had the audacity to continue enjoying it as she grew older, and to flaunt it (a privilege tabloid journalists regard as their own). Six months before her death, Cumming appeared naked on a television programme, and posed for a photograph topless but for a string of pearls – providing a perfect image to accompany the moralizing diatribes masquerading as obituaries. She published two volumes of memoirs (*The Love Habit* and *The Love Quest*) apparently detailing her sexual appetite and the measures she took to fulfil it.

Tabloids delighted in serializing her memoirs, then condemned her for the very life from which they had profited. Lest there be any doubt about the retributive nature of AIDS, the (generally calmer) *Daily Mail* soberly informs us, 'When she wrote of her countless lovers the Queen Mother forgave her relative. This week, alone, she died from AIDS.' The royals may pardon, God will not.

Sexually active and proud HIV-positive women are portrayed as highly culpable for their own infection, but the simple fact of having HIV infection (so long as it wasn't dentally acquired) drags any woman into this category. In order to acquire a life-threatening sexually transmitted infection she must be morally suspect and deserves to be tainted with the whore label. It is easy to pick on prostitutes and women who publicly celebrate their sexuality by writing erotic memoirs. The link between their gender and sexuality is so marked that, in media terms, they are fair game. They were fair game before AIDS, and all the epidemic does is to take moral approbation to a new height and provide a rationale for hatred. However, part of the 'queer paradigm' of AIDS is the fact that any HIV-positive woman, irrespective of the means by which she acquired HIV (infected by blood transfusion, from her bisexual husband, from shared injection equipment) is assumed to be a loose woman, sexually voracious, a whore; she becomes queer. While there is nothing intrinsically wrong with any of these states, many women often find it extremely distressing to be so perceived. No wonder then that many women with HIV who tell their story are at pains to defend their sexual history, 'I have never gone to bed with every boy who came on to me; I've been reasonably fussy', maintains one HIV-positive woman.[36] It's a short step from maintaining an image of purity to self-castigation when you know you have failed. Sandra Brea, a well-known Brazilian actress, announced that she had HIV in the summer of 1993. One of Brazil's leading sex symbols, she had previously spoken publicly about her enjoyment of sex. On announcing her HIV status she initially suggested she had acquired the infection from a blood transfusion. Later on – as it became clear she had acquired the virus sexually – she was heard to give vent to her guilt saying, 'Dona Aurora, my mother, must be jumping for joy in heaven.'[37]

In the midst of the 'told you so' discourse, Cumming at least received universal praise for stopping sex on receipt of her HIV diagnosis. One of the overriding public concerns with the HIV-infected woman is anxiety at her poisonous potential. Prostitutes and other commercial sex workers really feel the heat of this panic. One of the most grotesque examples of this particular prejudice is the story of Helen Cover.[38] In 1989, when an undercover police officer arrested her for soliciting (she offered to give him a blow-job for $25), Cover was front-page news in her home town of Syracuse, New York: 'Prostitution Suspect Has AIDS; Officials Try to Keep Her Jailed.'[39] They succeeded, and despite repeated appeals and medical testimony that HIV cannot be transmitted in this way, Cover was condemned as 'a menace, a hazard to society'.[40] She died less than a year later in Bedford Hills Correctional Facility. It is not only the individual HIV-positive woman who exchanges sex for money who comes under fire; commercial sex workers as a group (profession) are frequently represented as dangerous spreaders of disease – rarely as women vulnerable to acquiring disease from their punters. There is nothing new with this, and many have noted that this stigmatization replicates anti-syphilis campaigns at the turn of the twentieth century. To illustrate this, Berer reproduces an American World War II poster with a large head and shoulders shot of an attractive woman, three small images of men and the slogan 'She may look clean – but . . . Pick-Ups, "Good Time" Girls, Prostitutes . . . Spread Syphilis and Gonorrhoea', alongside a current Kenyan poster with a drawing of a man walking towards a skeleton dressed in classic prostitute clothes (stilettos and mini-skirt) with the slogan, 'What you see is not what you get . . . AIDS KILLS'.[41]

It is not necessary to leave the UK for demonic women in HIV-prevention campaigns, as is demonstrated by a notorious advertising campaign launched by the HEA in 1988. A full-page David Bailey photograph of a young, stylish, attractive woman appeared in national newspapers with the caption, 'If this woman had the virus which leads to AIDS, in a few years she could look like the person over the page.' Turning the page, the viewer finds the same image with the strapline, 'Worrying, isn't it?' Worrying for whom? Surely for HIV-positive women it is a source of encouragement. But the text which states that people 'can be infected with HIV for several years before it shows any signs or symptoms' is not directed at the HIV-infected. Instead it is a scare tactic for the uninfected straight male. It's the ultimate fantasy of the vagina dentata: one fuck with this gorgeous woman and you don't just lose your cock, you lose your life. Roberta McGrath notes that 'The [model's] fetishized face, the long hair, the jumper which falls off the shoulder are all signs of woman as a lure and seductress.'[42] This seductress doesn't just mess up your marriage – she kills.

These dangerous 'worrying' women lure innocent men who are seduced against their will. Ultimately these demons tend to be held responsible not only for infecting the unsuspecting male, but in turn the truly innocent party: his wife. The licentiousness of these women is shocking enough, but in some fantasies their evil is premeditated. The urban myth of AIDS revenge has become a global phenomenon: a man wakes up the morning after sex with a stranger to see a message written on the mirror in her lipstick. It reads: 'Welcome to the World of AIDS.'[43] Most facilitators of AIDS awareness workshops are used to being badgered with questions about people who test HIV-positive and then, in their anger, rush around trying to infect as many people as possible. Even Reuter gets in on the act with a report that police in Brazil are hunting twenty-seven HIV-positive prostitutes and homosexuals. These 'vampires of death' 'confirmed that the group's intention was to transmit Aids (*sic*) through sexual intercourse' according to a police official, while psychologists sought 'to persuade the members not to vent their anger at society by seeking revenge'.[44] The difficulties of adjusting to a positive diagnosis, making decisions about safer sex, and the range of psychological responses to a dramatic life event are conflated in this fantasy of psychopathic revenge sex.

These demonizing fantasies, culminating in the ultimate horror of revenge, neatly side-step the idea that 'it takes two to tango' and enable men – once again – to avoid sexual responsibility. This is ironic. While some men are coerced into sex by women, it is extremely rare (some might say physically impossible) for a woman to force an unconsenting man to have intercourse. An important feature of women's vulnerability to acquiring HIV is that consent to sex is not always mutual (this includes rape, abuse, coerced sex and harassment, and is influenced by complex factors and scenarios[45]). The recurrent image, however, is always the vampish HIV-infected woman (who will infect men) rather than the HIV-infected man who abuses a woman (making her highly vulnerable to infection) – despite the fact that the latter is both more common, and offers a more effective means of transmission. There can be no doubt that the locus of concern is men's vulnerability to HIV infection.

Normal people

The primacy of the male is apparent in the use of women to mediate a 'heterosexual epidemic', as discussed in Chapter 1. Over-sexed, demonized women cause generalized panic since they endanger the lives of straight men, targeting them with the message: AIDS is alive and kicking and coming your way. The following are examples of how the slippage from women to heterosexual panic is integrated in government statistics, by newspapers and HIV-prevention campaigns.

The 1990 release of the results of anonymized HIV surveys[46] in antenatal and GUM (genito-urinary medicine) clinics exemplified the government's heterosexualizing tendency. The Department of Health press release glossed over the horrifying figure that one in five gay or bisexual men in inner London tested HIV-positive, and so media reports dutifully ignored this fact. Instead, the press release and subsequent articles homed in on the discovery that as many as one in 200 women attending inner London antenatal clinics had HIV. Minister of Health, Virginia Bottomley, saw this as ample justification for public spending on education campaigns, and told journalists, 'Those who think AIDS and HIV only effect [*sic*] homo-sexuals and drug-takers need to think again.'[47] Her Chief Medical Officer then stated that the surveys 'reinforce our earlier messages that HIV and AIDS is increasing in the heterosexual population and is a problem which faces us all'.[48] Why did no one notice that HIV and AIDS was increasing among *women* and gay men? Why was there no targeted information suggesting how women – the major focus of the reports – could lower their risk? Acheson concluded his statement with his 'golden rules', which included, 'Avoid casual sex and try to stick to one faithful partner.' This is a particularly unhelpful rule for women, who have often been infected by staying faithful to one partner whose fidelity they are unable to control.

This displacement of women into 'the heterosexual population' was fundamental to World AIDS Day 1990, and local newspaper headlines expressed the real basis for the focus on women with classics like, 'AIDS alarm growing', 'Aids Day conference dispels myth of "gay plague" sickness'.[49] Respectively, the accompanying articles told that, 'women will be the target of health campaigners . . . not least because until recently AIDS has not been perceived as a female or heterosexual problem', and, 'World Aids Day in Bournemouth took a look at the disease from a female perspective. . . . Peter – diagnosed HIV positive six years ago – dispelled the myth of Aids as a "gay plague". "Anyone who has sex can get Aids," emphasised 27-year-old Peter.' It is not entirely clear how Peter was able to provide a female perspective, and he certainly did not appear to explain that any *woman* who has sex could get AIDS, nor how to combat the disease from a 'female perspective'. Rather, he is portrayed as propagating a message of generalized panic, and there is no clarity about whether he is heterosexual himself.

The *Sun* – tabloid newspaper par excellence – really does not know where it stands on AIDS. The epidemic includes all the juicy elements it loves and should make good copy, but at the same time they do not want it to interfere with the fun of their Page Three girls and Page Seven boys. They take the easy journalistic way out by drumming up a little conflict: one week Garry Bushell proclaims, 'there is no heterosexual AIDS explosion and never will be', the next week Michael Adler is pulled in to explain 'Why Anyone Can Catch AIDS'.[50] Adler, who is Professor of Genito-Urinary Medicine at the Middlesex Hospital, writes just before women's World AIDS Day. He defends his opening statement, 'AIDS is not a gay plague', by giving the examples of two of his patients: 'a 22-year-old secretary, who we will call Liz, had a one-night stand with a man she met at a club' and 'Joan, 45, who has two grown-up children. She became infected after intercourse with her bisexual husband.'

Why is it that when banging on the 'Anyone Can Catch AIDS' drum, doctors and journalists alike can usually only find women?[51] Is it that the only 100 per cent heterosexual (i.e. no other 'risk factors') patients are women? Is it that the women are more sympathetic characters? Could it be that they are more concerned to focus prevention messages at men than women? The misuse of women is usually based in unthinking compassion and the urgency of preventing the AIDS crisis, rather than malicious intent. Yet HIV-positive women become a commodity to promote a mainstream vision of how the AIDS crisis could develop, a vision which feeds policy makers' normalizing drive. The existence of HIV in women is not used to push information about AIDS to women, but rather in a generalized way. So Professor Adler continues by noting that HIV-positive women in Scotland, 'are perfectly ordinary people' – is this information directed at perfectly ordinary women, or at men who like having sex with perfectly ordinary women? He goes on to explain that this message is entirely general: '[M]ost men and women are infected by straightforward, normal sex. . . . Everyone must realise they are at risk – before it's too late.'

Since women are universally assumed to be heterosexual (lesbians are consistently invisible in any discourse, and bisexuality, male or female, is ignored or ridiculed), and the kind of women who get HIV must be the kind of women who put out, increasing rates of HIV among women come to symbolize a major threat to the 'heterosexual community' (whatever that is) rather than to women. 'Heterosexual' refers principally to men. The earlier newspaper article tells us ' . . . until recently AIDS has not been perceived as a *female or heterosexual* problem' (my emphasis), suggesting that heterosexuals are different from females. If we had a 'men and AIDS' campaign, this would (should) lead inevitably to discussions of gay men; it would probably also consider drug-using men, and men with haemophilia, and get to heterosexual men near the bottom of the list. The paucity of genuine models of masculinity mean that the principal route to straight men is through the generic concept of 'heterosexuals', or more simply through the body of a woman and the media roles afforded it. 'Since we live in a patriarchal society,' says McGrath, 'sex is most commonly signified by the female body, preferably white, heterosexual, young and healthy.'[52]

It is by no means only the media that misuses women in this

discourse – they are just the main ones who record their mistakes for posterity. The media is often criticized as if they are working out an explicit 'moral' agenda through the excessive nonsense of their AIDS reporting. Whilst in some domains (notably queerness and drugs) this may well be the case, most of the time the media rely on the voluntary and government AIDS industry for their information about AIDS, and these sources can be just as misguided. For example, a District Health Authority invites an HIV-positive woman into their schools to offer her 'personal perspective' of living with HIV. The worker tells a researcher that her rationale is to 'shock the boys into thinking they could have an attractive girlfriend like her'.[53] Although this may be the most explicit record of such behaviour, it is a fairly typical example of the tactics used by many in the AIDS industry.

A national AIDS organization runs a 'Women and AIDS' programme which goes around the country educating women's organizations, such as the Women's Institute, Townswomen's Guilds, Young Women's Christian Associations. At each of their sessions they invite an HIV-positive woman to talk about her experience of being diagnosed. At the conference to present the results of this programme to AIDS workers, women's organizations and the Princess of Wales (and hence the media), one of the women praised the programme for 'making AIDS real to her'. She had been impressed at how normal Caroline (the woman who spoke to her group) was, and how Caroline rushed to catch a train home to collect her child from school. 'I realized', she said, 'that it could happen to my daughter.'[54] This was hailed as an example of the success of the programme. These public-minded, influential women throughout the UK now realize 'it could happen to their daughters'.

This is doubtless a good thing, yet I wonder if this programme encourages women to explore the other ways AIDS could happen to them. Do they realize they could acquire HIV? Have they thought about their sexual relationships? Are their husbands faithful and entirely heterosexual? And what about their sons? How will they cope if one comes home to tell mum he's gay? Will they be impressed at how normal he is if *he* has HIV? The balance of probabilities suggests that these women will first encounter HIV in a gay son. How influential these women could be:

encouraging the board of governors to introduce comprehensive sex education in schools, ensuring that condoms are freely available to all adolescents, arguing for an equal age of consent for gay and bisexual men as for heterosexuals, ensuring the free supply of needles and syringes to anyone who injects drugs, arguing for human rights and health care for refugees, demanding equal respect for gay partnerships, countering prejudiced or homophobic articles on AIDS in the local press. These climate-setting women could create a climate wherein the diversity of human sexuality and desire is acknowledged and respected, where the realities of drug use are addressed from a public health perspective, where racism is confronted, and where the possibilities for HIV transmission to women and men are reduced by a supportive environment. Instead, it seems, they are trained to parrot 'heterosexuals get it too'.

What is so dispiriting about this tendency to demonize, infantilize and heterosexualize all of these stories of women with HIV is not just that it presents a false picture of the progress of the epidemic. Certainly, the intrinsic 'safety' of images of women with HIV is damaging the public perception of the epidemic. A colleague recently reported that an intelligent feminist just beginning to develop AIDS work was astonished to learn that women were not the most AIDS-affected constituency in the UK.[55] What is so sad is that the HIV-positive women who are misused in this way have mostly taken huge personal risks in being public about their condition. That this courage, which is often motivated by the 'higher good' and a desire to help others avoid infection, is so perverted, is tragic. Instead of allowing these women to speak out and for their true concerns to resonate, the policy-makers and dictators of public opinion pick and choose from women's lives and sell the story they believe the public most want or need to hear. That women continue to be highly vulnerable, biologically and socially, to this infection fails to interest them, since the idea of placing women at the centre of this (or any) discourse is seen as the pleading of special interest groups. Placing the reality of women's lives at the top of the agenda appears to be frankly unacceptable.

Notes

1. S. Sontag, *AIDS and Its Metaphors*, Farrar, Straus and Giroux, New York, 1988, pp. 65–6.
2. I have a collection of AIDS badges, most of which have feisty or rude slogans. The ones about women are unrelentingly dull with slogans like 'Say It!! Women get AIDS', 'Women, AIDS and the Future', 'Life Force: Women Fighting AIDS Inc.'
3. I'm not sure I did, until Frances Williams pointed this out to me.
4. An HIV-infected woman can halve the chance of her baby acquiring HIV by not breast-feeding. She can also take measures to lessen transmission during pregnancy and delivery, although this requires good knowledge and consideration from her healthcare providers. See Chapter 7.
5. By 31 December 1994 3201 women had been diagnosed HIV-positive, and 2142 of these women reported infection from sex with a man (105 were in the 'Other/Undetermined' category, but this generally reflects women who do not know the identity of the man who infected them). The figures are undoubtedly higher, since the majority of women who are infected have not taken the HIV antibody test.
6. Professor Anke Ehrhardt, 'Gender risk behavior intervention programs for women', plenary talk at 'AIDS' Impact: the 2nd International Conference on the Biopsychosocial Aspects of HIV Infection', Brighton, 8 July 1994.
7. J. Mills, 'Classroom conundrums', in L. Segal and M. McIntosh (eds), *Sex Exposed: Sexuality and the Pornography Debate*, Virago, London, 1992, p. 202.
8. C. S. Vance, 'Pleasure and danger: toward a politics of sexuality', in C. S. Vance (ed.), *Pleasure and Danger: Exploring Female Sexuality*, Pandora, London, 1992, pp. 23–4.
9. See, for example, R. McGrath, 'Health, education and authority: difference and deviance', in V. Harwood *et al.* (eds), *Pleasure Principles: Politics, Sexuality and Ethics*, Lawrence & Wishart, London, 1993, p. 161; T. Radcliffe, 'The invitation to meet Christ', in V. Cosstick (ed.), *AIDS: Meeting the Community Challenge*, St Paul Publications, Slough, 1987, p. 114; C. M. Myss and C. N. Shealy, *AIDS: Passageway to Transformation*, Stillpoint, Walpole, NH, p. 22.
10. One man with AIDS told me the story of walking past a woman in a shopping centre who was droning 'AIDS, AIDS, AIDS . . . ' as she tried to force leaflets on passers-by. As she accosted him he said, 'I've already got it.' She didn't react. In its zeal to raise awareness and prevent HIV, this special day overlooks the quotidian reality of people who are affected.
11. GMFA pointed out that in all the publicity supplied for the Family

World AIDS Day, gay men were rendered invisible. WHO expanded the concept of 'family' beyond the biological to include local communities, church groups, etc., but there was no recognition of queer friendship circles, the many 'pretend' families which fight AIDS on a daily basis.

12. There is a startling level of denial about homosexual and bisexual behaviour in the developing world, and most AIDS workers seem to buy the party line that homosexuality and HIV are only linked in the West. This is beginning to change with, for example, the Panos Institute review of men who have sex with men in the developing world.

13. Opining the insulting and drab nature of these slogans, Arne Husdal (a veteran international activist, who died in June 1995) challenged Mike Merson, head of WHO's Global Programme on AIDS, to let those affected choose these slogans in the future. This is not a challenge Dr Merson chose to take up. *EuroCASO Newsletter*, December 1993, p. 11.

14. This is the slogan on a T-shirt with an embroidered red ribbon on the front. The extent of red ribbon kitsch is mercifully muted in Britain (outside Soho). In America there are hundreds of bejewelled versions (Liz Taylor and Mathilde Krim are reported to have real ruby ones), as well as Christmas tree baubles, porcelain dinner sets and clothing. As this activist symbol has been twisted into a passive tool, ACT UP have printed up a T-shirt stating, 'Ribbons are not enough'. Few stores stock it.

15. K. Wellings, *AIDS Programme, Women and AIDS*, Health Education Authority, AIDS Programme Paper 5, March 1989, p. 5.

16. Kate O'Neill (THT Communication Manager), personal communication.

17. *Daily Mirror* and *Daily Star*, 3 September 1993; *Sun*, 22 March 1994.

18. *Daily Star*, 3 September 1993.

19. Quoted by J. Midwinter in 'Death-bed confession of the girl who got AIDS from dentist is dividing America', *Daily Mail*, 26 June 1994.

20. The circumstances of the 'Florida dentist' case are dramatic and confused. Acer alerted his patients (and the public) to his condition in a newspaper advertisement two days before he died. Half of his 2000 patients have been tested and six found to be HIV-positive. Did he infect all six? In areas of high prevalence (which Florida is), a random screening of 1000 people is likely to reveal some who are HIV-infected. With Bergalis, extensive DNA testing and genetic typing established that she and Acer shared the same strain of virus. But people from the same geographical area often share the same strain if they belong to the same network of transmission. Acer and Bergalis would have had the same strain of virus if they had had an HIV-infected sexual partner in common. Acer was dead by the time his patients' infections were

confirmed, and so it was impossible to confirm details about his practice. However, investigators concluded that hygiene measures were lacking and his practices were 'dirty'; some reports suggested these may even have been deliberate, 'revenge' infections. These conclusions were enhanced by Bergalis's protestations of virginity. See K. Alcorn (ed.), *AIDS Reference Manual*, NAM Publications, January 1995, pp. 100–1 for further information.

21. S. Churcher, 'Another victim of AIDS dentist', *Mail on Sunday*, 23 May 1993.
22. The phrase 'AIDS victim' is generally rejected in favour of the term 'People (living) with AIDS'. The AIDS industry has fought against terms such as AIDS victim and AIDS sufferer which place the disease before the person and imply that a person is in a state of constant suffering or victimhood. 'Victim' has also been misused to divide people with AIDS into the innocent (people with haemophilia) and the guilty (queers).
23. Midwinter, *op. cit.*
24. *Ibid.*
25. G. Corea, *The Invisible Epidemic: The Story of Women and AIDS*, HarperPerennial, New York, 1992, p. 320, quoting S. J. Porter, 'The People of the State of New York, respondent, v. Helen S. Cover, appellant', 1989. See also, P. Alexander and F. Delacoste, *Sex Work*, Cleis Press, San Francisco, 1987, pp. 248–63. (See also Chapter 8.)
26. *Daily Star*, 28 December 1994.
27. Edward King, personal communication.
28. *The Times*, 14 May 1993; *Mail on Sunday*, 16 January 1994.
29. These debates took place several times in plenary sessions at the 2nd International Conference on HIV in Children and Mothers, Edinburgh, Scotland, 7–10 September 1993.
30. Highland AIDS resource centre, Scotland, 1991.
31. Reuters report, 'Penalty enough', *The Times*, 21 July 1993.
32. Associated Free Press report, '£12m Aids award', *Guardian*, 1993.
33. A French HIV-positive man was jailed for ten years for raping two women – there is no mention of financial compensation. (Associated Free Press, reported in the *Daily Telegraph*, 28 September 1994.)
34. K. Alcorn, 'inSIGHT', *Capital Gay*, 26 March 1993.
35. *Daily Star*, 2 September 1993; *Sun*, 1 September 1993 and 2 September 1993.
36. Quoted by I. Kurtz, 'My name is Denise ... I'm HIV positive', *Cosmopolitan*, January 1991, pp. 68–9.
37. S. Branford, 'Sex, lies and a certain virus', *New Internationalist*, December 1993.
38. The shocking story of Cover's mistreatment is told in Corea, *op. cit.*, pp. 173–85.
39. *Syracuse Herald-Journal*, 29 January 1989.

40. Corea, *op. cit.*, p. 185.
41. M. Berer with S. Ray, *Women and HIV/AIDS: An International Resource Book*, Pandora, London, 1993, p. 41.
42. McGrath, *op. cit.*, p. 169.
43. Fumento has also encountered this myth: *The Myth of Heterosexual AIDS: How a Tragedy Has Been Distorted . . .* , Regenery Gateway, Washington, DC, 1993, p. 61.
44. 'HIV "vampires" wreak revenge', *Guardian*, 15 July 1993.
45. Men are, of course, raped and abused by other men, and some acquire HIV this way. This phenomenon is slowly gaining attention and some services, for example, those provided by the organization 'Survivors'. Male rape has always been capable of prosecution, but only acquired full legal recognition in 1994, with the first male rapist being imprisoned in 1995. His sentence was far longer than comparable sentences given to men who rape women, yet gay organizations failed to notice the homophobia (and sexism) inscribed in such sentencing.
46. The anonymized HIV surveys took place in seventeen London ante-natal clinics (eleven in inner London) and six GUM clinics (two in London). The surveys tested blood samples taken for other purposes and tested them for HIV. All identifying factors (except for gender, history of drug use and locality) were removed and the results were not given to patients. Patients were allowed to opt out of the survey.
47. *Daily Express*, 13 November 1990.
48. 'Virginia Bottomley announces first results of anonymised HIV testing', Department of Health press release, 17 May 1991, p. 2.
49. *Evening Star*, Ipswich, 29 November 1990; *Bournemouth Evening Echo*, 3 December 1990.
50. *Sun*, 31 October 1990.
51. The first (and thus far only) heterosexual man used to promote this line is 'Steve', who started to tell his story in HEA advertisements broadcast in 1991, and media pieces for World AIDS Day 1993. See S. Garfield, *The End of Innocence: Britain in the Time of AIDS*, Faber & Faber, London, 1994, pp. 215–24.
52. McGrath, *op. cit.*, p. 165.
53. R. Gorna, *From Soho to Southend: A Report on HIV/AIDS and Sex Education for Young People: What Is Happening in North East Thames*, North East Thames RHA, 1993, p. 43.
54. Participant at 'Women, AIDS and the Future' conference, London, 28 October 1992.
55. Simon Watney, personal communication.

Chapter three

Reservoirs of Infection

The statistics the popular culture chooses to promote most
heavily are the very statistics we should view with the most
caution. They may well be in wide circulation not because
they are true but because they support widely held media
preconceptions.

Susan Faludi[1]

By the end of 1994, 3201 women and girls in the UK were
known to have acquired HIV; 890 women had developed AIDS and
482 of these women had died.[2] These statistics ought to be easy to
come by. They are not. In the UK, epidemiological information
about HIV and AIDS is collected and disseminated by the Public
Health Laboratory Service (PHLS) AIDS Centre at the Communicable Disease Surveillance Centre (CDSC). Astonishingly, the bulk
of the current data does not record the most fundamental divide,
that of sex. Every month it is possible to find out how many people
with HIV or AIDS have been reported from each Regional Health
Authority, and the probable mode by which they acquired the
virus. It is not possible to tell how many women were diagnosed
with AIDS, or discovered they were HIV-positive that month
(although the cumulative total number of female AIDS cases is
given). Every three months the PHLS AIDS Centre produces
'unpublished quarterly surveillance tables' which go into a lot more
useful detail about current developments with the epidemic, yet still
only a minority of the tables fully analyse the statistics by gender
(for example, it is impossible to find out from these tables how
many women have died). The region of residence and probable

mode of acquisition of HIV, as well as the presumed sexuality of individuals (of some male individuals, that is), is seen as far more important than whether they are male or female. (Transsexuals apparently do not exist, contrary to the experiences of some community-based organizations.[3])

On their own, statistics showing the numbers of women with HIV or AIDS are fairly meaningless. For the individual woman who knows she is infected, it may be comforting to know she is not alone, and she may be diagnosed more speedily because her doctor has seen other women with the disease, but the precise numbers of other women who are infected is unlikely to be of major import-ance to her. Knowing the numbers of women with HIV or AIDS matters most to other people: policy-makers, scientists, politicians, epidemiologists, planners, opinion leaders, public health specialists, activists and the media. The numbers of women with HIV or AIDS acquires meaning for them by comparison. Current statistics are compared with those some months or years ago; the rate of increase is assessed; numbers of women with HIV are compared to total numbers of women; mortality from AIDS is compared to mortality from other conditions, especially among women of a similar age; and, most frequently, different groups of people with HIV or AIDS are compared with each other.

These comparisons are important in order to understand the current nature of the epidemic, to assess the potential vulner-abilities of women, and to ensure that women currently infected receive appropriate care and services. One of the areas which epidemiology explores is the 'type' of people who have been infected. As well as helping to plan for the future, this question has most relevance for a woman living with the condition since it allows her specific needs to receive attention.

There is a down-side to this and to all aspects of epidemi-ology which are reported in public. Describing the truth about who is currently infected often creates panic, and a tendency to find ways of making the disease more acceptable. In particular, acknowledgements of the clustered nature of the condition tend to be followed by vague predictions of an imminent 'normal' disease, a phenomenon usually entwined with heterosexualizing discourses. A common thread to discussions about the current extent of the

AIDS epidemic is that facts become overlaid with assumptions: political expediency overtakes personal reality. This expediency can be especially disheartening for women living with HIV, like Canadian Darien Taylor. She opines the mainstream media's representation of 'HIV in women either with sensational accounts of sex workers, which incorrectly scapegoat them as "reservoirs of infection" or with sentimental stories of "innocent victims". Women who test HIV-positive do not fit these stereotypes.'[4]

These stereotypes of contagion create fantasies of dangerous concentrations of HIV. Women are imagined as fearful reservoirs of infection – static pools of festering fluid that may be foisted on an unsuspecting public. The grouping together of individuals, which is an inevitable feature of epidemiology, cannot reflect the realities of which women are HIV infected and by whom. Epidemiological data is seriously limited and although the methods of collecting and presenting information about exposure to HIV have evolved, they still fail adequately to address the fundamental issues: how a person acquired the infection, and which types of people are currently infected.

Women with AIDS: dying of ignorance

AIDS is a very new disease. Many people are able to divide their lives pre- and post-AIDS, remembering how life was before they knew AIDS existed, before someone they love was infected, before the government splattered it all over billboards. Despite this fact, discussion of AIDS often posits a static condition rather than an evolving epidemic. There is a tendency for so much imprecise nonsense to be spoken about the current state of the epidemic among women (principally, that it is too small to matter), and so it is helpful to look back to the beginning of the epidemic in the UK and chart its evolution. This chart is created from the work of epidemiologists – scientists who track the changing patterns in diseases, especially infectious conditions.

Epidemiology is not a neutral, value-free activity. It

naturally touches on questions of broader significance. For instance, what counts as AIDS? What information is gathered about the lifestyles of people with AIDS? What assumptions are made about people with AIDS? How is this verified? How reliable is this information? What are the motivations for recording statistics in a particular way?

Statistics are notorious for their capacity to deceive, and one of the key confusions is often the terms 'incidence' and 'prevalence'. The incidence describes the number of new instances of a condition in a certain population within a specific period of time; the prevalence gives the total number of people with the condition in a certain population at a designated time. Thus, incidence gives an indication of the rate of increase, while prevalence shows the current scale of the condition.[5] So, for example, the AIDS incidence in 1994 is the number of new AIDS diagnoses made that year; the cumulative incidence of AIDS to 1994 is the total number of AIDS diagnoses declared since reporting began; and the 1994 AIDS prevalence is the cumulative incidence less the number of people who have died, i.e. the total number of people alive with AIDS in 1994.

The other major confusion lies in the different reliabilities of reports of HIV and AIDS cases. HIV reports track people who present voluntarily for testing, not the true HIV incidence. By contrast, AIDS cases are reported by clinicians caring for someone who has been diagnosed with symptoms of AIDS – the vast majority of whom will be in contact with medical services. There are many things which will bias the HIV data, including the fact that some (perhaps many) people who believe they are likely to have acquired HIV take the decision not to test unless they become unwell. For women, the data are further complicated by the fact that many HIV-infected women have no perception that they are at enhanced risk of exposure and so they may not have considered testing.

Epidemiologists seek out the connections between people with the same, or related, conditions. In many ways epidemiologists are medical detectives – once they have identified a 'suspect', they track them, following their direction and the impact they have. One of the remarkable tales of modern medicine is the speed at which a complex syndrome of conditions was linked, AIDS was identified, the gay connection made, routes of transmission established and the (main) causative agent identified.[6] This is not solely the story of doctors battling alone, but also the story of unprecedented links being forged between research doctors and communities struggling to understand what was besieging them. The fundamental question for epidemiologists was how people with these novel collections of symptoms were connected. Details about people's lives were essential in order to answer that question, as well as to see how the condition is spreading. From the outset it was apparent that the basic questions would more likely be answered in areas of highest prevalence – the larger the number of people, the less they will all have in common. Corea reports the thoughts of a physician with a large private practice in New York's Greenwich Village back in 1982, 'It was immediately obvious to Dr. Joyce Wallace that this new disease was sexually transmitted. Homosexuals were getting it and they weren't all eating at the same restaurant. If the disease was sexually transmitted, women would get it because women have sex. There was no known sexually transmitted disease that only affected one sex.'[7]

It was essential to exclude all other classic vehicles of communicable diseases. Shilts records how epidemiologists at the CDC initially hoped that GRID/AIDS might be caused by a lousy batch of poppers.[8] The most obvious link between gay men is sex, but that did not mean sex was the only possible cause of AIDS. The sex link became more obvious once people who were not gay, or who were female, developed AIDS. A small number of 'AIDS dissidents' continue to doubt that a virus or blood-borne pathogen is the cause of AIDS. Their views get far more publicity than their small number and poor methodology should determine, mostly out of the media's delight in any conflict.[9]

The principal means of avoiding AIDS were first described by gay men at a time when doctors were wary of making any statements about aetiology. At the end of July 1983, the epidemiologists in Britain would only say that 'group sexual practices and multiple sexual partners [are] thought to be important to the development of AIDS' and conclude that the reports of fourteen cases of AIDS in Britain 'provides no evidence of a UK epidemic . . . suggesting that the UK situation is simply part of the American epidemic'.[10] This vague approach hampered specificity, and inhibited a more thorough examination of the very real differences in the spread of the disease. The progress of HIV and AIDS in the UK has been continuously compared to the US epidemic, often with warnings that a similar situation is imminent. In fact, there have always been distinctive differences due to the remarkably different social structures and population profiles – something which is perhaps more apparent with the luxury of hindsight. For women, the differences are sharp. In the USA, the majority of women with AIDS are from black and Hispanic, poor, urban communities, and the majority have been infected through sharing drug-injecting equipment. In the UK, AIDS has always been associated with diversity: African immigrant women, women who have travelled abroad or whose lover is a bisexual man, has haemophilia or is from Africa, with some cases, principally from Scotland, associated with drug use. This is often concealed behind discussions about the far larger epidemic among women in the States – indeed, I have encountered British workers, fired up from international AIDS conferences, wondering how to develop initiatives to reach Latinas in the UK. The racial dimensions of AIDS in the UK are markedly different from those in the USA and not only because there are no large populations here of women from South America.

The early epidemiology of AIDS was troubled by American influence for good reasons. Inevitably, understanding AIDS was a matter of intelligent guess-work, and since more cases had been reported from the States, scientists naturally used that information as a guide. They had also been alerted to the fact that this new condition was likely to be similar to Hepatitis B in the way it was transmitted, and so they were looking at cases with the expecta- tion of finding parallels. One of the other dimensions which was fundamental to the statistics that were gathered was the political and media-driven excitement surrounding the new condition. As popular imagination was fired by new understandings of the dynamism of AIDS, so scientists turned to the data to see if there was a basis for popular understanding. This was particularly key to the ways in which assumptions were made about the sexual orientation of people recorded as having AIDS. When the public discourse focused on whether the risk of HIV and AIDS would be generalized, it was the epidemiologists' job to look at the data and see if that was plausible. The external constraints on this science led to repeated twists and turns in the ways the data were recorded, with ideology apparently overpowering science as the categorizations for people altered to reflect current explanations of what was happening.

In the very first three-page review of what was known about AIDS in the UK – published in July 1983 – the epidemiologists at the PHLS CDSC in Colindale, and in the Scottish Unit in Edinburgh, did not use the words 'women' and 'female'. The first fourteen cases recorded were all men: twelve were gay (one of whom also injected drugs – this was probably Terrence Higgins), one had haemophilia, and the other is later described as 'heterosexual with unknown risk factors'. They were aged between twenty and forty-five, ten lived in London and five had died by the time of the report. A limited definition of AIDS, from the American CDC, had been printed in letters appealing for reports in the *Lancet* and *British Medical Journal*, as well as appeals to microbiologists, venereologists and dermatologists and for information from death certificates. This resulted in details of six cases of KS (Kaposi's sarcoma – a rare cancer of the skin and internal organs characterized by reddish-brown marks, this condition now appears to be linked to a herpes-related virus and is seen predominantly in gay men and bisexual men and their partners, as well as in women and men from Africa where the condition is endemic), five cases of PCP (*Pneumocystis carinii pneumonia* – a rare pneumonia, occurring only in people whose immune systems are not functioning fully, and which can be fatal if not diagnosed promptly) and three other opportunistic infections (one case each of CMV, toxoplasmosis and oesophageal thrush – all conditions which do not occur in people with healthy immune systems). All of these men had 'no known underlying cause of cellular immune deficiency'.

Following this mid-1983 review of the first nineteen months of AIDS in the UK, the PHLS *Communicable Disease Report* (*CDR*) started to print a brief monthly update of AIDS case reports received. In these very early days, knowledge was severely limited.

Sex and blood seemed to be implicated, and American and African connections were strong. The definition centred on KS and PCP, and was flexible with other unusual conditions which might have been opportunistically occurring because of limited immunity; the updates usually concluded, 'Enquiries are in hand in relation to several suspected cases'.[11]

The first woman with AIDS was reported in September 1983, where she slips in as the fifth in a list of eight new reports: 'a 33 year old woman from north-west England who died in August 1983 with Kaposi's sarcoma and P. carinii pneumonia'.[12] It is telling that the first case of a woman was reported posthumously. Women are far more likely to have 'zero survival' than men – that is, to be diagnosed with AIDS at or after death. Whatever her doctors were treating her for, they obviously did not think this woman had AIDS until she died. (All the cases under investigation up to this time were in men.) It would be unfair to criticize doctors outside London for not considering such a rare and little-known condition in their diagnosis of a woman with lung and skin complaints, especially when fewer than thirty AIDS cases had been reported, nearly all in gay men in London. What is alarming is that this failure to consider AIDS as a diagnosis in women has continued for many years. By their next month's report, the scientists seem to have noticed that this woman's case might be a significant development in the British epidemic. They now provide information about her risk factors, telling us, 'The woman had multiple sexual partners'.[13] 'Multiple' is not defined. The fact that she had KS makes it extremely likely that she was infected sexually by a bisexual man, or that she was African.[14] Since neither her race nor her colour is recorded, we can safely assume that she was white British. At this early stage, the scientists appear to be trawling back through records to see if there are any undetected cases of AIDS. In November 1983 they report on 'a 26-year-old black Zambian woman with cerebral toxoplasmosis, who died in May 1983 and had neither received blood products nor engaged in drug abuse'.[15] By the end of 1983, scientists have identified a total of thirty-one cases of AIDS in Britain, and fourteen of the men and both women are dead.

The first report in 1984 brings the third case of AIDS in a

woman, and another zero survival (all other reported cases for that month and December 1983 – four gay men each – were alive at the time of the report). This forty-year-old woman from Uganda is classified as having AIDS after she died from KS and multiple opportunistic infections. In August 1984 there is a steep increase in the number of monthly AIDS cases, with fifteen new cases including 'a 49 year old white woman with Pneumocystis carinii pneumonia [who] had contacts with Central Africa'.[16] For the first time a woman with AIDS is reported alive! The next month a forty-three-year-old white woman who had lived in 'equatorial Africa' is reported dead from PCP; in November the same is reported for a fifty-four-year-old white woman 'who had travelled in Africa and the Caribbean'.

By the time the PHLS reviews cases again, in February 1985, these six cases in women form 5 per cent of the total AIDS reports. All but one of the six women is described as belonging to the category 'no known risk', a category which is congruent with many HIV-positive women's subsequent self-reports of their situation.[17] What is striking about these first women with AIDS in the UK is their diversity, the strong African connection, and the fact that they are all presumed infected from sex with men. This is a very different profile from the progress of the American epidemic among women, and a profile which continues to define the UK situation. These first six women were aged between twenty-six and fifty-four, two were black African (from Uganda and Zambia), and three of the white women had travelled in Africa (variously described by PHLS as the whole continent, central or equatorial) or the Caribbean. The other woman had multiple sexual partners (code for a sex worker?), and since blood transfusions are not mentioned, and drug use is denied, the assumption is that all were sexually infected.

The seventh woman with AIDS was reported alive in March 1985. She is believed to have acquired the virus when she was transfused with whole blood during a Caesarean section. The operation took place in Dubai in September 1984. This may seem an implausibly swift progression from infection to AIDS – given that most people live an average of ten years from infection with HIV until the first severe symptoms appear – but research shows that people who acquire HIV from whole-blood transfusions have very fast disease progression if the donor had AIDS at the time of giving blood.[18] Three months later, another woman was reported with AIDS. She had also received whole blood, this time during a colectomy. However, this sixty-six-year-old woman also had further risk factors: she is described as having a husband with haemophilia who 'is seropositive for HTLV3 antibody'. She is the oldest reported case to date. The ninth woman with AIDS was reported in August 1985, and she too is described as being 'a contact of a seropositive man'. No details are given about how he may have become infected.

The next month's *CDR* formally reports a change in the case definition stating that it has been amended 'to take into account the discovery of the causal agent HTLV3/LAV and the appreciation of the broader spectrum of disease associated with the virus'.[19] Led by the American epidemiologists, this is the first formal attempt to sharpen up the definition, and demonstrates how AIDS is in many ways a moving target. The principal concern identified by the PHLS in reporting this new definition is how many people will be reclassified. This concern sounds more political (bigger numbers require bigger resources) than scientific. The scientists state that this revision will change the status of less than 3 per cent of the total cases so far reported in the UK. The next month they state that the two men already identified as being HTLV3 antibody-negative have had their AIDS diagnoses revoked,[20] and two gay men with non-Hodgkin's lymphoma have been diagnosed with AIDS.

Over time, the shifting sand of the AIDS definition will come to have important implications for women. Indeed, some American activists claim that even by this early stage, women were seriously under-counted and many were dying without ever being counted as AIDS cases. Corea documents several examples of this,[21] and two leading American clinicians working with HIV-positive women identify mortality figures which give statistical support to Corea's anecdotes. Between 1981–86, the numbers of women dying of respiratory conditions greatly increased in New York, Washington DC and San Francisco (three epicentres of the AIDS epidemic) but not Idaho (the latter has low seroprevalence rates). It may well be that many of these women had undiagnosed AIDS – not just zero survival but zero recognition.[22]

The AIDS definition changed again in 1987 and then in 1993 (see Chapter 4 for more details); and at both times there was official angst about the potential impact on numbers. Predictably there were blips in the statistics, but not so great that this did any more than reflect the numbers of people who had developed serious disease associated with underlying HIV infection.

Returning to October 1985 in Britain, the *CDR* provides another gender breakdown of the AIDS cases reported so far. Of the total 241 reports, just 4 per cent – ten cases – have occurred in women. (Despite combing through all the reports, I cannot find out where that tenth case came from.) Some reclassifying has obviously gone on here (maybe one of the people previously described as male was really a woman?), and the modes of acquisition were identified as follows: one woman received whole blood, two had 'heterosexual contact' (no men are in this category), five were 'directly associated with sub-Saharan Africa' (one man in this category), and two women were 'indirectly associated with sub-Saharan Africa' (no men with this risk factor).

In December 1985 there is a particularly eccentric report of a thirty-six-year-old man with PCP who 'is not known to have had exposure to recognised risk factors, but who had multiple hetero-sexual partners including female prostitutes and who shared razors with intravenous drug users'.[23] He is the first case to be given an 'other' classification. The researchers do not seem convinced by the prostitute story (telling, since it would doubtless have been convenient to have a man identified as a 'heterosexual contact'), and that thing with razors sounds just a touch outlandish. The oddity of this report highlights the lengths to which people will go to conceal stigmatized behaviour, even where anonymity is assured. It also shows the willingness of researchers to find expo-sure routes that would parallel Hepatitis B. It also reflects the fact that the people taking exposure histories from people with HIV were doctors, and not necessarily trained in psychology or sexology.

The next report of a woman with AIDS (number eleven) is in March 1986 – some seven months after the last case. This is another zero survival – something last reported in 1984. It is also the first case of a woman identified as an intravenous drug user. Three men who injected drugs had previously been reported with AIDS – all were alive at diagnosis. One of the particular frustrations of this woman being reported posthumously is that there can be no way of checking the assumption that she acquired her infection from shared injecting equipment. It is just as plausible that she, like all but one of the other women, was sexually infected.

May 1986 brings another first, with the report of a baby girl born to a woman with AIDS. In April 1985 there had been a report of a twenty-month-old boy dying from PCP – he had received 'whole blood in Washington DC soon after birth', but this is the first report of a maternally infected child in the UK. Then in June 1986 there is 'a female child from Uganda who died with other opportunist infections'.[24] Following the new reports in June, there is a section announcing relevant new publications. The Department of Education and Science has produced an administrative memorandum and published, in March 1986, a booklet called *Children at School and Problems Related to AIDS* – the DHSS has distributed these to all doctors. These are not documents detailing how to develop sex education, nor to support children profoundly affected by the epidemic, rather they are designed to allay fears about contagion. This is somewhat strange given that there were no children living with AIDS in the UK at this time.[25] Children, like women, form a convenient smokescreen; this (mis)use of kids has not abated over time.

The July 1986 report does not include any new adult women with AIDS, but there is a curiosity which impacts upon the future categorization of cases. Suddenly the 'heterosexual contact' category swells by 150 per cent. Up to this point, no men have been identified in this way, but this is where CDR place three new reports (the others are all gay). Two of these men have apparently 'recently returned from Uganda and Mozambique'. All previous men with similar histories, and all the women with any African links, are counted as directly or indirectly associated with sub-Saharan Africa. Yet all of a sudden in July 1986 the statistics claim that more men than women have acquired AIDS from 'heterosexual contact'. The true picture appears to be precisely the reverse, but by scattering women with AIDS among several categories, like cannot be compared with like. To confuse things further, the third case of a man infected by 'heterosexual contact' is unlikely to be what it seems. The report describes 'a 36 year old man with Kaposi's sarcoma, who had recent multiple heterosexual contacts in Bangkok'. If the contact were that recent, it is extremely unlikely that he would already have progressed to AIDS. But apart from this, the presenting condition is a give-away. The description is suggestive of using the sex industry, but since he has KS it is far more likely that he was paying a male than a female. To this day this man is counted among the men who have acquired AIDS as a result of 'heterosexual contact'. How many other men who claim infection from sex tourism are concealing the true gender of the prostitute? If the report in July 1986 really wanted to show the numbers of men and women whose infection can be traced to 'heterosexual contact', the categorizing would be consistent and this would show a total of five men and ten women – that is 1 per cent of all men with AIDS and 77 per cent of all women.

In August 1986 the only new female case is a one-year-old 'born to seropositive parents'. In September, there is a twenty-five-year-old who seems to have been medically infected. She had abdominal surgery in Iran and then, in 1983, received blood transfusions in the USA. In this September 1986 report there is also an important reorganization of the statistics. Women and men can now be assigned to one of the following categories: homosexual/ bisexual, intravenous drug abuser, homosexual and intravenous drug abuser, haemophiliac, recipient of blood, heterosexual contact, paediatric (intra-uterine or perinatal infection), or other.[26] While this appears to bring together the 'heterosexual contact' with those people somehow associated with sub-Saharan Africa, it also obscures and conceals far more than it reveals. References to sub-Saharan Africa had come under fire for fuelling racism, but making explicit the African link can be important. The principal result of this reorganization has been to stress sexuality as the fundamental divide. An equally fundamental divide – race – has become obscured. Knowing the racial and national origin of people who have AIDS should highlight the needs for culturally tailored responses. It should also alert epidemiologists to consider whether 'heterosexual contact' is indeed the whole story.

There is increasing evidence that HIV exposure routes in Africa have not been properly reported, and that medically mediated transmission has been under-recognized. Research into AIDS in Africa has a fairly disgraceful history. While there have been noble and culturally sensitive research teams, African countries have also had more than their fair share of scientists engaging in 'imperialist scapegoating' and reporting on the 'poly-partner sexual activities' of allegedly promiscuous societies.[27] This is not the place to explore such colonialism, but it is startling that scientists so easily confirm their racist fantasies, while ignoring classic risk behaviour. One early research team in Uganda interviewed ten truck drivers who admitted homosexual behaviour. They reported to the *Lancet* that people were 'by western standards heterosexually promiscuous'.[28] Why was the real risk behaviour concealed? The denial of behaviour means there are no HIV-prevention messages addressing male homosexual or bisexual behaviour – an omission that endangers both men and women in Africa. The 1:1 ratio of male:female infections could be explained by this (if each man infects several women, after he has been infected by a man).

Another explanation, which also upholds the gender parity, may relate to the frequent use of injections and blood transfusions as medical treatment (especially for women who give birth and develop anaemia). WHO suggests that 10 per cent of African infections are due to medical routes of transmission, but it may be higher if blood is insufficiently screened for HIV, and medical equipment is unsterile and frequently reused because of poverty.[29] An association between HIV-positivity and repeated injections was noted as early as 1986, yet this seems to have slipped away from international concerns.[30] Where HIV transmission is related to contaminated blood supplies and a lack of sterile medical equipment, prevention measures are remarkably straightforward and cost-effective. Yet instead of focusing international aid on securing medical safety, the African AIDS crisis is written off. After all – so the argument goes – it is impossible to change heterosexual behaviour in countries where condoms would never be widely affordable even if they could be manufactured in such large quantities. If it is true that the African situation is more complex than widespread 'heterosexual AIDS', then the most trivial part of this political horror is that people are being sold a lie about sexual infectivity. There is constant reference to Africa as proof of imminent danger in the west, and yet some of this danger could be averted by a simple injection of cash to secure the blood supply – as well as addressing the more complex arena of behavioural change.

It may seem nitpicking to tear into the statistics at this stage, but it becomes far more important when numbers grow beyond the point where it is possible to track individual cases, and to where all manner of political predictions and analyses are made. Some three years after the first AIDS reports it is virtually possible to track every AIDS diagnosis. There is enough information to follow sex, age, geographical location and the most likely exposure category. As the cumulative total begins to top 500, the mass takes over and each individual becomes little more than a tick in a pre-determined box. It then becomes extremely important to know what assumptions determined those boxes, and governed the sorting of cases. The statistics that get flung around by media and policy-makers alike are statistics which muddle together, for example, a man with KS, a man who may have been infected by unsterile medical equipment in Africa, and one who had an HIV-infected wife – and they say all these men got AIDS as a result of 'heterosexual contact'.

The treatment of bisexuality is equally problematic. Most of the men diagnosed with AIDS are described as 'male homosexuals' – occasionally just 'homosexual' (no wonder lesbians feel invisible). However, in early 1985 a bisexual identity suddenly emerges. Yet it emerges in a tied category with no distinction made between the men who are homosexual and those who are bisexual.[31] Logically, bisexual should stand alone, but there could just as easily (perhaps more appropriately) be a category of 'bisexual and heterosexual men' if there were any real concern about transmission to women. The distinction of whether men are homosexual or bisexual has never been resolved in the statistics – they are just lumped together as disposable queers. In the long run, this cannot help women who are seeking to avoid, or living with, HIV and AIDS.[32]

The month after the major categorical reshuffle, PHLS change the classifications again. This time it is a tiny division of 'heterosexual contact' to state 'UK' or 'abroad'. This neatly avoids the stigmatizing use of the word 'Africa' (except that a note explains that ten of the twelve cases of 'heterosexual contact abroad' in this category are 'associated with sub-Saharan Africa'). It also neatly highlights what is supposed to be the major concern: 'heterosexual contact' within the UK. On top of the politics of classifying cases, October also brings with it two new reports of women with AIDS: a drug user (this time alive – did they ask her whether she might have been infected through sex?) and a woman who received whole blood four years ago (reported after she died). The next month – November 1986 – there were no new reports of women with AIDS. Yet this is a watershed month, as the UK government chose it to launch the start of the propaganda campaign 'to alert the public to the risk of Aids'.[33] This was the campaign which culminated in the infamous 'Don't Die of Ignorance' posters and the leaflet drop to all households. That month – forty months after AIDS started to be reported in the UK – the *CDR* presents a breakdown of the epidemic in the patient population which formed 2.8 per cent of the total case-load: women. Seventeen women had been diagnosed with AIDS, whereas 89.5 per cent of the cases of AIDS had occurred in gay men or bisexual men.

As Watney highlights, in this government campaign, the impact of AIDS on gay men, including the 536 already diagnosed with the disease, was 'totally and cynically erased from all public consideration'.[34] It was at this point in the history of AIDS that public health and political attention was focused on the potential of a heterosexual AIDS crisis. This focus came (inevitably) from the USA, when in October 1986 the right-wing Surgeon General published a report stating that transmission was likely to extend beyond the high-risk groups, and consequently AIDS was a major public health issue.[35] In alerting politicians to a doomsday scenario of generalized risk, this also ignored the reality. This trivializing of the current epidemic was achieved by shining the spotlight on women with AIDS – proof that gay men were not the only people infected, but also a cynical trick (and one which has oft been repeated).

But perhaps this was in women's interests? Unlikely. There would have been many ways to consider women's interests. For example, the review could have closely analysed how many of the men with AIDS have sex with women, or perhaps considered the practical and emotional needs of HIV-infected black women who are living away from their countries of origin, or perhaps they could have analysed gender differences in survival time. Instead, women were used to give good media copy. The media spotlight is on the epidemic because of the advertising campaign, and journalists are neatly steered towards the generalization of risk, and away from noticing the marginalized position of most people in the UK who have been diagnosed with AIDS. It has taken a few months for PHLS to get their statistics into order, but now they can help the media to see fifteen squeaky clean women (nearly all of whom got infected from 'normal' sex) and two baby girls.

Safety in numbers?

After this pivotal month, less and less information is given about the women who have AIDS, and there is a shift away from discursive reports describing individuals, to the tabular presentation of dry statistics. As the reports shift in style to a principally mathematical formula, so the text that accompanies the numbers becomes more political than descriptive. Instead of sharing the (limited) facts epidemiologists have about their subjects, anyone looking at these reports is plunged into analyses of the meaning of the disease. Yet it is no longer possible to check on the veracity of the information upon which these analyses are based.

The importance of developing new ways of splitting up the numbers is most vividly seen in the standard text of Department of Health press releases which accompany the quarterly AIDS figures. On the first page, immediately after recording the latest cumulative totals, they caution: 'trends in AIDS cases, their distribution between risk behaviour groups, and their geographical distribution, are *not* indicators of the current progress of HIV infection.' Lest there be any doubt about what this refers to, the commentary to the table which breaks down cases by transmission categories states, 'The proportion so far infected heterosexually is small. . . . But it is known that HIV infection can be transmitted between the sexes by vaginal intercourse, and the number of heterosexual infections is growing.'[36] The criticism of scare-mongering, so often laid at the feet of AIDS charities, is perhaps more appropriately directed at government officials. Certainly by 1990, the subtle emphasis of the Department of Health towards a 'heterosexual epidemic' has become overt. Half of the three-page press release for 11 April describes current statistics for AIDS and HIV cases in heterosexuals (respectively 6 per cent and 7 per cent of total reports). Five curt lines explain that cases of AIDS in homosexual and bisexual men 'account for 80 per cent of the total'.

From this point on, a special section is dedicated to describing rises in heterosexual AIDS and HIV; all other categories are rendered invisible. In 1991 this emphasis is strengthened by a change in the format of the tables. In part this responded to criticism from the AIDS industry at the stigmatizing use of 'risk groups', and so PHLS recategorize people according to how they are likely to have become infected, rather than who they are. Yet all this really does is to keep the imprecisions and add yet more focus to the potentials for 'heterosexual AIDS'.

Since 1991, people have been described as acquiring HIV from: sexual intercourse, injecting drug use (IDU), IDU and sexual intercourse between men, blood (differentiated between blood factor and blood/tissue transfer), mother to child, and other/ undetermined. The sexual intercourse category subdivides into 'between men' and 'between men and women' and then – be in no doubt about what really matters – the latter category has four sub-divisions. These are: 'high risk' partner (so much for ditching high-risk groups), other partner abroad, other partner UK, under investigation. There are also some new tables created 'to allow people better to gauge the current risks of unprotected sex'. Table 2 describes adults with AIDS according to three sexual orientations: homosexual men, bisexual men, heterosexual men and women (not split by gender). When it comes to HIV, there is only enough data for two sexual orientations: 'homosexual men/bisexual men' and 'heterosexual men and women'.[37] While it is good that they have grasped the difference between homosexual and bisexual

males, it is startling that all women are assumed to be heterosexual, and that this presumed sexuality is perceived as more vital
than their gender. From this point on, the basic categorizations
have remained stable. The constant category shifts highlight how
ideology underpins the compilation of statistics, not only the way
the numbers are used by popular culture.

Statistics mean nothing out of context. Epidemiology is all
about comparisons, and the comparison which still strikes me as
the most pertinent is not AIDS in women versus men, or competing exposure categories, or AIDS versus breast cancer, but AIDS
in 1984 compared with AIDS in 1994. The way the epidemic has
grown over the decade tells us the real-life impact of what is
happening. At the end of 1984, six women had been diagnosed
with AIDS in the UK. Two years later – when the UK government
launched its multi-media campaign – this had risen to fifteen
women and two girls. By the end of 1989, 100 women and 14 girls
had developed AIDS; 1192 women and 59 girls were known to be
HIV-positive.[38] That means the number of women with AIDS
nearly tripled in two years, and increased by a further 671 per cent
in the next three years. Five years later, in 1994, reports of HIV-
positive women topped the 3000 mark, with 3062 women and 139
girls testing HIV-positive.[39] Reported HIV cases have increased by
256 per cent, and there has been a 780 per cent increase in women
diagnosed with AIDS – to a cumulative total of 813 women and
77 girls.

Number crunching

The statistics in this book will inevitably be out of date by
the time it is published. Understanding the flaws in how they are
gathered is important to ensure a critical reading of the current
data. The most useful data available in the UK can be found in the
tables which are 'unpublished' every quarter, and I will use these
to consider what can be said about the women in the UK who were
known to have HIV or AIDS by the end of 1994.[40] There are two
basic pieces of information that are inscribed in statistics: who has
tested positive for HIV, or been diagnosed with AIDS; how women

will be vulnerable to future infection (which entails knowing how the current women became infected). The second type of information is more accessible than the first, which reflects back on the politics of data collection. Gathering information about a potential 'heterosexual epidemic' has consistently taken precedence over knowing about the women who are currently infected.

One of the key things that is known about women who are currently living with HIV or AIDS is their age – and they are consistently younger than men. Three-quarters of HIV-positive women are aged between twenty and thirty-four years, with 26 per cent aged twenty to twenty-four, 30 per cent aged twenty-five to twenty-nine, and 19 per cent aged thirty to thirty-four. By contrast, just 59 per cent of HIV-positive men are this age – 14 per cent, 24 per cent, 21 per cent in the respective age bands. For women and men with AIDS, the same differences are apparent. The peak ages for women to be diagnosed with AIDS are between twenty-five and thirty-four (52 per cent), while 57 per cent of men with AIDS are aged between thirty and forty-four. This suggests that many women are becoming infected at the start of their sexual careers. It could also be argued that this is true for men – following the theory that gay men postpone 'adolescence' until they are out – but it more likely demonstrates that men become infected when they are relatively sexually experienced. This may also reflect the fact that younger women have less bargaining power in sexual relationships, and may have additional societal vulnerabilities, such as likelihood of abuse or coercion. Young women also seem to have a greater biological vulnerability to HIV (this is discussed in Chapter 6). It is important to stress that while the majority of HIV-infected women are under forty, it is not exclusively a young woman's illness. Thirteen HIV-positive women, and eight who have developed AIDS, are over sixty-five years old. There is a popular de-sexing of older women, yet 16 per cent of cases of AIDS (140 women) and 7 per cent of the women known to have HIV (231 women) are over forty.

There is good information about the ages of women who have HIV or AIDS, but the data are less complete regarding where these women live. Geographical distribution of cases is recorded in tables which are more concerned about how people became infected than whether they are male or female (so that the category 'injecting drug use' is split between men and women, but 'blood' is not). This is odd, given that these tables should help local planners to determine the range of services to provide at local level. Although the data are not entirely reliable about the gender split, they suggest that the majority of women with AIDS and HIV are in London – like the men. Approximately 66.5 per cent of the women were diagnosed with AIDS in the Thames regions, as were 61.3 per cent of the women with HIV; 61.9 per cent of women with AIDS live in Greater London. This is slightly lower than the percentage of men – for example, 67.6 per cent of men diagnosed with HIV were in London. However, the geographical data are hard to analyse as it is well known that people tend to travel to (perceived) centres of excellence in London for their care, and they may be misregistered because of this. Certainly, service providers tend to identify that women with HIV and AIDS are scattered around the UK, and this makes sense in light of their modes of transmission. While gay men may be drawn to the capital, because of its tolerance and the political, social and sexual possibilities of the commercial scene, there is no reason why women who are vulnerable to HIV would experience a similar magnet. Indeed, the review of pre-1987 cases highlighted the broad geographical spread of women with AIDS.

The next thing that it would be useful to know is the race of the women. There is no way of knowing this from the statistics. Ever since 1986, when the African connection was actively concealed, there has been no way of telling the racial, national or cultural background of women diagnosed with HIV or AIDS. There are a few pointers based on reports from service providers. In early 1993, Positively Women's clients were (approximately) 48 per cent black African, 1.3 per cent Caribbean, 4 per cent mixed race, 42.7 per cent white European and 4 per cent other white (e.g. white American).[41] PHLS statistics do not give a racial breakdown of people with AIDS according to gender, but divide this information by exposure category. With some rough calculations these suggest that Positively Women's clients reflect the ethnic origin of women with AIDS or HIV in the UK.

Nearly all injecting drug users with AIDS (30 per cent of

whom are women) are identified in the tables as white, with just sixteen (of 591) of these people listed as black, Asian or Oriental, other or mixed. Similarly, 82 per cent of people with AIDS who have a 'high-risk partner' are white, as are 80.5 per cent of those with a UK partner (respectively 73 per cent and 44 per cent of people in these categories are women). However, the statistics are reversed in the category of people with AIDS who were infected by an 'other partner abroad', and this is especially pertinent as over 43.6 per cent of women with AIDS are identified as sexually infected by an 'other partner abroad'. Only 23.2 per cent of people in this category are white; 63.9 per cent are black, and 4.3 per cent are identified as Asian or Oriental. In turn it is quite possible that more than 64 per cent of the women in this category are black African (meaning that over 40 per cent of the men are white). White men are likely to have more opportunity to travel and have sex with a partner abroad than white women, and my close review of the statistics suggests that this category is a favourite with businessmen who want to conceal their sexual behaviour (like the one who was fond of Bangkok).

The 1986 shift away from noting direct and indirect connections to sub-saharan Africa was clearly not a success. It is ironic that this was (partially) intended to lessen racism, yet most people assume that the category 'other partner abroad' is simply code for black African. In fact it also incorporates people with white American, European and Australian sexual partners, as well as white people with black African partners – no one could know this from the vague coding. This was a classic piece of 'colour-blind' facile anti-racism which now backfires, leaving the number of black women with HIV or AIDS unknown. Where the number of black people is known (a total of 939, that is 9 per cent of the total diagnosed with AIDS by the end of 1994), not only is the gender breakdown lacking, but there is no way of knowing whether these are black British, Caribbean or African – all of whom will have distinctly different needs from care services.

The fascination with how people are assumed to have acquired HIV – so that public health officials could make neat statements about where the epidemic might go next – has disregarded the *needs* of the infected. The imprecise coding is problematic, but it does affirm that HIV and AIDS are principally sexual conditions for women, not linked to drug use: 564 women with AIDS (63.4 per cent of the total) and 2142 HIV-positive women (66.9 per cent) acquired the virus from sex. This includes the women categorized as 'other/undetermined'. In the USA, there has been a tendency to conspiracy theories, wondering why so many women are in this category (in the UK 1.8 per cent of AIDS cases and 3.3 per cent of women with HIV are placed here), with hypothesizing that they may have become infected from sex with other women. The truth is more mundane: most of these are women who do not know who infected them, and they are in this category while investigations seek to establish the man's identity or risk factors. This is coherent with Positively Women's finding that a third of the women did not know how they had become infected.[42]

The category 'other' also includes the four women who worked as healthcare providers and were proven to have acquired HIV after occupational exposure – in the UK no men have been found to be infected that way.[43] This appears to reflect the fact that women are more likely than men to work as nurses, and have the closest patient contact, and consequently an increased risk of exposure to infection by a very rare route. There are also lifestyle explanations for gender differences in blood-based exposure routes (routes which are now historical, as blood is screened in the UK): 1210 men acquired HIV (and 454 have developed AIDS) following exposure to HIV-infected blood products; only 11 women became infected this way (and 6 have developed AIDS). This is because haemophilia, the principal underlying condition requiring blood products, occurs principally in men. By contrast, more women than men have been exposed to HIV from blood transfusion or tissue transfer: 76 men tested HIV-positive from this exposure, and 37 have developed AIDS, compared with 80 HIV-positive women with 68 cases of AIDS. This may well be due to the fact that anaemia and complications in pregnancy, as well as gynaecological procedures such as hysterectomy, account for a good proportion of blood transfusions. The number of people exposed to HIV from blood transfusion is likely to be under-estimated due to the under-reporting of this exposure route for women and men from African countries.

However, the principal route of exposure for women is sex and in 1994, 564 women with AIDS knew the source of their sexual infection: 101 identified that he was 'high-risk' (he used drugs, was bisexual, or had received blood or blood products), 388 that he was 'abroad' and 52 that he was in the UK, with 7 under investigation and 16 other/undetermined. For HIV-positive women, this breaks down as 417 with high-risk partners, 1340 who have partners abroad, 202 in the UK and 183 in some way undetermined. A great deal of attention is always paid to the category 'other partner UK', and this is the category which the media think will demonstrate the onset of 'heterosexual AIDS'. If large numbers of women are found to be infected by an 'other partner UK' it would indicate that HIV has taken hold among heterosexual men who have never been transfused with infected blood products, shared drug equipment or been fucked by a man. In order for a 'heterosexual' epidemic to be sustained, there needs to be a sufficient number of HIV-infected men who have sex with women and vice versa. Myths of foreign contagion and a rigid hetero-homo divide suggest that this will not happen until tertiary heterosexual infections are established. The numbers are very small for this route (around 6 per cent of both HIV and AIDS reports), but it is not clear that this is really necessary for the epidemic to be sustained – it all depends upon whether sexual mixing continues between the groups originally infected.

Although the numbers of women who have acquired HIV from shared drug equipment are small, they are by no means irrelevant; 175 cases of AIDS (19.7 per cent) and 829 HIV-positive women (25.9 per cent) trace their infection to this. It is not clear whether it is actually the women who trace their infection to this or the people who collected the data. When an HIV-positive woman is known to have injected drugs it is often assumed that she got the virus from blood, but many of these women think it is more likely they got it from semen. Twenty-four per cent of the women in the Positively Women survey said they had injected drugs, but only 9.3 per cent believed they were infected this way. They may never have shared equipment or have always cleaned it, but not used condoms with their partner.[44] This is also borne out by what is known about the trends of HIV sexual transmission from male drug users. However, not all of the women infected this way risked being categorized as drug users since the majority may not have used drugs. A London survey found that 52 per cent (of 530) men who injected drugs had non-injecting female sexual partners – and the majority (70 per cent) never used condoms.[45] In 1994, 26 women who had sex with an injecting drug user tested HIV-positive; 35 women had tested positive in 1993, 37 in 1992, 30 in 1991 and 25 in 1990, with an additional 79 testing positive before in the previous decade.

There is also a small amount of information about the trends of sexual HIV transmission to women from bisexually behaving men. In 1994 just 7 women tested HIV-positive from sex with a bisexual man, but the previous year 27 women recorded this as their exposure route, with 19 in 1992, 10 in 1991, 11 in 1990, and a total of 48 in the 1980s. This appears to be just as significant a route as the numbers of women infected from IDUs. The total number of HIV-positive men who have sex with both women and men may be far greater than HIV-positive men who previously used drugs. Bisexuality is poorly researched and understood, but there are some indications that women may be highly vulnerable to HIV infection if the epidemic remains focused on gay men. One UK study of 930 gay-identified men found that 11.7 per cent had sex with a woman in the last year, and 5.6 per cent in the last month.[46] Since this behaviour is often stigmatized by the gay community, women's vulnerability may be greater, as these men are not educated about safer sex with women.

Women with HIV often record distress that people want to know 'how she got it', when what they really mean is 'who did you get it from?' The problem here is the classic one of women being defined by their relationships with men: 'who is he?' not, 'who are you?' It is not at all clear who these women are, and in terms of their sexual orientations or identities no one even hazards a guess. The word 'heterosexual' rarely rears its head, but this is not from any appreciation that women may have fluid or diverse sexual desire. There is just one table where lesbians and bisexual women are specifically mentioned, and this records good news for queer women. Between October 1986 and September 1994, 798 women who identified as 'homosexual or bisexual' went for the HIV test and none of them was positive. Before this is used to give queer women the all-clear, it is important to stress that these were just the women PHLS *knew* were queer. Positively Women's survey (of 75 women) included five women who identified as bisexual[47] – I wonder what the laboratories returning the test results to the PHLS thought they were.

The tables recording which kinds of people tested and how many came up HIV-positive show the proportions of a group of people who are infected, so that the statistics get closer to the real life they aim to chart. They are still restricted by exposure categories, rather than people's sense of identity, but they do at least discriminate between gender. In the eight years since testing started (October 1986), PHLS records the results of the first HIV tests taken by 117,521 women and 173,354 men. A total of 0.5 per cent of the women had a positive test result, compared with 2 per cent of the men. The highest prevalence rate is among babies born to HIV-positive women: 19.1 per cent of 152 baby boys and 11.2 per cent of 134 baby girls were found to be truly infected. This is not surprising as it fits within the known rates of transmission, and this is also a group which is likely to have a high rate of testing. What is shocking is that the next highest prevalence rate is not gay and bisexual men (8.5 per cent of 29,033 tested positive), but 'heterosexual: lived in/visited Africa': 13.4 per cent of the 1916 women, and 8.2 per cent of the 3232 men were HIV-positive on their first test. Yet more staggering, in the last three months, 21.7 per cent of the women in this category who tested had a positive result.

At a training session, I showed these statistics to a group of black women child-care workers, and they created an uproar. No one wanted to believe this could be true, and they suspected racist motives among the people collecting these data. One thing does seem certain: black African women are 'encouraged' to get tested in a way that white women never are – especially if they are pregnant. In the early days of the epidemic, women often reported that they had been tested for HIV without their consent, and certainly without pre-test counselling. This has declined sharply, but there are still examples of this terrible practice; all those cases identified by Positively Women since 1988 involved black African women.[48] Racism will be invoked by the discovery of high levels of HIV among black people – just as homophobia has been fuelled by the prevalence among gay men – but these data should alert black communities and their advocates to the fact that HIV is a devastating problem for African women in the UK today.

The HIV prevalence among groups who have been tested also reflects the differences in male-to-female and female-to-male sexual transmission of HIV. 6.1 per cent of 1215 women with an HIV-positive male sexual partner were infected; yet just 3.6 per cent of 663 men with an HIV-positive female partner were infected. Among women who had 'lived in/visited Americas' 2.3 per cent of 430 were HIV-positive, compared with 1.4 per cent of 697 men. This seems to confirm the rule of thumb that HIV is transmitted twice as efficiently from men to women as in the opposite direction (see Chapters 6 and 7).

HIV test results only reflect people who choose to get tested, whereas all people who develop AIDS symptoms are reported to PHLS. Yet neither statistic is ideal. The HIV cases are partial and subject to 'selection bias' (they also combine women who were infected at any time – some may have acquired HIV recently, others five years ago). The AIDS cases reflect women who were infected some ten years ago, and as such cannot give much information about the current dynamics of the epidemic. It would not be ethical to encourage people to take the HIV test in order to know how far the epidemic has spread (although some public policies seem to head in that direction), and so other mechanisms have been developed to estimate the current prevalence of HIV. The most credible data are derived from an unlinked anonymous HIV prevalence monitoring programme, which tests blood taken for other purposes after removing all identifying information (name, etc.) from the sample so that the test result cannot be traced back to an individual. Rates of HIV among women are derived from women attending genito-urinary medicine (GUM) clinics, women who inject drugs and use specialist agencies, women who seek terminations, and from blood taken from newborns (this gives information about whether the mother has HIV, not the baby). With the exception of women who are having terminations, data are gathered within London and in the rest of the country. The highest prevalence rates – with data gathered in 1993 – are seen in women who inject drugs and use services in London. 217 women were tested at these clinics and six were HIV-positive – a rate of 2.76 per cent; outside London the rate was 0.74 per cent.[49] Women who use GUM clinics – and who do not inject drugs – would appear to be at increased risk for HIV, since they have acquired STDs (sexually transmitted diseases). In London 0.57 per cent were HIV-positive, and outside London the rate was 0.09 per cent. This means that one in 176 women attending London clinics were HIV-infected, and, of these, 52 per cent had taken a named HIV test (i.e. they knew), either before or at the consultation where the blood was taken for this programme.

The data which always attract the greatest attention are the rates of infection among pregnant women (after or before delivery). The prevalence of HIV among these women is increasing, and in 1993 in London 0.18 per cent of them were HIV-infected (but only 0.004 per cent outside London – just six women). Within London there were sharp variations among districts, with nine districts showing rates over 0.2 per cent, the highest of which was 0.52 per cent. The researchers estimate that 70 to 80 per cent of these women are either from sub-Saharan Africa or were infected by a man from Africa. It is estimated that 12 per cent of women's HIV status was known by the healthcare staff (i.e. she had told them) and 7 of 24 infections were identified by named testing during pregnancy. It is possible that other women were aware of their HIV-positive status but did not tell the medical staff. In four hospitals which were known to have experience with HIV-positive pregnant women, or were offering voluntary named testing to substantial numbers of pregnant women, 16 of 43 infections were detected before or during the pregnancy.

Although pregnant women who continue their pregnancy receive a lot of attention, just one paragraph is given over to women who terminate their pregnancy. Women who end their pregnancy have higher rates than those who gave birth. These data were only gathered in London (from nine centres – compared with eighty-one centres where women give birth) and show a prevalence rate of 0.49 per cent, with one centre having a prevalence rate of

0.88 per cent. This means that 1 in every 205 women who terminate a pregnancy are HIV-infected. There is no information about whether these women are aware of their infection, and named HIV testing is not offered at these sites.

Jonathan Mann emphasizes that the HIV and AIDS pandemic 'is still very dynamic, unstable, and volatile; and its major impact is yet to come'.[50] In the UK, much has been learned about the current stage of the AIDS crisis and it is clear that the epidemic is far smaller than in comparable and neighbouring countries. By the end of September 1994, France had a total of 32,722 cases of AIDS, Spain had 27,584, and Italy had 24,511 – compared with 9865 in the UK.[51] At a global level, the situation is vulnerable to extreme and rapid change, but there are good reasons to believe that, unlike other parts of the EU, the UK has some structures in place (e.g. syringe exchanges) that will contain the numbers. Comparisons of the increasing statistics over time should express something of the shifting profile of the epidemic. Much has been made, and unmade, of the changing nature of the populations most affected. Gay men and bisexual men continue to form the (undifferentiated) core of the epidemic in the UK. Women and men who inject drugs have been infected, as have men and boys with haemophilia, but these infections have declined dramatically. In the last three months of 1994 just one woman and five men who injected drugs tested HIV-positive – although 36 female and 111 male IDUs developed AIDS in 1994 (but they would have been infected in the early 1980s). The striking shift in the 1990s has been the prevalence of HIV among populations with 'heterosexual' contacts outside the UK. This has principally been characterized as an African connection, and this is borne out both by service providers and the statistics, but it also includes contacts with the Americas and parts of Europe where HIV prevalence is highest (notably the southern countries). Overall, the ratio of male cases to female cases is changing significantly. In 1984, women were 5.5 per cent of the total AIDS cases. In 1989, women formed 7.1 per cent of the total AIDS cases and 10.7 per cent of HIV. In 1994 it is 8.6 per cent of total AIDS cases, and 13.9 per cent of people who have tested HIV-positive. This does not mean, in some political sense, that HIV is becoming a women's disease. It does mean that women are being infected at rapidly increasing levels, so much so that they are catching up the men who had a head start on them. This is not the kind of female ascendancy any feminist wants to see.

Notes

1. S. Faludi, *Backlash: The Undeclared War against Women*, Vintage, London, 1991, p. 26.
2. *Communicable Disease Report* (CDR), Vol. 5, No. 3, 20 January 1995, p. 13. When I was writing this chapter I considered contacting PHLS directly for inside information. I decided it would be more interesting to review the published data, as this might reveal more about the politics of women and AIDS. Since that time I have had the privilege of working with Doctors Angus Nicoll and Noel Gill from PHLS and recognize that had I contacted them they would have been able to answer many of my concerns. The presentation of epidemiological data is constantly evolving, and statistics are increasingly presented in more sophisticated ways which respond to many of the criticisms I make in this chapter. Many of the criticisms here refer principally to the ways in which government allows the scientific 'facts' to be presented to the public, not to the work of the scientists themselves.
3. In data compiled by the European Centre for the Epidemiological Monitoring of AIDS there is a footnote stating that (as of 30 June 1994) twelve transsexuals (presumably male to female) are counted in the cumulative cases of AIDS noted to occur in homo/bisexual males. There is no further information about these twelve people, such as their country of origin, age, date of report, etc. Since most countries do not have a sub-category for transsexuals we must assume this figure is far lower than the real number.
4. D. Taylor, 'Testing positive', in M. Berer with S. Ray (eds), *Women and HIV/AIDS: An International Resource Book*, Pandora, London, 1991, p. 12.
5. Based upon definitions from *A Dictionary of Epidemiology* supplied by the PHLS AIDS Centre.
6. Given the speed of discovery it is perhaps not surprising that in most countries there are small 'dissident' groups which question the HIV causation theory. What can often be frustrating about these groups is the suggestion that basic science is promoting a simplistic model about the pathogenesis of HIV and AIDS. In fact, scientific understanding about the development of HIV disease and AIDS is in a state of constant evolution.
7. G. Corea, *The Invisible Epidemic: The Story of Women and AIDS*, HarperPerennial, New York, 1992, pp. 8–9.

8. R. Shilts, *And the Band Played On*, Penguin, London, 1989.
9. The leading exponent of dissident ideas is Professor Peter Duesberg. He has a small but vocal discipleship in the UK, whose biggest coup has been to involve the *Sunday Times* in their conspiratorial fantasies. See E. King (ed.), *HIV & AIDS Treatments Directory*, NAM Publications, London, July 1995, pp. 36–42, for an excellent explanation of the arguments and their flaws.
10. 'Surveillance of the Acquired Immune Deficiency Syndrome (AIDS) in the United Kingdom, January 1982 – July 1983', PHLS Communicable Disease Surveillance Centre, Colindale, *CDR* 83/30, 29 July 1983, pp. 3–5.
11. For example, *CDR*, August, September and October 1983.
12. *CDR*, 83/39.
13. *CDR*, 83/43.
14. In *CDR*, 83/39, the case is recorded of 'a 45 year old heterosexual male from the Dominican Republic with Kaposi's sarcoma'. It is unlikely that the first woman was infected by this man since the *CDR* reports tend to note any sexual connections between cases.
15. *CDR*, 83/47.
16. *CDR*, 84/34.
17. See, for example, *Women Like Us*, Positively Women, London, 1994, p. 12, where 76 per cent of these clients of Positively Women stated that they did not think they were 'at risk' at the time when they probably acquired HIV.
18. J. W. Ward, 'The natural history of transfusion-associated infection with human immunodeficiency virus: factors influencing the rate of progression to disease', *NEJM*, 321:14, 1989 pp. 947–952; cited in K. Alcorn (ed.), *AIDS Reference Manual*, NAM Publications, January 1995, p. 102.
19. *CDR*, 85/39, 27 September 1985. In turn this references CDC, 'Revision of the case definition of Acquired Immune Deficiency Syndrome', *MMWR*, 34, 1985, pp. 373–6.
20. Doubtless, Duesbergites (and others who dispute that HIV – then known as HTLV3 or LAV – is necessary for AIDS to occur) will see in this fact some important support for their theories. However, there have always been people who have manifested the diseases which are now known as opportunistic infections of AIDS, and have had underlying immune imbalance (for example, people who have had organ transplants). AIDS became defined because of the increased clustering and frequency of these disease patterns, not because a previously unknown disease was identified.
21. For example, Corea, *op. cit.*, p. 57.
22. Mortality figures cited in K. Anastos and C. Marte, 'Women – the missing persons in the AIDS epidemic' in N. F. McKenzie (ed.), *The AIDS Reader*, Meridian, New York, 1991. Cited in D. Vowles,

'Positive choices – ethical dilemmas: a study of the advice and coun-selling offered to HIV positive women on reproductive decision making', unpublished MSc dissertation, London, 1994, p. 13.

23. *CDR*, 85/52.

24. *CDR*, 86/26.

25. The last age-based table of statistics dates from July 1985, by which time there was just one report: the twenty-month-old boy, and he had died. From October 1985, ages are no longer routinely given. In February 1986 it is reported that an eleven-year-old boy died, and had previously received blood transfusion in Portugal. Cases in people under twenty are sufficiently unusual that they can be expected to attract comment.

26. *CDR*, 86/39.

27. See, for example, R. M. Packard and P. Epstein, 'Medical research on AIDS in Africa: a historical perspective', in E. Fee and D. M. Fox (eds), *AIDS: The Making of a Chronic Disease*, University of California Press, 1992.

28. D. Serwadda *et al.*, 'Slim disease: a new disease in Uganda and its association with HTLV-III infection', *Lancet*, 2, no. 8460, 19 October 1985, pp. 849–52; cited in Packard and Epstein, *op. cit.*, p. 353.

29. There are also reports that in Japan husbands and wives are fre-quently injected with the same needle – leading to high rates of Hepatitis C; Russ King, personal communication.

30. J. M. Mann *et al.*, 'Risk factors for Human Immunodeficiency Virus seropositivity among children 1–24 months old in Kinshasa, Zaire', *Lancet*, no. 8508, 1986, p. 676; in Packard and Epstein, *op. cit.*, p. 363.

31. In November 1983 a thirty-one-year-old bisexual man with PCP and CMV is reported posthumously. Then twelve months later twelve men newly diagnosed with AIDS are described as 'homosexual/bisexual', with no precision as to how many are which (let alone whether this is what they or their doctors think they are).

32. Obscuring the risk factors also means men are discouraged from understanding and taking responsibility for their own risks of acquisi-tion. It also promotes an inaccurate view of HIV-positive women's infectivity, which is ultimately harmful for women living with the virus.

33. J. Carvell, 'Cabinet Aids drive aimed at all homes', *Guardian*, 12 November 1986, quoted in S. Watney, *Policing Desire: Pornography, AIDS and the Media*, Methuen, London, 1987, p. 136.

34. Watney, *ibid*.

35. C. Everett Koop, *Surgeon General's Report on Acquired Immune Deficiency Syndrome*, US Public Health Service, 1986; cited in E. King, *Safety in Numbers*, Cassell, London, 1993, pp. 173–4.

36. For example, press releases on 11 July 1988, 11 October 1988 and 9 January 1989.
37. Department of Health press release, *Quarterly AIDS Figures*, H91/22, 21 January 1991.
38. Department of Health press release, *Quarterly AIDS Figures*, 90/14, 11 January 1990, Tables A and C. These statistics included infections in Scotland for the first time, reflecting high levels of exposure related to sharing equipment for drug injecting.
39. PHLS AIDS Centre, unpublished quarterly surveillance tables, No. 26, December 1994, Table 1.
40. All subsequent statistics are based upon the PHLS AIDS Centre unpublished quarterly surveillance tables, No. 26, December 1994, Tables 1, 6–8, 10, 11, 13–16, 20, 23, 24, 29. The best source of reliable statistical data is the THT library, open to visitors on weekday afternoons by appointment.
41. *Women Like Us*, p. 10. PHLS statistics published in September 1995 analyse cases of 'heterosexual transmission' by contact with different regions of the world.
42. *Ibid.*, p. 12.
43. THT library archives. Also, Richard Foord, personal communication.
44. *Women Like Us*, p. 12.
45. M. Donoghoe *et al.*, 'Sexual mixing between drug injectors and non-injectors: potential for heterosexual transmission of HIV', Centre for Research on Drugs and Health Behaviour, Abstract WS-C09-3, IX International AIDS Conference, Berlin, 1993.
46. P. Weatherburn *et al.*, *The Sexual Lifestyles of Gay and Bisexual Men in England and Wales*, Project Sigma, 1992, London.
47. *Women Like Us*, p. 11.
48. *Ibid.*, p. 16.
49. E. Rubery *et al.*, *Unlinked Anonymous HIV Prevalence Monitoring Programme in England and Wales*, Department of Health, London, January 1995.
50. J. M. Mann *et al.* (eds), *AIDS in the World*, Harvard University Press, Cambridge, MA, 1992, p. 18.
51. PHLS AIDS Centre, unpublished quarterly surveillance tables, No. 26, December 1994, Table 30.

Chapter four

What Is AIDS?

For Lela ... getting an official AIDS diagnosis was almost
a relief. ' ... Before, I felt like I was a trivial woman with
all sorts of minor ailments and that all I needed was to get
my head in a better place in order to heal.'

Quoted in *M. Callen*[1]

ACT UP in New York is notorious for its pithy campaigning,
with lines like 'AIDS is a Disaster – Women Die Faster' and 'Women
don't get AIDS – they just die from it'. Both slogans summarize
medical findings that the time from an AIDS diagnosis to death is
shorter in women than men, so much so that far more women have
zero survival – that is, they are diagnosed with AIDS posthumously.
These slogans were used to demand that the AIDS definition include
conditions which are specific to women. The AIDS definition has
many functions, and one of them is to reflect the natural history of
HIV disease (a description of conditions associated with the course
of disease). In women this is still poorly understood, and research
into natural history started remarkably late. Many HIV-positive
women and their healthcare providers simply do not know whether
the conditions they have are due to the underlying HIV infection
or not, and this has consequences for treatment as well as for
the expectations they have about the development of the disease. The
poor knowledge about the natural history of HIV disease in women
means that HIV-related illness may not be considered as a diagnosis
for a woman who has never taken the HIV test and sees a doctor
because of, for example, persistent vaginal thrush which is unre-
sponsive to treatment – whereas any doctor worth his/her salt will
encourage a gay man with purple blotches to consider HIV testing.

Life expectancy

It is extremely difficult to say to someone with HIV or AIDS what their prognosis is after diagnosis – not simply because this is a gloomy topic, but also because the general nature of AIDS is unpredictable. It is not linear, and this uncertainty can cause great anxiety as well as hope. For most people the graph of the syndrome is a roller-coaster – illness is followed by the steep climb back to health, then some time later another condition may hit. Sometimes the graph is more of a ski slope, often accompanied by a phenomenon described as 'death by duvet' (someone is diagnosed with AIDS, decides this is the end, crawls under the duvet, and gets one sickness after another until she dies). The classic course of illness is varied and scientific information is also ever-changing, as is illustrated by studies which have looked at survival rates for people with HIV. Those which distinguish between sex and mode of transmission when analysing the data, have been summarized by Drs Anastos and Vermund.[2] They show that, in the early years of the epidemic, survival for women with AIDS was much shorter than for men. One of the first studies, published in 1987, looked at over 5000 men and 500 women in New York City and found that 81 per cent of white gay men with KS were alive one year after their AIDS diagnosis, whereas only 20 per cent of black women IDUs were alive twelve months after a PCP diagnosis.[3] When the data are controlled to remove such factors as KS (people with KS have a longer survival time than people with other opportunistic infections, and KS is far rarer in women than gay men), and to allow for comparable treatment protocols, the finding is consistent: women die faster.

The studies conducted to mid-1991 all show the same trend, but the median (mid-point average) time from diagnosis to death varies between the studies with average survival between 3.8 months and 19.6 months for women and ranging from 11.4 months to 21.8 months for men. These studies are often used as the basis for statements about life expectancy, but it is the trends which are far more meaningful than the absolute numbers. The lowest figures (3.8 and 11.4 months) come from an Australian study which considered data up to July 1987 looking at less than 600 people, twenty-one of whom were women.[4] It showed that, by a very early point in the Australian epidemic, ten women had died less than 3.8 months after their AIDS diagnosis, and ten women lived longer than that. It does not say why some women died more quickly, what the main differences from men were, or how long women with AIDS can expect to stay well. This study (and most of the studies by the time they are published) do not apply directly to people currently living with AIDS. In order to know that the median survival for men was 11.4 months, the Australian study had to consider people diagnosed before July 1986. Since this time there have been remarkable life-prolonging advances in diagnosis, prophylaxes and treatments, especially for opportunistic infections. These survival studies are often squeezed to yield far more information than they are designed to tell. For example, the fact that the highest survival time figures come from an analysis of women and men receiving antiretroviral therapy (in a study of over 7000 people [including 139 women] in San Francisco until 15 May 1991) is used by some to argue that antiretroviral therapies (like AZT, ddI and ddC) work. This may be true, but all it says definitively is that of the people in this particular study, the women who received antiretrovirals survived, on average, 13.2 months longer than those who did not – for men it was an extra 7.2 months.[5] Was it the antiretrovirals, or closer monitoring, earlier diagnosis, the approach of their doctors, or better access to care? Given that the effect of the antiretrovirals is significantly different between the sexes, it is unlikely that they alone are the cause of the longer life expectancy. The main suggestion to be drawn from these data is that these women who are taking antiretrovirals are getting something which women do not usually get, but men do. The access point to antiretrovirals includes CD4 cell counts, and anyone taking antiretrovirals is closely monitored (because of the heightened possibilities of adverse events). It is entirely possible that these features are just as significant as the therapies themselves.

Turning to the survival studies from 1992 and beyond, little or no difference is seen between the sexes regarding length of survival. There is even some suggestion that with optimum treatment women might progress to illness more slowly than men.

The studies suggesting this reversal are small and based upon monitoring CD4 cells which, although a vital part of the monitoring and clinical care of individuals, are increasingly thought to be an incomplete marker for research.[6] However, what is clearly observed is that survival times lengthen and 'the gender gap has apparently narrowed as the epidemic progresses'.[7] However, the key question remains unanswered: is it nature or non-nurture? Are/were women dying faster because the course of HIV disease in women is more severe, or because women are not getting adequate diagnosis and treatment for their HIV-related conditions? In order to answer this question it is useful to know two things: does the pathogenesis (how HIV causes disease) or natural history differ between HIV-infected women and men? And are there differences in the ways HIV-positive women and men access care?

Access to care

Reporting on the studies on survival differences presented at the 1992 International AIDS Conference, I wrote that the information 'supports the thesis that social factors are to blame. . . . Significantly, studies have consistently shown that the survival rates in the US for people of color are less than for whites; and those for drug users are less than for gay men. Women, people of color and drug users all tend to have more limited access to care.' London doctor Anne Johnson commented that, 'the explanation may not be intrinsic to women, but may be more due to late diagnosis and quality of access to care.' And Harvard doctor Deborah Cotton explained, 'the differences in access to care [between women and men] are so great that they are a more likely explanation than biological differences.'[8]

The theory runs that the main reason why women and 'people of color'[9] die faster is not genetic but a lack of care. If HIV-positive women had better medical services they would be diagnosed sooner, treated better and live longer. Studies in the USA prior to the AIDS epidemic suggested, however, that women in fact seek care earlier and more frequently than men, and that this includes people in drug treatment programmes. Anastos and Vermund speculate that this may not be true for all sub-groups of women, and that those with poorer access to care are the women who are most vulnerable to HIV.[10] The more important question must be whether if women seek healthcare, their clinicians are considering HIV as a possible diagnosis. In another setting, Anastos suggests that women in general do access primary healthcare, but that there still appears to be late diagnosis of HIV and AIDS. Fewer women than men who present with PCP will have this diagnosed at their first clinic visit. Since effective treatment relies on early diagnosis (and anyway the condition should be entirely preventable), this is a major failure.[11]

The first study in Britain[12] to explore the question of different groups' access to care has surprising results. Porter and her colleagues at the PHLS AIDS Centre reviewed information on 4127 adults with AIDS reported between 1989 and 1992. For 3293 men and 263 women the dates of both their HIV and AIDS diagnoses were known, and the researchers analysed these data to see which people had been aware of their HIV-positive status at least nine months before developing AIDS. They confirmed that prior knowledge of HIV status has important implications for clinical monitoring and access to prophylactic therapies.[13] Of people who knew they had HIV for less than nine months 12.9 per cent died within one month of their AIDS diagnosis, whereas only 6.1 per cent of people who had known about their status for more than nine months died during the month of their AIDS diagnosis. Overall, 34 per cent of women knew they were HIV-positive at least nine months before they developed AIDS, whereas this was the case for 52 per cent of the men (and 54 per cent of gay men and bisexual men). However, when the findings were analysed according to routes of transmission, the gender balance reversed. Among people who had probably acquired HIV through 'heterosexual sex', 29 per cent of the women knew they were HIV-positive, but only 17 per cent of men; of drug injectors, 66 per cent of women knew they were HIV-positive compared to 49 per cent of the men. Porter's findings are so contrary to received wisdom that they are expressed in a confusing double negative: 'After controlling for other factors, women were less likely to have been unaware of their infection than men.' The study surmises that men may have less awareness of their infection than women since 'women have more frequent contact with health care services'. It also reflects anecdotal reports that many women repeatedly seek HIV testing.[14] It seems that women are often panicked by AIDS-awareness campaigns into HIV testing simply because they are sexually active with men – not because, say, they have gynaecological symptoms which healthcare workers think may be HIV-related. Whatever the quality and gender-appropriateness of the healthcare in the UK, women are relatively well aware of their HIV status before they develop AIDS. Porter's study suggests that the argument that women with AIDS die faster because they 'lack access to healthcare' may be too simple for a British scenario.

The American scenario

Most of the research on treatment, medical and scientific aspects of HIV and AIDS and nearly all of the studies on different survival times with AIDS come from the USA. This has important implications for applying this information to HIV-positive women and men in the UK and Europe, let alone in the developing world. Most Americans assume that they are writing for other Americans, or at least that their readership understands the complexity of what is imaginatively described as their healthcare 'system'. As (to most people's utter despair) the British NHS slides in that direction, most British people have some insight into how the USA does (or does not) organize these things, but it is worth dwelling a little on the reality of the current situation. In the USA, the fruits of good health insurance are not single rooms, a television and a choice of menus (although this may be on offer), but access to your choice of doctor and excellent, technologically advanced medical care. Good health insurance cover is usually linked to permanent employment: the benefits often extend to children and spouse (hardly ever taken to include a same-sex partner) and are most comprehensive for people in a career job. Anyone who lacks proper health insurance or has health insurance which excludes cover for their critical condition (someone with HIV or AIDS cannot insure that 'pre-existing condition') cannot access the basic elements of healthcare which most Britons take entirely for granted. This is the situation for the majority of poor women and men, and many others. The lack of universal healthcare in the USA must rate as the most profoundly uncivilized feature of a so-called civilized nation – poor access to healthcare can still mean no healthcare except in an emergency.

So when Americans say that women have poor 'access to care' they do not just mean that women put their needs second, have a higher pain threshold or defer going to the GP, they may also mean that the woman has no medical services – she may never see (the equivalent of) a GP because she has no GP. The basic source of free healthcare is the emergency room (casualty department) of a hospital, and some hospitals in poor areas have closed their emergency services to block people from turning them into free primary healthcare facilities.[15] Using the emergency room as a general practice is not encouraged, and there is certainly no continuity of care, or option to see the same doctor. Americans with the least resources qualify for Medicaid – a basic insurance which is only accepted by some doctors and which limits the number of prescriptions a person is allowed in a twelve-month period; a person with AIDS can easily reach the ceiling within three months. If you do not have insurance and cannot afford, say, $3000 per month for your various prophylactic drugs, the pharmacy will not give them to you. Each element of medical care is detailed and costed and few doctors will want to admit an uninsured patient to the $1000 per day hospital bed, or order expensive tests, unless it is strictly necessary. The system is so remarkably complex that the savvy have found ways through it, but these are often complicated, time-consuming and draining, and guidance through the maze is rare.[16] Since a massive proportion of US government spending on health pays for research, entering a research trial is now one of the easiest ways for a poor or uninsured American with HIV or AIDS to access thorough medical care and monitoring. The poor and vulnerable can become research 'guinea pigs' by default: it is the only way to get quality healthcare.

These are only small, imprecise examples of the complex and confusing nature of the American 'system', yet the depth of the inequity is fundamental to their response to AIDS and the issues they highlight. Corea comments that, 'The AIDS virus [*sic*] thrives on precisely what permeates the U.S. medical system: the notion of "otherness". This is also called "sexism," "racism," and "homophobia" – words too puny and mild-mannered to convey the savagery they represent.'[17] When Americans highlight that AIDS affects the 'others' in society (poor women, 'people of color', prisoners, gay men, drug users) they are not just highlighting that it hits people whose humanity is undervalued, but that these are the very groups which are least likely to have any decent medical care. American activists' rhetoric which pits 'white gay men' against other people with AIDS is not only expressing basic hierarchies of oppression (men have more power than women, whites more than blacks), but that this group of people with AIDS is more likely to have healthcare than other affected groups – and if they do not, they are more likely to have access to a media and friends who can guide them through the bureaucratic systems to find care.

These factors, and the sharp divides within society which create such economic chasms between communities, are not replicated in Britain. The demographics and social characteristics of different groupings, communities and societies have profound effects upon the directions AIDS can take. Homophobia, sexism, racism and class politics oppress the people most vulnerable to and affected by AIDS, and in Britain and in Europe these things express themselves differently, more subtly than in the USA. Like the American medical system, sexism, racism, and homophobia permeate the NHS, but they do so in a very different way. This means that these 'isms' need to be confronted in different ways. For example, HIV affects black communities in Britain very differently from in the USA. The oppression of black communities functions differently and is rooted in different histories in the USA and the UK, and these result in different constructions of prejudice, ghettoizing, oppression, drug use and poverty, which influence the spread of diseases like HIV. The needs of the Ugandan refugee woman in London are different from the black woman in New York's Bronx, and sliding their needs together can create a simplistic understanding of the effects of racism. The black woman in Britain may have difficulties accessing care because of cultural insensitivity, a lack of translation facilities (although Positively Women's research suggests this is not a major issue), but the only black women who are restricted to medical care through accident and emergency departments are those with student or tourist visas (or who have overstayed when a visa has expired). Healthcare is more fundamentally inaccessible to many black American women (and Latinas and poor white women) than it is to black British women. Poor access to care for women in America may mean no access to care. If British HIV-positive women do have comparatively good access to care, the question that remains is whether they have access to good *standards* of care.

I am not aware of any study comparing standards of care for HIV-positive men and women in the UK, but there is some useful information from a review of the hospitalization of 735 HIV-positive men and 30 women in Vancouver, Canada. The Canadian epidemic among women is closer demographically to the British epidemic than the situation in the USA. In Canada, HIV is not so closely connected to poor, drug-using women of colour, and a high percentage of Canadian HIV-positive women acquired their infection sexually (as in the UK). Canada also has a universal health service, free at the point of access, making comparisons with Britain about treatment access more appropriate. Strathdee's Vancouver study[18] – like Porter's – found the reverse of the typical American scenario: HIV-positive women were hospitalized more than men. Over the three years of her study, the rates per 1000 patient years were 422 stays for men, and 658 for women – that is a 1.54 times higher rate for women. People with PCP, and with low CD4 counts, were also more likely to be hospitalized, as would be expected. However, the women who were hospitalized tended to have higher CD4 counts than the men, be younger, and not have AIDS-defining illnesses. Strathdee noted that women were more likely to receive AZT monotherapy (while men received combination therapies), to be treated by less experienced doctors (who had fewer than five HIV-positive patients), and to be cared for in more rural settings. These are all barriers to care, despite women apparently seeking healthcare more frequently than men. The emphasis on monotherapy is significant given the preliminary results of the Delta trial, which found longer survival and less disease progression in people receiving combination therapies, compared with those who received just AZT. Indeed, it may be that the women were in hospital more frequently not because they were receiving better care, but because the doctors lacked experience of treating women with AIDS.

What is AIDS?

Activists need simple and focused rallying points. For American activists concerned about women and AIDS in the early 1990s, the AIDS definition became the logical target. Activists charged that the medical neglect of HIV-positive women, and the paucity of research into the natural history of HIV disease in women, had led to under-counting cases of women with AIDS because the definition had not shifted to recognize AIDS in women. They were concerned for two reasons: the diagnosis of AIDS is a key access point to services and government benefits, and women were suffering from illnesses that were not being taken seriously because they did not fit into some arbitrary list of what constituted AIDS. Indeed, many HIV-positive women were dying before they ever received an official diagnosis of AIDS, whereas this was rare for HIV-positive men. Several issues were rolled together in the fight over what defined AIDS. The acronym 'AIDS' can describe the wide impact of the medical condition and its social consequences, can be perceived as 'a death sentence' by an individual, is used by scientists as a marker of severe immune damage, may be used by service providers as an access point to services, and still describes serious – often life-threatening – clinical conditions occurring because of underlying HIV infection.[19]

AIDS is so new that understanding of what it is shifts constantly. The first descriptions of AIDS were necessarily vague. In 1983 (before HIV was discovered), clinicians were asked simply to report any opportunistic infection or KS with 'no known underlying cause of cellular immune deficiency'.[20] The definition developed over time, and in 1987 the CDC defined four stages to HIV disease: Group I described acute infection or seroconversion; Group II was asymptomatic disease; Group III defined PGL (persistent generalized lymphadenopathy) and Group IV defined AIDS. CDC IV had a number of subdivisions (relating to whether the person was proven to have HIV infection) and listed twenty-three different opportunistic infections which might occur when the immune system is damaged.[21] This was a fairly mixed bag of conditions reflecting the changing patterns of illness, especially those seen in drug users. Most of the conditions included in the AIDS definition got there by pure observation: people with HIV and their doctors would notice how their health had changed since the diagnosis and conclude that this was how the new disease manifested itself. By the time HIV-positive women's conditions were starting to get the attention they deserved, the standard of proof had risen significantly. This was not necessarily some conspiracy to exclude women, but was based on some sound reasons. One of the activist battlegrounds was to recognize vaginal thrush as a symptom of AIDS. Many HIV-positive women have repeated, serious bouts of vaginal thrush which are hard to treat. However, this is also one of the most common symptoms that all women experience. It would be a disaster if every woman who got thrush became a 'worried well', convinced that she was HIV-infected and demanding monthly HIV antibody tests, all of which she disbelieved. Yet it is equally a disaster that HIV-infected women are not taken seriously and are encouraged to believe that significant causes of morbidity which reduce their quality of life are irrelevant. Many of the conditions which HIV-positive women experience are common symptoms of ill health in women, and this means that understanding of what medically constitutes AIDS needed to move beyond anecdotes.

The battle between anecdotes and scientific proof is complicated because 'AIDS' is not a neutral, value-free term. Programme planners for the VIII International AIDS Conference seriously considered holding a scientific session entitled 'What is AIDS?' to reflect the confusion and diversity of opinion. At the conference, some of the most carefully watched sessions and posters were those dealing with the AIDS definition. Women activists were getting angry and demanding that the definition include conditions specific to women, especially gynaecological complications. At the round table session on 'The CDC Surveillance Definition', AIDS history was made in the exchange between Dr Jim Curran and Theresa M. McGovern.

Since 1990 Curran (who is Director of the American CDC HIV/AIDS Division) had been a constant target for noisy demonstrations because of his unwillingness to agree that the AIDS definition should expand and include conditions which occur only in women.[22] McGovern calmly described her legal practice with low-income clients in NYC, and how many of the women, drug users and 'people of color' she saw were desperately sick or had died without ever receiving the benefits and entitlements which depend upon qualifying as disabled – a qualification which is based on the CDC definition of AIDS.

'We believed our clients when they told us they had AIDS,' she told the conference, 'and we looked through the major medical journals to find any evidence that HIV was linked to these illnesses.' She reviewed the illnesses her clients had, the arguments CDC had used to resist including new conditions in the definition, and their flawed logic, and concluded, 'The definition must be expanded to include anyone with 200 or less CD4 cells, recurrent bacterial pneumonia, pulmonary tuberculosis and cervical disease. This is a wise and supportable compromise.'[23] After the activists' noise and applause had died down, Curran stood up and said (in so many words), 'Sounds good to me'. The next year, these conditions swiftly became integrated in the new American definition of AIDS.

The battle of the AIDS definition was won at Amsterdam – but was it really such a victory? In their conference summaries, clinical scientists, epidemiologists and social scientists all high-lighted it as a key development, gathering approval from the audience. In his review, Dutch epidemiologist Coutinho reminded the Conference that the definition of AIDS in Africa was also troubled, but questions of whether to adopt the 'Bangui' or 'Abidjan' description dropped into the background.[24] The 'sexy', in-your-face ACT UP activism is often the most theatrical, inspiring event at international meetings, and it does have a tendency to get stuck in American (sometimes New York) politics. In Europe, activists and scientists agreed to differ from the Americans. Both sides of the pond agreed a core definition of symptoms, which enables epidemiological data from both continents to be compared. Only the Americans wanted to define a person who had less than 200 CD4 cells as having AIDS; for Europeans it seemed too arbitrary to use a surrogate marker for such a life-changing medical diagnosis. In New York this may have been the only way for poor people to get the benefits they needed, but most benefits in Europe are not so rigidly tied to the CDC definition of AIDS.[25] The psychological implications of telling a healthy person she has

AIDS underpinned the resistance of European activists (and some Americans) to the idea of an AIDS definition turning on a blood test of dubious predictive value. The diagnosis of AIDS becomes a catastrophic event in a person's life, but it may not necessarily be bestowed when clinically there is a catastrophe. Anastos points out that the point 'when someone gets sick is not a random point in time – it indicates failure of the immune system'.[26]

The 1993 definition was reorganized into three categories to reflect the different stages of immune failure. Category A describes seroconversion, asymptomatic infection and PGL; Category B includes symptomatic illnesses which are not in themselves life-threatening, such as shingles; and Category C lists life-threatening symptoms. Of significance for women, Category B now includes 'candidiasis of the vagina and/or vulva which is persistent, frequent, or responds poorly to treatment', 'cervical abnormalities of moderate or severe extent or cervical cancer' and 'pelvic inflammatory disease, particularly if complicated by tubo-ovarian abscess'. Category C lists the conditions previously assigned to Group IV, and adds recurrent pneumonia, pulmonary TB and invasive cervical cancer. Despite the apparent victory over the AIDS definition, the more fundamental questions had still not been answered: what is the clinical course of HIV in women?

The spectrum of illness

The notion of 'AIDS' is a historical artefact. It was essential to describe this new clustering of symptoms as soon as possible in the early 1980s, to facilitate the identification of any linked cases. As researchers and clinicians began to see more cases, to understand better what they were encountering, and as the prime cause – HIV – was identified, the complexity of this medical condition became clearer. In essence, the disease of AIDS has three mechanisms: as the immune system ceases to function fully, old conditions re-emerge (the protective cellular memory is damaged); new conditions can cause harm which have no, or little, effect on people with healthy immune systems; and HIV itself weakens the immune system and can also cause direct harm to organs of the body, including the brain.

While necessary for counting and delineation, the whole idea of being diagnosed with AIDS is troublesome. For most people an 'AIDS' diagnosis is far more severe than 'HIV', yet even with the most sensitive definition AIDS can mean many things: it can be the woman who had PCP four years ago and since then has been in remarkable health and climbing mountains; it can be the man who was hospitalized for meningitis, then developed cryptosporidiosis and, before that was fully cured, has now got MAI too; it can be the woman who has had no symptoms except dizziness for a couple of months, goes to hospital where her speech and mobility begin to fade, and they get progressively worse until she dies of PML two months later. The whole concept of 'AIDS' is so inscribed with social, psychological and cultural baggage that it will never be jettisoned. Yet for a long time it has been clear that 'HIV disease', which describes a spectrum of varying illness, is a far clearer description than this idea of a shift from mild (HIV) to severe (AIDS) illness.

The only way to understand properly the course of HIV disease in women – and to assess whether HIV-positive women develop different diseases from HIV-negative women, and from HIV-positive men – is to conduct studies comparing the disease over time. Since the progress of HIV disease in men has been studied from the early 1980s, cohorts (groups) of women are necessary to see if there are any differences. Natural history studies compare HIV-positive women with HIV-negative women who have similar histories of drug use and sexual activity, and the same demographics (e.g. race and socio-economic status). This is because these factors can also have an impact upon health, in particular gynaecological conditions, such as menstrual problems and STDs. In the USA, two large longitudinal studies are now under way to look prospectively at the natural history of HIV disease in women, by monitoring over time how the disease develops. In April 1993 HERS (the HIV Epidemiology Research Study) began enrolling 800 HIV-positive and 400 matched HIV-negative women. WIHS (the Women's Interagency HIV Study) is now enrolling 2000 HIV-positive and 500 matched HIV-negative women. Compared to the quantity of research addressing children, and perinatal transmission, scientific research on women is sparse and began very late. Acquiring this knowledge is not some academic exercise, but is required to enable health carers to intervene effectively and for the HIV-positive woman to take control of her life. There are two main gender specific questions. Are there HIV-related conditions which occur in female organs and systems? Do general HIV-related conditions occur differently in women?[27]

• *Investigating gynaecological conditions*

The paucity of information about the effect of HIV on the organs which men lack is a mixture of historical accident, embarrassment and neglect. The fact that men were first infected with HIV has meant that how this new condition affects cervices, vaginas, wombs and female hormones was not as pressing as it might have been had women and men been equally affected from the outset. This fact has been stretched, however, to conceal continued neglect and embarrassment. As Anastos and Vermund comment, 'Protestations that in developed countries there were inadequate numbers of women to study are not tenable.'[28] If researchers in New York could study the survival rates of over 500 women with AIDS in 1986, why couldn't they study the nature of their disease? Corea shows how, in the USA, pelvic examinations have not been offered routinely to women with HIV, and that gynaecological measures have not been included in research protocols. In early 1995 an American woman living with HIV stated that for the last nine years she had participated in a study co-ordinated by the National Institutes of Health. She has never been given a pelvic exam on that study.[29]

The argument that the failure to look at gynaecological conditions in HIV-positive women is somehow linked to the small number of HIV-positive women does not convince Corea, who shows that pelvic exams were rarely part of routine care for women with HIV.[30] Since early HIV services were designed to respond to a disease mostly affecting men, gynaecological services were not integrated into HIV care from the start. Clearly this is no longer reasonable. HIV services have always had to integrate a wide range of specialties (genito-urinary, virology, immunology, pulmonary, oncology, dermatology, etc.) to deal with this complex syndrome, and it is now overdue for gynaecology to form a part of this. There seems to be no small dose of the 'ick' factor in the neglect of gynaecological conditions, and this is by no means a problem restricted to the USA. Anna, a twenty-seven-year-old healthcare worker in Oslo, Norway, had chronic, persistent vaginal candidiasis for five of the six years since she was infected with HIV. By 1992, her doctors had never given her a pelvic exam. 'I have a feeling they're a little bit embarrassed. I just say I have something itchy and they write a prescription.' She has never even been advised about Pap smears, and has never had one.[31] Corea reflects on the attitudes of physicians in Brooklyn in 1988, 'None of the infectious disease docs wanted to do gyn exams. Those exams were gross. Besides, some commented, "Women are going to die from their HIV disease before they'll die from any cervical problems so why should we bother to do this?"'[32]

For years now, women with HIV and their advocates have known that there are gynaecological complications, including menstrual abnormalities, urinary tract infections, vaginal thrush, pelvic inflammatory disease and cervical (pre-)cancers. It would be bizarre if these conditions did not flare up as the immune system becomes deficient, yet for a long time researchers appeared to cling to the idea that these were only seen because HIV-positive women were the kind of women who get more gynaecological problems (because they are 'promiscuous'). So Dr Deborah Cotton commented on the – then unproven – link between HIV and cervical cancer, 'The risk factors tend to be the same: women having early sex, and women with multiple partners.'[33] Slowly the research is rolling in at international conferences to affirm that many gynae-cological conditions are linked to HIV: they are more frequent, persistent or resistant to treatment. In turn prophylaxis and treatment protocols are put in place. At least the CDC now advises that all women should have a pelvic examination, including a Pap smear, upon diagnosis with either HIV or AIDS – why then hasn't the UK Department of Health circulated this guidance? The International Community of Women Living with HIV and AIDS (ICW) has twelve demands including one for 'education and training of health care providers and the community at large about women's risks and needs. Up-to-date, accurate information concerning all issues about women living with HIV and AIDS should be easily and freely available.'[34]

Few experienced AIDS doctors would now be likely to dismiss a patient's concern about a gynaecological problem, but it is not clear that all are automatically considering it. Twenty-six-year-old Tanja has had far more acute and depressive bouts of PMS in the four years since she was infected, but her doctor in Germany has never asked about menstrual or gynaecological issues (nor suggested cervical smears), and she has not raised them. 'When you first get your diagnosis, you're so frightened. I kept thinking "Maybe he'll ask me about my periods so I can find out what's going on".'[35]

The problems many HIV-positive women encounter include more frequent and heavier periods, spotting in between periods, increases in premenstrual symptoms (including breast pain, cramps, fluid retention, anxiety and depression), light or absent periods and early onset of menopausal symptoms. Denenberg notes that these are often avoided by health carers who may have 'a subconscious opinion that women with HIV infection become "asexual" or should not have sex and therefore do not have concerns about menstruation, menopause and sexuality. In fact, HIV-positive women have the same concerns and desires as other women.'[36] Denenberg considers that these menstrual problems may not be analysed sufficiently because (like Corea's Brooklyn doctors) health professionals assume HIV-positive women will die before such symptoms could cause serious harm. She points out that these do need to be worked up since they can mask or be mistaken for the symptoms of opportunistic infections, they may be precursors of more serious conditions, and of themselves they may cause significant morbidity – for example, heavy bleeding can lead to anaemia (as well as increasing risks of HIV transmission and, for some women, restricting their sex lives).

Although menstrual problems have often been reported by HIV-positive women, there is still no definitive evidence that these are linked to HIV. One well-controlled study of 301 HIV-positive and 286 HIV-negative women found startlingly high levels of menstrual irregularities, with just two-thirds of the women having normal menstrual cycles: 1.5 per cent of the women had over fourteen periods in a year, 20 per cent had less than ten periods and 7 per cent did not bleed for over three months. Over one in ten women had at least one period that lasted more than a week, and around 3 per cent had one or more periods lasting less than two days. Five per cent of the women had some bleeding after vaginal intercourse. Despite all these problems, there were no statistical differences between the HIV-positive and HIV-negative women, nor were there any noticeable trends towards differences. It is possible, therefore, that the problems HIV-positive women report reflect the fact that all women have extensive menstrual problems; these may even be more common among women who are highly vulnerable to HIV (e.g. drug-using women). However, there were some methodological problems with the study, in particular because it relied on women remembering details about their menstrual cycle over the past twelve months.[37]

One of the symptoms which may be indicated by menstrual problems is pelvic inflammatory disease (PID). PID is an inflammation of the upper genital area, around the pelvis. It can be caused by one or a number of bacteria, especially untreated STDs such as chlamydia and gonorrhoea. PID can cause fever, fatigue and acute, dull pain in the abdominal area and lower back. If left untreated, it can lead to bleeding in between periods, extremely painful periods and trouble walking due to the pain. PID has been reported as leading to infertility in up to 25 per cent of women with the condition,[38] and in rare cases it can even be life-threatening. The association with HIV is extremely unclear, with research sometimes claiming that it is worse or more resistant to treatment in HIV-infected women, sometimes that there are no major differences in terms of the severity of the condition and the effectiveness of treatment. This is an issue that is unlikely to be resolved until there are good data from large cohorts, like HERS and WIHS. Every year one million women in the USA develop PID. One study showed that 6 to 10 per cent of all women (and 16 to 30 per cent of African-Americans) with PID attending emergency rooms were HIV-infected. Women with HIV responded slightly less well to initial treatment, but four to ten days after commencing treatment they were as well as uninfected women.[39]

PID is an infection of the reproductive tract. Many reproductive tract infections (RTIs) are silent and symptomless and become chronic in women, whereas in men there are frequently visible or painful symptoms early after infection. Most HIV-infected women who acquired HIV sexually have been vulnerable to acquiring STDs, which are the cause of many RTIs. Early research suggested that women with HIV had a higher prevalence of hard-to-treat RTIs than uninfected women. However, more rigorous research, including preliminary reports from the HERS study, has found very low levels of STDs and no differences between HIV-positive and HIV-negative women.

The initial findings from HERS were echoed by findings from the long-standing New York Cervical Disease study, with both groups showing virtually the same statistics. The two studies gathered data on a total of 706 HIV-positive and 531 HIV-negative women and found that none of the women had gonorrhoea, around 4 per cent had chlamydia, about 6 per cent syphilis, between 10 per cent and 22 per cent had trichomonas (TV), and around 37 per cent had bacterial vaginosis (BV). One worrying feature was the low awareness the women had of their conditions. All of the clinicians detected that the women with BV had an abnormal discharge, but only 25 per cent of the women were aware of this; with TV, 75% per cent of the clinicians noted the discharge, but only 31 per cent of the women.[40] This emphasizes the importance of regular gynaecological monitoring and care for all women, and is a useful reminder that even if there are no major HIV-related differences, women still need excellent medical care.

The most common gynaecological complaint from HIV-positive women has been vaginal or vulval candidiasis (thrush), and this is often a problem at high CD4 levels, before women are likely to develop any other symptoms linked to HIV. With thrush there is a definite link with HIV, and oral and oesophageal thrush have always been a part of the definition. The first results from the HERS study[41] showed that a large number of women had some colonization with candida (i.e. the fungus was present), and this was more common among HIV-positive (72.3 per cent) than HIV-negative (56.9 per cent) women. Nearly 41 per cent of the HIV-positive women had vaginal candidiasis (i.e. the fungus caused disease), whereas only 22 per cent of the HIV-negative women did. With rectal candidiasis there was a smaller, but significant, difference: 42 per cent of HIV-positive women and 31 per cent of HIV-negatives. Oral candidiasis was found in a very large percentage of the women: 62.3 per cent and 45.4 per cent respectively, and there was a link with lower CD4 cells. The high prevalence of vaginal candidiasis has implications for the treatment of oral and oesophageal candidiasis which occur at lower CD4 counts. In particular, there can be severe problems if a woman becomes resistant to other systemic treatments used for vaginal thrush. If vaginal thrush is treated aggressively, and strains of candida become resistant to drugs like fluconazole, then women may have no treatment options if they go on to develop more severe conditions at other sites.

• *Genital cancers*

The other gynaecological condition which appears to have a well-proven link to HIV is cervical cancer. Most of the research focuses on cervical (pre-)cancers, but cancers and lesions can occur at any part of the genitals – a woman's cervix, vagina, vulva, clitoris, anus or peri-anal area. Invasive cervical cancer (ICC) has become an AIDS-defining condition, but it appears that the cervical changes which may be precursors of cervical cancer are really the conditions that are more prevalent among HIV-infected women – not invasive cancers themselves. The fear that thousands of HIV-positive women would die of cancer does not seem to have been realized, and this may be due to good cervical screening protocols, or that the initial cervical changes were never likely to progress to cancer. During 1994, there were 14,801 new cases of women with AIDS reported in the USA, and of these women, only 164 were reported as having AIDS because they developed ICC – that is just 1.2 per cent of the new cases. In Europe during the first nine months of 1994, 42 women were diagnosed with AIDS because they developed ICC – that is 1.8 per cent of women diagnosed over that timescale.[42]

Although this is good news, there is accompanying bad news. In HIV-infected women, ICC – and its precursor CIN (see below) – respond poorly to treatment. The failure rate for treating genital pre-cancers in the general population is around 10 per cent, but failure rates of up to 80 per cent have been seen among HIV-positive women. One study, using loop electrosurgical excision (also known as LEEP), succeeded in removing lesions from only 44 per cent of 34 HIV-positive women; the treatment worked for 87 per cent of the 80 HIV-negative women. Studies of other therapeutic options – cryotherapy, laser treatment and cone biopsy – also show high levels of failure in HIV-positive women. These problems are not just related to the cervix; Abercrombie also found it difficult to treat lesions on the vulva. Of fifteen low-grade HPV lesions found in HIV-positive women, six were treated with trichloroacetic acid (TCA) and five recurred, whereas only one of the nine lesions which were untreated caused persistent disease. Six high-grade lesions (VIN 2 or 3) were treated by LEEP or laser and all recurred. However, none of these lesions progressed to invasive cancer during the period of review.[43]

Nearly all women who have genital (pre-) cancers are infected with HPV (human papilloma virus), a common STD that can cause genital warts. Genital warts can be diagnosed by examination, but HPV infection is often present when warts are not. HPV is thought to be one of the causes of genital cancers, but there are at least seventy different strains of HPV, only some of which are definitively linked with genital cancers. These are described as oncogenic types – principally HPV strains 16, 18 and 31. Some strains are associated principally with warts, and are not linked to cancer; these are HPV types 6, 11, 42, 43 and 44. Pre-cancerous changes of the cervix are called dysplasias or are graded as CIN 1, 2, 3 – CIN stands for cervical intraepithelial neoplasia. CIN 1 is the mildest change, affecting around 25 per cent of the epithelium, and giving a 7 per cent risk of progression to cancer; CIN 2 affects around 50 per cent of the epithelium, and there is a 50 per cent risk of spontaneous progression to cancer; CIN 3 is the most severe: the bulk of the epithelium is affected, there may be carcinoma in situ, and some believe this represents a 100 per cent risk of spontaneous progression to cancer. Other genital lesions are referred to as VIN (of the vulvar), VAIN (vaginal), AIN (anal) and PAIN (peri-anal). In America, the terms High or Low Grade SIL (squamous intraepithelial lesions) may be used, but this is just another way of grading these changes. Low Grade SIL (LGSIL) is broadly equivalent to CIN 1, and High Grade SIL (HGSIL) is equivalent to CIN 2 or 3. The term 'condyloma' describes less severe changes.

Although these lesions are typically referred to as 'pre-cancer', this is an imprecise term. It may be that the lesions themselves are the problem, and that many stabilize rather than leading on to more serious, life-threatening disease. It could also be that they do progress, but progress so slowly that HIV-positive women have died of other conditions before the cancer can cause harm. Perhaps one of the greatest ironies of long-term survival is that as HIV threatens life more slowly, other life-threatening conditions are given the opportunity to emerge. Joel Palefsky, expert on genital cancers, states ironically, 'I hope people with HIV will live long enough for cancers to become more common.'[44]

Palefsky has stated that one of the most reliable studies found CIN in 23.5 per cent of HIV-positive women, but only 0.6 per cent of HIV-negative women (the group was well-matched for demographics and risk factors). A study of the prevalence of CIN in women in different parts of the USA concluded that between 23 per cent and 48 per cent of HIV-positive women had these lesions.[45] Data are also beginning to show that women with HIV are more vulnerable to cancers and lesions of the vulva and vagina. The New York Cervical Disease Study (which has studied 400 HIV-positive women and 400 demographically matched HIV-negative women since 1991) found forty-six vaginal or vulval lesions in HIV-positive women, but just six in HIV-negative women. They calculate that, compared with uninfected women, HIV-positive women have a six times greater risk of developing cervical condyloma, 5.5 greater risk of developing vulval condyloma, and 4.5 greater risk of vaginal condyloma.[46] Another study suggests that HIV-positive women are twenty-nine times more likely to have VIN (vulval intraepithelial neoplasia) than women who are not infected.[47]

The risk factors for CIN (and other neoplasias) are consistently shown to be: HIV infection, CD4 counts under 200, HPV infection, and being older than thirty-four years. Smoking is associated with genital cancers, and there is some link with chlamydia. In US studies, African-American women are more at risk than Caucasian women – this is not a biological difference, but because black women have poorer access to medical care, and consequently do not have Pap smears which would pick up early changes. The link between HPV and CIN is not total, but HPV is an important marker indicating that a woman is at higher risk of developing genital cancers. HPV is more common among HIV-infected women. Using the highly sensitive PCR (Polymerase Chain Reaction) test, initial results from HERS have found that 64.5 per cent of HIV-positive women are infected with HPV, compared with 30.9 per cent of HIV-negative women. The Southern Blot assay (which is less specific) found a similar difference: 34.2 per cent compared to 13.5 per cent.[48]. This is not just a cervical matter: PCR screening for HPV in a cohort of women found that 56 per cent had HPV at the cervix and 77 per cent at the anus. Reporting these findings, Palefsky suggested that although anal neoplasias are relatively uncommon – and of lower grade than cervical neoplasias – the anus may be a reservoir of infection. Moreover, he says, 'The anus is an ignored area in the care of women, but it is an important sexual organ.'[49]

It is reassuring that data are beginning to trickle in on the natural history of HIV disease in women. In 1995 it was a delight to attend a conference on women and HIV packed full of preliminary scientific results, rather than playing 'hunt the women's poster session' at generic meetings. It will take a number of years before there is full information, and knowledge is confirmed, but it already appears that there are differences between HIV-positive women and men (surprise) and between HIV-positive and negative women. There are also a lot of similarities. One of the results of the studies appears to be that all women (at least, all women at high risk of acquiring HIV) have an incredibly high rate of gynaecological complications. Where differences are not seen between HIV-positive and negative women, this does not mean that HIV-infected women do not have these medical problems – just that they are not necessarily linked to the virus.

• *Screening for genital lesions and cancers*

Invasive genital cancers are life-threatening, and can be most easily avoided if they are treated very early in disease progression.

Early detection is easy, and it is for this reason that all women are encouraged to have at least three-yearly Pap smears. These involve taking a small scraping of cells from the cervix, and looking at the cells under a microscope to see if there are any changes suggesting cancer could develop in the future. In the USA there was concern from activists that the overall standard of gynaecological care for HIV-positive women was insufficient. There were additional concerns that early studies had suggested that Pap smears might be missing pre-cancerous changes, and these could be picked up more quickly using a colposcopy. This involves placing a microscope in the vagina to look at the cervix, and it can be accompanied by biopsy, where a small piece of tissue is cut for further examination. As a procedure, colposcopy is more precise, but it is also expensive and requires specialist staff to carry it out – staff who are rarely present in generic HIV clinics in the USA.

The interventionist nature of colposcopies has led to a number of studies aiming to assess the relative merits of the two procedures. Colposcopies are intrinsically more sensitive, but the key question is whether Pap smears could fail to detect CIN so that women would risk developing cancer before interventions could be offered. There had been problems with the methodologies of previous studies, but these were overcome in an excellently controlled study by Dr Carol Brosgart.[50] This looked at 75 HIV-positive and 21 HIV-negative women who attended a clinic for CIN screening, and found four times as many abnormalities among the HIV-positive women, by both Pap smears and colposcopies. Twenty-four of the HIV-positive women had positive results by colposcopy, but only fourteen of them had positive results by Pap, which suggests that the Pap smear is 58 per cent sensitive, i.e. a false negative rate of 42 per cent. In the general population, Pap smears have a false negative rate between 20 and 50 per cent. On further investigation, Brosgart found that the fourteen positive smears corresponded with all the high-grade CIN and pre-cancers. The ten women who were only positive by colposcopy had low-grade CIN or were false positive and none required treatment. Consequently, Brosgart concluded that Pap smears are 100 per cent sensitive to screen for CIN in HIV-positive women. Forty-three per cent of the women with negative Pap smears had potentially oncogenic (cancer-producing) strains of HPV, and she proposes that baseline HPV typing might predict which women would benefit from more frequent screening.

The American CDC have produced guidelines for screening HIV-positive women which state that women should receive Pap smears at diagnosis and then every six months; if there are any abnormalities these must be investigated using colposcopy. No UK specific guidance has been issued, but many HIV-positive women report that six-monthly colposcopies are routine at their clinics which are more able to provide the service. For many UK clinicians, less constrained by the appalling healthcare system of their Stateside colleagues, there can be a tendency to cautious over-investigation. Yet colposcopies are a more invasive procedure, which often cause greater discomfort and bleeding than Pap smears, so are they really necessary?

One AIDS specialist states that among his female HIV-positive patients 'I have yet to meet a woman who wants a colposcopy', and he fears that introducing routine colposcopies would send his patients running. It looks like the American activists' stress on colposcopies has set an agenda that may not be appropriate outside their shores. Indeed, in contrast to the American neglect of pelvic exams, this doctor quotes one of his HIV-positive patients who says, 'I am fed up with spreading my legs for the medical profession.'[51] The depressing findings about poor treatment outcomes (especially at low CD4 levels) suggest that current efforts to detect and treat genital cancers may be misguided. 'Screening and treatment for cervical disease in anybody is not a pleasant procedure,' states Palefsky, 'the clinician and the patient need to make choices about how aggressive to be in preventing morbidity and mortality. Where the woman is not going to benefit in terms of prolonged survival or comfort, it may not be useful to continue aggressive screening.'[52]

Trials and errors

Important as it is to define HIV disease progression, it is of little use to know what the symptoms are if treatments are not available. The American ACTG (AIDS Clinical Trials Group) only started its first trial involving the female urogenital system in late 1992.[53] No wonder no one knows how to treat HIV-positive women who develop CIN or invasive cancer. The clinical and treatment knowledge about HIV in women is poor because the research cake is rarely divided in a way that addresses some of women's most pressing concerns. Breakthroughs are hailed in respect of using AZT to prevent babies from becoming infected, but still no one knows whether AZT interferes with women's menstrual cycle. It is easy to see which study would get the greatest media coverage, but why has no researcher looked at this most basic quality of life issue for women?

Inevitably, HIV-positive women will have complications men don't have, in the organs men don't have. Yet the notion 'that clinically important differences between men and women are the rule rather than the exception [is] a biologically implausible assumption'.[54] This is important, and it is critical that in the rush to rebalance the research agenda, activists do not pit men and women against each other as if they are different species. Still, there are some theoretical reasons to wonder if there may be a few clinical differences between HIV disease in women and in men – is there an interaction between, say, the endocrine and immune systems? This would be highly sex specific, and there is no way of knowing. By 1990, the only study on HIV and the endocrine system excluded women and just looked at testosterone in men.[55] There are even more basic differences that should be explored, and are not. In general, drugs may work differently in women than men – for example, because of women's lesser body mass, and since the hormonal system may alter the metabolism of drugs. Yet information about this is hardly ever gathered in the course of clinical trials. There are two reasons for this: trials which include women may not analyse their data according to gender, and some trials have excluded women because of alleged 'child-bearing potential' – if women are included they are required to use contraception, even if they state they are celibate or lesbian. At the beginning of 1995, the US FDA (the agency responsible for approving new drugs) proposed new regulations stating that all trials must analyse their data by gender, and that women may only be excluded from trials where evidence exists that a new compound could harm women's reproductive capacity. These changes ought to make a difference, but activists will need a beady eye.[56]

Notes

1. Cited in M. Callen, *Surviving AIDS*, HarperCollins, New York, 1990, p. 128.
2. K. Anastos and S. Vermund, 'Epidemiology and natural history', pp. 154–6, in A. Kurth (ed.), *Until the Cure: Caring for Women with HIV*, Yale, 1993; see also R. Gorna, 'Research into women and AIDS: where is it?', *World AIDS News: The Newspaper of the Harvard-Amsterdam Conference*, 24 July 1992, pp. 4–5.
3. R. Rothenberg *et al.*, 1987, 'Survival with the acquired immuno-deficiency syndrome: experience with 5,833 cases in New York City', *NEJM*, 317: 1297–1302, quoted in Anastos and Vermund, *op. cit.*, pp. 154f.
4. B. Whyte *et al.*, 1989, 'Survival of patients with the acquired immuno-deficiency syndrome in Australia', *Medical Journal of Australia*, 150: 358–62, cited by Anastos and Vermund, *op. cit.*, p. 155.
5. G. F. Lemp *et al.*, 1992, 'Survival for women and men with AIDS', *Journal of Infectious Diseases*, 166: 74–9, cited by Anastos and Vermund, *op. cit.*, p. 155.
6. The Concorde trial, which compared beginning AZT early or later in disease, found that, although early intervention had a positive effect on CD4 cells, this was not translated into clinical benefit in an analysis which looked over three years. Researchers and treatment activists are now sceptical about using CD4 cells alone to monitor treatment efficacy. However, CD4 cells remain a vital element of clinical care.
7. Anastos and Vermund, *op. cit.*, p. 156.
8. Gorna, *op. cit.*
9. In the USA, 'people of color' seems to be the preferred term. In Britain, debates about the best term are constant and I use the term 'black communities' in the way Americans would use 'people of color', that is, to describe all non-white races. Individual racial or ethnic groups will be stated where significant.
10. Anastos and Vermund, *op. cit.*, p. 154.
11. Session 18, First National Conference on Human Retroviruses and Related Infections, Washington, DC, 12–16 December 1993.
12. Porter *et al.*, 'Factors associated with lack of awareness of HIV infection before diagnosis of AIDS', *BMJ*, 3 July 1993, 307: 20–23; Thanks to Professor Ian Weller who brought this to my attention at the IX International AIDS Conference in Berlin.
13. Subsequent studies suggest that knowledge of HIV infection prior to

an AIDS diagnosis may change the course of disease, but not increase overall survival time. M. C. Poznansky *et al.*, 'HIV positive patients first presenting with an AIDS defining illness: characteristics and survival', *BMJ*, 1995, 311, pp. 156–8.

14. Personal communications from several health advisors – they note that there is often a rise in women seeking HIV tests around the time of high-profile publicity, for example around World AIDS Day. The PHLS graphs which show test-seeking behaviour record people by exposure category rather than gender.

15. Dr P. Bialer, personal communication.

16. Probably the best American book on the topic is R. Rimer and M. Connolly, *HIV+: Working the System*, Alyson, 1993.

17. G. Corea, *The Invisible Epidemic: The Story of Women and AIDS*, HarperPerennial, New York, 1992, p. 4. Corea credits Sandra Elkin with the conception and phrase 'politics of otherness'.

18. S. A. Strathdee *et al.*, 'Predictors of hospitalization in women and men with HIV-disease', Abstract TC2-120, 'HIV Infection in Women: Setting a New Agenda' conference, Washington, DC, 1995.

19. Many of these ideas are based on a paper I wrote with Dr Jurgen Poppinger: *A New AIDS Definition for Europe*, Internal Briefing paper, European AIDS Treatment Group (EATG), 1992.

20. 'Surveillance of the Acquired Immune Deficiency Syndrome (AIDS) in the United Kingdom, January 1982 – July 1983', *CDR*, 83/30, 29 July 1983.

21. See E. King (ed.), *HIV & AIDS Treatments Directory*, NAM Publications, London, July 1995, pp. 6f.

22. See for example, Corea, *op. cit.*, pp. 273–94.

23. Theresa M. McGovern, 1992, 'The CDC Surveillance Definition', round table presentation at the VIII International Conference on AIDS, Amsterdam, July 19–24. McGovern is Director of the HIV Law Project at the AIDS Service Center in NYC, and member of ACT UP. Her paper includes extensive references confirming the association of pulmonary TB, bacterial pneumonia and cervical cancer with HIV.

24. Roel Coutinho, p. 29, in R. Gorna (ed.), *Conference Summary Report: VIII International Conference on AIDS/III World STD Congress, Amsterdam, The Netherlands*, Harvard AIDS Institute, 1992.

25. Most UK state benefits turn on the idea of a person being disabled and/or having a terminal prognosis. THT's welfare rights service has taken a central role in lobbying to ensure that the needs of people with symptomatic HIV and AIDS are well understood by those awarding benefits.

26. Opening plenary session, 'HIV Infection in Women: Setting a New Agenda' conference, *op. cit.*

27. This is not the place for detailed medical information, in particular

since it changes so frequently. E. King gives comprehensive up-to-date information on the medical aspects of HIV, and *AIDS Treatment Update* reports new advances. For an overview, see the joint leaflet from THT and Positively Women, *Positive Women: A Guide to Symptoms and Treatments for Women Living with HIV and AIDS*. A comprehensive guide on women has been prepared by family nurse practitioner Risa Denenberg, *Gynaecological Care Manual for HIV Positive Women*, 1993, Essential Medical Information Systems Inc., USA. Volume 6, Number 7 (summer/fall 1992) of GMHC's *Treatment Issues* is a special edition on women (eds. M. Caschetta and G. Franke-Ruta) and is still one of the most thorough overviews. Excellent information is contained in F. D. Johnstone and M. Johnson (eds), *HIV and Women*, Churchill Livingstone, Edinburgh, pp. 17–35. Kurth, *op. cit.*, includes important information in: M. Young, 'A primer of health care', pp. 19–34; R. Denenberg, 'Gynaecological considerations in the primary-care setting', pp. 35–46; K. Anastos and S. Vermund, 'Epidemiology and natural history', pp. 144–64.

28. Anastos and Vermund, *op. cit.*, p. 162.
29. Rae Lewis-Thornton, opening plenary address, 'HIV Infection in Women: Setting a New Agenda' conference.
30. Corea, *op. cit.* See, for example, pp. 81, 159f., 196, 225f.
31. Gorna, *op. cit.*
32. Corea, *op. cit.*, p. 160.
33. Gorna, *op. cit.*
34. The twelve statements (in essence a charter of demands) were issued following the first ICW pre-conference, meeting before the VIII International AIDS Conference in Amsterdam, July 1992. This involved nearly 100 women from fifty-five countries and all continents of the world.
35. Gorna, *op. cit.*
36. R. Denenberg, 'Female sex hormones and HIV', *AIDS Clinical Care*, September 1993, Vol.5, Number 9, p. 70.
37. T. Ellerbrock *et al.*, 'Characteristics of menstruation in HIV-infected (HIV+) women', Abstract TP-449, 'HIV Infection in Women: Setting a New Agenda' conference.
38. J. Wasserheit, 'The costs of reproductive tract infections in women', in M. Berer with S. Ray, *Women and HIV/AIDS: An International Resource Book*, Pandora, London, 1993.
39. Abstract 250, 'First National Conference on Human Retroviruses and Related Infections', *op. cit.*
40. S. Cu-Uvin *et al.*, 'Prevalence of genital tract infections in HIV seropositive women', Abstract FC1-178; T. Ellerbrock et al., 'Genital tract infections in HIV-infected (HIV+) women', Abstract FC1-180, 'HIV Infection in Women: Setting a New Agenda' conference.
41. P. Schuman *et al.*, 'Candida colonization in women at risk for HIV

infection', Abstract FC1-176, 'HIV Infection in Women: Setting a New Agenda' conference.

42. See R. Gorna, 'Women's treatment update', *AIDS Treatment Update*, Issue 29, May 1995, pp. 1–7.

43. M. A. Chiasson *et al.*, 'Cervical disease in HIV-infected women – prevalence, incidence, risk factors, detection and use of loop electrosurgical excision for treatment', Abstract FC2-208; P. D. Abercrombie *et al.*, 'Vulvar intraepithelial neoplasia (VIN) in HIV-infected women', Abstract FC2-209, 'HIV Infection in Women: Setting a New Agenda' conference.

44. J. Palefsky, Session 102, First National Conference on Human Retroviruses and Related Infections, Washington, DC, 12–16 December 1993.

45. J. Palefsky, 'Anogenital cancer and HPV', Abstract TC2-121, 'HIV Infection in Women: Setting a New Agenda' conference.

46. Chiasson *et al.*, *op. cit.*

47. Abercrombie, *op. cit.*

48. D. Warren, 'Genital human papillomavirus (HPV) infection and squamous intraepithelial lesions (SIL) on Pap smear in women at risk for HIV infection', Abstract FC2-207, 'HIV Infection in Women: Setting a New Agenda' conference.

49. Palefsky, *op. cit.*

50. C. Brosgart *et al.*, 'Papanicolaou (Pap) smears versus colposcopy as screening tests for cervical intraepithelial neoplasia (CIN) in HIV seropositive women', Abstract 079B, X International Conference on AIDS, Yokahama, Japan, 7–12 August 1994.

51. Dr Ray Brettle, personal communication.

52. Palefsky, First National Conference on Human Retroviruses, *op. cit.*

53. ACTG 200 compares 5-FU with standard treatment for high-grade cervical dysplasia. J. A. Korvick, 'Trends in federally sponsored clinical trials', p. 101, in Kurth, *op. cit.*

54. M. Angell, *NEJM* editorial, Vol. 329, No. 4, p. 272.

55. Corea, *op. cit.*, p. 244.

56. Terry McGovern, 'HIV Infection in Women: Setting a New Agenda' conference.

Chapter five

Victims or Victors?[1]

I have had the privilege of not having to remain silent. . . .
Because of what AIDS has been made to represent, most
women are not able to make that choice. Our voices are not
heard. We live in isolation and fear of discovery. We remain
invisible.

Kate Thomson[2]

The goal should be to live a normal life. You should be
allowed to be sick with this stupid disease, without making
it a crime to be sick.

Anna[3]

Serious medical conditions have a tendency to subsume the
person. When someone is sick, the body takes over and there is
often an intense focus on the minutiae of the daily struggle with
disease, leaving little energy for the many other facets of an
individual's life. The person can become her disease. And the two
are often reduced to a simple bio-medical model. So, for example,
a woman may state 'I've been HIV for four years' or simply 'I'm
HIV'. This construction is not unusual, and it reveals an alarming
level of identification between the self and the virus which
threatens to cause havoc within the body. Far more common than
this type of personal owning of disease, is the external representation of a woman as all virus: she is described as an 'AIDS patient',
'AIDS sufferer' or 'AIDS victim' – even if she is HIV-positive and
asymptomatic. AIDS discourse has frequently focused on deconstructing the terminology used to describe people living with the

virus. The term 'AIDS patient' has a very restricted relevance to the bio-medical context. When an individual is hospitalized or under treatment, it may make sense to describe her as a patient, yet people with an AIDS diagnosis spend less than 20 per cent of their time in hospital.[4] The variability of HIV disease is inadequately described by 'patient' and 'sufferer' terminology, and affords far more importance to the clinical condition than is its place in daily life.

The most common descriptor is 'AIDS victim', a much (mis)used phrase which subsumes the individual to a state of cowering victimhood – overwhelmed by this monstrous (fatal) condition which precedes the person. In its place, the AIDS industry promotes the phrase 'person living with AIDS' (or HIV), which sometimes is reduced to the acronym PLWA or PWA (hardly more humanizing). This phrasing at least has the obvious benefit of enabling the person to precede the medical condition, and indicates that it is something which can become integrated into an individual's life. Rejecting victimology is not only an AIDS consideration – disability activists resist the tendency to identify people by their disability, and feminists have similarly rejected the term 'rape victim' in favour of 'rape survivor'. Interestingly, there is a shift by some campaigners to restate the victim concept, emphasizing that women (or men) who are raped will not inevitably survive the experience, and removing any suggestion that they could share responsibility for the assault. In the endeavour to re-empower the person who has suffered misfortune, there can be a swing too far which negates the pain of the experience, so that living with AIDS is banalized to the level of living with an annoying flatmate. The first person with AIDS I cared for was a sharp-tongued AIDS activist, and when he was hospitalized I remember him railing against the language he had promoted, complaining that he wasn't living with AIDS, he was suffering.

Most people facing a life challenge such as HIV infection will initially be victims of their condition, yet this does not preclude the potential of transformation 'from victim to victor'. For many women, accessing the power to effect this is painful and difficult, yet achieving such empowerment frequently improves not only the quality, but perhaps also the quantity of life.[5] The journey from victim to victor is often a spiritual or psychic one. Along each of these personal journeys many women will encounter practical stumbling blocks which are shared with other HIV-positive women. One of the major challenges of HIV and AIDS is that its newness makes knowledge scant. This is a problem for all people with HIV and AIDS, and is particularly acute for women. The medical and scientific questions which remain unanswered and unasked are significant, but the broader psychosocial impacts of HIV on women are of equal or greater importance – and they are desperately under-studied.[6]

The invisible woman

Isolation and invisibility 'unite' women living with HIV. The impact of AIDS on women is very different from that on gay men in urban environments. For gay men there is a terrible impact on their pre-existing communities: friends and lovers are also infected, grieving is commonplace. What makes AIDS so appalling for gay men is also what brings the possibility for peer support and a shared cultural identity. This multiple impact certainly does not appease the pain or make the horror any less, yet one problem for most women with HIV is that they do not share in a community experience. When they meet other women with HIV they may have nothing in common but the virus.

Men with haemophilia and HIV will usually have attended the same clinic all their lives, and although their relationships with healthcare workers can be jeopardized by the fact of their infection, they do have those pre-existing links as well as links with other people with haemophilia and HIV. When a gay man is diagnosed HIV-positive he may already know someone who has HIV or AIDS, or know someone who knows someone, or go to a support group where he meets someone with similar interests or lifestyle. It is not uncommon for gay men to meet old friends and lovers when they join support groups. Gay men often live in large cities, since these offer more social and sexual opportunities. For different reasons many (although by no means all) injecting drug users live in urban environments, and for social, economic and pragmatic reasons they may cluster in discrete geographical areas (e.g. near a drug supply).

Prior connectedness is far rarer for women. A woman may know the man who infected her, but beyond that, sexual and social networks are more dispersed. Women often live far from other people with HIV, as well as from medical and social services. Since they are more randomly infected, a higher proportion of women may live in rural environments and be distant from specialized care services – for example, one woman has to be driven over 100 miles to attend her hospital appointments.[7] It is not unusual for a woman to receive a positive HIV diagnosis and tell no one. Denise, a white British woman, described her reaction six months after her test result was positive:

> It was like having a nervous breakdown. I wanted sympathy, but you just can't walk up to people and tell them you're HIV-positive. You carry on with the same routine, go to work, go to shops, go to the same pub. But you're different, and you know that you're different. Yet nobody else knows. I used to get an urge to jump up in the tube and shout, 'Listen, everybody, guess what? I'm HIV-positive!' But I had to keep it to myself and pretend nothing was wrong. That was what frightened me at first: the isolation.[8]

She has 'done nothing wrong'; why should she be so stigmatized and isolated? The isolation functions in several ways. Her rarity makes the HIV-positive woman 'a freak': she is a 'special case', an 'innocent victim' to the media and a novelty to many healthcare providers; and the rarity of her condition in her pre-existing friendship circles impedes her access to peer support and information. 'It's a vicious circle:' as Thomson and O'Sullivan explain, 'until women (and men) can more easily be open about their status, they will remain hidden and 'other'. But until they can be out without undue fear of reprisals and ostracism, they aren't able to do so.'[9]

It is rare that women with HIV already belong to communities where others are visibly experiencing the same health crisis, and many women report shame and a sense of freakishness immediately after their diagnosis. Isolation is reported by a vast range of women. For example, Susan, a black African woman living in London says:

> I've never told anybody. Sometimes I get depressed, but still I've never talked to anyone from my country about it, not even my parents. . . . I get so angry I can't talk about it – sometimes when I'm sitting on a train or in a bus I feel like shouting aloud because I'm so frustrated. Even when I'm with my friends at a party, I break down and cry. I look at all the people and think how they don't know I have the virus and how miserable it makes me that I can't tell them.[10]

Betsy, an American woman, says:

> I love to be around lesbians, it's important to me to have lesbian friends in my life that I can connect with. And if they cannot accept the fact that I'm HIV-positive it's real hard. Cause if I have to hide that, it takes too much energy. So, I have gotten lots of friends out of my life. . . . And I'm finding myself feeling real lonely.[11]

Such loneliness and isolation can be as motivating as it is depressing. Sheila, a white Scottish woman, describes her experiences of seeking support in 1986:

> I had nobody to tell about all my feelings who could turn around and say, 'God, I know how you feel, I've been through it too.' I went to a few HIV/AIDS support groups which were very gay-orientated . . . my needs weren't being met. I was always the only woman. . . . Some of the men quite subtly and nicely told me it was a refreshing change because they talked about different issues when I was there. I was isolated; they thought of me as being so different that it didn't really matter where I was from, or what I had done.[12]

Frustrated by her isolation and otherness, Sheila made a flyer advertising for other HIV-positive women and eventually she was joined by one other woman, then Kate Thomson, and soon they co-founded the UK self-help group 'Positively Women'. As well as providing direct services for HIV-positive women, Positively Women exists to smash the invisibility and confront the isolation that separates HIV-positive women from each other.

Since isolation is so fundamental to most HIV-positive women's experience, and as the UK epidemic is relatively small, the only connections available to HIV-positive women may well be with women from different backgrounds. There are attempts to organize some more focused groups for African women, but even these are linking women from a huge number of countries in a vast continent, and with immense linguistic diversity – the seventy-five women in Positively Women's survey spoke a total of twenty-seven different languages.[13] This creates practical problems for support, and there are also practicalities relating to transport, time (many women do not like to travel after dark, and others cannot meet in the day because of work) and childcare. Women may not want to bring any children to a creche at a support group, but may lack the finances or personal support for them to be cared for at home. The practical constraints reflect the fact that support groups for people with HIV have emerged from a male model. There is a feminist model for women's groups, but many HIV-positive women are alienated by this and resist those groups. For women, acknowledging a need for support can feel like a failure, and this is one reason why informal support networks may be most powerful. Some support groups have been organized around meals, or services have provided practical facilities (such as washing machines) so that women do not need to make an overt statement of need.[14]

Of course, it is not the case that HIV-positive women never know others outside the confines of self-help groups. For drug-using women (and men), there may be more cohesion and prior community than for HIV-positive women in general (although the 'underground world' of drug use is nothing like the queer world). Drug use can be common in areas of socio-economic deprivation; and on some housing estates in Edinburgh, for example, there are very high levels of HIV.[15] However, such proximity is not always supportive, but may bring with it fears of broken confidentiality. Among refugee women from some African countries this can be a particularly acute concern. They may be housed near people from their own country, but as HIV is frequently stigmatized within refugee communities, this may present more problems (confidentiality) than benefits (mutual support). The sub-community of these women and their families is quite small and the potential for a network of connected women can be high. Some healthcare professionals report that their patients are so anxious about confidentiality that they refuse to use the services of translators (who may know the women) and are nervous at being identified in clinic waiting rooms – leading the staff to arrange a general waiting area for several different clinics.[16] The potential for breaches of confidentiality is often quite subtle and does not involve naming a person as HIV-positive. For example, an HIV specialist community nurse was enraged to discover that a television report showed her attending an AIDS conference, as she feared this could compromise her anonymity when visiting patients at home.

Fears about confidentiality are common to most people living with an HIV diagnosis, and they may be especially acute for women, and for mothers who fear the impact of AIDS stigmatization on their children's well-being.[17] The (apparent) rareness of HIV in women underpins these heightened fears and the isolation most women experience. Yet these features of living with HIV are constructs of a society which heaps scorn on women who are already faced with two more fundamental issues: mortality and infectivity. The HIV-positive woman has been diagnosed with a medical condition which, at the current time, has life-threatening consequences; she can also pass on this condition. This combination of features is fundamental to why HIV is so different from, say, breast cancer, and its significance is evident in the ways HIV-positive women are treated. Is the focus on them, on how to cope with a life-threatening diagnosis, on the measures they can take to enhance their well-being, on the support they need, the planning they might do? Or is the focus on their infectivity, the implications of their infection for those around them, the danger they pose? In the name of women with HIV, there is a constant conflation between potential and actuality, between a life-threatening condition and the transmission of its prime cause, between prevention and care. The woman with HIV is constantly up against the ways in which her condition is used by others. AIDS in gay men may be used as symbolic of the disgusting nature of gay sex, the perversion and abnormality of their lifestyle. AIDS in women becomes symbolic of the general threat – or if the woman is black or a drug user, a symbol of the 'perversion' and 'abnormality' of her lifestyle. She becomes a warning to the uninfected, like the 'worrying' woman in the HEA poster.[18]

AIDS is not 'normal' and this is, principally, because of the nature of the condition and who it affects: its newness, fatality, transmissibility and queerness. Since AIDS is new, information is lacking, and what exists often changes. The newness also under-pins the wild fantasies and constructions of the media and commentators. AIDS is life-threatening; it may not always be fatal (it is too new to know for sure), but it usually is, and this fact determines the necessary direction of services, and underpins the reaction of individuals and their loved ones to a diagnosis. The transmissibility of HIV affects a woman's needs from two perspectives: how she acquired HIV, and how she may transmit (or has transmitted) it. She may have a range of emotions around these areas, which will be both rational and irrational. The efforts of workers and commentators are over-focused in this area: there may be an incessant curiosity about how she became infected which ignores the emotions this causes for her. Her potential for transmitting the virus may be emphasized over the probable fatality of her condition. Finally, the queerness of AIDS jumbles together the fatality and transmissibility (especially sexual) with the communities hardest hit by AIDS. Much of the fear, stigma and panic of AIDS is created by this queerness, resulting in the perception of AIDS as the worst possible life-threatening condition (for example, an acquaintance expressed relief that she thought she had AIDS, but 'only' has cancer; her life expectancy is less with cancer, but for her it is not such a terrifying condition).

The combination of these features with each woman's psyche and life experiences will define her needs. In order to give a more concrete sense of how these features combine, I will use four case histories of women who are HIV-positive in order to explore some of their needs. These examples are composite pictures – which I use in training sessions – based upon interviews with women, their talks, writing and psychosocial research:[19]

Suzie is twenty-two. She grew up with her mother and brothers on the same housing estate outside Edinburgh where she now lives. She always hated school and was absent a lot. When she was fifteen she started to use heroin with her brother and his friends. At the outset she took very little and they would just share their supply with her. When she became Mick's girlfriend she began to use more, and he would inject her. As her habit developed she would turn tricks to get the money to buy her own supply. She mostly shared her works with Mick but, when they were in short supply, the original group of friends would share needles. A year ago, one of her friends overdosed and died. This scared Suzie and a few months later she went to a drug rehabilitation centre. She was tested and found to be HIV-positive. Mick, who is still using heroin, took the test and is also HIV-positive. They split up, but he often calls Suzie to shout at her, call her a whore and blame her for infecting him. Suzie misses her friends and is finding it very hard to stay in the rehab, but she hopes that if she completes it she might settle down and have a baby.

Jane's life was disrupted by the civil war in her home country, Uganda, during which time she was tortured and raped. Two years ago, at the age of twenty-eight, she came to London with her sister and two children. Her husband stayed in Kampala with her two older children. She was pregnant when she arrived, and went to an antenatal clinic where they carried out a lot of medical tests which she did not fully understand. The staff told her that she was HIV-positive and should consider an abortion. She had the baby. Jane's health is very varied, but she finds it hard to find time to see the doctor, and doesn't really understand what he is saying. When she takes her daughter to the clinic she gets some health advice. Her daughter is HIV-infected and had pneumonia when she was four months old. She is quite weak now, and is small for her age. Her sister (who does not know about their HIV status) thinks this is because Jane did not breast-feed – something she never understood. Her refugee status has not yet been granted, but advice staff at THT are helping her and she now has a small council flat in east London. Jane tries to go to the African women's support group at Positively Women whenever she can get transport, although she is nervous that she will meet someone she knows there.

Fiona is a twenty-five-year-old artist who lives in Leeds. She has been out as a dyke since she was at art college. She spends a lot of time going to clubs with her queer friends. She has relationships with a few women, and doesn't want a main full-time lover at the moment. Sometimes, when she's done a lot of ecstasy, she has sex with one of her best friends. He hasn't told any of his friends about this and she is a bit embarrassed and worried that if her friends knew they would reject her. They don't really talk about it to each other much – it's just something that 'happens' if she stays over. He tested HIV-positive six months ago after his ex-lover developed PCP, and she has just received a positive test result. He took her to his support group but there were only men there – when she went in one of them said, 'Oh look, our first dyke!' She left in tears and doesn't know where to go for support.

Amanda is sixty. She works part-time as a secretary and lives in the London suburbs. She is married and has three children and two grandchildren. Ten years ago she had a blood transfusion after a hysterectomy. Four years after the operation she was informed that the blood might have been HIV-infected, she was tested and found to be HIV-positive. She had continued to have a full sex life with her husband; he has been tested and is HIV-negative. Since receiving her diagnosis they have not made love: she feels 'dirty' and is terrified of infecting him. She has also had vaginal thrush for the past four years, but hasn't told him or her doctor. Apart from this her health has been generally good and she sees her GP only every six months. She has been losing weight over the last year, and at her last appointment he suggested starting AZT and ddI but she has refused – she is worried that people will ask why she is taking these pills, and that it will remind her of her condition. She and her husband try to laugh at the AIDS jokes his colleagues tell. She cannot say the word 'AIDS' and has not told any of her children, friends or work colleagues about her infection. She hopes that she will die without anyone having to find out about the cause.

Although these are not true stories, they are familiar scenarios reflecting the UK epidemic. Of course they should not be taken to suggest that, say, all women who have taken heroin since they are fifteen have done sex work or all women from Uganda are HIV-infected. There are other common scenarios too: like the woman who tests HIV-positive and has no idea what her risk factors were (was her second boyfriend bisexual? had her one-night stand shared needles?), or the girlfriend of a man with haemophilia, or the woman who tests HIV-positive in prison, or the woman whose child is rushed into hospital with pneumonia and tests positive, or the wife of a man who has concealed his bisexuality throughout their marriage, or the woman who lived a bohemian life in New York's Greenwich Village in the mid-1980s . . . There is not really a common thread between these women's diverse lives.

Whether or not a person is queer, once diagnosed HIV-positive s/he becomes queer in the sense of being outside of what is allowed to be normal. For women who have never had this sense of themselves (aside from the general sense of being abnormal because of not being male) HIV may trap them in a closet of secrecy at the very time they are most in need of help. The common response to HIV is one that suggests it is something to be ashamed of: shame and stigma is something which many gay men and drug users will have experienced before their diagnosis, but one that may be new to many women. The queerness of women with HIV is visible in the case studies: Jane's queerness is expressed in the demands for secrecy and fear of broken confidentiality. Suzie's lifestyle may seem 'queer' to people outside of her culture, but this is unlikely from her perspective. When she is diagnosed with HIV she is isolated from her social group and becomes both 'queer' and feared. She confronts her friends' fears about whether they too are HIV-infected. Fiona has embraced the positive sense of queer before her diagnosis, but now finds herself outside her community – suddenly she has more in common with gay men than lesbians. For Amanda, AIDS is the only queer thing in her life; everything else is mainstream. There may well be a conflict within herself – the queerness she may previously have despised is now a part of her, inscribed in her blood. One woman described how, immediately after her HIV diagnosis, 'I just felt so filthy, really dirty. Unclean. I kept washing myself and having baths, thinking maybe I could wash it away.'[20]

People do not lose their existing attitudes when they are diagnosed with HIV, and the more diversity there is among a group of people, the more difficulties there may be in achieving adequate support.[21] How might Amanda feel about Suzie's lifestyle? These women would be unlikely to meet if it were not for their shared HIV status – the challenges they face overcoming prejudices may be immense. When an HIV-positive woman goes to a general HIV support group she can often find (like Fiona) that she is the only woman in the group. If she goes to a women-only support group, she may find that the lifestyles of the women present are diverse. One woman described some of the HIV-positive women who attend her support group in Toronto. They included a young lawyer at a prestigious firm, an ex-sex-worker and IDU, a West Indian woman infected by blood transfusion, a mother of a two-year-old whose husband had just died, a diabetic woman who cared for her partner who was an ex-sex-worker and IDU, a health worker and mother of three who found out about her husband's bisexuality when he developed AIDS, a widow from Eastern Europe who had adult children, and a young woman infected ten years ago by one of her first boyfriends.[22]

What is startling is the diversity of lifestyles – while gay men are a diverse bunch too, there is more common ground derived from the struggles of fighting pre-AIDS oppression. American commentator Cindy Patton observes, 'For people . . . who are already familiar with the 'coming out' and 'telling your story' models from gay liberation and Alcoholics/Narcotics Anonymous, respectively, HIV antibody positivity becomes a new and critical aspect of identity which is important to speak about publicly.'[23] Integrating 'HIV' into a sense of personal identity is often foreign for women: group sharing (a fairly American practice for a start) may be a totally unfamiliar exercise, on top of which is the unnatural act of seeking support for oneself. Rachel only sticks with it because it gives a rare opportunity to meet other women with HIV. She observes, 'It *is* depressing. This isn't what I really want to do at night – sit around talking about HIV with a group of women I have nothing in common with except HIV! I'd rather be out dancing!'[24] The fact that women from such diverse backgrounds find ways of providing support for each other is one of the transforming and extraordinary features of the AIDS crisis.

The isolation and queerness of an HIV diagnosis, and the diversity of women's lifestyles, often create acute needs, but there are other major concerns. Issues around the transmissibility of HIV are complex, and the rarity value of women with HIV can lead to voyeurism. Many women experience constant enquiry into the mode of their infection, and one American activist recounts this exchange:

> Vivian had to see a new dermatologist for an HIV-related skin problem. The doctor entered the room with a couple of residents, looked at her chart, and said, 'Sex or drugs?'
> 'Excuse me?' Vivian said.
> 'Sex or drugs?' he repeated.
> 'I don't do drugs anymore,' she said, 'And sex with you? I don't think so.'[25]

Perhaps the doctor had scientific reasons why he needed to know if Vivian currently uses drugs, or whether she was infected by a bisexual man (to consider a diagnosis of KS) – but as a first question? This line of questioning is usually about curiosity, not medical need. It is also a particularly stupid line of questioning, since few women infected as a result of drug use are likely to answer honestly to such an aggressive approach. If a woman has no history of drug use, then the questioning often leads to the risk factors of the man who infected her. This information may be important for epidemiologists, or to help a counsellor explore her support needs and feelings about how she became infected, but it is extraordinary that healthcare workers frequently believe they have a claim to such intimate information. It is rare for a caring professional to quiz a woman with breast cancer about whether she smoked, breast-fed or took the pill. The (necessary) high public profile about the modes of HIV transmission appears to have led to an inappropriate level of curiosity about each individual woman's mode of acquisition.

The simplicity of the public message on HIV transmission has left many women confused about their infectivity, especially through sex. One of the needs which many HIV-positive women articulate (within a 'safe space') is for more and better information about sex – and this is something women rarely receive on diagnosis. Many women have internalized messages that they should not be sexual. Tanja, a German student, was diagnosed when she was nineteen and the doctor said nothing about how it might affect her sex life. Sexuality is her biggest concern since being diagnosed. 'I can't develop it further,' she says, 'HIV is like a big blockade. I'm also so afraid I'll infect my partner.'[26] Another woman states that her diagnosis 'stopped me from having sex. I have no interest in forming a relationship, as no partner will accept my HIV status.'[27] The Positively Women research also showed that a lot of women misunderstood safer sex, with extreme sadness at changing or losing their sex lives, and a tendency towards excess caution. Women made statements like, 'I don't want to have sex anymore for fear of passing it on to others', 'There is no such thing as safe sex except no sex and condoms can always break' and 'I worry about kissing – I know the facts, but psychologically I have problems.'[28] This is out of all proportion with what is known about the infectiousness of HIV. It is very hard for women to transmit HIV sexually, and yet many of these women are sacrificing their sex lives and making themselves very unhappy. It has been documented that the male sexual partners of HIV-positive women are far more likely to practise safer sex or abstain from sex than the (uninfected) female partners of HIV-positive men. Moreover, in discordant couples where the woman is HIV-positive there are more psychological problems, and more divorces than in those couples where it is the man who is infected.[29]

Individuals frequently have extreme responses to such life-changing events as an HIV diagnosis, and American activist and nurse-practitioner Risa Denenberg notes, 'A common response to the discovery of HIV infection – among both women and men – is to shun sexual relations for a period of time. This often is a symptom of depression and altered self-esteem.'[30] However, many HIV-positive women seem to be maintaining celibacy. Is it guilt at becoming infected, rage, fear of transmitting HIV, fear of rejection if they tell new partners, or just poor information? Certainly research is lacking about specific rates of infection with different sexual activities, but there is also a sense that the information which exists is being withheld from women. Denenberg goes on to state that, 'HIV-positive clients need support and encouragement to attain healthy and safe relationships where affection and sexuality are experienced.'[31] The majority of HIV-positive women do not seem to be getting this support from their healthcare professionals, or even from ASOs. Certainly, doctors appear to tell women far less about sex than they do when informing gay men about HIV. Tanja says of her doctors, 'It's like a taboo, or maybe they don't think I like it. They are men and they can't understand us women, and even if they try it's difficult. And with HIV, which belongs to sexuality, it's even more so.'[32] Tanja's experiences with her doctor have been echoed by other HIV-positive women, many of whom report that the extent of sexual counselling after a positive result is a doctor telling her, 'Don't get pregnant'. The infantilization of HIV-positive women's sexuality is not solely the province of the media.

The fatality of AIDS is often presented as the major issue with which people have to contend. There is often an exaggerated image of HIV-positive people walking around with a permanently heightened consciousness of their own mortality, yet many women may already have so many financial and practical challenges that their HIV status is just another challenge. For example, one woman in the Positively Women survey states that 'the worst [time] was being told my children might not come to live in England'.[33] For women refugees, geographical displacement frequently has a far greater impact on their well-being than does their health status. Many HIV-positive women were living in poverty before diagnosis, and often report extremely poor standards of housing, alongside acute practical and financial needs. For some women these practical needs have to take precedence. For example, a woman may not access the best standards of medical care for her HIV status, because the benefits of that service are outweighed by the time and expense of travelling across London with three small children in tow. The AIDS industry was designed in response to a catastrophic condition occurring in a population not noted for major pre-existing concerns with health and poverty.

Many of the models for responding to AIDS come from the response to gay men, and these may not translate automatically to women. As the epidemic becomes rooted in communities where ill health and poverty already exist, the balance of attention may need to shift. For Jane, is her AIDS diagnosis more disturbing than the traumas of rape and torture and the horrors of the civil war which led her to take the extraordinarily difficult step of leaving part of her family and her homeland? Unless she is given centre stage, it would be easy to define her needs for her and decide what ought to be most upsetting. Fiona's needs – as a young woman with career hopes – may well fit into the gay model, whereas Amanda's – an older woman who has achieved the life she wanted, and is acutely concerned with social reputation – probably will not. Some women face other life-threatening factors which override the potential of HIV to cause death a decade down the line. There is a painful irony for women (and men) who are diagnosed as they start the difficult process of ending drug addiction: what motivation will Suzie have to stay off drugs if she was doing so to avoid death by overdose?

The horror of what AIDS can mean often leads to a focus on all the potential negative implications of a diagnosis with HIV infection. This focus may not be generated by the women them-selves, who are living with the changed reality of knowing they have the virus in their bodies. The focus on the horror can often restrain an HIV-positive woman in a position of patronizing victimhood, rather than empowering her to make choices about how to live her life well.

Women who are in contact with self-help organizations like Positively Women are not typical of all HIV-positive women. Those who reach out to find others with the same medical diagnosis are often on a path towards 'victorhood'. They frequently report that adjusting to this changed life situation provided a sense of meaning to life. One woman went so far as to describe her HIV diagnosis as 'a trial from God – I am now fighting it and I will not give up'.[34] Few women afford the virus quite such a positive role, but many have described a process of development, with the woman learning to place herself more in the centre. This does not mean that HIV is 'a good thing', or that people who have made positive changes no longer suffer any negative effects of AIDS. However, it is important to consider this perspective, which is rarely seen amidst so much media-generated gloom. Sixty per cent of the HIV-positive women in the Positively Women survey felt that life had, in some way, changed for the better since their diagnosis. As one woman said, 'I'm still trying to work it out. Spiritually I value life, and the importance of living day by day. It's difficult, frightening, but good.'[35]

Testing positive

For women the responses to this new medical diagnosis are not only problematized by general public perceptions of AIDS (which they may well share), but also by the manner of diagnosis. One of the defining differences between HIV-positive women and men is that the men will tend to have taken a decision to get tested, whereas women are less likely to choose to test – they may be 'encouraged', coerced, or have the diagnosis thrust upon them.

This is particularly alarming given that few women are likely to prepare for a positive result, since 76 per cent of HIV-positive women did not perceive themselves to be at risk of infection at the time when they became infected.[36] 'I think everybody who has had unprotected sex in the last ten years must deep down somewhere know that they are at risk from HIV,' says Rebecca, 'But there's a very big step from that to actually making a decision to have a test. I certainly never made a decision to have a test – I was actually diagnosed because I gave blood.'[37] By contrast, Mary was tested when her child became ill, and Angela found out that she was HIV-positive two years after hospital doctors had taken a lot of blood tests. Describing a subsequent routine procedure, a doctor asked her, 'Didn't you know you were HIV?' when she queried why they were planning to use gowns, masks and gloves.[38]

Increasingly, women are being offered the test to reduce the risk of HIV transmission to an unborn child, and consequently discovering that they have a life-threatening disease at the same time as anticipating a new life. Despite most professionals' assumptions that HIV-positive women will terminate their pregnancy (although six of seven babies will be born uninfected), over 90 per cent of women continue with the pregnancy, and many choose to conceive again.[39] In Positively Women's survey, nearly half of the women said that they had been pressured either not to become pregnant or to have an abortion.[40]

Frequently, the test is promoted or offered to women for reasons which seem to reflect the healthcare providers' concerns, rather than the best interests of each woman. The HIV antibody test is a diagnostic tool, not an intervention to prevent HIV. All the test achieves is to provide an individual with information about whether she has been infected with a virus which is likely to have life-threatening consequences. It is often assumed that a woman should want to get tested, but does she really want to know if she has HIV? Gay men who are used to the day-to-day realities of AIDS often know people who have different experiences of testing: some may know that they are HIV-positive; some will have decided not to test although they think it likely that they are infected; some will have tested HIV-negative. In general, they will have been exposed to a range of attitudes to testing, and know that a person should think carefully and choose whether they want to have this information. One HIV-positive man described his test result as 'like somebody telling you you are going to be in a serious, serious car crash, probably in about ten years' time. And you've got to live those ten years knowing you're going to be in a car crash, waiting for it to happen.'[41]

For women, the process of HIV testing can be characterized as one of encouragement underpinned by a patriarchal 'doctor knows best' attitude – in sharp contrast to the approach for gay men, which is embedded in a rhetoric of choice and individual decision-making. One way in which 'doctor knows best' is the doctor who tells the little woman not to worry her head about something as unlikely as AIDS. Kate Thomson describes how she was misdiagnosed as HIV-negative and 'told off by the doctor. I was "an hysterical woman, wasting NHS resources. Women don't get AIDS."'[42] Although this attitude is becoming less common, several women report being discouraged from testing (or told not to worry about the result) because their healthcare provider assumes she cannot be infected. Such patronizing behaviour may lead to undue and unnecessary suffering for HIV-infected women whose medical conditions remain undetected. For example, one woman, complaining about her GP, states 'I had HIV symptoms for four years which the doctors didn't pick up on.'[43]

If a woman has symptoms, knowing whether she is infected with HIV may help to make the right diagnosis, and to ensure she receives appropriate medical care. Yet the HIV antibody test can give no information about how long a woman has been infected, nor when she is likely to develop AIDS. If a woman is healthy, with no symptoms, the reasons for taking the test are more complex, as will be the implications of the result.

Receiving a positive diagnosis to the HIV antibody test is the beginning of a woman's personal journey of living with HIV. The manner in which the test is undertaken, and in particular, whether she has consented to the test, are likely to affect the adjustment a woman makes to this new life situation. While receiving a positive result is a shock for most women, if she has not requested or agreed to a test then the impact of the diagnosis is likely to be particularly difficult. In the Positively Women survey, nearly 60 per cent of the HIV-positive women did not give their fully informed consent to taking the HIV test; although 82.7 per cent gave 'consent', only 42.7 per cent received pre-test counselling that would have informed them about the nature of the test, and what they were consenting to. It is alarming that there was a strong link between race and a lack of consent. Since 1990, all of the women in the survey who did not give their consent to testing, and two-thirds of the women who were not counselled, were African. This backs up anecdotal reports from service providers that African women are being summarily tested. This is further supported by evidence from the same survey showing that the majority of African women were tested in hospital, rather than at GUM clinics where the understanding of HIV is far greater. Finally, just 65.3 per cent of the women were counselled *after* receiving a positive test result. Since this is life-changing information, with serious implications for the woman's health and well-being, it is shocking that one in three women were expected to adjust to this alone.[44]

Sexual women

The current girlfriend, wife or lover of an HIV-positive man will often be expected to take the test immediately after he is diagnosed (if she hasn't taken it before or simultaneously) and she will often want to. Women who have been informed that an ex-lover is HIV-infected also often rush to get tested – and the usual advice to consider carefully whether to get tested tends to be jettisoned in such a scenario. HIV-positive women often have concerns arising from the circumstances of their tests, and kneejerk reactions to take the test will also have consequences for women who test HIV-negative. An HIV-positive diagnosis is a life-long thing, whereas an HIV-negative diagnosis is not. Testing HIV antibody-negative simply demonstrates that a person had not been infected with the virus three months before the test. This says nothing about whether she will avoid infection in future months or years. There is a tendency to divide people into HIV-positive and HIV-negative and to perceive these as stable states. Where it is recognized that there is another group – those who have not tested – it is assumed that these people are HIV-negative, irrespective of the individuals' self-assessments.

A negative result may be treated as a once-for-all result, or a sticking plaster: at least she is safe. The test result may be treated as celebratory, and there may be little time to reinforce prevention messages. It can be difficult for the HIV-negative partner of an HIV-positive man (or woman) to adjust to her diagnosis: she may be guilty that she is uninfected, angry that he is positive or that he exposed her to infection, in mourning at the end of an unsafe sex life or grieving the loss of future conception. Health professionals and friends may assume that, *of course*, she will now practise safer sex, and she may have few opportunities to explore the complex reasons why discordant couples often do not do so. She will be very lucky if she finds any tailored interventions or resources to support her and her lover in adopting safer sex.[45] There may be rational and emotional reasons why a woman has unsafe sex with her HIV-positive lover (insisting on latex feels like rejecting him, she doesn't want to survive him, he'll beat her if she doesn't, she wants a child, she 'loves him to death' . . .), but with the near-universal assumption that she would be 'mad' not to have safer sex, who will support her in her choice or even help her to explore her feelings?

The sexual and emotional needs of women in relationships with people with HIV are inadequately explored. The classic scenario which is presented is of the woman who discovers that her husband/lover is HIV-infected, several years into the relationship. The challenge that is described is how the woman adjusts to the clause in their contract stating 'for better and for worse, in sickness and in health'; and researchers note that women are less likely to abandon their male HIV-positive partners than vice versa.[46] Yet there are also (not surprisingly) women who choose to enter rela-tionships with men who already know they are HIV-positive. There are very few accounts of the needs of women partners of HIV-positive men, and I could locate none by British women. (But the British public are well educated by the soap opera *EastEnders*, with its storyline about Ruth, a feisty Scots woman, who marries HIV-positive Mark Fowler after meeting him at an AIDS hospice.)

American (lesbian) AIDS activist Zoe Leonard has described some of the angsts and conflicting feelings she faces, which include her battle with irrational fears of infection, the thrills of playing with safer sex, and panic at the long-term possibilities of loving a man who is currently asymptomatic and HIV-positive. She says:

> It's one thing to learn to fuck safely and quite another to feel committed to someone that you are afraid might get really sick or die. I think: can I do it? Will I have the patience, will I be adequate? What if he really does get sick, what then? . . . can I handle feeling this responsible? Do I want to take care of him? And what if he really does die? What about that? . . . I wonder, do I just thrive on drama?

Do I have a martyr complex, or a death wish? Did I fall for him because of his status? Do I want to get infected; is this my most recent and subtle form of self-destruction? Friends and family are anxious, ask me about *it*. They tell me I'm crazy, and speak of illness and health in hushed tones.[47]

Caring women

Women whose loved ones are HIV-positive deserve the opportunities to experience and express their most unreasonable responses and needs, in order to offer their love and care. One of the things that sometimes happens to all this emotion, the complexity of love and concern, is that it gets squashed into statements like, 'We are all living with AIDS'. This is not true.

Often support groups are run for all women affected by AIDS, and I wonder how these can respond adequately to so many different women's needs. How can a mother recall burying her son to a woman who has just got over PCP? Or a sister grieve and rage that she will lose her beautiful brother, with a woman who is thinking positive and praying her unborn child will not be infected? One of the things many women and men with HIV need is hope, yet 'thinking positive' can become a tyranny, or slide into denial, for their loved ones struggling to adjust to the probability of a new time-frame and loss. There are practical and resource reasons for these groups to operate in this way (two bereaved mothers in one locality are not enough to sustain a self-help group), but there are rarely support groups for 'all men affected by AIDS'.

It is only by acknowledging the specific needs women have around AIDS, the multiple ways it changes lives, that women can cope with the turmoil it causes. The effects of AIDS on those women who are profoundly impacted by the epidemic, who are living with the AIDS crisis on a daily basis, are important and need greater attention, and they are fundamentally different from the needs of women who are diagnosed HIV-positive. There is frequently a sense that women have chosen to care about AIDS, rather than having it forced upon them like, say, gay men. Sometimes this is true (although it denies the fact that some gay men are remarkably negligent about AIDS), but this also conceives of a gay world which is divided and distant from the world which women occupy. Although women are as frequently the relatives, friends and carers of other people with HIV, it is useful to focus on the care for gay men, mostly because they are the majority of people with HIV and AIDS, but also because relationships between women and gay men are complex.

The Sexual Lifestyles survey confirmed that, 'Women tend to be more accepting than men of same-gender relationships.'[48] This difference was particularly marked in respect of women's attitudes to gay men. In the survey, 70.2 per cent of men stated that they thought sex between two men was always or mostly wrong, but this attitude was shared by 'only' 57.9 per cent of women; 64.5 per cent of men said they thought sex between two women was always or mostly wrong – an attitude shared by 58.8 per cent of the women. This suggests not only that women are the more tolerant – of a fairly intolerant bunch – but also that people tend to dislike something which they may perceive as personally threatening. So the women were more at ease with gay men than with lesbians – whereas for men it was the reverse.

A lot of women like (or accept) gay men, but the response of gay men to women sometimes feels like an attraction-repulsion thing: women are sexually undesirable, over-emotional 'fish', at the same time as being these glorious caring goddesses who can dress in sparkly frocks and make-up and drink a lot of Bollinger. Some gay men live a separatist life, isolated from the women in their family and choosing not to connect with women (an easier choice to fulfil than for separatist women, but that's another story). These gay men will not have informal women carers – and probably should never be given women as formal carers (for both their sakes). The majority of gay men and bisexual men are not isolated from women. Some are married, or have current or past female lovers. These women (and any children they have) are in a strange position – they tend to be ignored or ridiculed in a gay milieu and pitied in the media. These women may feel rejected by their lovers and energetically conceal their situation, either out of dislike for their male partners' lifestyle or an irrational sense of shame, as they may be perceived as sexually inadequate. Many gay men will have close, 'confidante' women friends – who may or may not be 'fag hags' (efforts to reclaim this pejorative, rather aggressive term seem doomed, despite Penny Arcade's best efforts[49]). All gay men have families. While some families have rejected their queer children, others have not. Where a gay man is not out to his family, or they have rejected him, often he is out to or accepted by a female relative (sister or mother) who may carry the burden of supporting him, negotiating with other family members or hiding his ill-health from them. For the families who accept their gay relative, life can still be difficult: how does his mother get support from the homophobic vicar? Is his sister expected to confront every colleague's queer joke? Part of the Far Right's anti-gay fantasy is that their homophobic hatred only hurts queers, who don't count because they're a minority. This blocks out the toll on the friends and relatives of queers – many of whom are women.

The diagnosis of HIV or AIDS may force a gay man out to his family, confronting them not only with society's anti-gay prejudice, but also their own. Whether or not it should be, the revelation of a son, brother, grandson or nephew's homo/bisexuality is often a traumatic event, so that many relatives have to adapt to two new circumstances – his queerness and his HIV – at a time when their own anxieties and distress can rarely be given attention or take centre stage. Where the child or sibling's HIV is not related to homosexuality, it is still a queer diagnosis. The woman whose coffee-morning friends sympathize when her daughter develops breast cancer may have different responses to a daughter who has AIDS – does she use drugs? Is she 'that sort of girl'? Did her mother bring her up properly? The taint of the queer disease does not only cover the person infected, but also their immediate family: there is something wrong about a loved one developing AIDS, it is a diagnosis that is discussed in hushed tones. For the friend or relative who cares, the burden of secrecy may be as painful as the burden of her loved one's illness or death. She may internalize the notion that her own needs are irrelevant, and she is unworthy of attention. For example, one woman described the stress of caring for her brother thus:

> What was unbearable was having to keep it from the rest of the family. I got no support from my brothers or my

mother. So I told my husband and my best friend. I hated the secrecy and deceit – I found it horrendous because everything was on my shoulders.[50]

Working women

Most women have been trained into caring roles from childhood, and in that sense it is 'natural' that friends and relatives turn to them for support, or that they have turned to a 'caring profession' for income or as volunteers. Many women work and volunteer with AIDS service organizations (ASOs), and in other parts of the AIDS industry. Indeed, ASOs were created by gay men in allegiance with the women (of all sexual orientations) who loved them and cared about their well-being. Currently, more than half of the Terrence Higgins Trust staff and 40 per cent of volunteers are women, and in many other agencies there are large numbers of women buddies, nurses, health advisers, social workers, counsellors and complementary therapists. At the outset, many of the AIDS doctors were gay men, and while men continue to occupy most of the consultant positions, there are increasing numbers of women paediatricians, junior infectious disease doctors, Genito-Urinary Medicine doctors, and GPs caring for people with HIV and AIDS. Women are epidemiologists, statisticians and other researchers and scientists. They work in health-promotion units, needle exchange schemes, as sex education advisers to schools and as HIV-prevention outreach workers. Some bring the expertise of living with HIV, or experiences of sex work or drug use, others have formal trainings in health education, teaching, social work or science. As workers, women have been involved in AIDS since the start.

The discovery of the public health threat now known as AIDS is credited to Dr Michael Gottlieb, who published a short report of five cases of PCP in young, previously healthy gay men in 1981.[51] There is no doubt that Gottlieb's role in making the connection among these patients was a vital advance. Yet there were other equally important contributions to this earliest stage of medical detective work, and this is not published and rarely remembered. Randy Shilts recalled how, in mid-1983, workers at the CDC wrote on a paper napkin and then pinned it to an office door. It read, 'In this office in April 1981, Sandra Ford discovered the epidemic that would later be known as Acquired Immune Deficiency Syndrome.'[52] Have you ever heard of Sandra Ford before? Most of the AIDS mafia who know all about Gottlieb haven't either. Apart from the entries in Shilts's book, her role has been lost.

Sandra Ford was a drug technician at the CDC and one of her roles was to process requests for the (then) unlicensed drug, pentamidine. Pentamidine is a treatment for PCP – in 1981 this was a rare pneumonia occurring principally in people with leukaemia, or who had been immune-suppressed to receive transplant organs. Requests for the drug were sufficiently rare and specific for Ford to be alerted when the drug was repeatedly requested in early 1981 from physicians who could not identify the reason for their patients' underlying immune deficiency. When she heard about investigations into bone sarcoma in homosexual males in New York, Ford wrote a memo to her boss describing the nine recent pentamidine requests she had received and thus, claims Shilts, 'alerted the federal government to the new epidemic'.[53]

The story of AIDS is a story of many individuals' unsung contributions, and I do not wish to suggest there has been any active conspiracy to conceal Ford's role. I doubt if anyone has tried to write Ford out of history, but I have searched hard and can only find Shilts's record of her. Sandra Ford, like so many women, found herself in a background job. Whether it was less ambition, lack of educational opportunities, practical considerations or the family-career balancing act, this thorough and efficient scientist was writing memos not scientific papers. The issue is not simply whether she should have been writing scientific papers, but that women's contribution is concealed because little besides published work is valued. Many women make immense contributions to the AIDS crisis, but they rarely slog away writing articles, papers or books, and so their role is rarely recorded. Ford found a vital piece of the jigsaw, making her contribution fairly formidable. For other women the roles may be less groundbreaking, but they are essential and influential nevertheless.

The AIDS industry can have just as powerful a glass ceiling as many a more mainstream field. It is useful to reflect on women's positions in AIDS work, not simply to gripe and demand career advancement, but to point out that women's AIDS work is usually invisible. This has important consequences for support needs with such tough work – and work which often involves women supporting men. For feminists, support needs may have to address the fact of taking care of so many men, and always working below men. Indeed some queer women have come under fire for looking after men in this way – why aren't they devoting their energies to women's causes? Why are they mopping up after men again?[54] In ASOs, men tend to be running the show, there is often a strong homoerotic culture and most of the clients are men. Even the women who are fully aware of what they've bargained for may find this overwhelming at times. I have been amazed at how often a gay colleague would expect me to listen to a meticulous description of where he cruised last night and every last sexual act he did with his trick, and who would then run away looking nauseous if I mentioned the word 'period'.

The point is not just that men are difficult to work with (of course they are) but that in AIDS work, women are usually fighting someone else's battle – yet it is rare for women to explore the contradictions this creates.[55] Unless women operate within a women-specific service, or an agency for another core group (like drug users), they will be fighting for men to love (or at least have sex with) men – something which fairly effectively locks women out of the loop. It is virtually impossible, and certainly undesirable, to work in the AIDS field if you do not like gay men or respect their struggle. Even if women are working in a women-specific service, they cannot avoid gay men since the fact of the impact of AIDS on gay men has defined responses to AIDS.

It is not only that men have the power and visibility in AIDS work, but that gay men have a powerful case for maintaining this to reflect the disproportionate impact they suffer – otherwise it is evidence of 'de-gayed' invisibility.[56] It is impossible to fight AIDS without fighting homophobia, even when the fight is for straight women. For women, the problem is that most of these gay spokesmen fail to make the connection between gay men's oppression and vulnerability to HIV, and women's oppression and vulnerability to HIV.[57] Gay men's valid claims to respect for the impact their community has suffered from AIDS can ignore the real sufferings of individual HIV-positive women, or lead women to get stuck in a familiar 'my needs are irrelevant, I am unworthy' script. How can I yell at a gay man dealing with the daily indignities of AIDS about his misuse of the words 'cunt' and 'rape'? And how can I maintain my self-respect and his dignity if I don't? Traditional hierarchies of oppression are complicated by new hierarchies of suffering. Many women volunteers and workers have suffered incredible levels of loss through AIDS, yet the whole phenomenon of multiple grief is perceived as a gay thing. Undoubtedly women suffer a different type of loss from that of gay and bisexual men who 'face this epidemic head on, eyeball to eyeball every time [they] have sex',[58] but this does not mean that women's multiple grief should be ignored or trivialized as it so often is.[59]

Addressing the ways in which women are 'victims' of the AIDS crisis, it is important to think more broadly than the women who are already infected. Although women living with HIV and AIDS must remain central to any analysis, beyond this core group of over 3000 women there are waves of impact reaching out to many thousands more women. From the inner circle of women living with HIV, the waves extend out to the women whose lovers are HIV-positive, to the mothers, sisters, daughters, grandmothers and aunts, out further through the close friends and friendship circles of people living with HIV, through to the volunteers, other informal carers and caring professionals. The waves of impact are not hermetically sealed from one another – the best friend of a woman with AIDS may also be the lover of an HIV-positive man; the woman whose uncle is diagnosed with HIV may be a helpline volunteer; the social worker might have lost two brothers to AIDS. The red ribbon rash tends to affect just as many women as gay men. When I see these women sporting a twist of red on their lapels I wonder, are these sisters? HIV-positive women? Buddies, mothers, lovers, health-promotion workers, best friends, or lesbians? Or simply women with a sense of solidarity, or displaying a commitment to safer sex?

Women have been profoundly affected by AIDS, and most

of these women have played an invisible role in the epidemic – their work is low-profile and hidden, or the impact is personal and individual. In the shift to reassert the gay dimensions of the AIDS crisis in Britain, there is also a real danger that the sexual vulnerabilities to HIV faced by small groups of women may have become ever more hidden from them. It is relatively easy to focus on the impact on women when they are already diagnosed with HIV or AIDS, or when they have entered into a caring relationship with someone who is diagnosed. Far less attention is paid to an equally fundamental impact of AIDS on women: the threat that HIV may pose to women's enjoyment of their sex lives. By denying the sexual dimension of the epidemic, not only are women's lives endangered, but women are also cast into simplistic nurturing or 'victim' roles which avoid the rich complexity of women's experiences.

Notes

1. The phrase 'From Victim to Victor' was coined by Dietmar Bolle as the slogan for the 5th International Meeting of People Living with HIV/AIDS, held in London, September 1991.
2. S. O'Sullivan and K. Thomson (eds), *Positively Women: Living with AIDS*, Sheba, London, 1992, p. 119.
3. I interviewed Anna, a twenty-seven-year-old healthcare worker from Oslo, Norway, at the European meeting for people with HIV in Göttingen, Germany, May 1992. The interviews with her (and Tanja and Josephine) were for the daily newspaper at the VIII International Conference on AIDS, Amsterdam, July 1992.
4. Cited by S. Watney, 'Taking liberties' in E. Carter and S. Watney (eds), *Taking Liberties*, Serpents Tail, London, p. 15.
5. See, for example, M. Callen, *Surviving AIDS*, HarperCollins New York, 1990, for a balanced account. There are many less rigorous claims about how a 'positive attitude' can translate into healing, and some (such as Louise Hay's work) risk plunging people into victimhood by implying that illness is a sign of insufficient self-love.
6. This is reviewed in J. M. Ussher, 'Paradoxical practices: psychologists as scientists in the field of AIDS', pp. 130–133 in C. Squire (ed.), *Women and AIDS: Psychological Perspectives*, Sage Publications, London, 1993.
7. Julie Amos, personal communication.
8. Quoted by Irma Kurtz, 'My name is Denise . . . I'm HIV positive', *Cosmopolitan*, January 1991, p.68f.
9. O'Sullivan and Thomson, *op. cit.*, p. 7.

10. *Ibid.*, pp. 38–9.
11. Quoted in *Woman to Woman*, Lyon-Martin Women's Health Services, The National Lesbian/Bisexual HIV Prevention Network, June 1995, p. 4.
12. O'Sullivan and Thomson, *op. cit.*, pp. 19–20.
13. *Women Like Us*, Positively Women, London, 1994, p. 10.
14. Kate Thomson, personal communication.
15. For an excellent description of one such estate, see John Sturrock's photo essay in S. Mayes and L. Stein (eds), *Positive Lives: Responses to HIV – a Photodocumentary*, Cassell, London, 1993, pp. 22–37.
16. Dr Diana Gibb, personal communication.
17. This is documented in, for example, L. Sherr *et al.*, 'Psychological trauma associated with AIDS and HIV infection in women', *Counselling Psychology Quarterly*, Vol. 6, No. 2, 1993, pp. 99–108; *Women Like Us*, p. 52; E. A. Preble and J. Foumbi, 'The African family and AIDS. A current look at the epidemic', *AIDS*, 5, suppl. 2, 1991, pp. 5263–7.
18. See Chapter 2, pp. 61–2.
19. Personal testimonies of women with HIV and AIDS can be found in O'Sullivan and Thomson, *op. cit.*; I. Rieder and P. Ruppelt (eds), *Matters of Life and Death*, Virago, London, 1989; A. Rudd and D. Taylor (eds), *Positive Women: Voices of Women Living with AIDS*, Second Story Press, Toronto, 1992; A. Richardson and D. Bolle (eds), *Wise Before Their Time*, Vintage, London, 1993; ACT UP NY Women & AIDS Book Group, *Women, AIDS and Activism*, South End Press, Boston, 1990. See also, L. Sherr *et al.*, *op. cit.*; *Women Like Us*; L. Sherr, 'Psychosocial aspects of providing care for women with HIV infection', in H. Minkoff and J. Dehovitz (eds), *Women and AIDS*, Raven Press, New York, 1993.
20. Sarah (England) quoted in Richardson and Bolle, *op. cit.*, p. 63.
21. This has often been a difficulty for gay men and men with haemophilia, with the latter blaming gay men for donating infected blood, and gay men resenting the 'innocent victim' status of haemophiliacs.
22. D. Taylor, 'Testing positive in Canada', *HealthSharing*, Spring 1990, reproduced in M. Berer with S. Ray, *Women and HIV/AIDS: An International Resource Book*, Pandora, London, 1993, p. 13.
23. C. Patton, *Inventing AIDS*, Routledge, 1990, p. 120.
24. Rachel, quoted in R. Rimer and M. Connolly, *HIV+: Working the System*, Alyson, 1993, p. 187.
25. M. D. Banzhaf, 'Doin' it for themselves: how women can deal with physicians', *Positively Aware*, May 1993, p. 20.
26. R. Gorna, 'New direction for women's traditional responsibilities', *PAACNotes*, September 1993, Vol. 5, No. 9, pp. 384–5.
27. *Women Like Us*, p. 25.

28. *Ibid.*, pp. 24–8.
29. M. Kamenga *et al.*, 'Evidence of marked sexual behaviour change associated with low HIV-1 seroconversion in 149 married couples with discordant HIV-1 serostatus – experience at an HIV counselling center in Zaire', *AIDS*, 1991, 5, pp. 61–7; cf. J. Tice *et al.*, 'Impact of HIV testing on condoms, spermicide use among HIV discordant couples in Africa', 6th International Conference on AIDS, Abstract SC 694, p. 262.
30. R. Denenberg, 'Gynaecological considerations', in A. Kurth (ed.), *Until the Cure: Caring for Women with HIV*, Yale University Press, 1993, p. 44.
31. *Ibid.*
32. Personal communication.
33. *Women Like Us*, p. 20.
34. *Ibid.*, p. 29.
35. *Ibid.*
36. *Ibid.*, p. 12.
37. Quoted in Richardson and Bolle, *op. cit.*, p. 45.
38. *Ibid.*, pp. 46–9.
39. See M. Kamenga *et al.*, *op. cit.*; L. Sherr, in Minkoff and Dehovitz, *op. cit.*; L. Sherr, *HIV and AIDS in Mothers and Babies*, Blackwell Scientific Publications, Oxford, 1991; A. Sunderland *et al.*, 'The impact of HIV serostatus on reproductive decisions of women', *Obstetrics and Gynecology*, Vol. 79, No. 6, June 1992, 1027–31; M. Temmerman *et al.*, *AIDS Care*, Vol. 2, No. 3, 1990, 247–52.
40. *Women Like Us*, pp. 22–3.
41. 'Steve', quoted in S. Garfield, *The End of Innocence: Britain in the Time of AIDS*, Faber & Faber, London, 1994, p. 218.
42. O'Sullivan and Thomson (eds), *op. cit.*, p. 98.
43. *Women Like Us*, p. 31.
44. *Ibid.*, pp. 15–18.
45. A small number of resources are being developed to meet the sexual health needs of HIV-positive gay men. Even where they refer to the target audience as including bisexual men, information about protecting women is never included. No resources are currently available for women.
46. D. Worth, 'Women at high risk of HIV infection', in D. Ostrow (ed.), *Behavioural Aspects of AIDS*, Plenum Medical Books, New York, 1990.
47. Z. Leonard, 'Safe sex is real sex', in ACT UP NY Women & AIDS Book Group, *op. cit.*, pp. 29–30.
48. K. Wellings *et al.*, *Sexual Behaviour in Britain: The National Survey of Sexual Attitudes and Lifestyles*, Penguin, London, 1994, p. 253.
49. Most persuadingly promoted in her show *Bitch! Dyke! FagHag! Whore!*, ICA, London, 30 September 1993.
50. Cited in P. G. Keogh *et al.* (Sigma Research), 'The support and

resource needs of gay men with HIV/AIDS, their partners and their carers', unpublished, March 1995, p. 17. In this study the majority of the sixteen carers who participated in the interviews were women – two mothers, eight sisters, two friends (gender not stated) and four partners (gender not stated, but probably male).

51. M. S. Gottlieb, *Morbidity and Mortality Weekly Reports* (*MMWR*), CDC, 5 June 1981.
52. R. Shilts, *And the Band Played On*, Penguin, London, 1989, p. 323. He also describes Ford's role on pp. 54, 61, 63, 66, 80, 160.
53. *Ibid.*, p. 66.
54. In their World AIDS Day piece which recognized the work of some lesbians and bisexual women in AIDS work, the *Pink Paper* felt compelled to ask why we weren't involved in breast cancer activism. C. Treasure, 'Women's work', 1 December 1993.
55. Women who have explored some of these elements of their work include K. Deverell and J. Bell, 'Some thoughts on being straight women in a men who have sex with men project', Keele University, Department of Sociology and Social Anthropology (mimeo), 1993; K. Deverell, 'Fact-finder, fag hag, fellow and funambulist: differing identifications and their impact on the research process', in press; J. M. Ussher, 'Paradoxical practices: psychologists as scientists in the field of AIDS', in Squire, *op. cit.*, pp. 126–46.
56. See, for example, P. Scott, *Capital Gay*, 22 May 1992.
57. Keith Alcorn is one of the few to write about this: 'Why women lose out when Aids organizations are de-gayed', inSIGHT, *Capital Gay*, 14 May 1993 (although he did not acknowledge the women who informed his argument, because their arguments had not been published . . .).
58. S. Watney, letter to *Outlines*, US, June 1992.
59. One gay man responded to my concern about this by suggesting women were whining, 'Oh these nasty gay men are cruel – they keep dying on us and making us sad.' In the face of such violent cynicism, it is hard to hold on to the belief that women's needs are valid and deserve attention.

Chapter six

Vessels

Straight sex cannot give you AIDS – Official.

Headline in the Sun[1]

Women are always shown as vectors of transmission. Women get the blame for HIV – rather than being shown that we're at risk.

Joanne Manchester[2]

One of the great truths, and great fallacies, of HIV transmission is: 'It's not who you are, it's what you do.' The review of epidemiology shows that the likelihood of a woman having a sexual partner who is HIV-infected *is* linked to 'who he is' (I use the pronoun advisedly). Some sub-groups and communities have been disproportionately affected. However, no woman acquires this virus *because* of who she, or her sexual partner, is. A woman becomes infected because of 'what she does' – and because she does it with someone who is infected with HIV (and in turn became infected because of what he did, not who he was).

This chapter explores in detail the mechanisms of the transmission of HIV *to* women, and the research upon which this knowledge is based; transmission *from* women is reviewed in the next chapter, 'Vectors'. The socio-economic factors which determine risk, such as the power men may have over women, and the fact that their behaviour determines the likelihood of men being infected, are discussed elsewhere.

When they are not being blamed as vectors, HIV-positive women may be represented as 'vessels', the recipients of infected fluid. The woman as vessel is a dangerous container of infectious fluid – and, potentially, of an innocent babe within that fluid. The woman as vessel is also represented as semen recipient – a passive being without agency or desire in respect of sex. The reality is that, in sexual contexts, women with HIV are far less likely to transmit the virus than men with HIV. The rationale for exploring this is not to suggest that women are 'innocent victims' and men inviolable, but rather to give women the knowledge and power to assess for themselves the risks they face and pose. Women and girls deserve to know that HIV transmission is not as simple as the prevention message that says, 'Gay or straight, male or female, anyone can get AIDS from sexual intercourse.'[3]

The basics

Information develops over time, and by the time this book is published there will doubtless be new developments; these will be found in the *AIDS Reference Manual*.[4] Before turning to the more complex scientific details, it will be helpful to summarize the essentials of what is currently known and agreed. Although there are gaps in knowledge, and some points of conflict, the core facts have been confirmed since understanding of AIDS began in the early 1980s.

HIV is a fragile virus and it does not survive well out of the body. In order for HIV to be transmitted, it must be able to leave the body of a person who has HIV in sufficient quantity for infection to occur, and there must be an appropriate route for it to enter the body of another person. (It may seem self-evident, but HIV can only be transmitted from a person who is infected with the virus.) In laboratory tests, HIV can be isolated from many body fluids. However, in reality HIV is only present in sufficient quantity for transmission in a very few fluids. These are: blood, seminal fluid (including pre-ejaculate), cervical and vaginal fluids (secretions/mucus/juices – including menstrual blood) and breast milk. No cases of HIV transmission involving other body fluids have been reported. If there is only a minute quantity of one of these body fluids then infection is extremely unlikely. However, the minimum quantity of a fluid for infection is not defined and this would be difficult to assess. The concentration of HIV varies according to the fluid, the infectivity at different stages of disease progression, and different strains of the virus.

Finally, the virus has to enter another person's body through an appropriate route. The virus needs to infect white blood cells (lymphocytes [CD4 cells, CD8 cells] or macrophages) in the blood of the other person. Intact skin is an excellent barrier against HIV and is sufficient to prevent infection. HIV can enter the blood directly by an invasive surgical procedure (blood transfusion or organ transplant), from contaminated injection equipment or through a cut or sore. It can also enter the bloodstream through mucosae (mucous membranes), principally in the cervix, vagina, rectum, urethra and under the foreskin. HIV can be absorbed through CD4 receptors on the surface of white blood cells, called lymphocytes, or on dendritic cells and Langerhans cells, which are present in these membranes. If membranes are damaged transmission may be easier, but it may occur whether they are damaged or not. Sometimes these principles are summarized as 'Quality, Quantity and Route', and there are only three efficient routes for HIV transmission: penetrative sex, blood contact (including shared drug injecting equipment) and from a woman to her baby.

The basis of knowledge

The scientific facts about HIV transmission are often treated as if they are neutral and fixed. They are not. Since AIDS is such a new phenomenon, the body of scientific information is constantly expanding. There is no solid rock of long-standing knowledge, but rather a constant process of learning as the epidemic unfolds. In general 'scientists hate committing themselves without adding confusing caveats',[5] and most are necessarily cautious about definitive statements about HIV transmission until there is a greater volume of evidence (which depends upon more time passing). Sadly, this academic caution is often misused to create an unreasonable level of distrust resulting in comments like, 'We really know nothing. Scientists may soon discover we can catch it from kissing.' Of course, anything *is* possible, but it is worth recalling that the first safer sex guidelines were established before HIV was discovered, before it was even clear that a sexually transmitted virus was the prime cause, yet advice given over a decade later remains broadly in line with these original guidelines.[6] The trend over fifteen years of the pandemic is towards a greater understanding of how difficult it is to transmit HIV, to a greater refinement of knowledge about the circumstances in which HIV is most likely to be transmitted and to safer-sex guidance becoming ever less stringent.

Information about the dynamics of HIV transmission has developed from two sciences: epidemiology and biology. Within epidemiology there are three basic knowledge sources: prospective studies, retrospective studies and case reports. Prospective studies gather a cohort of people and study them over time to see how many transmit or acquire HIV, and what the routes and co-factors of transmission are. Retrospective studies ask (or make assumptions about) how a group of people who are HIV-positive became infected; and case studies consider an individual. Biological information is gleaned from basic scientific research into HIV based on *in vitro* (laboratory) studies into the nature of the virus: how long does it survive, which cells does it infect, etc. Finally there is important information to be gained from what is already known about other blood-borne pathogens (such as Hepatitis B) and STDs, as well as the basics of physiology and how the body acquires infections.

Each of the methods of gathering information is limited in some way. Biological information depends upon creating models in the laboratory, yet these can rarely comprise all the features which make up the complexity of a sexual encounter. With retrospective studies there are problems of recall about behaviour. This does not mean that people actively lie, but rather that memory is by necessity highly selective, especially regarding behaviour that may have happened a number of years ago, that is not easily coded and named, and that may be stigmatized. Some reports also show bias with people seeking to 'please' the researcher by concealing risky behaviour, or reaching a state of self-denial through shame of exposure. Several cases of this have been documented in respect of alleged oral sex HIV transmission.[7] Case studies are often the most appealing and easily understood form of reporting, but these do depend on the quality of interviewing, and it can be dangerous to generalize from an individual report. With prospective studies there is the ethical 'problem' that they must promote safer practices to the cohort, but this may have the consequence that people will be less likely to engage in the unsafe practices which would enable them to contract HIV.[8]

As well as the technical provisos, there can also be problems with the use made of results from epidemiological research. WHO's Henning Mikkelsen suggested that 'epidemiologists are good at counting and colouring',[9] and while some of these eminent scientists may find this a touch reductive, there is a tendency to reduce their sophisticated efforts to a bunch of numbers. When translating information about HIV transmission and different sexual activities into real life decisions, statistics about the per incident rate may be seductive, but they are not always helpful. Ultimately, the question is whether an activity is efficient, inefficient or impossible, in respect of transmission. With routes which are efficient, there is a further question of whether there are factors which render them less efficient, or even impossible. Some people may base decisions according to the statistical odds of transmission, but this can often become twisted and lead to false assumptions (for example, if a certain activity had a 1 per cent chance of transmission, this would *not* mean that it was safe to do it ninety-nine times). The particular circumstance of potential transmission to a baby may be an exception since pregnancy is a rare activity, and so basing decisions on statistics may make sense. Ultimately, the statistical rates of transmission are of most use for seeing the relative risks and making assessments on that basis: receiving an infected blood transfusion is very risky, giving cunnilingus is not.

I will describe some of the rates of HIV transmission which have been calculated, but it is critical to use caution in interpreting these. They are based upon research which is necessarily imperfect, and subject to shifting circumstances, and this may influence the rates which are derived from studies.[10] Statistics are calculated principally with regard to scientific interest rather than individuals' real-life decision-making, and they must be interpreted in that light. An over-reliance on any one source (such as retrospective case studies) or one particular study can lead to incorrect conclusions. The basic information about how HIV is transmitted is established by bringing together the information from all these sources. In many ways, understanding HIV transmission is a creative exercise in combining these different types and strands of knowledge to develop usable information.

Blood (and drugs)

Transmission of HIV is most effective through blood, and the likelihood and mechanics of transmission by this route are gender neutral. There are three ways in which HIV transmission is effected by blood: infusions of blood and blood products, contamination through shared equipment (e.g. syringes) for drug use, accidental contamination through sharps (e.g. needles). At an epidemiological level, there are gender differences: men are more likely to receive HIV in blood products, women are more likely to be infected through blood transfusions. In respect of shared injecting equipment, more male drug users are infected than women, because more men inject drugs. However, women are more likely to acquire HIV accidentally as healthcare workers, since nurses (mostly women) have less training and encouragement to adopt safer practices than do doctors (mostly men). These differences are dependent upon socio-economic factors, and the prevalence of other health conditions which require blood products (haemo-philia), or transfusions (pregnancy-related anaemia), rather than physiology.

HIV in blood is transmitted equally efficiently into female and male bloodstreams. A person acquires HIV when the virus infects the lymphocytes in the blood. When HIV-infected blood is injected into the vein of an uninfected person in any of the above ways, the virus can easily reach these cells. For sexual transmission to occur, the virus first has to pass through the intermediary of CD4 receptors on cells in the mucous membrane (either dendritic cells or Langerhans cells) before it can infect the lymphocytes. The direct access to lymphocytes is why 'blood-to-blood' transmission is by far the most efficient route.

In considering HIV transmission, it is necessary to place transmission events in context and compare the relative efficiency of different routes. Even this most efficient mode of transmission is not 100 per cent effective – that is, an uninfected person will not always acquire HIV if HIV-infected blood is placed in their bloodstream. In one study, of 220 people who received HIV-infected blood transfusions, 85 people remained HIV-negative after receiving the blood.[11] The 135 people who acquired the infection were more likely to have received large quantities of blood from donors who developed AIDS within two and a half years of giving blood (i.e. they had more advanced disease). From this one study it would not be correct to state that there is a 60 per cent rate of transmission of HIV by blood transfusion. However, it does show that HIV transmission is not inevitable even in such extreme, easily measurable and favourable conditions.

With injecting equipment shared for drug use, the likelihood of acquiring HIV from a person who is HIV-infected will be less than for blood transfusion, on a single exposure, although there are no clear estimates. One reason why it is difficult to estimate the chance of infection is that most people who share drug-injecting equipment do so repeatedly, making it hard to assess a per incident rate. The number of blood transfusions an individual receives is generally known. The individual likelihood of infection by shared drug injecting equipment is lower because relatively small amounts of blood are passed on, and they are not always delivered directly into the bloodstream. Blood from the first injector remains in the needle and the barrel of the syringe after it is 'flushed' (so that all the drug enters the bloodstream), or in other parts of the 'works' (the common collective name for all paraphernalia used to inject drugs). HIV can then be passed on if another person uses the same works without cleaning them (works can be cleaned by flushing with bleach twice and then with water twice). The likelihood of transmission will alter significantly, dependent upon the levels of virus present in the blood. At least 5000 infectious particles of HIV have been isolated from just one millilitre of infected blood, and it is stated that with high viral load (i.e. when HIV is replicating), HIV infection can occur with quantities of blood which are invisible to the naked eye.[12]

It is possible to estimate the rates of transmission of HIV through medical accidents, since most healthcare workers are required to report work-related incidents where HIV transmission is possible. A UK review of all reported HIV-related injuries showed that only 0.38 per cent of health professionals, accidentally exposed to HIV-infected fluids in the course of their work, have themselves acquired HIV.[13] The risk from needlestick injuries is believed to be lower than that associated with sharing needles for injecting drugs; it has been estimated that needlestick injuries contain one-seventh of the quantity of blood injected when sharing drug injecting equipment.[14] This is an over-simplification,[15] and does not automatically suggest a per incident rate of transmission for drug-injecting equipment of 3 per cent. The estimate does not allow for different forms of medical accident: many needlestick injuries are skin punctures, rather than direct injections of blood into a vein (which tends to occur when injecting drugs). It also fails to allow for varying stages of infectivity. Once again the quantity of blood and infectivity of the virus, as well as the site of the injury, will have an impact on the real-life likelihood of acquiring HIV in such a scenario.

Sex

Few people ever get the blood of another person into their bloodstream; by contrast, few people never have sex. Thus, although the per-incident risk of transmission from blood-borne routes is highest, the vast majority of cases of HIV transmission are mediated by the far more common activity: sex. Even if the per-incident risk is lower, the cumulative effect renders it a far higher risk for most people. Sex may be common, but it is also shrouded in myth and misunderstanding, and wariness about describing practices in detail (let alone the motivations for engaging in the practices). The risks of sexual HIV transmission are remarkably poorly understood when compared with what is known about the risks of transmitting HIV to an infant, and this is a good example of where science has served us poorly, by failing (thus far) to provide clear information about such a vital area.

The science writer Phyllida Brown, who has reported on the epidemic since its earliest days, points out, 'One of the most critical aspects of the AIDS epidemic is also the least researched and most poorly understood – the mechanisms by which HIV spreads during sex.'[16] The paucity of reliable information is partly due to a lack of pressure from activists, with a willingness to accept the imprecisions available, but there are also problems raised by the scientific community.[17] Certainly, sexual risks will be harder to define than maternal ones, and they are not a popular focus for grant applications. It is easy to imagine the tabloid response if a research team announced that they had completed their work on the HIV risks of breast-feeding and were turning their attention to oral sex – although this is a scientific direction that would be of immense help to HIV prevention work, individuals living with HIV, and their sexual partners. At the 1992 International AIDS Conference, organizers hoped to run a session on oral sex, yet no scientist would agree to participate. Individuals were willing to be interviewed for the conference newspaper, but refused to discuss their perspectives with their scientific peers. Some scientists claimed that it was an inappropriate discussion since proper studies had not been undertaken, while others stated that there was no risk from oral sex and the whole topic was irrelevant and had been hyped by activists (notably lesbian activists).[18] Whatever the validity of these researchers' critiques, it remains extraordinary that, whilst tens of thousands of scientific papers have thus far been presented to ten international conferences on AIDS, there has never yet been a session which addresses this highly contested issue, which is a significant and immediate concern for many people.

There is a tendency to biological reductionism among researchers considering sexual transmission, with the complexity of sexual repertoire limited to anal intercourse, vaginal intercourse and oral sex. Partly this is because common sense dictates that these activities may involve a risk of HIV, but it is also a simplistic way of capturing behaviour which tends to be anything but simple or linear. The scientific focus tends to consider biological co-factors such as menstruation, circumcision and the presence of other STDs, yet what is consistently absent is any attempt to measure transmission differences linked to real-life factors such as the use of violence or coercion, or the length of the sexual encounter. Inevitably this is a troubled area, since they are seeking to assess HIV risks with activities which do not easily lend themselves to precise definition, let alone mathematical analysis. As Felicia Stewart points out, 'Sex is not just a mechanism for transmitting disease',[19] and undoubtedly the social, cultural, psychological and economic contexts within which sex happens are the most important elements for individuals having sex. Despite my criticism of scientists for biological reductionism of sexual acts to anal, vaginal and oral, I will describe, in a mechanistic fashion, these same activities, attempting elsewhere to place this in a broader, real-life context.

This chapter will describe how a woman may become infected from sex with an HIV-infected man. In order to avoid excess repetition, information about whether a woman may become infected from sex with an HIV-infected woman is described in the next chapter (which looks at transmission from an HIV-infected woman). I start with sex with men since women are infinitely more vulnerable to acquiring infection from men than women. The (biological) concerns about whether an HIV-infected woman can transmit sexually to another woman also touch upon many of the concerns of HIV-infected women who have sex with men. The principal sexual risks of acquiring HIV are related to the presence of HIV in semen, and so this will be the initial focus. This is followed by a review of the three key sexual activities for HIV: vaginal intercourse, anal intercourse and fellatio (oral sex). First I will consider the biology of how HIV could enter a woman's body: through the female genital tract, the anus, and the mouth and gastro-intestinal tract. Then I look at epidemiological studies of HIV transmission from men to women to see what is known about the real-life risks. In all cases I will consistently describe sexual scenarios where the HIV-infected person is a man, and the person vulnerable to acquiring HIV is a woman.

One important reason for dwelling on the mechanics is that a proper understanding is essential to combat lay beliefs and forms of 'magical' thinking which can be extremely unhelpful for individual decision-making. One model which is often promoted by professional AIDS educators is the idea of an 'exchange' or 'mingling' of body fluids. Such phrasing encourages people to think of sexual HIV risks as akin to conception: like the ovum and the sperm, the joining together of two people's sexual fluids creates a third entity, in this case HIV. This can lead some people to imagine that HIV can be created where neither partner is infected.[20] It is important to stress that HIV is not 'exchanged': it is given or it is received, not both. This is not a trivial point, as there is often a lay sense that both people's fluids have a role to play. They do not, but both partners are important. The 'giver' of HIV needs to give a sufficient amount of a fluid which contains sufficient quantities of the virus. The 'recipient' needs to have the potential for the virus in that fluid to infect her; she needs to be vulnerable to acquiring HIV.

• *Semen*

After blood, semen provides the most effective vehicle for the virus. In infected people, HIV is contained in body fluids in two forms: as free viral particles and cell-associated virus. Free viral particles are pieces of HIV which exist in a fluid without becoming attached to any cells; whereas cell-associated virus means that the HIV is integrated within the infected cell in the fluid or attached to its surface. HIV most frequently infects lymphocytes, a kind of white blood cell (but it can also infect other cells which have CD4 attachment sites). Consequently, body fluids which contain a high concentration of white blood cells (like semen) are the fluids which are most likely to be capable of containing enough HIV for transmission, because the virus becomes attached to and integrated within these cells. In these same fluids, free virus can also sometimes be found. Basic scientists have tested all body fluids to try and detect whether HIV is present (and if so in what quantities), and have established that it can be transmitted in blood, sexual fluids and breast milk.[21]

In one millilitre of blood, as I have said, there may be over 5000 HIV-infected lymphocytes. In semen it is estimated that the

average concentration is between 500 and 1000 infected lymphocytes per millilitre (ml), although rates over 5000 have been
recorded.[22] Most papers state that the average male ejaculates 5ml
of semen, around half a tablespoon, but this can vary a great
deal.[23] There have also been reports of infectious HIV in pre-
ejaculatory fluid (pre-cum), which led some scientists to speculate
that infection could occur even if an HIV-infected man does not
ejaculate inside the woman. However, the virus was detected in
pre-cum using very sensitive tests which may find virus which
is at a level too low for transmission to occur. The scientist who
identified HIV in the pre-cum of six out of nine HIV-positive men
gathered samples between a few drops and 1ml (estimating an
average of around 0.5ml, half a teaspoon, of pre-cum in a sexual
encounter). It is unclear whether there would be a sufficient
concentration of the virus for transmission to occur, and other real
life studies suggest that this is unlikely (see below).[24]

Spermatozoa – also known as sperm – is the active ingredient
in conception; this is contained in seminal fluid, and the combination
of sperm and seminal fluid is described as semen. A critical question
(especially for women who want to conceive) is whether HIV is
found in the seminal fluid or the spermatozoa or both. This
has important implications for developing technologies for HIV-
negative women who wish to become pregnant from a (potentially)
HIV-positive man (e.g. microbicides should ideally be available in
both non-contraceptive and contraceptive formulae). There is still
no definitive answer, but it seems that most HIV is found in the
seminal fluid in both cell-associated and free virus forms. At least
two research groups have shown that HIV can bind to the cell
membrane of the spermatozoa, when free viral particles are incub-
ated with sperm in the laboratory. However, it was found on no
more than 20 per cent of the sperm heads, even though very precise
tests were used.[25] One group used PCR (polymerase chain reaction,
a highly sensitive test) and found HIV DNA in the sperm of 33 per
cent of samples from HIV-infected men,[26] but a previous study
had found no HIV in sperm from infected men, although virus
was present in 87 per cent of the seminal fluid.[27] There has been
some question as to whether men with vasectomies could
transmit HIV. Although men who have vasectomies have fewer

cellular components in their ejaculate, seminal and prostatic fluids contain sufficient white cells for HIV to be present. A study of four men who had vasectomies found high concentrations of white blood cells containing infectious HIV in one asymptomatic man, although the other three had low white blood cells and HIV was not found.[28] HIV can definitely be present in this seminal fluid, and vasectomies are decidedly not an effective means of HIV prevention.

Although HIV can become attached to the sperm, it appears that it is rarely transmitted in the sperm. One group found that HIV bound to the sperm, but it did not replicate within it and instead infected lymphocytes (in the fluid). If the virus does not replicate then it cannot cause infection. However, this group inferred that HIV-positive men should be barred from donating semen for artificial insemination.[29]

Results from studies of women who have been impregnated with sperm from HIV-positive men contradict this. Many clinics which carry out alternative insemination use techniques to separate the motile spermatozoa from the seminal fluid, in order to increase the likelihood of conception occurring. In Milan, one laboratory has verified that 'gradient centrifugation followed by a swim-up procedure effectively removed HIV-1 infected cells from the semen of HIV-seropositive men'.[30] Using this technique of 'spinning semen' or 'sperm washing' they have inseminated thirty-six HIV-negative women with sperm from their HIV-positive partners, none of whom has seroconverted. (Seroconversion basically means acquiring infection. It describes the process whereby antibodies to HIV develop in the blood (serum), so that the status of the blood shifts from negative to positive, according to tests for HIV antibodies. Sometimes descriptions mention a person's HIV 'serostatus', that is, whether they are negative or positive.) By 1993, at least seventeen women have conceived through the Milan lab's technique, twelve babies have been born and none of the babies or their mothers acquired HIV. Worldwide, only twelve women have been reported as infected from artificial insemination, principally from semen provided by fertility clinics prior to HIV testing.[31] Doubtless many cases have not yet been reported, but it is striking that there are so few reports. Perhaps the standard procedures for isolating the most fertile spermatozoa simultaneously removed the infectious

HIV. The studies so far suggest that HIV is in the fluid but that 'the sperm does not carry [enough of] the germ'.[32]

INCREASING INFECTIVITY

The infectivity of any body fluid alters in a person with HIV over time, and the most important changes relate to disease progression. There are also fluctuations which are linked to the presence of other STDs. It has long been known that STDs, in either partner, increased the likelihood of HIV being transmitted. Initially it was assumed that this was because STDs which cause ulcers or lesions (e.g. herpes) made it easier for HIV to enter the woman, or increased the quantity of infectious fluids (maybe including blood) in the HIV-infected man. However, further research has found that HIV is also transmitted more readily where the man has non-ulcerative STDs. It is believed that this is because any STD increases the levels of white blood cells present in the genital area, including the urethra. This then means that there are also greater concentrations of white cells and consequently higher levels of HIV present in semen.[33]

The highest levels of HIV are found in people who are sero-converting (that is, during the first few weeks and months after infection), and this is the time when transmission is most likely. Viral load is also high in people who have developed symptoms or have low CD4 counts (usually below 200 – the cut-off point for beginning PCP prophylaxis). Testing for virus in the blood, researchers generally find high levels of replicating (i.e. infectious) HIV during seroconversion and then later in the disease, as CD4 cell counts decline, and especially when the person has developed symptoms of AIDS. The period between these two events, of asymptomatic HIV infection, has generally been understood as a time of low infectivity, with the virus kept at a low level by the immune system. The work of scientists such as David Ho and Anthony Fauci on the pathogenesis of HIV disease (that is, the understanding of how HIV develops within the body and causes disease), has reoriented thinking to an awareness that the virus is constantly replicating, but that this replication is relatively con-tained in the blood. Instead, it is suggested that HIV is replicating within the lymph nodes where it is held in some balance by the immune system, which is able to destroy the thousands of new HIV particles which are produced every day.[34] One of the key questions is whether, during asymptomatic infection, HIV is replicating in sexual fluids at sufficient levels to permit transmission. Using PCR one small study of thirty-six men found HIV in the semen of 81 per cent of these men, and the researchers stated that the presence of HIV was not related to the disease stage or CD4 count of the men.[35] However, this seems to be contradicted by the bulk of research which finds a link with the stage of illness.

The variable infectivity of semen has the most important impact on rates of HIV transmission. This has been demonstrated using mathematical models to explain the initial rates of infections among cohorts of gay men in the USA. These cohorts showed a slowing of new infections from 1984, and this had been assumed to relate to the introduction of safer sex interventions. Although these initiatives clearly had an important role, Koopman, Jacquez and their colleagues state, 'Most HIV transmissions between homosexual and bisexual men occurred during primary infection before antibody developed.'[36] Although HIV is evidently present during different times in the disease process, highest viral load occurs during primary infection, and this is invisible in studies of HIV-positive men because primary infection is the time before antibodies develop, and therefore before they are eligible for the cohorts.

In respect of viral load, there are four main phases that can be identified with HIV infection: primary infection, asymptomatic HIV-positive, symptomatic HIV-positive (from when CD4 counts begin to fall below 400) and AIDS. The third phase is when viraemia begins again, as viral load rises in people with HIV before AIDS-defining symptoms emerge (and there may be no symptoms at all during this time).[37] The suggestion is, therefore, that by no means all, but most HIV transmission occurs during the first, third and fourth periods of a person's illness. In the fourth phase (AIDS) sexual activity is often reduced, which means that fewer infections are likely to occur at this time, even though the person is highly infectious. Although viral load (viraemia) rises with disease progression (and continues to do so until death) it does not reach the same levels as during the initial one to two months of seroconversion. Koopman and Jacquez claim that the risk of acquiring HIV from anal sex is 176 times greater if the infected man is seroconverting compared to all other phases of his illness; the risks from other sexual acts (e.g. fellatio) are also greater during seroconversion (this is discussed in more detail below).[38]

What is particularly alarming with these findings is that most infections may be taking place at exactly the time when the HIV-infected person cannot know that he or she is infected. This is consistent with what is known about other viruses (e.g. flu virus), where the highest infectivity occurs immediately after infection and before symptoms appear (and in HIV, before sufficient antibodies for detection are present). What is different about HIV is that 'the virus persists and gradually initiates a new process that leads eventually to immunosuppression with renewed infectiousness and ultimately death'.[39] One study found that 40 per cent of men with CD4 counts between 100 and 200 had high viral load in semen, and this was the case for 87 per cent of men with CD4 counts below 100.[40] Although viral load rises as CD4 cell counts drop (and disease progresses) many therapeutic interventions used to delay the progression of the disease aim to impact on viraemia. Most studies have found that antiviral therapies (such as AZT, ddI and ddC) reduce the infectivity of the virus in semen; this is to be expected since they reduce viral load in blood. However, (as in blood) resistant strains of virus have been found in semen and there have been cases of transmission. This is important because it means that women (and men and infants) can become infected with strains of HIV which will not respond to treatment with those antiviral therapies.[41]

In summary, basic research into HIV and semen finds that seminal fluid is a highly efficient vector of HIV. It is most likely that the seminal fluid (including pre-ejaculate) contains more virus than the sperm itself. High concentrations of HIV can exist in seminal fluid and these vary within an individual. Fluctuations of viral load (infectivity) in semen are closely linked to changes in viral load within the blood, but they are not solely dependent upon the stage of a man's illness. By far the highest levels of HIV are found in semen during the period of seroconversion. Viral load is far lower during the asymptomatic phase of the disease, levels of

HIV in semen then rise as CD4 counts fall and when he develops AIDS. Both ulcerative and non-ulcerative STDs also increase the viral load in semen. High enough levels of HIV for transmission may also be found in seminal fluid at other times. Antiviral therapies can have an effect on the level of HIV in seminal fluid; they may reduce concentrations of HIV, but if he becomes resistant to the drug this resistant strain can also be sexually transmitted.

Semen may be an extremely efficient (if variable) vehicle for the virus, but the question now is to determine the most efficient sites of entry for the virus to enter a woman's bloodstream. In summary: the cervix provides an easy access point for HIV to enter the bloodstream, as does the rectum, and perhaps the vagina, but the mouth and throat are relatively well protected against infection. What does this mean in practice? Perhaps the best information comes from cohorts of discordant couples, where just one person (known as the 'index') is initially HIV-infected. Researchers follow the couples' behaviour to see whether the other partner becomes infected, and if so, what seems to account for the infection. However, it is hard to arrive at statistical estimates of the risks faced by women from individual sexual activities because few people engage in only one type of act. This is further complicated by the fact that most cohort research assesses rates in terms of 'heterosexual transmission' (that is, men and women are lumped together so that it is impossible to see who is infecting whom) or compares 'male-to-female transmission' with 'female-to-male transmission' (lumping together a range of different activities). These studies also exclude couples where both are infected before the research begins, even if the source and direction of transmission is known. Even after trawling through the texts of these papers, it is frequently impossible to disentangle the activities or the genders, but I will try (although I am necessarily forcing some artificial divides between this chapter and the next).

• *Vaginal sex*

By vaginal sex I mean the penetration of the vagina by a penis, which may include the ejaculation of semen. Some people will use the term 'vaginal sex' to refer to other activities – such as using fingers or sex toys in the vagina – and these are discussed in the next chapter. Reports of the high risk of HIV acquisition by women who have anal sex with HIV-infected men has led some to deny the risks inherent in vaginal sex and characterize all HIV-infected women as having been infected through anal fucking. Responding to a health education campaign purporting to represent an HIV-positive woman, Reginald Murley, a former president of the Royal College of Surgeons, notoriously stated that the woman was unlikely to get HIV unless she 'allows herself to be buggered'.[42] This is nonsense, but dangerous nonsense which appears to have worked its way into common understanding. One of the curiosities of HIV transmission is that many people have an uncanny tendency towards perceiving a danger only with the activities they would like to be risky. Such an approach fails to appreciate that risk is a relative term, not an absolute.

While it is beyond doubt that vaginal sex is an efficient route of HIV transmission (and the most frequent), the exact mechanisms by which HIV enters the body are subject to disagreement, and this disagreement leads some people to claim that vaginal sex is an inefficient route of transmission. Compared with anal sex, there is no difference in the infectious fluid entering the vagina and so it is the exact site of entry for HIV which is disputed. Researchers suggest that during vaginal sex the part of a woman's body which is most vulnerable to HIV is the cell population in the transformation zone of the cervix. HIV may also enter through cuts or abrasions to the vaginal wall. What is unclear is whether HIV can attach to intact, untraumatized vaginal walls. As previously described, HIV can enter the body by becoming attached to the dendritic or Langerhans cells, these and white blood cells are present in the mucosa of the rectum. The outer surface of a healthy vagina has a relatively thick stratified squamous epithelium (squamous is the type of cell; epithelia are the type of tissues which line body cavities that are open to the body surface).[43] These mature squamous cells contain few white cells and consequently are unlikely to be a site to which HIV can become attached.[44] However, some studies have suggested that HIV can enter directly through the vaginal wall. In particular, one study showed HIV-infection in a woman who did not have a cervix, and a study showed that animals which had undergone hysterectomy could be infected.[45] The question of how HIV is transmitted in vaginal sex has important implications for HIV prevention. If HIV enters principally through the cervix, then female-controlled barrier methods, such as cervical caps and diaphragms, will offer useful protection. Despite the practical importance of this, the question remains controversial, and most scientists refuse to be drawn on it, tending towards profound disinterest.

Although there is some support for the idea that HIV can infect directly through the vagina, many researchers would be inclined to agree that 'an intact vaginal wall gives some protection against infection'.[46] Others would go further, and claim that an intact vagina and cervix provides a very robust and normally effective barrier to HIV infection.[47] Certainly the walls of the vagina are remarkably strong in comparison to the rectum – after all, they are sufficiently elastic to act as a birth canal and allow an infant to pass through. However, many women do not always have an intact vaginal wall, although they will usually be unaware of this. Trauma is not uncommon during vaginal sex, and this can damage both cervix and vagina, making HIV acquisition more likely, since there is easy access to the lymphocytes in the blood. Trauma may be caused in a range of circumstances. Some women find that the friction of penetration can cause trauma if they do not have sufficient natural lubrication. This dryness may occur because the woman is post-menopausal, and many pre-menopausal women also experience fluctuations in lubrication with their menstrual cycle (and this is often perceived as an unmentionable, taboo topic). Of course, a woman may also lack lubrication simply because she is not aroused (also taboo), perhaps because she is coerced into sex. Bailey notes that young women may have little vaginal lubrication because early adolescent sex is 'a time of in-expertise and emotional ambivalence'. In some cultures 'dry sex' is customary, where lubrication is deliberately removed from the vagina (e.g. by using cloths, herbs or detergents).

Some women will experience trauma from 'rough sex' which is consensual, from penetration with sex toys, fingers or a fist, or even by using tampons (which can cause drying or abrasions). Women who have recently given birth, especially if there has been tearing, or even episiotomy, may also bleed during intercourse. For many women, trauma to the genitals is caused by non-consensual sex, which may involve violence, assault or rape. Bleeding and tearing can also occur if a woman has experienced infibulation, excision or clitoridectomy ('female circumcision'). Despite increased public health attention being paid to these practices, and the impact on women's health, there appear to be no peer-reviewed articles addressing HIV transmission concerns for women who have been 'circumcised'.[48] On top of the many awful health impacts for 'circumcised' women, the implications are likely to be significant for HIV: not only is bleeding during vaginal intercourse common, but if anal sex is substituted for vaginal sex (because the consequences of infibulation make vaginal sex too difficult), then women's vulnerability to HIV is enhanced. In addition, there may be HIV risks involved in carrying out the procedures where sterile instruments are not available (especially where the procedure is carried out covertly).[49]

The integrity of the female genital tract can also be affected by benign conditions (such as cysts on the cervix) and lesions caused by other STDs.[50] The presence of genital ulcer disease in women is clearly associated with HIV acquisition; this includes chancroid, syphilis, warts and genital herpes. Non-ulcerative STDs also increase the likelihood of acquiring HIV. This is because inflammation caused by these infections bring macrophages and lymphocytes to the surface, and the presence of these white blood cells in the genital tract increases vulnerability to HIV. This has been reported for several STDs, including bacterial vaginosis,[51] chlamydia, gonorrhoea and trichomoniasis. Trichomoniasis may also increase risk by causing thinning of the epithelium (the tissue lining the genital tract). There have been reports that defloration is associated with HIV transmission. In the European Study Group on Heterosexual Transmission of HIV (ESG) five women experienced vaginal sex for the first time with the HIV-infected man in the cohort; two of these five women acquired HIV.[52]

Older women, who are post-menopausal, may be at increased risk of acquiring HIV for two biological reasons. The hormonal changes of menopause create a thinning in the vaginal wall (suggesting that white cells are closer to the surface – as in the rectum) and also reduce vaginal lubrication. If a woman does not use additional lubrication she is more vulnerable to trauma with the friction of sex. Although little biological research has been carried out about this,[53] epidemiological studies do show a connection. For example, the European Study Group found that the women over forty-five years had a 3.9 times higher risk of acquiring HIV than the younger women.[54]

Pubescent girls also have an enhanced risk of acquiring HIV. There may be many socio-economic reasons for this. For example, younger women may be more vulnerable to coercive sex or rape; they may have less economic and practical access than older women to condoms; some may need to exchange sex for money, drugs or housing; in some societies they also tend to have sexually experienced, older male partners (who are more likely to be HIV-infected). In addition, there are important biological reasons why the genital tract could be more vulnerable to infection. What Bailey describes as 'the passage of adolescence' is a period of change when the body matures and a girl develops the capacity to conceive.[55] During the eighteen months to six years of sexual maturation, changes take place in the vagina and the transformation zone of the cervix. In the year before menarche (the onset of menstruation), the pH of the vagina becomes lower and squamous cells grow to cover the existing columnar cells, and offer protection from the increasing acidity of the vaginal environment. Columnar cells are vulnerable to attachment by sexually transmitted pathogens, and white cells are associated with the transformation zone. In the time before mature squamous cells form the outer surface of the vagina, these girls are at greater risk of infection if they get HIV-infected semen in their vaginas.

Changes are also happening to the cervix, and these are significant. The cervix, at the top of the vagina, forms a type of barrier to protect the uterus, with cervical mucus 'plugging' the entrance during most phases of the menstrual cycle. The mucus changes during the cycle to allow the cervix to function as a channel, enabling sperm to reach the ova (during ovulation), and menstrual fluids (and on occasions babies) to leave the womb. The transformation zone of the cervix is the place where different types of cell meet: mature squamous cells, and columnar and metaplastic cells. These latter cells are accompanied by a lot of white cells, including dendritic and Langerhans cells, and so this area is vulnerable to infections, including HIV. It is this part of the genital tract which appears to be most susceptible to HIV in all women. In adolescent women the vulnerability is greater because the transformation zone is itself in transformation. Initially the transformation zone is on the outside of the cervix (i.e. the part that faces into the vagina), but as women age it moves into the cervical canal, and so becomes more protected.[56]

Heightened vulnerability of the cervix is not only a concern for young women. The transformation zone becomes more exposed if a woman becomes pregnant, when the cervix shifts (everts) and more columnar cells become exposed. There is also some suggestion that the cervix may be rendered more vulnerable by oral contraceptive pills. Hormonal contraception may lead to cervical ectropion (where the transformation zone turns outwards), more candida and chlamydia infections, and 'oestrogens depress most, if not all, the major functions attributed to the cell mediated immune system'.[57] There is also concern that the IUD (intrauterine device) may cause trauma and disruption of the epithelial when it is inserted through the cervix, as well as generally causing heavier bleeding. It is not proven that there is an association between these contraceptive measures and HIV vulnerability, and this area needs further research.[58] Some research suggests that if the epithelium of the cervix is fully intact it will provide protection against HIV, although the paper describing this also showed that virulent strains of HIV would be able to infect these cells, and stated that 'a disruption in the natural barrier of the genital tract epithelium may enhance HIV transmission'.[59] The problem with translating such laboratory studies into real life is that it would be extremely difficult for a woman to know at any given time whether the natural barriers in her genital tract were disrupted or not.

Finally, the component of the genital tract which may have a bearing on whether a woman acquires HIV is her genital secretions. The cervical and vaginal secretions (mucus/fluids) present in a healthy vagina are naturally acidic, between pH 3 and 6, and it is known that HIV is deactivated at or below a pH of approximately 5.4 – that is, the vaginal environment has a natural virucidal quality. However, this pH is raised (i.e. becomes more alkaline) in the presence of semen, which itself is naturally alkaline. The vagina also becomes less acidic in the presence of infections (e.g. STDs), and during hormonal changes mediated by contraceptives, pregnancy and breast-feeding. In addition, the pH of vaginal fluids alters during the menstrual cycle, with fluids becoming more alkaline during menstruation.[60] It has also been suggested that these fluids become more alkaline during ovulation.[61] I have not located scientific papers referring to this although it would make sense (it would enhance the likelihood of the sperm reaching the ovum). This may suggest why the likelihood of a woman acquiring HIV varies with her menstrual cycle (a few studies have suggested that she is more vulnerable if she has vaginal sex during her period, although these studies may be confusing the risks to men and to women). The acidity of the vagina is likely to reduce the viability of HIV in semen, and so it could be more infectious if the vagina is alkaline before the ejaculation of semen.[62] This is probably more important in respect of HIV-positive women and their liability to transmit HIV, and is discussed in the next chapter.

Some reports have documented women who became infected from having unprotected vaginal sex just once with a man infected with HIV.[63] Although there are several reports of unique infection, it is also clear that repeated exposure to HIV heightens the risk of acquiring HIV. This is not because of a dose response, but rather due to repeated unprotected sex heightening the chance of having sex when the situation is most favourable to transmission (e.g. when he has high viral load). The ESG calculates that a woman who has unprotected sex with an HIV-infected man less than ten times has a 10 per cent chance of becoming infected, and this rises to 23 per cent if they have unprotected sex more than 1447 times. (Unfortunately they do not state what kind of sex, and so I assume they mean vaginal.) Yet the chance from a single unprotected encounter is calculated at just 0.054 per cent.[64] In reality this statistic is irrelevant, since it says nothing about the length of intercourse, frequency of ejaculation, infectivity of the virus, etc.

The viral load of an infected person (which is linked to the stage of illness) appears to be the single most important factor influencing HIV transmission in any circumstance. All of the 'heterosexual' cohorts report associations between women acquiring HIV and unprotected vaginal sex with a man who has AIDS or very low CD4 cell counts, although describing the exact risks is complicated by the different ways of defining stages of disease progression.

Over four years, beginning in March 1987, 556 HIV-positive men and women (the index partners) and their 'heterosexual' partners were recruited to the ESG at centres in eight European countries. Initial reports considered how many of the female partners of 400 HIV-positive men had been infected, and how. Eighty-two women acquired HIV from their index partner, and there was a relatively high rate of HIV acquisition, because most infections (all but seven) happened before the couples joined the cohort, when many may not have been aware of a risk.

The ESG initially calculated a 5.4-fold increased risk to women if the man has what they call 'full-blown AIDS' (based upon 42 women [out of 155] who seroconverted) whereas a study of the sexual partners of drug users in New York City found a far greater difference: if the man had AIDS or ARC (AIDS-Related Complex) the risk was 16.8 times greater.[65] In this study there were 72 women who became infected (out of 142 partners of HIV-infected men), and this may give us better information since the epidemic is older in the USA than in Europe (so there are more men who are ill). In 1992 the ESG calculated a 2.7 times greater risk of transmission from a man described as 'in an advanced stage of HIV infection', and the most recent paper suggests an overall (not gender-specific) rate of 48.7 per cent if the index partner has AIDS (or CD4s < 200), compared with 7.8 per cent if she or he is asymptomatic, or has CD4s > 200.[66] These findings are clearly impacted by the low level of seroconversions – just eight women and four men acquired HIV during the four years of the study.

Safer behaviour has been adopted by the majority of couples in cohorts like the ESG, but there are other theories about why cohorts show low levels of transmission, and these concern the changing nature of the infectivity of the virus. Jacquez, Koopman and their colleagues have examined a vast range of discordant couple cohorts, and state that 'risk depends on whether or not sex acts occurred during a highly infectious period. . . . The findings of very low transmission probabilities in discordant partner studies are readily explained if most of the infected partners are antibody-positive and symptom-free, so that the infected partners are in the long asymptomatic phase of low infectiousness'[67] This group have assessed a number of mathematical models and a range of co-factors which may explain the curve of the epidemic, and their conclusion is that viraemia during primary infection and as disease progresses are the most important factors. This is a compelling theory which makes good empirical sense, both explaining why not all sexual partners acquire HIV, and also alerting as to how swiftly this may change. For example, cohorts of HIV-positive men with haemophilia have shown very low rates of transmission to their wives and girlfriends, even when condoms have not been used. One study published in 1988 followed thirteen HIV-positive men with haemophilia and their regular female partners for the last three years. During the study the researchers estimated that the couples had vaginal sex a total of 3000 times (but no anal sex), and condoms were used only 1000 times. None of the women acquired HIV.[68] This can easily be explained by factoring in the time consideration: men with haemophilia were infected between 1980 and 1985, and with an asymptomatic phase of at least ten years, most men will only begin to express high levels of virus again in the 1990s. One of the problems with universal messages which pretend that every act of intercourse has an equal risk is that people affected by HIV know this is not true. One doctor recounts that he sees male partners of HIV-positive women who reject condom use because their friends (who also have HIV-positive girlfriends) have not seroconverted[69] – this may well be just a matter of time and, as with primary infection, the re-emergence of viraemia is invisible in an asymptomatic person with HIV.

In addition to the critical area of viral load, there are other proven correlations. One which is well-reported is the link between having another STD, especially one which causes ulcers, and risks of acquiring HIV. The ESG's first paper suggested that a history of STDs in the past five years creates a 3.1-fold increase in risk for women.[70] A later analysis described the differences according to whether the STD caused ulcers, with a risk of 12.8 per cent if neither partner had a STD, 33.3 per cent if one had a non-ulcerative

STD, and 40 per cent if there was an ulcerative STD.[71] Unfortunately, these rates are not gender-specific (i.e. it refers to either acquisition by, or transmission from, a woman) nor are they act-specific (it appears to refer to unprotected anal or vaginal sex). Another definitive risk for women is bleeding during sex. Seidlin found this increased the overall chance of women becoming infected 4.9-fold: 69.2 per cent of women who bled acquired HIV, compared with 41 per cent of the women who had no bleeding during sex.[72]

Case studies have also reported women who acquired HIV from vaginal sex in 'low-risk' circumstances (i.e. with no other co-factors such as the man having AIDS, other STDs, or the woman bleeding during sex).[73] Thus, although the risk in such situations is technically lower, it is still high enough to be a risk that I would not want to take. Finally, although there is concern about HIV being present in pre-cum, the ESG found that HIV was not transmitted if the HIV-infected man withdrew before ejaculation.[74] *Coitus interruptus* is a notoriously poor contraceptive measure, and cannot be recommended as anything more than a theoretical HIV-prevention strategy (the intention to withdraw is all very well, but not always achieved).

• *Anal sex*

Anal sex is used here to mean penetration of the anus by a penis, which may include the ejaculation of semen. Some people will use the term 'anal sex' to refer to other activities (such as using fingers, tongues or sex toys in the anus – these are discussed in the next chapter) and terminology can often become confusing. This is one reason why many AIDS workers use the term 'fucking' to be precise about the activity which is reported to have the highest risk of HIV transmission (when a condom/femidom and lubricant are not used). In turn this can become confusing since fucking also refers to vaginal sex (penetration of the vagina by a penis) – a confusion that led one edition of the *National AIDS Manual* to refer to anal fucking and vaginal screwing. Such pedantry is unlikely to be helpful, but it should underscore the importance of precision when communicating HIV-prevention messages.

Anal sex is often neglected in messages which address women (or 'heterosexuals'). The activity is not infrequently referred to as 'gay sex', despite the fact that it is well known as a pleasurable and contraceptive activity for many women. In the Sexual Lifestyles survey, 12.9 per cent of British women claim to have tried this activity and 5.9 per cent of all women interviewed had anal sex in the last year. Anal sex was reported more frequently by younger women (aged sixteen to twenty-four), women who were in stable relationships (married or cohabiting) and those who had more sexual partners. For example, anal sex had been tried by 27 per cent of the women who had sex with more than ten men in the last five years. However, anal sex is stigmatized (and was illegal for women and men at the time of the Sexual Lifestyle interviews) and the researchers believe that it was probably under-reported.[75]

There have been some criticisms of the methodology of the Sexual Lifestyles survey, and there are indications that the prevalence of anal sex has been radically underestimated. This could be due to imbalances with sampling, and in particular the study's sample may not be representative of people currently most vulnerable to HIV. Studies of discordant male–female couples (where one person is HIV-positive) record prevalence rates for anal sex between 12 per cent and 45 per cent – far higher than Sexual Lifestyles reports. For example, the ESG found that 12 per cent of 378 couples had anal sex at least once.[76] The most reliable American cohort of 379 couples (conducted by Nancy Padian) shows that 37 per cent of the women partners of HIV-positive men had anal sex with that man, as did 36 per cent of the men whose female partner was HIV-positive.[77] Data from these and other discordant couple studies either show that Sexual Lifestyles have underestimated the prevalence of anal sex among the whole population, or that the sub-group of HIV-positive people are more likely to have anal sex than HIV-negative people. It may be that men whose behaviour is bisexual (and who consequently have higher rates of HIV than entirely heterosexual men) are more likely to have anal sex with women, but there are no published data to prove this. A survey of 1000 British men, who had sex with both women and men in the last year, found that 44.4 per cent of these men had anal sex with a woman during that time, and 34.2 per cent had anal sex with both women and men in that year.[78] This suggests quite powerfully that the level of HIV risk to women from anal sex is far higher than that suggested by the Sexual Lifestyles survey.

Of all sexual practices, anal fucking is assumed to be the most risky for HIV (and indeed for several other STDs, such as gonorrhoea). As described earlier, for transmission to occur, the virus has to infect the lymphocytes which are found in the blood.[79] Anal sex is an efficient mode of transmission because the mucous membrane offers an easy route for the virus to reach these cells. It is also particularly risky because the mucosa of the rectum is very delicate. The rectum can quite easily be damaged during anal sex, through the friction of fucking – in particular because the anus does not lubricate as extensively as the vagina. Trauma (i.e. cuts or abrasions) can also be caused by using fingers, sex toys or a fist before fucking, or because of medical problems (like piles, warts, herpes, or lesions caused by STDs). It is often assumed that HIV transmission occurs in anal sex because the tissues of the rectum are damaged and there is bleeding. There is very little information about the realities of anal penetration. It may be that the (frequent) references to anal trauma refer principally to defloration. That is, fucking a virgin anus causes trauma, as does fucking a virgin vagina. When a (wo)man frequently has anal sex, trauma and damage may be uncommon.[80] Although cuts or tears in the rectum will increase the risk of a woman acquiring HIV, dendritic cells and Langerhans cells are actually present on the surface of the rectal mucosa, and consequently there is a direct vulnerability to HIV through CD4 receptors on these cells. The concentration of white blood cells (which increases vulnerability to infection by HIV) increases when a woman has STDs, but infection is also common in the absence of any additional factors.

Unprotected anal sex with HIV-infected men is assumed to be the most risky activity, and King states, 'In virtually every instance, gay men who become infected with HIV today report having had unprotected anal sex.'[81] However, attempts to establish the precise risks of receptive anal sex are complicated. Few women who have anal sex never have vaginal sex, and most gay men have both receptive and insertive sex (i.e. they both fuck and get fucked – indeed, it is this fact that may well account for the initial rapid spread of HIV in gay communities).[82] Most cohort studies of gay men find that rates of HIV are higher among men who have had receptive anal sex (been fucked) than those who have only practised insertive sex (fucking), although this is not to suggest that 'insertive' anal sex is risk free.

Studies of women and men have found that women who have anal sex as well as vaginal sex are more likely to acquire HIV than those who only have vaginal sex. I am not aware of any study where women have had only anal sex with their HIV-positive male partner, but anal sex does seem to be an efficient way of increasing the risks inherent in vaginal sex. It may be that the increased risk relates to choice of partner (e.g. bisexual men) rather than the choice of act. The study of the sexual partners of HIV-infected drug users in New York City found that women who had anal and vaginal sex with an HIV-positive man were 10.8 times more likely to acquire the virus than women who only had vaginal sex. Only 33 of the 73 women who acquired HIV had anal sex, so this was by no means the only possible mode of transmission. Of the 92 women who did not have anal sex (but did have vaginal sex) with their HIV-positive male partner, 52 remained HIV-negative; by contrast, just 17 of the 50 women who had both anal and vaginal sex remained HIV-negative.[83] However, these numbers are too small for definitive conclusions to be drawn.

The ESG initially calculated that women who had both anal and vaginal sex were 5.1 times more likely to be infected than women who only had vaginal sex (42 women had both anal and vaginal sex with the index).[84] Two years later, the ESG measured the numbers of new infections and the sexual practices among the couples in the cohort. Their analysis found a smaller risk for anal sex: 27.8 per cent for women who had both unprotected anal *and* vaginal sex, compared with 11.7 per cent for just vaginal sex. However, this is linked to the changing nature of the study: just eight women were still having unprotected anal and vaginal sex with their HIV-positive male partners (of whom two became infected) and 65 were having unprotected vaginal sex, six of whom seroconverted.[85] Once people are enrolled in cohorts (which involve HIV testing and interviews every six months) their knowledge of HIV and motivation for safer sex are likely to increase. Consequently, safer behaviour is common and new infections tend to be rare, so that broad conclusions about infectivity cannot be drawn.

It can be difficult to assess the risks of different activities because many people do more than one of them. Women who become infected (e.g. in the ESG) and have had both anal and vaginal sex are assumed to have acquired HIV from the anal sex. This is not just intuition, since researchers carry out 'multivariate analysis' (where numbers are large enough) and this shows that women who have anal and vaginal sex have an additional risk. If anal and vaginal sex were equivalent risks then there should not be a higher rate for the women who have both. The intrinsic risks of anal sex vary according to the man's infectivity and Jacquez assigns relative risks to the different stages of disease and suggests that the changing risks from one incident of (presumably receptive) anal sex can be summarized thus:[86]

Disease stage	Percentage	Max. probability
Primary infection	5% – 30%	3 in 10
Asymptomatic HIV+	0.01% – 0.1%	1 in 1000
Symptomatic HIV+ CD4s < 400	0.1% – 1%	1 in 100
AIDS	2%	1 in 50

• Fellatio (oral sex)

In 1986 Norman Fowler, then Secretary of State for Social Services, allegedly asked a meeting preparing the UK government's first AIDS campaign, 'Oral sex? Do we know how many people *do* this sort of thing?'[87] If his government had not withdrawn funding from the Sexual Lifestyles survey, he might have found out a little sooner. The answer that emerged was 'the majority'. The data on fellatio (the sucking or licking of a man's penis, which may lead to ejaculation) suggest that this is a common part of many women's sexual lives: 64 per cent of women had ever given oral sex (sucked a man), and 44 per cent had done so in the last year. Wellings states that 'Some experience of either cunnilingus or fellatio was reported by 75.2% of men and 69.2% of women, while 24.5% of men and 19.9% of women reported cunnilingus or fellatio in the last week.' Both women and men reported slightly more cunnilingus (licking the vulva and clitoris) than fellatio, and any oral sex was far more likely in younger women and men: over 60 per cent of people aged eighteen to forty-four had oral sex in the last year, but this was the case for just 35 per cent of those aged forty-five to fifty-nine. Oral sex certainly seems to be becoming more frequent: of the interviewees aged sixteen to twenty-four who had experience of vaginal sex, 85 per cent also reported oral sex, and 79 per cent had oral sex in the last year.[88]

Probably the most confusion about HIV transmission concerns oral sex. This section will consider fellatio because there is absolutely no risk to a woman if an HIV-infected man licks her (there is insufficient HIV in saliva to cause infection[89]) and HIV risks of cunnilingus are discussed in the next chapter. Although semen is a very efficient vehicle for HIV, ingestion of infected fluids is an inefficient route of HIV transmission, because the lining of the mouth is relatively strong, saliva has protective qualities, and these are backed up further by gastric fluids. The mucosa of the female genital tract is more robust than the mucosa of the anus, and intact mucosa in the mouth is even more protective. In his inimitable (offensive) way, Fumento describes this in terms of the 'natural' functions he affords different orifices:

> The anus is not made to take anything in, while the vagina is made to occasionally receive the male organ. But mouths are built to take in regularly all manner of things, hot and cold, hard and soft, animate, formerly animate and never previously animate.'[90]

It is perhaps for theologians to debate whether God really designed humans so that oral sex would be the privileged, safest, sexual activity. However, this does at least highlight the intuitive fact that most of us regularly introduce things into our mouths that could make us sick, but do not. In terms of HIV, this is more than intuitive – there are very few white blood cells present on the surface of mucous membranes of the mouth or throat.

The protective capacity of the oral cavity is not only due to the mucosa. Saliva and gastric juices (where the mouth's contents are ingested) provide a second line of defence which makes the mouth a less vulnerable site. Saliva has qualities that some have described as antiseptic, and a protein in saliva has been identified which is able to protect against HIV. McNeely has identified a protein called secretory leukocyte protease inhibitor (SLPI) – a naturally occurring protease inhibitor[91] – that is able to stop HIV from entering lymphocytes. SLPI (attractively pronounced 'slippy') seems to protect against HIV by binding to the white blood cells, and preventing the virus from causing infection. Curiously SLPI does not react with CD4 – the receptor on the surface of white blood cells that attaches to HIV – but with another, unidentified molecule.[92] It is not yet known what quantities of SLPI are necessary to deactivate quantities of HIV which may be present in semen (or vaginal and menstrual fluids). If infected fluids were to reach the stomach, it is assumed that the highly acidic gastro-intestinal juices would deactivate HIV (as HIV cannot survive at a pH below 5.4).

Although the biology suggests that the mouth is a very poor site of entry for HIV, it does not render transmission by this route impossible. The integrity of the mouth's lining may often be damaged, with gums bleeding (especially after brushing teeth), and ulcers and cuts on the surfaces of the tongue, cheeks and other mucosa. Lips may also have cuts or lesions, e.g. cold sores (this may not be relevant if ejaculation takes place within the mouth, but could be pertinent in respect of transmission from e.g. vaginal fluids). As with other surfaces, cuts and abrasions in the mouth will inevitably enhance the likelihood of HIV being acquired. Inflammation of the throat could also be a point of entry, and this can arise from throat infections, allergies, smoking or STDs (e.g. gonorrhoea).[93] Alcorn points out, however, that 'continuous swallowing or peristalsis ensures that anything ingested will be in contact with damaged tissue for only a short time'.[94] Some people worry about the potential for HIV to enter the bloodstream through stomach ulcers, but it does seem unlikely that HIV would still be infectious at this point, having been exposed to saliva for an extended period of time and then encountering acidic gastric juices.

Sadly, heterosexual cohorts offer little information about any HIV risks of oral sex. This is principally because other activities provide a masking effect, and few women only suck. Some cohorts suggested a link between the people who acquired HIV and people who had oral sex. However, on closer analysis it became apparent that this is because there is a consistent link between having anal sex and oral sex. For example, Fischl (a well-known clinical researcher) suggested that oral sex might be a risk by a rather simplistic reading of epidemiological data. She found higher rates of HIV among the women who had both vaginal and oral sex compared with women who only had vaginal sex.[95] Yet this is easily explained by the fact that all of the women in her study who had anal sex also had oral sex (although the opposite was not true). The link between oral and anal sex was also identified in the Sexual Lifestyles survey: of the men and women who had anal sex in the month before interview, nearly 80 per cent had also had oral sex during that time.[96] This highlights the importance of a critical reading of scientific studies. The technique of multivariate analysis assesses which of a number of potentially significant factors are most common among people who seroconvert. So, for example, the ESG found that oral sex was significant in a univariate analysis, but not so in the multivariate analysis 'because of a strong association between oral and anal sex'.[97] For Fischl (or the ESG) to argue that oral sex was risky would have implied that fellatio was more risky than *anal* sex.[98] Without the balance of biological probabilities of transmission, one can reach conclusions which illustrate more about the lifestyles of people who engage in risky behaviour than which *is* the risky behaviour. So, for example, several studies suggest that poppers (amyl nitrate) may have an impact upon the acquisition of HIV. Does this mean: a) poppers are responsible for HIV transmission; or b) people use poppers to relax the muscles in the rectum before anal sex, which is responsible for HIV transmission?

Despite the problems of masking in cohorts, the fact that the majority of people in cohorts have adopted safer behaviour does give some useful information. The 1994 paper from the ESG describes that there was no HIV transmission among '39 partners who had unprotected oral sex while consistently using condoms during vaginal intercourse'.[99] Since this lumps together both male and female index partners, clearer information about fellatio comes from gay men's studies. Gay men who do not fuck have always been a part of cohorts, and information about these men provides powerful evidence about the low risk of oral HIV transmission. King reviews evidence from cohorts in detail,[100] and shows that the principal cohorts of gay men in the USA, Canada, Australia and the UK conclude that oral sex 'carries very little or no risk for HIV transmission'.[101] These findings are buoyed up by the fact that, since the emergence of AIDS, many gay men have abandoned unprotected anal sex in favour of sucking (for example, in Project Sigma's cohort of British gay men, 60 per cent reported oral sex in 1988 and this went up to 75 per cent in 1991[102]). Yet rates of HIV transmission among gay men have been falling, and this would be extremely unlikely if oral sex was an efficient means of transmission. It is also significant that Hepatitis B virus does not appear to have been transmitted by oral sex, despite the fact that this virus is 8.6-times more likely than HIV to be transmitted among gay men.[103]

This all looks very good news, but unfortunately there are some reports of men and women who have acquired HIV from sucking. There have been fourteen pieces of research which indicate that fellatio may have been responsible for HIV transmission, although five of these include reports which have subsequently been shown to be false.[104] It is worth dwelling briefly on examples where reports have been shown to be false as this indicates why assessing the risk from oral sex is so difficult. A Dutch cohort of 102 HIV-positive gay men (for whom the time of infection was known) completed a questionnaire and face-to-face interviews about their sexual activities during the year before they seroconverted. On the questionnaire, twenty men said they had not had anal sex, and appeared to have been infected through oral sex. However, during the interview eleven of these men said they had been fucked, and five that they had fucked. Only one man, out of 82, who said he had been fucked before seroconverting contradicted his statement at interview. Four of these 102 seroconverters may therefore have acquired HIV from fellatio, but the study also highlighted that 'a psychological barrier in reporting the practice of anogenital receptive intercourse may lead to an overestimation of the [orogenital] transmission rate'.[105]

Alcorn suggests four reasons why men and women may not report unprotected anal intercourse:

> Shame at failure to practise safer sex; 'forgetting' in order to blot out the memory of risky sexual activity; desire to please researchers by demonstrating an adherence to safer sex guidelines; refusal to acknowledge taboo sexual practices, i.e. anal intercourse.[106]

This is not to suggest that people necessarily 'lie' or deliberately intend to mislead, but rather that the stigmatization of unprotected sex is huge within communities most vulnerable to acquiring HIV. At a conference to mark the tenth anniversary of AIDES (the French national ASO) a young volunteer with their gay men's health education group explained the difficulties he had in explaining to his peers that he was infected with HIV after becoming involved in HIV-prevention work. Olivier explained how he considered telling people that a condom had broken, because the reactions of his friends and colleagues were so condemnatory when he told them he seroconverted just six months ago. Ultimately he stated that despite knowing all the information, and being actively involved in HIV-prevention work, he still got fucked without a condom because 'sexuality isn't just a technique'.[107] In the USA, there have recently been a number of anecdotal reports claiming HIV infection from fellatio. It is perhaps telling that many of these reports come from men described as 'well-known activists'[108] – would it be possible for them publicly to acknowledge fucking without a condom?

Although some reports of HIV being transmitted by fellatio are masking more risky activities, there do seem to be a small number of women and men who have acquired HIV from getting semen in their mouths. One study described two women who apparently had no risk factors other than oral sex with a man with HIV: one man was in the late stages of HIV disease and was p24 antigen positive (so he had high viral load); the other man had herpes and bleeding lesions on his penis (hardly an appealing prospect).[109]

Another study reported that two gay men had previously tested HIV-negative and reported only oral sex with ejaculation as a risk to explain how they acquired HIV. Both men had a history of allergies which could have caused inflammation in the throat. However, the researchers were wary stating that the men may have concealed more risky behaviour or even had false positive tests.[110] Another study suggested that oral sex to ejaculation was the route of HIV transmission to two men who had gum disease.[111]

Case reports and anecdotes are extremely attractive since they personalize the issue and appear to reflect real life in a way that cohorts, by their very scale and scientific rigour, can not. Yet case reports are also the most unreliable form of reporting, and often appear in medical journals as letters, rather than as articles which are peer-reviewed. King points out that 'these isolated cases often attract attention which is out of all proportion to their significance, while the more reliable conclusions from large cohort studies are overlooked.'[112] Yet there are apparently reliable reports of a total of seventeen men and two women acquiring HIV from fellatio. This activity is clearly a low risk. No cases of transmission from fellatio have been recorded when ejaculation did not occur.

Transmission only appears to be possible in certain defined situations, that is when a woman is vulnerable because she has poor oral health and she gets semen in her mouth (there are no reliable reports where ejaculation does not happen) from an HIV-infected man who is highly infectious. The infectivity is likely to be the most important factor. As we have seen, viral load is highest during primary infection (immediately after he acquires HIV) and in the late stages of illness. The estimates offered by one group of researchers suggest that the risk of transmission from fellatio is generally no more than three in 50,000, but that during primary infection oral sex becomes 523 times more risky, rising to as high as one in thirty. The work from this group also suggests that the risks of oral HIV transmission from men who are symptomatic or have AIDS is still low: around three in 5000 for men with CD4 cell counts less than 400, and three in 2500 for men who have developed AIDS.[113] Therefore, there may be times when some women will want to take precautions for oral sex, such as not getting semen in their mouths from partners who develop AIDS.

• *Other sex*

As should already be apparent, HIV is not automatically transmitted even through the most intimate acts. When the most infectious fluid, semen, contacts the most vulnerable site of entry (e.g. the rectum) HIV has its best chance, but transmission is still not inevitable. Despite this, many women will have concerns about other activities, especially if they are in sexual relationships with men (or women) they know to be HIV-positive. It is impossible to list every sexual activity every woman enjoys (or at least does), but the *AIDS Reference Manual* is a reliable and comprehensive source for up-to-date information on a wide range of sexual practices and their HIV risks. The information already provided on the infectivity of fluids, and the vulnerability of different sites of entry, should be sufficient to estimate the efficiency of HIV transmission from sexual activities other than fucking and sucking.

A woman is most likely to acquire HIV from getting infected semen in her vagina (such that it can reach her cervix) or her anus. Every other act is definitely safer. Hesitation at stating that all other activities are *safe* is purely due to the scientific caution that bedevils such a new area.

It has always been known, for example, that kissing does not transmit HIV and the discovery of SLPI adds additional reassurance. Yet early panics and individual angst have sustained some fear of kissing, and maybe this is code for fear of intimacy with people with HIV. For some people, extreme situations (like AIDS) demand extreme measures (like giving up sex), even where these are absolutely not warranted by scientific fact.

Scientific information about sex is extremely reassuring: HIV is not especially infectious. Knowledge about sexual transmission needs then to be contextualized in epidemiological data about the ever-increasing reach of this disease. Even though very few sexual activities are efficient viral transmitters, and despite the small risks with individual acts, HIV has established itself remarkably quickly: many of those acts are repeated on a regular basis, and many people still resist the simple measures necessary for protection. The good news that HIV is not readily transmitted should not become a rationale for sinking into complacency and avoiding safer sex.

Journalist Steve Connor comments that HIV 'itself is not particularly infectious, but its delayed action combined with its transmission during the most compulsive human activity can cause the complacency and denial that makes it such a great threat'.[114]

Notes

1. Quoted in S. Garfield, *The End of Innocence: Britain in the Time of AIDS*, Faber & Faber, London, 1994, p. 192.
2. Statement to the 'All Party Parliamentary Group on AIDS' meeting on Women & AIDS, House of Commons, London, March 1994. Joanne is one of the co-ordinators of the ICW (International Community of Women Living with HIV/AIDS).
3. This was part of the strapline to the UK government's initial poster campaign from 1986-7; quoted in Garfield, *op. cit.*, p. 117.
4. The *AIDS Reference Manual* is edited by Keith Alcorn and published by NAM Publications. This is updated regularly as new research on HIV is presented.
5. 'Pass Notes No. 601: DNA', *Guardian*, 12 April 1995.
6. R. Berkowitz and M. Callen, *How to Have Sex in an Epidemic: One Approach*, News from the Front Publications, New York, 1983.
7. E. King, *Safety in Numbers*, Cassell, London, 1993, pp. 99–114; K. Alcorn (ed.), *AIDS Reference Manual*, January 1995, pp. 91–5.
8. For example, the 'Heterosexual Transmission of HIV-1' cohort in Scotland was closed after four years because there were 'not enough' seroconversions (new HIV infections). These cohorts need to be sustained over time to have any useful information, since it is entirely possible that safer behaviour will not be sustained, and the infectivity of the index cases will alter. Moreover, if protected intercourse really was universal in the cohort, useful information could be gleaned about the status of 'low-risk' activities, like oral sex.

   (These ethical concerns are also a major issue for the design of primary vaccination studies, including microbicidal research. Unethical prospective studies could give such powerful information that the temptation exists to run them. Researchers have a tendency to fall prey to this temptation in the developing world more readily than in their own industrialized countries.)
9. H. Mikkelsen, Presentation to 'AIDS Hotlines for Countries of Central and Eastern Europe', WHO Workshop, Warsaw, 13–16 December 1991.
10. The research that might get closer to answering real-life questions could never be approved for practical and ethical reasons. Such research might monitor (say) a number of HIV-positive men and their HIV-negative female partners and divide them into sub-groups

who would restrict themselves to a given sexual practice under certain (unprotected) conditions.

11. J. W. Ward, 'The natural history of transfusion-associated infection with human immunodeficiency virus', *NEJM*, 321:14 (1989), pp. 947–52, cited in Alcorn, *op. cit.*, p. 78.

12. Alcorn, *op. cit.*, pp. 78, 97, referencing D. D. Ho *et al.*, 'Quantitation of human immunodeficiency virus type 1 in the blood of infected persons', *NEJM*, 321:1621–5 (1989); J. A. Levy, 'Pathogenesis of human immunodeficiency virus infection', *Microbiological Reviews*, 57, pp. 185–289 (1993).

13. N. Gill *et al.*, *Occupational Transmission of HIV: Summary of Published Reports*, May 1992, PHLS AIDS Unit, CDSC, Colindale. See also C. Becker *et al.*, 'Occupational infection with HIV', *Annals of Internal Medicine*, 110:8, pp. 653–6 (1989).

14. M. D. Gaughwin *et al.*, 'Bloody needles: the volume of blood transferred in simulations of needlestick injuries', *AIDS*, 5:8, pp. 1025–7 (1991).

15. Mike Bailey, personal communication.

16. P. Brown, 'HIV and the straight sex connection', *New Scientist*, 5 June 1993, p. 11.

17. Scientists are sexual beings themselves, and appear to be embarrassed by issues which have a personal dimension. This is intensified by the fact that most are conservative, middle-class, white, heterosexual, Anglo-Saxon males. Mike Bailey, personal communication.

18. R. Gorna, 'Everything you always wanted to know about oral sex . . . but you won't find it here', *World AIDS News: The Newspaper of the Harvard-Amsterdam Conference*, 20 July 1992, pp. 4–5 ; personal communications when researching the article.

19. F. Stewart, 24 February 1995, closing speech to 'HIV Infection in Women: Setting a New Agenda' conference, Washington, DC, 1995. Dr Stewart is Deputy Assistant Secretary for Population Affairs at the US Department of Health and Human Services.

20. Apparently many callers to THT's Helpline are unaware of the importance of one person being infected for transmission to occur. Debbie Vowles, personal communication.

21. HIV is also in sufficient quantities for transmission in amniotic fluid, cerebrospinal fluid and transplants of tissues, organs, skin and bone marrow. These only pose a (theoretical) risk for healthcare workers carrying out invasive procedures, and transplant recipients. In the UK, all donors of body fluids or parts are tested for HIV.

22. 'Mechanisms of transmission from men to women', *AIDS Newsletter*, Bureau of Hygiene and Tropical Medicine, 1992, 7(12), p. 14, reporting a state-of-the-art review by Deborah Anderson at the VIII International Conference on AIDS.

23. Alcorn, *op. cit.*, p. 78. Anecdotal reports suggest that this is often an underestimate.

24. J. Pudney *et al.*, 'Pre-ejaculatory fluid as potential vector for sexual transmission of HIV-1', *Lancet*, 340:8833, p. 1470 (1992). The potential for transmission seems unlikely given the findings that withdrawal before ejaculation seemed to protect women from infection (I. de Vincenzi *et al.*, 'A longitudinal study of human immunodeficiency virus transmission by heterosexual partners', *NEJM*, 1994, 331: 6, pp. 341–6). However, this referred to vaginal sex, and the same effect may not be seen with the more delicate walls of the rectum. One would expect the chance of transmission to be greater with high viral load. I am not aware of any studies that would clarify this further.

25. O. Bagasra *et al.*, 'Interaction of human immunodeficiency virus with human sperm *in vitro*', *JAIDS*, 1988, 1(5), pp. 431–5; E. Dussaix *et al.*, 'Spermatozoa as potential carriers of HIV', *Res. Virol.*, 1993, 144(6), pp. 487–95.

26. O. Bagasra *et al.*, 'Detection of HIV-1 proviral DNA in sperm from HIV-1 infected men', *AIDS*, 1994, 8(12), pp. 1669–74.

27. J. H. Mermin *et al.*, 'Detection of human immunodeficiency virus DNA and RNA in semen by the polymerase chain reaction', *Journal of Infectious Diseases*, 1991, 164 (4), pp. 769–72.

28. M. P. O'Leary 'Eliminating HIV from seminal fluid', *JAMA*, 25 March 1992, 267(12), p. 1677; D. J. Anderson *et al.*, 'White blood cells and HIV-1 in semen from vasectomized seropositive men', *Lancet*, 31 August 1991, 338, pp. 573–4.

29. E. Dussaix *et al.*, *op. cit.*

30. A. E. Semprini *et al.*, 'Insemination of HIV-negative women with processed semen of HIV-positive partners', *Lancet*, 340: 1317–19 (1992); also A. E. Semprini *et al.*, 'Reproductive counselling and assistance to HIV-discordant couples', IX International Conference on AIDS, Berlin, July 1993, Abstract WS-B32-2.

It is unclear whether such techniques will ever be made available to couples in the UK. The willingness of a hospital in Birmingham to offer *in-vitro* fertilization treatment to an HIV-positive man and his HIV-negative wife was greeted with condemnation by many sectors of the media, and headlines such as 'NHS storm over AIDS man's baby' and 'AIDS rotter Roy wants test-tube baby' (both *Sunday Express*, 22 August 1993).

31. J. Bignall, 'News: HIV infection from donor semen', *Lancet*, 345, 18 March 1995, p. 719.

32. Zena Stein MD, 23 February 1995, statement at 'HIV Infection in Women: Setting a New Agenda' conference. Stein – and her colleague Anke Ehrhardt at the HIV Center, Columbia University, New York

– have been pursuing this question vigorously; it has major implications for the development of a non-contraceptive microbicide.

33. See, for example: M. Laga, 'Interactions between STDs and HIV infection', Transcript 28, August 1992; M. Laga *et al.*, 'Non-ulcerative sexually transmitted diseases as risk factors for HIV-1 transmission in women: results from a cohort study', *AIDS*, 7:1, January 1993, 7: 95–102; de Vincenzi *et al.*, *op. cit.*

34. D. D. Ho *et al.*, 'Rapid turnover of plasma virions and CD4 lymphocytes in HIV-1 infection', *Nature*, 373 (6510), pp. 117-26, 12 January 1995.

35. K. A. Hamed *et al.*, 'Detection of human immunodeficiency virus type 1 in semen: effects of disease stage and nucleoside therapy', *Journal of Infectious Disease*, April 1993, 167, pp. 798–802.

36. J. S. Koopman *et al.*, 'HIV transmission probabilities for oral and anal sex by stage of infection', PoC 4101, VIII International Conference on AIDS, Amsterdam, 19–24 July 1992; J. A. Jacquez *et al.*, 'Role of the primary infection in epidemics of HIV infection in gay cohorts', *JAIDS*, 1994, 7, pp. 1169–84. I am indebted to Edward King and Keith Alcorn for bringing these important papers to my attention.

37. *Ibid.* (Jacquez), Figure 4, p. 1174, based upon I. M. Longini Jr *et al.*, 'The dynamics of CD-4+ T-lymphocyte decline in HIV-infected individuals: a Markov modelling approach', *JAIDS*, 1991 (4), pp. 1141-7.

38. Koopman *et al.*, *op. cit.*

39. *Ibid.*

40. P. L. Vernazza, 'Detection and biologic characterization of infectious HIV-1 in semen of seropositive men', *AIDS*, 8:9, pp. 1325–9 (1994), cited in Alcorn, *op. cit.*, p. 78.

41. Hamed, *op. cit.*; D. J. Anderson *et al.*, 'Effects of disease stage and zidovudine therapy on the detection of human immunodeficiency virus type 1 in semen', *JAMA*, 267, pp. 2769–74 (1992); T. R. O'Brien, 'Inverse association between zidovudine therapy and the isolation of HIV in the semen of HIV-positive men', *Seventh International Conference on AIDS*, Abstract No. MC 3092 (1991) – cited by Alcorn, *op. cit.*, pp. 78–9.

42. R. Murley, *Daily Mail*, 7 November 1989, p. 6, quoted by R. McGrath in V. Harwood *et al.* (eds), *Pleasure Principles: Politics, Sexuality and Ethics*, Lawrence & Wishart, London, 1993. A fine example of this displacement was the reaction of the media to the discovery that a young man with HIV and haemophilia (whom the media had vilified for allegedly knowingly infecting a number of women) had anal sex with several women who acquired HIV. This is discussed in King, *op. cit.*, pp. 242–5.

43. *AIDS Newsletter*, reporting Anderson, *op. cit.*

44. D. L. Draper *et al.*, 'Scanning electron microscopy of attachment of *Neisseria gonorrhoeae* colony phenotypes to surfaces of human genital epithelia', *Am. J. Obstet. Gynaecol.*, 138:818, 1980, cited in M. Bailey, 'The passage of adolescence: preliminary exploration of some biological factors of adolescence and health', unpublished, Geneva, April 1993.

45. P. D. Kell *et al.*, 'HIV infection in a patient with Meyer-Rokitansky-Kiister-Hauser syndrome', *J. Roy. Soc. Med.*, 1992, 85:706-7; C. J. Miller *et al.*, 'Mechanism of genital transmission of SIV: a hypothesis based on transmission studies and the location of SIV in the genital tract of chronically infected female rhesus macaques', *J. Med. Primatol.*, 1992, 21:64-8. These studies are cited by J. E. Howe *et al.*, 'Contraceptives and HIV', *AIDS*, 1994, pp. 861-71.

46. *AIDS Newsletter*, reporting Anderson, *op. cit.*

47. Mike Bailey, personal communication.

48. M. Berer, with S. Ray, *Women and HIV/AIDS: An International Resource Book*, Pandora, London, 1993, p. 362, cites three papers which were presented at meetings held by the Inter-African Committee in Addis Ababa in 1989 and 1990. One study apparently compared African countries where 'female circumcision' is regularly practised with countries where it is rare, and found no difference in HIV prevalence rates. Other factors may have contributed to this conclusion and I have not been able to locate the paper (cited in Alcorn, *op. cit.*, p. 88).

    A useful overview of the practice (which does not address HIV) is N. Toubia, 'Female circumcision as a public health issue', *NEJM*, 331:11, pp. 712-16, 1994.

49. Some of these links with HIV are mentioned in A. Walker and P. Parmar, *Warrior Marks: Female Genital Mutilation and the Sexual Blinding of Women*, Jonathan Cape, London, 1993.

50. Laga *et al.*, *op. cit.* Also, K. Holmes, 'STD as a co-factor for HIV infection', state-of-the-art lecture at First National Conference on Human Retroviruses and Related Infections, Washington, DC, December 1993.

51. C. R. Cohen *et al.*, 'Relationship between bacterial vaginosis and HIV seropositivity among female commercial sex workers in Chiang Mai, Thailand, 1992', poster 55, presented at First National Conference on Human Retroviruses and Related Infections, Washington, DC, December 1993.

52. European Study Group on Heterosexual Transmission of HIV (ESG), 'Comparison of female to male and male to female transmission of HIV in 563 stable couples', *BMJ*, 304 (March 28), pp. 809-13 (1992).

53. United Nations Development Programme Report, cited in 'Youngest women at risk', *WorldAIDS*, No 30, November 1993, Panos Institute.

54. ESG, 1992, *op. cit.*
55. Discussion of the biological implications for adolescent girls are based on Bailey, *op. cit.*
56. Seventy-four per cent of sixteen- to twenty-year-olds have the transformation zone on the outside surface of the cervix, whereas this is the case for 50 per cent of twenty-six-year-olds and no women over sixty, according to A. B. Moscicki *et al.*, 'Differences in biologic maturation, sexual behaviour and sexually transmitted disease between adolescents with and without cervical intraepithelial neoplasia', *J. Pediatrics*, 115:487–93, 1989; cited in Bailey, *op. cit.*, p. 3.
57. C. J. Grossman, 'Regulation of the immune system by sex steroids', *Endocr. Rev.*, 1984, 5, pp. 435–55; cited in Howe *et al.*, *op. cit.*
58. See Howe *et al.*, *op. cit.*
59. Patrick *et al.*, 'Human immunodeficiency virus infection of early passage cervical epithelial cultures', *International Journal of STD and AIDS*, 1993, 4, pp. 342–5.
60. B. Voeller *et al.*, 'Heterosexual transmission of HIV', letter, *JAMA*, April 8 1992, 267 (14), pp. 1917–18; discussion, pp. 1918–19.
61. C. Camlin, 'Dams be damned!', p. 44, *QW*, 20 September 1992.
62. S. D. Holmberg *et al.*, 'AIDS COMMENTARY: Biologic factors in the sexual transmission of human immunodeficiency virus', *Journal of Infectious Diseases*, July 1989, 160 (1), pp. 116–25; J. B. Cohen *et al.*, 'Sexual and other practices and risk of HIV infection in a cohort of sexually active women in San Francisco', abstract WP.57, Proceedings of the Third International Conference on AIDS, Washington, DC, Bio-Data, 1987.
63. A. M. Johnson *et al.*, 'Transmission of HIV to heterosexual partners of infected men and women', *AIDS*, 3(6), June 1989, pp. 367–72.
64. A. M. Downs *et al.*, 'Per-contact HIV transmission rates in heterosexuals' IX International Conference on AIDS, Berlin, 6–11 June 1993, Abstract PO-C11-2859.
65. M. Seidlin *et al.*, 'Heterosexual transmission of HIV in a cohort of couples in New York City', *AIDS*, 1993, 7:1247–54.
    Results from any study of drug-using couples tend to be treated with caution as infections may be due to shared equipment rather than sex. However, in this study the researchers carried out physical examinations to remove this variable.
66. de Vincenzi *et al.*, *op. cit.*
67. Jacquez *et al.*, *op. cit.*
68. M. E. Van-de-Ende *et al.*, 'Heterosexual transmission of HIV by haemophiliacs', *BMJ*, 1988, 297, pp. 1102–3.
69. Ray Brettle, personal communication.
70. ESG, 1989, *op. cit.*
71. de Vincenzi *et al.*, *op. cit.*; see also ESG (1992), *op. cit.*
72. Seidlin *et al.*, *op. cit.* In general, it is thought unlikely that HIV can

be transmitted into a wound that is expressing blood (one HIV trainer likens this scenario to two hosepipes pouring water at each other). However, when a woman bleeds during intercourse this may indicate more extensive trauma, so that there are wounds in the genital tract which are not bleeding, and consequently are vulnerable to acquiring HIV.

73. See, for example, K. Henry, 'Documented male-to-female transmission of HIV-1 after minimal vaginal exposure in the absence of other co-factors for infection', *Minn. Med.*, 74 (10), October 1991, pp. 32–4.

74. de Vincenzi *et al.*, *op. cit.*

75. K. Wellings *et al.*, *Sexual Behaviour in Britain: The National Survey of Sexual Attitudes and Lifestyles*, Penguin, Harmondsworth, 1994, pp. 148–75.

76. de Vincenzi *et al.*, *op. cit.*: 130 of the index partners were women and 248 were men.

77. N. Padian *et al.*, 'Female-to-male transmission of human immunodeficiency virus', *JAMA*, 25 September 1991, 266 (12), pp. 1664–7. The index partners of these 379 couples had a range of primary risks (including bisexual men, IDUs, men with haemophilia and transfusion recipients) and comprised 307 HIV-positive men and 72 HIV-positive women.

78. P. Weatherburn *et al.*, *Behaviourally Bisexual Men in the UK*, Sigma Research, London, 1995. Apparently condoms were used for less than half of these acts.

79. They are also found in the lungs, brain, kidneys and gastrointestinal tract; this is unlikely to be a concern in a sexual context.

80. Mike Bailey, personal communication.

81. King, *op. cit.*, p. 104.

82. Wellings suggests that women and men who have anal sex nearly always report other sexual activities, including vaginal sex (p. 154, *op. cit.*). Watney states that 'the gay man is truly polymorphous: he may fuck and be fucked, and is as much at home in the one fantasy-position as the other' (*Policing Desire*, Methuen, London, 1987, p. 28). Project Sigma report that, of the gay men in their cohort who had anal sex in the previous twelve months, 60.6 per cent were both insertive and receptive, 22.5 per cent exclusively insertive and 16.9 per cent exclusively receptive. P. Weatherburn *et al.*, *The Sexual Lifestyles of Gay and Bisexual Men in England and Wales*, HMSO, London, 1992. See also, Wellings, *op. cit.*, Figure 5.18, p. 224.

83. Seidlin *et al.*, *op. cit.*

84. ESG, 'Risk factors for male to female transmission of HIV', *BMJ*, 298, pp. 411–15 (1989). This first study showed a 5.8-fold increased risk related to anal sex, based on preliminary data from 42 infected female partners of 153 men. The subsequent paper gives

a larger picture, but since it was later it may also reflect the impact of health education messages, as well as women being aware that their partner was at risk for HIV.

85. de Vincenzi *et al.*, *op. cit.*
86. Based on Jacquez *et al.*, *op. cit.*
87. Garfield, *op. cit.*, p. 118.
88. Wellings, *op. cit.*, pp. 149, 151, 154–5, 156–7.
89. Alcorn, *op. cit.*, p. 92.
90. M. Fumento, *The Myth of Heterosexual AIDS: How a Tragedy Has Been Distorted by the Media and Partisan Politics*, Regnery Gateway, Washington, DC, 1993, p. 55.
91. Protease inhibitors are a class of antiviral drugs which are showing some promise in slowing replication of HIV, especially when used in combination with other compounds. Nearly twenty different versions of this drug are in development (which suggests that pharmaceutical companies think this may well be a money spinner).
92. T. B. McNeely *et al.*, 'HIV inhibitor identified in saliva – secretory leukocyte protease inhibitor: a human saliva protein exhibiting anti-HIV activity', Paper 90, Session 18, Second National Conference on Human Retroviruses and Related Infections, Washington, DC, 30 January 1995.
93. W. Chen *et al.*, 'Allergy, oral sex, and HIV' (Letters), *Lancet*, 339 (8793), pp. 627–8 (1992); A. B. Murray *et al.*, 'Coincident acquisition of Neisseria gonorrhoeae and HIV from fellatio' (Letters), *Lancet*, 338, p. 830 (1991); cited in Alcorn, *op. cit.*, pp. 91–5.
94. Alcorn, *op. cit.*, p. 92.
95. M. Fischl *et al.*, 'Evaluation of heterosexual partners, children and household contacts of adults with AIDS', *JAMA*, 1987, 257:640–4, cited by Fumento, *op. cit.*, p. 56. Fumento's reading of epidemiology is technically very good, although it is so laden with offensive conclusions about people that it is painful to read.
96. Calculated from Wellings, *op. cit.*, Figure 4.4, p. 153.
97. ESG (1992), *op. cit.*
98. The only study that makes a comparable claim is J. I. Wallace *et al.*, 'Fellatio is a significant risk behavior for acquiring AIDS among New York City streetwalking prostitutes', VIII International Conference on AIDS, Amsterdam, July 1992, Abstract PoC 4196 (cf. Abstract PoC 4560). They conclude 'oral receptive sex is more risky than vaginal sex among crack using streetwalkers' and provide biological plausibility by explaining that crack pipes damage the gums, tongue and lips, as well as making women hyper-sexual. However, their study records no data on anal sex, and does not carry out any multivariate analysis. They also explain their finding by noting that HIV-infected women perform more oral than vaginal sex – but this could

equally suggest that the women know they are HIV-positive and have chosen not to sell vaginal sex.

99. de Vincenzi *et al.*, *op. cit.*, p. 344.

100. King, *op. cit.*, pp. 99–114. See also, the review in Alcorn, *op. cit.*, pp. 91–5. Alcorn includes a comprehensive listing of fourteen papers from cohorts and case studies that show no detectable risk of oral transmission (these all concern fellatio), and fourteen which indicate a possible risk. (This includes five studies where reports of HIV transmission during fellatio have subsequently been shown to be false, and four studies concerning possible HIV risks from cunnilingus, one about rimming and one about deep kissing.)

101. R. K. W. Lau *et al.*, 'Trends in sexual behavior in a cohort of homosexual men: a 7 year prospective study', *International Journal of STD and AIDS*, 1992, 3, pp. 267–72; quoted in King, *op. cit.*, p. 104.

102. Project Sigma, *Update*, London, March 1992; cited in King, *op. cit.*, p. 103.

103. King, *op. cit.*, pp. 104–5, citing L. A. Kingsely *et al.*, 'Sexual transmission efficiency of hepatitis B virus and human immunodeficiency virus among homosexual men', *JAMA*, 1990, 264 (2), pp. 230–4; M. T. Schreeder *et al.*, 'Hepatitis B in homosexual men: prevalence of infection and factors related to transmission', *Journal of Infectious Diseases*, 1992, 146, pp. 7–15.

104. Alcorn, *op. cit.*, pp. 94–5.

105. I. P. Keet *et al.*, 'Short communication: orogenital sex and the transmission of HIV among homosexual men', *AIDS*, 1992, 6, pp. 223–6.

106. Alcorn, *op. cit.*, p. 91.

107. Olivier, speech to '*Les Assises de AIDES: dix ans de lutte contre le SIDA, dix ans de solidarité*', 25 September 1994.

108. See, for example, G. Rotello, 'Watch your mouth', *OUT*, June 1994, pp. 148–68.

109. V. Puro *et al.*, 'Male-to female transmission of human immunodeficiency virus infection by oro-genital sex', *J. Clinical Microbiology and Infectious Diseases*, 1991, 10 (1), p. 47.

110. W. Che *et al.*, 'Allergy, oral sex, and HIV' (Letters), *Lancet*, 7 March 1992, 339 (8793), pp. 627–8.

111 A. Lifson *et al.*, 'HIV seroconversion in two homosexual men after receptive oral intercourse with ejaculation: implication for counselling concerning safe sexual practices', *AJPH*, 1990, 80; 12, pp. 1509–11.

112. King, *op. cit.*, p. 108.

113. Based on Koopman *et al.*, *op. cit.*, and Jacquez *et al.*, *op. cit.* These are my own very rough estimates deriving from Koopman's statement that anal sex is 176 times more risky during primary infection than at all other times combined. I used the crude estimate (from Jacquez) of 0.1 per cent risk of HIV transmission through anal sex

at 'all other times combined'. Koopman says that oral sex is 523 times more risky during primary infection than at all other times combined, and that overall anal sex is 5.3 times more risky than oral. The confidence intervals are so huge (for the rates Jacquez describes for anal sex) that in the absence of more detail I could not arrive at accurate figures that would tally back exactly.

114. S. Connor, 'The terror is infectious', *Independent*, 20 April 1995.

Chapter seven

Vectors

We are treated as vectors of transmission to men and foetuses.

Maxine Wolfe[1]

Women with HIV are often perceived as 'vectors', liable to transmit to more vital 'communities'. Instead of seeing each woman as an individual living with the virus in her body, she is frequently seen as a link in the chain of infection, a body through which infection passes, a vector. A vector is a 'carrier of disease or infection from one organism to another',[2] and it is in this light that the concept of women as 'vectors' is offensive.

The dictionary definition explains that the nature of a vector is 'a quantity having both magnitude and direction'. This can be useful in the context of HIV since it highlights the giver-receiver relationship, and that the direction and scale of the virus are critical to whether transmission occurs. In order to move away from the negative discourse of woman as vector, caught between two other people with HIV, she needs to move centre stage. How did this individual acquire HIV infection? How might she transmit HIV infection? And what are the gaps in knowledge? Many HIV-positive women are fearful of their own infectivity and shut down their sexuality[3] – they believe the media image that they 'pose a threat to men'. This chapter reviews when and how HIV-infected women may 'pose a threat' to men, women and children – and discovers that, in gender-related contexts, women are relatively poor transmitters of the virus.

Sex

The previous chapter showed how vulnerable women are to acquiring the virus from HIV-infected men, either through vaginal or anal sex. These routes of transmission will also be worrisome for women living with HIV, since they could become re-infected with new strains of HIV – and other STDs – from unprotected vaginal or anal sex with a man with HIV. There are an increasing number of reports to suggest that being re-infected with a more aggressive strain of HIV will hasten progression to symptoms of AIDS, and to death.[4] Even if her partner is not HIV-infected, an HIV-positive woman will also want to protect herself from other STDs which can be more severe and resistant to treatment for her. In particular, HPV (associated with cervical cancer) and chlamydia and gonorrhoea (linked to PID when untreated) could cause additional life-threatening health problems for HIV-infected women.[5] These concerns are important, and are relatively easily addressed – technically speaking – since infections can be prevented by using barrier methods: condoms, femidoms, diaphragms and caps.

This chapter focuses principally on the risks of HIV transmission from a woman with HIV to her male and female sexual partners. Although the principal focus is the most risky activities (vaginal and anal fucking), I also give some detail about other sexual activities which have concerned women with HIV infection and the women and men who may be having sex with them; some of these activities may also concern a woman who is having sex with a man who has HIV. I will first review in turn the infectivity of a woman's genital fluids – vaginal and cervical secretions, and menstrual blood – and then consider the vulnerability of male genitals to acquiring infection, before turning to what is known about HIV transmission and different sexual activities. The infectivity of blood, and the vulnerability to infection of female genitals as well as the mouth were addressed in the previous chapter, which is frequently cross-referenced. Finally, I review the core knowledge about transmission from an HIV-infected woman to a baby, and some of the strategies that exist to prevent this – some of which are more heavily promoted by the medical profession than others.

All studies addressing the sexual transmission of HIV between women and men conclude that female-to-male transmission is less efficient than male-to-female transmission. (I am not including studies from Africa which have suggested an equal risk for transmission in either direction, because there are significant methodological limitations which make it unlikely that these data are transferable. Few African studies ask about anal sex or acknowledge that men may have sex with other men. Sexual transmission rates are also likely to be higher than in Europe since there is far higher prevalence of untreated STDs.)

Since both anal and vaginal sex are practised by many of the people in these studies, these expressions of risk are often generalized and cannot provide precise information about individual acts. It is estimated that the virus is between two and twenty times more likely to be transmitted from an HIV-infected man than from an HIV-infected woman. The exact scale of difference regarding the direction of transmission is hotly debated. Padian found the largest difference in her cohort where just one man became infected (out of 72 men with HIV-positive female partners, i.e. 1.4 per cent), compared with 61 women (of 307 who had HIV-positive male partners, i.e. 19.9 per cent).[6] This massive difference was queried in a letter from Haverkos, who looked at the rates from sixteen studies and suggested that male-to-female transmission was really just 1.9 times more risky (in the USA and Europe). In reply, Padian disagreed with his methodology, and also identified problems with results from the European Study Group (which claimed a 1.9-fold difference in their 1992 paper): 68 per cent of the cases of female-to-male sexual transmission in the ESG were in couples where the woman injected drugs – in these situations blood-borne infection cannot, she suggested, be ruled out. She also emphasizes that drawing comparisons by combining data from discordant-couple studies is unwise, since all have different methodologies and co-factors.[7] One key difference in co-factors, pertinent to female-to-male transmission, is that uncircumcised men may be more vulnerable to acquiring HIV: the majority of American men do not have foreskins, whereas circumcision is less common in Europe.

The majority of scientists appear to favour the ratio of a two-

or three-fold greater risk to women. Yet it is not clear if this is due to scientific precision, or anxiety about the impact these findings may have on prevention messages. Certainly the implications are important, and any scientist discovering lower probabilities of HIV transmission from women frets that 'prevention should not be compromised by the false belief that men are not at risk'.[8] The risk women pose has repeatedly been exaggerated to panic men (presumably out of fear that men will refuse safer sex unless they are panicked). In the light of what is known about women's infectivity, it is shocking that the sexual pleasure of so many HIV-positive women is needlessly restricted. Somewhere a balance is necessary, a balance that encourages men to protect women by using condoms without so exaggerating the risk of infection from HIV-positive women that they become dangerous vectors in their own and others' eyes.

• *Vaginal fluids*

There are distinctions to be made between vaginal secretions and cervical secretions regarding the concentration of HIV. For brevity I will describe both as 'vaginal fluids' and use the term 'secretions' when I am differentiating between secretions coming from different sites. (After all, both types of secretions tend to mingle and leave the body together in real-life situations.)

In considering how a woman acquires HIV, the previous chapter described how a healthy vagina is naturally acidic, having a pH between 3 and 6. This is a level that deactivates HIV and so vaginal fluids have been described as providing a natural barrier to HIV. This has important consequences for HIV transmission from infected women. Although HIV can definitely be found in vaginal fluids, studies have shown that they are a relatively poor vehicle for HIV when compared with fluids which are rich in white blood cells (like blood and semen). The first two reports of 'HIV' in vaginal fluids were published in the *Lancet* in May 1986. Wofsy considered that 'only small amounts of the virus were present' as it took a long time to culture 'AIDS-related virus' from the vaginal fluids of four of eight women (and one sample was of menstrual blood). Vogt tested samples from fourteen women (seven of whom were viraemic) and found 'HTLV-III/LAV' in just four samples, three from women who had developed symptoms.[9]

The reason why HIV may be rare in vaginal fluids appears to be the lack of host cells for HIV, as well as the acidic environment. One study tested the vaginal fluids of five HIV-negative women throughout three menstrual cycles. Researchers found that, 'White blood cells, including lymphocytes and macrophages, are infrequently present in cervicovaginal secretions of healthy women except during menses; the vaginal environment may effect their function.'[10] This group also looked at vaginal fluids from eighteen HIV-positive women – five of whom had symptoms and six had AIDS. They compared these with samples from five HIV-negative women. They discovered that HIV host cells (i.e. lymphocytes and macrophages) were only present in HIV-negative women during menses and the proliferative phase. Among the HIV-positive women, the highest levels of host cells were seen among the women who were symptomatic but did not have AIDS. However, HIV p24 antigen was not detected in any of the samples, suggesting infectious virus was low in these fluids.[11]

This is not to suggest that HIV is not present in vaginal fluids, but rather that the level is generally low. Menstruation certainly seems to increase risk, but there are other circumstances which enhance levels of HIV. In one study, seventy-seven vaginal and eighty-four cervical secretions from ninety-seven HIV-positive women were tested for HIV DNA by PCR.[12] They recovered virus in the vaginal fluids of nearly one third of the women and found that the fluids were more infectious if women used the oral contraceptive pill (11.6-fold greater risk), had cervical mucopus (6.2-fold) or cervical ectopy (5.0-fold) or were pregnant (4.5-fold); and these links were even stronger following a multivariate analysis and controlling for age. Hormonal changes, including the contraceptive pill, pregnancy and having passed through the menopause, increase the prevalence of white blood cells, as do infections and damage to the genital tract. This study also found that HIV was far more likely to be present in fluids from the endocervix than the vaginal wall, with the virus found in 33 per cent of cervical and 17 per cent of vaginal samples. This is consistent with what was described in the previous chapter regarding the comparative vulnerability of the cervix and the vagina.

• Menstrual fluids

As most women (and quite a few men) know, menstrual blood is not the same as venous blood, and it is not wholly correct to describe it as blood. Rather, the lining of the womb and the unfertilized ova are expelled from the body, on average once a month, and on average yielding about 40 ml of fluid. Although they are not as dense in white blood cells as blood from the veins, menstrual fluids do contain a large quantity of white blood cells, and as such may be efficient vehicles for HIV. They are certainly more efficient than regular vaginal fluids, with one researcher commenting, 'Most women do not normally secrete cells from the cervix that can host HIV except during menses.'[13] As well as the far higher concentration of lymphocytes that may be infected with HIV, the pH of vaginal fluids alters during the menstrual cycle, with fluids becoming more alkaline during menstruation.[14] It has also been suggested that these fluids become more alkaline during ovulation, which would allow semen to survive longer and pass through the cervical canal to reach the ovum for fertilization. This process is also facilitated by changes in cervical mucosa.

One early study of seven HIV-positive women suggested that there was no menstrual pattern to the isolation of HIV from vaginal fluids.[15] However, this was rejected by other researchers who noticed that data from this initial study showed that during the first ten days of the menstrual cycle six samples (46.2 per cent) were able to culture virus, whereas only one sample (9.1 per cent) taken during the second half of the cycle contained HIV.[16] Indeed, all of the studies (biological and epidemiological) show compellingly that HIV is far more likely to be present during menses than at other times in the menstrual cycle.

Paglia points out that 'Most early cultures hemmed in menstruating women by ritual taboos. . . . Menstrual blood is the stain, the birthmark of original sin, the filth that transcendental religion must wash from man.'[17] Sex during menstruation remains the subject of taboos, embarrassed silence or distaste – despite the fact that for many women this is a time of high erotic charge. The link with HIV does not mean that sex during menstruation is diseased or dirty sex, but rather that this is a time when condoms are particularly important. Sadly, very few HIV prevention materials mention sex during bleeding, let alone advise on how to enjoy it safely.

• *Penis*

The previous chapter showed that the cervix is vulnerable to infection with HIV, as are the anus and, to a lesser extent, the vagina. On rare occasions the mouth and throat may also be sites for HIV to enter the body. In order for an HIV-infected woman to transmit the virus to a man, there needs to be an entry site. Since epidemiologists have identified vaginal and anal sex as the risk activities for men (and from what is known about the transmission of other STDs), HIV must be infecting men through their penises. Strangely, there is very little research on how HIV attaches itself to the male genital mucosa – certainly nothing like the (albeit small) quantity of information looking at whether HIV enters through the vagina or the cervix. It is assumed that the virus has a point of entry through the mucous membranes on the glans of the penis and in the urethra (the small opening through which both semen and urine pass). The vulnerability to infection is clearly lower than for women, as the surface area that can be infected is smaller. With the urethra, not only is the area small, but when the man ejaculates he essentially 'flushes' out any infection (unless it has already had time to become established). The virus may also enter through any cuts or abrasions, but these are not essential for transmission because the delicate mucosal membranes contain the dendritic cells and Langerhans cells which facilitate infection.

Men who are uncircumcised have a higher risk of acquiring HIV, because the skin which is exposed when the foreskin is drawn back is more delicate (if a man is circumcised, it becomes tougher through exposure to abrasion). During fucking, the woman's sexual fluids (blood in anal sex, vaginal or menstrual fluids during vaginal sex) become 'trapped' between the glans and the foreskin so that the skin on the glans is exposed to the fluid throughout intercourse and after withdrawal. The frenulum (where the foreskin attaches to the penis) can bleed with the movement of the foreskin, and this would enable HIV to become attached. There may also be a link with balanitis: the white fungus (smegma) that can grow on the penis and produces some inflammation.[18] The association of HIV with uncircumcised men is important, to the extent that some have recommended circumcision as a public health measure. However, few would recommend this since condoms are far simpler, and the link is by no means absolute – circumcised men do acquire HIV when the virus enters through the urethra or the delicate mucosa at the tip of the penis. Factors which increase the presence of white blood cells on the surface of the glans (like STDs) will increase the vulnerability to acquiring infection, as will any lesions, cuts or abrasions. It is not unusual for there to be slight cuts or abrasions on the penis, for example, as a result of the friction of penetration.

• *Vaginal sex*

The acidity of vaginal fluids, combined with the low concentration of white cells that may be infected by HIV, makes vaginal sex a relatively inefficient route of transmitting HIV to men. The mechanisms by which men can acquire HIV during vaginal sex have already been hinted at in the descriptions of biology. The risk appears to be activated by ejaculation when the alkalinity of semen renders HIV viable in vaginal fluids, especially in the secretions at the cervix (which have the most white cells). Vaginal sex is not only a risk because ejaculation lowers the pH, but also because the mucous membrane at the tip of the penis usually comes into contact with the cervix, where the more infectious fluids are found.

Although the evidence (and it is slight) suggests that healthy vaginal fluids contain very little HIV, men would be wrong to infer from this that there is no risk to them from vaginal sex. Anything that raises the pH of the vagina and increases the white cells in vaginal fluids (like STDs or bleeding during sex) will make transmission more likely. Most women and men will be unaware of having conditions which increase the quantity of white blood cells in vaginal fluids (except for menstruation). STDs are notoriously silent in women (whereas men tend to get symptoms); hormonal shifts associated with the pill are not always apparent; and bleeding is relatively common, but tends only to be apparent post-coital. Planning specific protection from these enhanced risks is, therefore, rarely feasible, whereas consistent use of condoms and lubricant is achievable.

Sexual HIV transmission from women to men receives some research attention because the risks are not well quantified and it is relatively rare in Europe and the USA. This may well be a function of time and sexual lifestyle. Studies show that all women have, on average, significantly fewer sexual partners than men[19] (especially gay men[20]). Women who are HIV-infected tend to have acquired the virus in relationships where they were monogamous. During seroconversion – the time of highest infectivity – a woman is therefore more likely than a man to have sex only with the man who infected her, and not pass on the virus (whereas gay culture places a higher value on multiple partners, and the frequency of partner change was a critical factor in the early transmission of HIV). However, in many instances, an HIV-infected woman will not still be having sex with this same man when she reaches her second stage of high viral load (i.e. when she becomes symptomatic), since he was infected first and he may have died by then. This means that most transmission from women to men will only happen (and be detected) at this second stage, some ten years after the woman became infected (there will be some transmission during the asymptomatic phase – but rates are likely to be significantly lower). The majority of early HIV infections in industrialized countries were in men, few of whose sexual partners were women, so many HIV-infected women are currently at earlier stages of disease progression and consequently less likely to transmit, for both biological and psychosocial reasons.

Nearly all of the cases of transmission to men are reported from women who have high viral load due to disease progression. In the 1992 report from the ESG, the clinical status of the woman increased the likelihood of transmission 17.6-fold – a startlingly high odds ratio. Initially 19 (of 159) men acquired HIV from their HIV-positive female partner, which gives a transmission rate of 12 per cent.[21] When the group was followed for the next twenty-four months, 47 men used condoms inconsistently and four of them became infected; there was a definite link with disease stage. The ESG estimated the risk of acquiring HIV from one instance of vaginal sex at '5 per 1000 if the index partner was in an advanced stage of infection and 0.7 per 1000 . . . if the index partner was asymptomatic'.[22] This estimate (of 0.5 per cent compared to 0.07 per cent) was of either-direction transmission, i.e. data from men and women were lumped together, but Padian points out that previous evidence denotes an important gender difference. In her own study, the one woman who transmitted HIV to a man had AIDS, and she suggests that 'clinical status could have a stronger effect on transmission from women than from men, and . . . as the epidemic matures and more women become symptomatic, we might observe more female-to-male transmission.'[23]

The man who seroconverted in Padian's study also experienced regular bleeding during sex (both from his penis and her vagina) and this connection has been made in other studies. An even more important co-factor is vaginal sex during menstruation. All studies suggest that there is a strong link with transmission – the ESG suggested a 3.4-times increased risk.[24] Some studies have shown links with STDs (both ulcerative and non-ulcerative, since they increase the amount of white cells in vaginal fluids), but this was not proven by the ESG. By contrast, women with a history of candidiasis seemed more likely to transmit (four of ten women with candidiasis transmitted, according to the ESG 1992 report). This may be because candida makes the vaginal environment more alkaline, or the woman may have lower CD4 cell counts and the candida is a marker for her high viral load. Most studies have shown a connection between the length of the relationship and the likelihood of a man acquiring HIV. The ESG suggested that the probability of a man acquiring HIV from a women is 7 per cent for between 17 and 462 unprotected sexual contacts, and this rises to 36 per cent if he has unprotected sex with her more than 910 times. This may well be for the same reason why frequent partner change was significant for gay men: the longer the relationship, the more chances of having sex during a time of high viral load.[25]

• Anal sex

During anal sex, there are also significant differences between the HIV risks to the penetrator (male) and penetrated (female). HIV can be transmitted from the woman in blood, which is often present in the rectum because of the friction of fucking. It is worth recalling that this may be small quantities of blood which (as in transmission via injecting equipment) may cause infection even when too small to be seen. However, 'insertive' anal sex is a less efficient way of acquiring the infection than getting a small amount of blood directly into the bloodstream. One point worth stressing (although it ought to be self-evident) is that men do not acquire HIV from anal sex because of faeces – if there is blood in faeces then there may be a risk of HIV, but it is *blood*, not shit, that mediates HIV. Certainly there can be other health risks associated with anal sex play, but anal sex does not cause disease because it is 'dirty'. Cindy Patton and other cultural critics have written at length about the germophobia and erotophobia which have troubled responses to AIDS.[26] The generalized distaste towards the anus as a sexual organ has led to strange fantasies about transmission and talk of 'unnatural acts' – fantasies that also surround fucking during a woman's period. Commentators like Fumento maintain that the AIDS/anal sex link shows that an organ 'designed' for expelling matter should not be used for receiving semen. This argument must beg the question whether the vagina is 'designed' for receiving semen or expelling a baby. The concept that parts of the anatomy may have multiple uses, and indeed that the whole body can be sexual, seems to be lost on these men.

It is remarkably difficult to assess the risks of a man acquiring HIV from anal sex with a woman who has HIV. Alcorn states that it is a 'dangerous myth . . . that the man doing the fucking (the insertive/active partner) will not get infected',[27] but he is not willing to even guess at the different level of risk involved. There are studies showing that gay men who only fuck are infected,[28] yet most HIV-infected gay men have been fucked. There are theoretical reasons to believe that vaginal sex may be more risky to men than anal sex with a woman (perhaps the opposite of the situation for women), since there are usually more fluids present in the vagina than the rectum. Yet it is hard to interpret findings from epidemiological studies of sex between women and men in order to assess this. Studies suggesting that the men who have had anal sex appear to have a higher risk of acquiring HIV than the men who do not[29] may be masking the fact that these men may be more adventurous in all their sexual practices and engage in, for example, vaginal sex during menstruation. (Wellings, for example, suggests that 'hetero-sexuals' who have anal sex may have 'skills . . . for expressing sex-ual pleasure through a range of different activities'.[30])

In 'heterosexual' cohorts, only a small number of women tend to be the index partner (HIV-positive), and with a relatively low rate of transmission to men, numbers are often too small for analysis. An Italian study concluded that anal sex was 4.6 times more risky for men, but in this group there were only fourteen sero-conversions among the 224 male partners of HIV-positive women. The group also saw an increased risk depending upon the woman's disease stage, and with such small numbers it is entirely possible that this, rather than anal sex, was the major risk factor.[31] Another problem with reports from cohorts is that researchers have a tendency to conflate men and women, describing the efficacy of transmission for individual activities, or they conflate activities and report on female-to-male and male-to-female transmission. This may well generate useful information for building models describing the course of the epidemic, but it is not much use for people living with HIV, their partners, and HIV-prevention work.

If it is not possible to define a risk for men to acquire HIV from anal sex with a woman, it is at least clear that transmission is not inevitable. One study describes 31 couples (where the woman was HIV-positive) who had 'a mean of 3.3 sexual intimate contacts per week without the use of condoms' over an average of 54 months. Of the couples, 41.2 per cent had anal sex, but none of the men became infected, despite the fact that 24 of them were uncircumcised and nine reported penile lesions.[32]

• Cunnilingus (oral sex)

This section does not consider fellatio because there is simply no risk to a man if an HIV-infected woman sucks him; there is insufficient HIV in saliva to cause infection. Three papers have suggested that a man acquired HIV when receiving fellatio, but these 'eccentricities' (as King calls them) have been shown to be false reports which tell us more about the unreliability of case reports than about transmission routes.[33] This section will consider cunni-lingus and whether a (wo)man who goes down on an HIV-infected woman could acquire the virus. It is helpful to consider this here, after showing the relative rarity of sexual HIV transmission from women, since this is a topic that has created disproportionate levels of anxiety, disagreement and aggressive debate. This attention has mostly been spearheaded by some groups of lesbians, but since women's tongues and mouths are no different from men's, lesbian campaigns inevitably had an impact on all women (these campaigns are the subject of Chapter 10, 'Dam Those Dykes').

Among HIV-positive women (and their sexual partners) the unresolved debate and poor information about cunnilingus has led to incredible levels of sexual distress. In the UK survey of seventy-five HIV-positive women, concerns about the risks of oral sex and their lack of reliable information were repeatedly raised. It was startling how many women referred to this as a major source of difficulty and loss following their HIV diagnosis.[34] If this anxiety was not created by 'lesbian safer sex' campaigns (and I rather suspect it was), then it certainly has been fuelled by them. Safer sex campaigns targeted at lesbians have tended to stress the use of dental dams (squares of latex) to cover the vulva during cunnilingus and prevent vaginal fluids entering the mouth of the woman licking. Is this really necessary?

When considering the biology of the mouth and throat (in the last chapter) it was clear that this is an inefficient, but not impossible, entry site for HIV. In trying to understand HIV risk, cunnilingus is often lumped together with fellatio, as if the bringing together of a mouth and a set of genitals makes the nature of the genitals and their secretions irrelevant. The different physiologies matter and, unlike fellatio, cunnilingus offers an inefficient vehicle for HIV (vaginal and menstrual fluids), as well as an inefficient entry site for HIV (the mouth). The acidity of vaginal fluids, combined with their low concentration of HIV, makes vaginal sex a relatively inefficient route of transmitting HIV to men. What risk there is, is intensified by the fact that the alkalinity of semen renders HIV viable in vaginal fluids, especially in the secretions at the cervix. In cunnilingus, by contrast, the fluids that are being ingested by the man or woman doing the licking, are still acidic and unlikely to contain sufficient concentrations of HIV. If oral sex is happening during the HIV-infected woman's period, the menstrual fluids are more likely to contain HIV (and perhaps this would also be the case if oral sex happens after ejaculation, when fluids may be less acidic), but this is still a far lower concentration than in semen or venous blood.

Even if the vaginal fluids are at their most infectious, it is hard to see how infection could occur through oral sex since there are relatively small amounts of fluid (and they are not even heading in the right direction). Case reports of fellatio with an HIV-infected man, show that in those very rare cases where there may have been transmission, ejaculation in the mouth was essential (as indeed ejaculation is for vaginal transmission). This suggests that quite a high dose of fluid has to travel at speed in the direction of mucosa – and even then transmission is extremely unlikely. In general, cunnilingus creates fluid which is more diffuse, and which has fewer opportunities to enter the body. It is suggested that HIV could be transmitted during cunnilingus if large quantities of vaginal juices were able to pass through broken skin around the mouth and chin. It might be prudent to tell men not to shave immediately before or after going down on a woman. Barriers may be considered by women and men with severe eczema or other skin diseases which cause disruption to the integrity of the skin – but the cuts or abrasions would need to be extensive. Some people have raised concerns about cold sores (herpes lesions) around the mouth; it is not wise to engage in barrier-free cunnilingus with these as the risks of transmitting genital herpes are high. Some women have also raised concerns about female ejaculate, a liquid which appears to originate from a gland in the vagina and which some women produce when the G-spot is stimulated. Large quantities of this fluid (some report as much as a pint) can spray out of the vagina during orgasm. Remarkably little is known about female ejaculate, but it seems unlikely that it would contain a high concentration of white blood cells (which could contain HIV) since it is not viscous.[35] An additional concern raised by a few lesbians is that they have oral sex for longer than other women and produce more fluid. There is no research to back this up, and non-lesbian women have found this a bizarre argument.

Biologically, the risks of transmission through cunnilingus are remote, and this is strengthened by the fact that there are no reliable reports from epidemiological studies of transmission by this route. Indeed, the best evidence available from a cohort suggests that transmission does not happen. In response to anxiety expressed by lesbians, an Italian group conducted a prospective study of eighteen HIV-discordant lesbian couples who completed a three-month sexual diary and attended assessments for six months. This study was reported in a letter to the *Lancet* and, although detailed information was not given, it appears from a graph that all women had oral sex during the three months. No barriers were used and none of the HIV-negative partners acquired the virus.[36] Although this does look promising, the study was short and this emphasizes why information from other, less specific, cohorts is important.

As mentioned earlier, 'heterosexual' cohorts tell little about any HIV risks of oral sex, because other activities provide a masking effect. However, there could be useful information from discordant couples who consistently use condoms, since the Sexual Lifestyles survey suggests that most will be having oral sex. Another way of assessing if cunnilingus (or at least sex between women) is implicated in HIV transmission has been to discover what proportion of HIV-infected women are lesbian or bisexual. This is difficult because most epidemiologists fail to record this information. However, in 1992 an American retrospective study interviewed 106 women discovered to be HIV-positive through the blood transfusion service. This found that just three of these women reported sex with women, and all three had classic risk factors: either injecting drugs or sex with men.[37] These extremely encouraging results mean that the only possible evidence for HIV transmission from cunnilingus would have to be derived from case studies and personal anecdotes which (as documented with fellatio) are notoriously vulnerable to reporting bias.

One report described a sixty-year-old man who claimed that he was infected when he went down on a commercial sex worker.[38] However, it subsequently emerged that she was HIV-negative and the man had concealed a history of sharing needles to inject drugs. This is a telling case history, since it demonstrates that people may conceal risky behaviour – but why? Perhaps he considered injecting drug use to be the most stigmatized of his activities, or perhaps he felt guilty about using commercial sexual services and perceived HIV infection as a logical 'punishment'. Indeed, many helplines habitually receive calls from people with guilt-ridden unwarranted AIDS anxiety connected to stigmatized behaviours, usually sex with sex workers, or men who have had sex with men. If the person taking the case history is not sensitive to such motivations, incorrect conclusions will be inevitable. Lesbians may be especially vulnerable to (internalized) pressure to conceal stigmatized behaviour which is inconsistent with their sexual identity (sex with a man) or which is rejected by their community (injection drug use). Yet, numerous studies reveal that both activities, in particular sex with men, are remarkably common. One lesbian, prominent in work around lesbians and AIDS, described the way she simply forgot that she had injected drugs, because this was a period of her life that seemed distant at the time she was asked about her drugs history.[39]

Case studies from lesbians have inevitably shown problems with recall about risk activities. One report described a couple where a thirty-seven-year-old lesbian died of AIDS, having denied sex with men or injecting drug use. Her lover tested HIV-positive and maintained that she acquired HIV from oral sex, since she had not had sex with a man or used drugs either. The problem with this case is that the relationship is presented as hermetically sealed, and no plausible explanation has been given about how the first woman became infected.[40] The fact that she had Kaposi's Sarcoma is good evidence to suggest she acquired HIV from sex with a bisexually behaving man. Since evidence about the first woman's infection was not properly gathered, it brings into doubt the reliability of the whole report. Another group referenced this case study in their report two years later of apparent transmission from a twenty-five-year-old drug-using lesbian to her twenty-six-year-old lover. This explained how HIV first entered the relationship; the question is whether it was then transmitted within the relationship. The twenty-six-year-old denied drug use, but on questioning it transpired that she had sex with at least three men, one of whom was bisexual. She had sex (using condoms) with the bisexual man in August 1984 – four months before she tested HIV-positive. However, she also reported apparent symptoms of seroconversion illness four to six weeks after starting her relationship with the twenty-five-year-old woman, and reported that their sexual activities included oral sex during this woman's period.[41] Was that the route of transmission, or did the condom break with the bisexual man?

Calling into question these case studies – or, even more daring, personal anecdotes of oral sex transmission (which all seem to arise from the USA) – is extremely fraught. It has become commonplace to probe and question reports of men who say they acquired HIV from sex with a woman. (Are we *sure* Magic Johnson isn't concealing some homosexual behaviour? Fumento certainly is not.[42]) Yet, questioning claims of 'woman-to-woman' transmission is perceived as distinctly unsisterly, and brings down aggressive accusations that the questioner is disbelieving of HIV-positive women (and I have never encountered a man who claims to have been infected by cunnilingus). Yet the evidence all points away from oral sex being an efficient route of transmission from an HIV-infected woman. Just maybe, if she was menstruating during primary infection, and the man or woman licking her had broken skin around and in the mouth, HIV transmission might happen. Yet compared to penetrative sex, oral sex is clearly in an entirely differ-ent, and lower, league of risk, with cunnilingus trailing along far behind the extremely low risk of fellatio.

• *Sharing sex toys*

Amidst all the polemic about whether an HIV-infected woman can transmit the virus to another woman through sexual acts, dental dams have often obscured the sexual act between women that may facilitate transmission. Sharing sex toys in the vagina has a slighter more plausible risk than oral sex. The fluids which are most likely to contain HIV are cervical secretions, which are produced at the top of the vagina. HIV in cervical secretions (or menstrual fluids) could be transmitted on the tip of the sex toy from the HIV-infected woman's cervix, and then introduced to another woman's (vulnerable) cervix if the toy is not cleaned and is switched to the other woman immediately. Although there is a theoretical risk here, vaginal fluids are relatively inefficient vehicles for HIV transmission in the absence of seminal fluid.

Some people believe that if any of the reports of woman-to-woman HIV transmission are borne out then it is this route, not cunnilingus, that is responsible. This also makes good biological sense since other STDs, like chlamydia, may be transmitted this way, but not through oral sex.[43] Responding to an early report of oral-sex transmission to a lesbian, Peter Greenhouse wrote to the *Lancet* stating 'orogenital contact not involving semen is most unlikely to be responsible for HIV transmission between women', but urged researchers detecting unusual modes of transmission to ask about the 'shared use of sex toys', which he defines as a high-risk activity.[44]

The most likely case of HIV transmission between women was reported from the USA in 1993. A twenty-four-year-old woman tested HIV-positive when her thirty-eight-year-old, former IDU, female lover died of AIDS. The two lived together in a monogamous relationship from November 1987 until the older woman's death in July 1989. In December 1987 the younger woman developed herpes lesions in her vagina, and in April 1988 she developed symptoms typical of a seroconversion illness. Other blood tests after her lover died suggested that infection could have happened around this time. The women's sexual practice included sharing a vibrator, and this offers a good biological explanation for transmission: the thirty-eight-year-old would have had high viral load during the two years before her death, and the twenty-four-year-old had a good site of entry for the virus with lesions in her genitals. Despite this technical description, and the seductive nature of case reports (they often read a little like soap operas), the authors of this study have reviewed all other relevant data and urge caution. Their message is: '[Seroprevalence] studies, combined with the sparse number of individual case reports, suggest that female homosexual activity is an inefficient mechanism of HIV transmission.'[45]

• *Rimming*

Having dealt at length with fellatio and cunnilingus, I will briefly consider the other mouth-to-genital act: anilingus, or rimming. Rimming is the term for licking around the opening to, and the base of, the anus. This activity does have risks for pathogens which are transmitted by the oral-faecal route, including pathogens (like salmonella) that may be especially dangerous for people living with HIV. Since HIV is not present in faeces, rimming cannot be a risk activity for HIV.[46] Even where HIV may be present in blood, the quantities of blood in faeces are so small as to be irrelevant, and since the mouth is not an optimal site of entry, this is clearly a safe activity for HIV. In some current guidelines from the USA promoting what they call 'safe sex', prohibitions against these acts exist, despite the fact that these fly in the face of scientific knowledge about HIV. Germophobia and erotophobia rear their ugly heads with any sex play involving faeces or urine. 'Dirty sex' becomes 'bad sex' which in turn becomes 'diseased sex'.

• SM *and broken skin*

The practice of sadomasochism (SM) by some women, in particular some lesbians, created fearsome debates in feminist communities during the 1970s. There was a polarization between women who perceived SM as indicative of the root of women's oppression, and women who enjoyed the erotic diversity of SM and the opportunities to test sexual and power boundaries. Although some conflict between these different positions is sustained, the aggressive attitudes towards women who enjoy SM seem to have abated in some sectors of the women's community. In the wider population, some people believe that sexual activity that draws blood or causes pain is reprehensible, but overall there is more awareness and discussion of sex involving power, games and fantasy. At the time of writing, pain induced for sexual pleasure is probably illegal in Britain, following rulings in the Operation Spanner case which criminalized consensual SM sex.[47] Rubin points out that 'When fears of incurable disease mingle with sexual terror, the resulting brew is extremely volatile.'[48] Represented as 'bad sex', it inevitably slides into 'diseased sex', despite the fact that most SM, bondage and fantasy sex are among the safest possible varieties of sexual acts.

Some people raise anxieties about HIV transmission through open wounds. There are no cohorts or case studies which can give reliable information about this, partly because the questions are not asked, partly because no one has presented with this as their presumed mode of HIV infection. Common sense dictates that getting HIV-infected vaginal fluids, menstrual fluids, semen or blood into an open wound is ill-advised. However, what is known about transmission of HIV to healthcare workers also shows that even this would not be an efficient route of transmission. A fresh cut or wound to the skin is rarely an efficient site of entry for HIV as the wound tends to expel blood rather than absorb another person's fluid. The basics of HIV transmission warn against HIV-infected blood or sexual fluids entering another person's (un-infected) bloodstream. This can easily be avoided by ensuring that skin is intact, and where it is not, that blood and sexual fluids do not come into contact with any wounds. Information from studies of healthcare workers is most pertinent here, and this underscores how unlikely it is for HIV to be transmitted in SM scenarios.

• Fingers and fists

Intact skin is a barrier, so much so that a lesbian campaign in Toronto, Canada proclaims, 'Your skin is a condom.'[49] There are no reports of anyone acquiring HIV from putting fingers, or fists, in the anus or vagina of an HIV-infected woman or man. Anal fisting created anxiety (especially early in the epidemic), doubtless because of germophobia and moral panics about activities some find unusual. Yet there also seemed to be an epidemiological association, with HIV more prevalent among gay men who fisted. On investigation it turned out that this actually revealed that a man was more vulnerable to acquiring HIV from being fucked if he had first been fisted, since he was more likely to have abrasions to the rectum which facilitated the entry of HIV in semen. No link has ever been shown between fisting a woman's vagina and acquiring HIV, and it is extremely unlikely to be risky. Not only does the vagina have more robust mucosa than the rectum, but vaginal fluids are not highly infectious, especially in the absence of semen. Moreover, there is no efficient route of entry for these fluids. As for the woman who is fisted, if this causes trauma, and an HIV-infected man then ejaculates in her (damaged) vagina, the likelihood of her acquiring HIV will be enhanced.

Most discussion of fisting has focused on whether the person fisting could acquire HIV from a (wo)man's vagina or anus, and some safer sex guidelines have promoted the use of latex gloves as protection. The only scientifically justified caution to women or men who fist, is to those who have eczema, or extensive non-intact skin for other reasons. One report of HIV transmission in the healthcare setting described a nurse who had severely broken skin on her hand and arrested the bleeding of an HIV-infected man for several minutes. It appears HIV in his blood had an easy point of access to her lymphocytes as it flowed directly into her blood-stream. No cases of this type have been recorded from sexual acts, but it is just on the bounds of possibility if the integrity of the skin were truly disrupted.

There has also been a report of an unusual case of a man who seems to have become infected by *being* fisted.[50] He denied anal or oral sex in the past several years, and had very restricted sexual practices with the man who apparently infected him. The man who was fisting had frequent ulcers on his hand, and was symptomatic with AIDS during their sexual relationship. Although this is thought to be an authentic case, it is noteworthy that the report was in 1986 and sexual history taking may not have been sophisticated.

• *Relative risks*

The existence of rare instances of such extreme cases of transmission does not change the fact that, in respect of sexual transmission, most women and men acquire HIV from getting semen in the vagina or anus, and some men acquire it from getting vaginal fluids, menstrual fluids and/or blood in the urethra, through the glans of the penis or under the foreskin.

As the epidemic reaches massive proportions, there are inevitably more reports of infection through extremely low-risk but biologically plausible routes. Fumento points out that 'in a large enough group of anything, there will occur events that seem at first too strong to be coincidence unless one looks at the entire group as a whole.'[51] This does not mean that these activities are any higher a risk than previously thought – it simply reflects the economies of scale. For example, an Australian writer reflected on the news that a man acquired HIV from using his partner's semen as lubrication when masturbating, saying, 'The odds on this must be about one in a million. . . . Does this mean that mutual masturbation cannot be described as "safe"? . . . Most of us happily do things which carry a small but statistically measurable risk of leading to death.'[52]

It can become invidious to constantly compare risks. The vast array of risks surrounding the individual make it easy to oscillate between total inertia and total paranoia. All women will make different choices about risks which are acceptable in their lives, and will have different concerns. For some people, the tiny HIV risk from fellatio may be terrifying; for others this is far less important than the lung cancer risk from cigarettes. For some the psychological risk of bearing an infected child is lower than the risk of dying childless. And so on. Risk is relative.

Babies

I have dwelt at length on sexual transmission, because information is not readily available, and many of the salient points need further research. Since sexual activity is less easily quantified or described than, say, vaginal delivery of a child, it is indeed more complex to define risks of individual activities. Scientists claim that it would be hard to construct *in vitro* models that could mimic many sexual acts. This may well be true, but it does seem strange given their abilities to pursue far more complex research directions.

In the arena of maternity, research is well advanced, and I have deliberately chosen not to go into great detail about HIV transmission to children (and prevention of this). This book is about women; since children are a key concern for many women I will summarize some of the information. However, there is extensive, reliable information about pregnancy and babies which is fairly easy to access,[53] and I do not wish to shift the focus from women themselves. The privileging of babies over their mothers has a long history. Faludi describes in chilling detail how in recent years '[a]s the foetus's rights increased, the mother's just kept diminishing'[54] to the point where women have been forced to submit to Caesarian section, or have been denied potentially life-saving therapies, often in futile attempts to save the child. Although these extremes have not yet been documented with HIV-infected women, the current vogue for antenatal HIV testing has many activists alarmed at the potential for interventionist policies. Indeed, a headline in a newspaper that prides itself on its balanced reporting shrieked: 'Doctors failing to prevent Aids babies';[55] the article did not mention the need to prevent women from acquiring HIV.

Although there is an extreme lack of balance with the representation of women as dangerous vectors to foetuses, attitudes from the healthcare profession seem to have shifted extensively in recent years regarding childbearing by HIV-positive women. In the past, these attitudes were characterized as judgemental and prohibitive, with frequent tales of coercive abortion and even forced sterilization. These attitudes have begun to shift. Positively Women found that there was pressure to abort or not conceive placed on 70 per cent of women who tested HIV-positive before 1988, but this pressure was only experienced by 34.4 per cent of women diagnosed between 1990 and 92.[56] Currently – in places treating large numbers of HIV-positive women – the approach tends to be to offer the most up-to-date scientific information and to support women in making choices about conception, or continuing with a pregnancy (although horror stories are still reported, principally from African women). By contrast, sexual decision-making is rarely afforded the same respect for any women. This may not be entirely reprehensible given that such different factors come into play: decisions about each sexual act are unlikely to be planned and premeditated in the same way as many conceptions (especially conceptions by women who know themselves to be HIV-positive).

The goal for most HIV-positive mothers and their healthcare providers will be to prevent transmission to the child. In order for this to happen there must first be certainty about when transmission occurs, and what factors may decrease or enhance the likelihood of it happening. Researchers have perhaps achieved more of practical value in this domain than in any other area of AIDS research (which makes it strange that efforts are currently intensified into dotting the 'i's of this knowledge, rather than turning to other areas where the 'i's are still unknown). It is now established that transmission from mother to baby can occur in three ways: during pregnancy – the foetus may be infected by HIV in the mother's blood crossing the placenta; during delivery – the infant may be infected by HIV in the mother's cervical secretions or blood during childbirth; during breast-feeding – the infant may be infected by HIV in the mother's breast milk or blood.

Research in this area is one of the most rapidly developing, and the overall rates of transmission are much lower than was initially assumed (it was initially represented as an inevitability). Rates vary in different areas of the world, with African research showing the highest rates, and this appears to be linked to the higher frequency of poverty, malnutrition and breast-feeding, and the fact that more of the women who give birth and breast-feed may be seroconverting or have developed AIDS. Probably the most reliable information (and the most pertinent to the British situation) has been gathered by the European Collaborative Study (ECS) which has analysed data from 1254 mother-baby pairs. This has established that 14 per cent of babies become infected during pregnancy or delivery. A further 14 per cent of infants are infected with HIV if they breast-feed. Infants whose mother herself becomes infected at delivery or during breast-feeding (from unprotected sex, or blood from medical interventions) stand a higher chance of acquiring HIV from breast-feeding, estimated at around 29 per cent.[57] These risks from breast-feeding exist in addition to the 14 per cent risk of HIV transmission during pregnancy and birth (i.e. the total risk to an infant whose mother is infected in the last trimester could be as high as 44 per cent).

• *How does transmission happen?*[58]

There are still some debates about the timing of transmission. Overall, it is believed that, where a child is breast-fed, there is a similar risk involved as during the time from conception to birth. In respect of that time, it appears that most transmission occurs during birth (intra-partum) or immediately before delivery, perhaps mostly after the onset of labour. In a review of the topic, Stephane Blanche proposed that '35 per cent would be infected before birth and 65 per cent during'.[59]

In the womb (*in utero*), the foetus is connected to the mother by the placenta, but their bloodstreams are separate. Sometimes HIV crosses the placenta and infects the foetus. Precisely how and when this transmission might occur during pregnancy is poorly understood, yet tests performed on aborted foetuses suggest that it could occur as early as twelve weeks.[60] *In utero* transmission may be more common if the placenta is damaged by infections, perhaps including untreated STDs.[61] One important finding is the presence of HIV in cord blood, indicating that the virus can cross the placenta.[62]

In the first eighteen months of the child's life, the usual test for HIV antibodies will not be able to distinguish between the mother's antibodies and the child's. The mother's antibodies are always transmitted to the child – the key question is whether the virus has also been passed on. Tests on the blood of newborns have therefore aimed to assess whether the infant is infected by looking for the *virus* with tests that are very sensitive. (These are expensive and difficult to perform, and consequently only available at a few specialist centres.)

Some infants will have a negative viral test immediately after birth, but are later found to have the virus. It is believed that these babies were infected late in the womb or during delivery, which is why the test could not immediately detect the virus, which was just starting to replicate. Some infants have been found to be virus-positive immediately after birth, suggesting that these babies were infected very early on in gestation. Babies who are fast progressors may also have been infected early. (The term 'fast progressors' describes the 25 per cent of HIV-infected newborns who develop AIDS in the first year of life.)[63]

Newborns may be infected during birth by prolonged exposure to HIV in their mother's blood, cervical and vaginal secretions. It is believed that the child may acquire the virus through abrasions on the skin, and also by ingesting infected blood or cervical secretions. The newborn's mucosa in the mouth is not fully formed at birth, or in the first months of life, and so this could provide a site for the virus to enter which is not vulnerable in adults.[64] Some studies suggest that vaginal delivery is more risky than Caesarian section (C-section), and this has become the focus of debate. One of the bases for considering that C-section has a protective effect is that where twins are born vaginally, more first-born twins (50 per cent) are HIV-infected than second-born (19 per cent), with the hypothesis that the first infant had far longer exposure to infected fluids in the cervical canal and vagina.[65] It is logical that vaginal delivery would be more risky than C-section, since this has been demonstrated for other viral conditions, such as hepatitis B and herpes simplex virus.

Many of the cohort studies looking at mother-to-child HIV transmission have also reported a lower rate of transmission with C-section. In 1992, the ECS suggested that the odds of transmitting by C-section compared with vaginal delivery in the ratio of 1 : 0.56. However, the confidence interval (the extent to which this statistic could have been due to chance) for C-section was between 0.3 and 1.04. That means C-section could lower the risk by as much as 70 per cent, or it could even be slightly more risky than vaginal delivery.[66] The ECS carried out a meta-analysis, looking at all published data considering this, and concluded that C-section may halve the risk of transmission, but that this was still not a definitive conclusion.[67] There are significant implications for morbidity and mortality with C-sections, and many researchers have raised concerns at an apparent rush to recommend C-sections to women with HIV.[68] Women who have C-sections are liable to all the problems associated with surgery, including bacterial infections, and it is more difficult to have future vaginal deliveries (and many HIV-positive women do go on to have another child). One estimate is that sixteen HIV-positive women would need to deliver by C-section to prevent one infant from acquiring HIV.[69] In the context of herpes simplex virus, it has been estimated that the cost of using C-section to avert a single case of transmission to an infant is $2.5 million per child, and between one and ten mother's lives would be lost for every two children saved.[70]

While the protective value of C-sections for HIV-infected women remains unproven, there are clear links between prolonged exposure (over four hours) to ruptured membranes and HIV transmission. Intuitively this would make sense, since the infant has more exposure to infected fluids.[71] There are also links between higher rates of HIV transmission and invasive procedures, including forceps, scalp electrodes, episiotomy and vacuum extractors. This link is strongest in centres which are not experienced with these techniques.[72] It is possible that the pregnancies were complicated (making transmission more likely), so the procedures were used – the procedures themselves did not necessarily facilitate transmission. One association with increased rates of transmission is delivery of babies before thirty-four weeks of gestation.[73] This appears to suggest that babies who are infected may be premature – backed up by findings that a high proportion of miscarried foetuses are also HIV-infected.

All of the research on HIV transmission to infants consistently states that the child is most likely to acquire HIV in the womb or during delivery if the woman has high viral load or poor immunity, that is, if she is recently infected or she is in the late stages of disease. Markers include low CD4 cell counts, symptoms of AIDS, p24 antigenemia, and other measures of viral load such as HIV culture, and RT QC-PCR to quantitate HIV-1 RNA plasma levels.[74] Some researchers have found that placental inflammation increases the risk of transmission, and one group found that high CD8 cell counts (with normal CD4 counts) was linked with transmission (high CD8 cells may reflect that a woman has been infected very recently).[75] Other infections, including STDs, and poor nutritional status and general health – in particular Vitamin A deficiency, which may be an indication of poor immune function[76] – are associated with a higher risk of transmission.

• Breast-feeding

One of the strange features about HIV and breast-feeding is the deep resistance many people have had to hearing the information about transmission. The tendency has already been noted for people to acknowledge danger only in the activities which they would like to be risky, and nowhere is that more evident than in respect of breast-feeding. Breast-feeding is a healthful, inexpensive and psychologically beneficial method of feeding infants which has been hijacked by international commercial interest. Women's activists have long been alert to scandals involving the promotion of formula feed to women in the 'developing' world (as well as to women in British maternity wards). In situations where clean water is a rare luxury, formula-feeding can be lethal to a child, yet the practices of some companies (Nestlé being the one which is complained about most) lead to children getting hooked on the product, women ceasing to produce their own milk, and financial misery as well as health problems. No wonder, then, that any news suggesting breast-feeding could be harmful is scrutinized closely. Are findings about HIV just some new plot to undermine the benefits of this natural act?

Conspiracy theories have a tendency to overstay their welcome, and in this case the initial healthy scepticism has dragged on too long. Sadly, breast-feeding really does pose a risk of HIV transmission to babies born to women with HIV – but this does not presage the end of breast-feeding. Since 1987, WHO guidelines have consistently stated that the risks from bottle-feeding in areas where the water supply is unsafe outweigh the risks of HIV infection from breast-feeding.[77] However, where bottle-feeding carries little physical health risk, the HIV risk from breast-feeding (when a woman is known to be HIV-infected) is greater than the disadvantages associated with bottle-feeding.

It is telling that the policy implications of HIV transmission during breast-feeding are so great that they necessarily precede a description of the mechanisms of transmission. Within the scientific literature, articles and letters have been volleying back and forth, replete with anxiety about the public health guidance which would emerge.[78] The presence of HIV (then HTLV-III) in breast milk was established as early as 1985,[79] and in 1988 the UK implemented HIV testing for all breast-milk donors (this was controversial, not only because of fears that this would discourage women from high-risk groups from breast-feeding, but also because the pasteurization process alone should be sufficient to deactivate HIV).[80] It was to be expected that breast-feeding would be an efficient mode of HIV transmission given that other viruses (CMV, HTLV-I, hepatitis B) are easily transmitted by this route.[81]

Infants can acquire HIV when breast-feeding from virus in the breast milk and also in blood, from bleeding, cracked nipples or breast abscesses.[82] The concentration of HIV appears to be particularly high in colostrum and early milk.[83] Although it is impossible to distinguish between the ingestion of blood and breast milk when an infant is breast-feeding, reports of HIV transmission associated with breast abscesses would suggest that risks of transmission are increased in the presence of blood. Virus in the breast milk (or blood) can infect the child through white blood cells on the surface of the mucosa in the infant's mouth. Children are not just mini-adults, and newborns are still in the process of physiological development (a development process that takes many years, as highlighted by earlier descriptions of the adolescent female genital tract). The skin lining the mouth is still immature and may not be intact (for example, if the child is teething) and this makes the child vulnerable to acquiring HIV. Adult mouths are more robust, and experienced at resisting infections, and it would be highly unlikely that an adult would ever ingest so great (and frequent) a quantity of infected fluid as a breast-fed infant will drink. (Some people have made inaccurate comparisons between breast-feeding and oral sex, and some women and men have expressed anxiety about ingesting breast milk in sexual contexts.[84] Adult infection by this route is highly implausible.)

The existence of breast-feeding HIV transmission has been established from case reports, mostly of women who received infected blood transfusions at the time of delivery, thus seroconverting during the first days of the child's life, and breast-feeding during the highest viral load.[85] It is clearly established that the likelihood of transmitting HIV during breast-feeding rises when the woman has high viral load, especially when seroconverting, but also at low CD4 counts and when she has developed symptoms of AIDS.[86] Several cohorts have confirmed the risks established from case studies. This has been more complicated, as it depends upon comparing women who choose to breast-feed with those who do not, and this is not something that can be randomized. However, the potential methodological problems with cohorts have mainly been overcome, in part because of the introduction of early viral testing which may suggest the timing of infection. The ECS carried out a meta-analysis of studies assessing the risk of breast-feeding and concluded that the risk of transmission when the woman was HIV-infected before conception is 14 per cent, compared with 29 per cent when the woman is infected postnatally (or *intra-partum*).[87] These findings appear to have been universally accepted – the only problem that remains is how to integrate them in public-health and HIV-prevention policies. And it is to the prevention of HIV that we turn next.

• *Interrupting HIV transmission to babies*

Some opportunities to reduce HIV transmission to babies should already be apparent from the overview of the modes by which infection occurs. The most effective way to 'prevent AIDS babies' is to prevent women from acquiring HIV in the first place.[88] Given that women who become infected during pregnancy or breast-feeding are at increased risk of transmitting to the baby, safer sex (and drug use) should be promoted to pregnant and lactating women – but it rarely is. The second most effective approach to prevent babies from acquiring HIV is for HIV-infected women not to have babies; this is highly unrealistic for many women. If women are infected and want children then there are a number of mechanisms which reduce the risks of their babies acquiring HIV – although there is no mechanism which can give a 100 per cent guarantee of infection not occurring.

The highest likelihood of HIV transmission to a baby in Europe is during breast-feeding, followed by delivery, and finally during gestation. Alternatives to breast-feeding are an efficient mode of preventing HIV transmission, and this is a realistic strategy where safe alternatives exist. However, this strategy is only useful where women know (or highly suspect) that they have HIV, as the general health gains of breast-feeding are so great. Since breast-feeding must be recommended where there is not a safe water supply (i.e. in most developing countries), there have been discussions about alternatives to bottle-feeding. Aside from using wet nurses who are HIV-negative, there are no realistic strategies. Some (male) researchers suggested that it might be possible for women to just avoid breast-feeding when there was colostrum, or expressing breast milk which would be pasteurized and then fed to the child.[89] However, these suggestions are rejected by most (women) researchers who find them unrealistic and overcomplicated. The recommendation to HIV-positive women not to breast-feed may not always be an easy one for women to adopt – especially if members of their family or culture perceive breast-feeding as culturally essential.

After breast-feeding, HIV transmission is most likely during the delivery of the baby. As noted earlier, Caesarean section (C-section) appears to confer a protective effect, perhaps by as much as half. Despite the fact that the researchers themselves are not convinced of the data, the appearance of this study in 1994 seems to have resulted in a rush for C-sections to be offered to, and accepted by, HIV-positive women. It is alarming that women are having C-sections based upon a hunch, or to assuage any guilt or anxiety at being pregnant, and therefore undergoing invasive and potentially dangerous procedures.

One option for reducing transmission risks during delivery would be to 'clean' the birth canal using a vaginal lavage. Several products have been proposed, and these include chemicals under investigation as microbicides to prevent HIV transmission during vaginal intercourse. These include chlorhexidrine, betadine, Nonoxynol 9, benzalkonium, acidifying solutions and surfactants. Another approach would be to keep the vagina at a low (acidic) pH throughout the labour and birth process.[90] Trials into such logical and cheap approaches have been nudged out of the way by the apparent efficacy of systemic approaches, such as AZT (see below). Some of these products for vaginal lavage have been used successfully for other conditions (there were very few adverse events in a trial of 7000 women using chlorhexidrine in Norway and Sweden), yet attention has focused on more interventionist methods.

Researchers have proposed a randomized trial to assess the different risks of C-sections and vaginal delivery, where HIV-positive women would be randomly assigned by the researchers to give birth either by Caesarean or vaginally. Scientists claim that this is the only reliable way to check that different rates of transmission are due to the procedure, rather than confounding variables if the women chose for themselves how they would give birth. Scientifically the methodology may be sound, but it raises alarming ethical and practical concerns which the researchers appear to be resistant to addressing. The idea that women will yield responsibility for such an intimate choice to others is strange, and this is complicated further by the fact that the trial methodology is likely to involve covert coercion. The 'opportunity' to participate in the trial will be discussed with HIV-positive women from their first booking at an antenatal clinic and then discussed with them at each subsequent visit; allegedly this is to enable them to consider the choice carefully. Despite the fact that the majority of HIV-positive expectant mothers in the UK are of African descent, researchers have not made budgetary provision for interpreters. The trial was planned for women living in Europe, but the realization that insufficient numbers would be likely to participate means that HIV-positive pregnant women in Soweto will also be enrolled. This is quite extraordinary, given that one of the key risks with C-sections is post-operative infections, which will be especially dangerous for HIV-positive women who return from a shiny new Soweto hospital to homes without running water.

The tendency to experiment on women in the developing world is nothing new. There were also plans to conduct a randomized trial of breast-feeding versus formula feed among HIV-positive women in Rwanda. A lot of data on pregnancy, breast-feeding and HIV came from Rwanda, where seroprevalence among women was very high. The trial was never realized because of the war. It would have randomized children to either feeding option, and the women would have been supplied with formula feed and clean water.[91] Concerns about the ethics of the trial focused on the disruption this intervention would cause within the women's cultures (including problems of confidentiality) and the dangerous lay beliefs about formula feed that could arise. The marketing of formula feed in 'developing' countries has turned on promoting it as a Western, healthy option, and the conduct of this trial would likely have reaffirmed such messages.

Such randomized trials may give more precise academic statistics for conference presentations, but do they really assist women in making complicated real-life decisions? Psychologists have urged the researchers to include components to the trial which would assess the impact of these interventions on women's well-being and decision-making capacities. These have consistently been rejected in favour of the hard science of knowing numerical rates of transmission – rather than what this means for the women who might be passing the virus on to their children.[92]

In these 'placebo-controlled' trials where the guinea pigs are pregnant vectors, all the learning from AIDS-treatment activism dissolves: researchers propose protocols which are entirely unacceptable to the community, refuse to negotiate, and adopt the patriarchal stance of 'Doctor knows best'. When experimental AIDS treatments are proven to be tolerable and safe, but efficacy is unproven (as is the case with 3TC and several protease inhibitors, at the time of writing), Open Label trials are developed.[93] Under such programmes, researchers and people living with HIV or AIDS share the risks of unproven therapies. Science is then enriched by data being gathered on people who choose to try out an approach which may benefit them, but may also entail unforeseen risks. So why is this approach not used for C-sections, antiviral therapies and other pregnancy-related interventions? The underlying rates of HIV transmission from a woman to her child are extremely well documented. It would be easy to gather data on the birth outcomes of HIV-positive pregnant women who chose a range of approaches, and this could soon reveal whether a particular approach lowered the HIV-transmission rate. In such a vital area as the health of a future generation, apparently women have to be protected from making such decisions for themselves – despite the fact that doctors have no better evidence upon which to base their advice than is easily accessible to HIV-positive (would-be) mothers.

The best-publicized intervention to reduce HIV transmission to the newborn is AZT, as reported from ACTG 076. This American trial was controversial from its inception. Corea documents how, in 1990, American treatment activists were frustrated to find that discussions about the planned trial represented women as 'fetus-carriers', made no plans to chart the effects of the drug on women, and withdrew AZT from women as soon as they had given birth. As women had been excluded from earlier trials of AZT – a move that blocked not only scientific learning about the effects of AZT on women, but also excluded women from the sole free point of access to the drug – the whole approach seemed cynical to activists. ACT UP's Linda Meridith characterized the trial's message to HIV-positive women as: 'Don't get pregnant if you want access to clinical trials – but we will only include you in a trial if you are pregnant so that we may study the effects of treatments on your fetus.'[94] Activists succeeded in changing the protocol so that women could continue with AZT after the child was born (if they wished), but the trial never collected adequate data on the effects of AZT on women, especially gynaecological effects.

The results of 076, released to great fanfare in 1994, restored popular faith in AZT.[95] The trial had aimed to enrol 748 women, but results were analysed based on data from 477 women who had given birth to 421 infants; all women had CD4 cell counts over 200. The trial was double-blind (neither the women nor the doctors knew who was receiving AZT). The women were equally assigned to two groups. One group received 500mg of AZT tablets daily between fourteen and thirty-four weeks of pregnancy, followed by an infusion of the drug during labour, and the infant was then given AZT syrup for the first six weeks of life. The other half of the women and infants received placebo (sugar-pill) tablets, infusions and syrup. Thirteen HIV-infected infants were born to women in the AZT arm, with 40 born to women receiving placebos. This gave respective transmission rates of 8.3 per cent and 25.5 per cent – an apparent two-thirds reduction due to taking this antiviral.

At all subsequent International AIDS Conferences, speaker after speaker has spoken of the results of ACTG 076 as a break-through in the management of HIV in women. AZT's tarnished image was restored and it was back on the pedestal as a wonder drug. Is it? AZT has a highly controversial image (which it will probably never shake off) veering between characterizations as the magic bullet, poison by prescription, or the cornerstone of HIV therapy. Cynics might detect in all the 076 hype a simple relief that the drug at least does *something*.

This is not the place to discuss whether AZT is an effective treatment for HIV disease,[96] but it is hardly surprising that AZT showed a positive effect on HIV-transmission rates. The drug works by slowing the replication of the virus, and it is the level of virus which is most closely associated with whether HIV is transmitted. What remains disputed is whether AZT is a therapy that should be recommended to pregnant HIV-positive women, and whether they should be recommended to follow the full 076 protocol. The strange thing is that worldwide physicians seem to have interpreted 076 as giving definitive information that such an approach is warranted – based on data about just *fifty-three* HIV-infected babies. The risks of breast-feeding have only gradually been established, after evidence has been gathered on hundreds of babies infected by this route. Yet, based on one trial, official documents now imply that, to prevent transmission, AZT is more effective than not breast-feeding.[97]

The debate that has followed the results from 076 has tended to focus on any (unknown) long-term effects of AZT to the uninfected offspring of women who took the drug during pregnancy. Oddly, these concerns have been highlighted by feminist activists, as if concern for the foetus should be the major feminist issue. This is ironic given that teratogenicity (harm to the foetus or newborn) is also a fundamental worry to pharmaceutical companies making such a product, and the major reason why women's access to all experimental medication is restricted. In the post-thalidomide era, every pharmaceutical company errs heavily on the side of caution with allowing women access to drugs. For women, perhaps the bigger concern is why they are being used as vehicles for surrogate treatment. The use of antivirals during pregnancy perceives women as potentially dangerous incubators that need regulating with sophisticated products. The reason why the 076 protocol originally withdrew women from AZT after they had given birth was because the drug was not intended for their health. The majority of women will be happy to engage in measures that will safeguard the health of their child, but the fusing of the interests of woman and child are excessive. No one has ever suggested that adults would be willing to take toxic drugs in order to prevent the sexual transmission of HIV – why is it automatically assumed that foetus-carriers will be compliant? One of the fundamental questions about using AZT in pregnancy must be whether it harms the woman's health – as well as whether it truly does safeguard the child's. If a woman with high CD4 counts takes AZT during pregnancy might she 'use up' any potential future benefit for herself? What are the implications if she develops AZT resistance? These questions were not asked in trials such as 076 – principally because scientists have focused solely on whether HIV-transmission rates are reduced, and whether the babies are damaged by the medication. However, the results of the multi-centre Delta trial (which compared AZT monotherapy with combinations of AZT and ddI or ddC for treating adults with HIV) suggest that women's long-term health potential will be damaged by taking AZT alone in pregnancy. Combination therapies have a clear benefit over AZT monotherapy – but the benefit is only seen if the woman never previously took AZT.[98]

With so many gaps in knowledge, and the apparent harmful consequences of monotherapy, the rush to embrace AZT, and to ignore other potential interventions, does seem far too hasty. There are many other antiviral therapies in development, and there is good reason to believe that some of the less well-known varieties (produced by less well-off firms) could be far more use. One product that appeared to have great potential is nevirapine which causes a swift and impressive reduction in viral load.[99] However, this is soon followed by resistance and the drug shows little promise for long-term therapy. This means it could be an ideal candidate, since the effect is time-limited (as is pregnancy) and using it would not interfere with a woman's future treatment options (since she would not be prescribed nevirapine for her own health). The importance of identifying products which make a more impressive dent in viral levels is strengthened by some closer inspection of the initial data from 076. Informal comments by the principal investigator of 076,[100] combined with a small study on mother-to-child transmission which included some women on 076, suggest that the level of viral load is a far more significant factor than AZT use in determining whether women transmit HIV to their babies.

Weiser described a small study of thirty HIV-positive pregnant women whose viral load was measured during pregnancy, and the child's HIV status was established.[101] Eight of the women transmitted HIV (27 per cent), and these were the eight women with the highest viral load detected by PCR tests – at delivery, all eight women had between 10^5 and 10^6 copies of HIV-1 RNA per ml plasma. What was also significant about these tests is that they were done at several stages during the women's pregnancy and the levels seen early remained relatively stable. This means that, using PCR, it is possible to predict ultimate HIV transmission from early on in pregnancy. Nineteen of the thirty women in this study received AZT at some time during their pregnancy. Most of these women took AZT intermittently, but two of the women were enrolled on 076, and so they received a full dose. Women who took no anti-virals, or who remained on consistent therapy (e.g. they had been taking AZT before they became pregnant) had stable viral load, but the effect of beginning AZT during pregnancy was not always the desired one. One woman (enrolled on 076) began taking AZT while pregnant, and had an initial five-fold drop in her viral load. However, she then quickly developed resistance to AZT and transmitted HIV to her baby. Weiser measured AZT resistance in the women and found that three women had resistant virus, two of whom had high viral load and transmitted HIV. This is not to suggest that AZT was necessarily harmful (the link between AZT resistance and high viral load is chicken and egg), but Weiser's analysis did demonstrate that there was no link between using AZT and transmitting HIV, nor between using AZT and the level of viral load.

While the spotlight has been on the nice little earner produced by Glaxo-Wellcome, some of the simpler, more realistic strategies have been neglected. Viral load increases as health status declines, and one of the key indicators of poor immune function as well as poor nutrition is deficiencies of the micro-nutrient Vitamin A. In Malawi, 474 HIV-positive women were followed during their pregnancy and until the child was one year old.[102] Vitamin A levels in their blood were measured and 69.2 per cent of the women were found to be Vitamin A-deficient (having less than 1.05 mol/L). The women were divided into four groups and the transmission rates from woman to child were assessed (the child's HIV status was assessed at 12 months). Women who were very deficient in Vitamin A had a 32.4 per cent transmission rate; 25.2 per cent of women who were deficient transmitted; women with acceptable levels had a 16 per cent transmission rate; and only 7.2 per cent of mothers transmitted who had sufficient Vitamin A. Over a quarter of the children died by the end of the first year, and this was also strongly associated with whether the mother was Vitamin A-deficient; Vitamin A deficiency also doubled the risk of death for the mothers.

These findings are very significant. They do not suggest that HIV-positive pregnant women should take Vitamin A supplementation, since high doses can be toxic, and this is a known teratogen. There are also theoretical concerns that high levels of Vitamin A could increase HIV viral replication. The connection between Vitamin A deficiency and HIV transmission and higher mortality is not necessarily a causative link. Vitamin A deficiency seems to be linked with impaired immunity to HIV. It is also associated with placental pathology (allowing infections), increases levels of HIV in breast milk and increases the susceptibility of the birth canal to bleeding and trauma during vaginal delivery. Deficiency in this micro-nutrient may be indicating other nutritional problems, or be a marker for general immune deficiency. Vitamin A is known to be central to good immune function, and in developed countries Vitamin A deficiency is rare as many food products have vitamin supplementation. However, American research found more Vitamin A deficiency among drug-using HIV-positive women with CD4s under 200, especially women who use cocaine.[103] The findings from this preliminary research suggest that HIV-positive women who hope to conceive would be well advised to pay attention to their nutritional status and avoid becoming vitamin-deficient.

In terms of HIV-positive women, the accumulating evidence suggests that there is concrete advice that can be given to women about the timing of conception and the likelihood of HIV transmission to the baby. This is an area which seems to cause anxiety, and healthcare workers resist discussing it in too much detail – what if they are encouraging the infection of one in seven babies? Although no one can predict with certainty when or whether a woman would transmit HIV to a child (or indeed to an adult), there is an increased risk at low CD4 cell counts and with high viral load. The implications are straightforward: HIV-positive women who want children should be encouraged to become pregnant early on in their disease (although not during the period of seroconversion). Women also need to maintain their general health status and be supported in having optimal nutrition. If women have low viral load before conceiving, or in the first trimester of pregnancy, the likelihood of HIV transmission is extremely low. Indeed, at least one researcher is willing to define a level (10^5 copies of HIV-1 RNA per ml plasma) below which she believes HIV transmission is not likely to occur. The challenge arising from this mass of scientific information is whether foetus-carrying HIV vectors will be afforded their basic human right to found a family – and to make their own choices about how to minimize the risks of morbidity and mortality within their own, and their babies', bodies.

Notes

1. Maxine Wolfe, 22 February 1995, opening speech to 'HIV Infection in Women: Setting a New Agenda' conference, Washington, DC, 1995. Wolfe is a long-standing feminist, lesbian and AIDS activist, whose association with New York's ACT UP dates back to March 1987.
2. *The Concise Oxford Dictionary of Current English*, 7th edition, Oxford University Press, 1982.
3. See, for example, *Women Like Us: Positively Women's Research into the Needs and Experiences of Women with HIV*, Positively Women, London, 1994, pp. 24–8.
4. D. Wiley *et al.*, 'Monotonic rapid decline of CD4+ cells related to anal receptive intercourse with ejaculation in a cohort of HIV-infected men who have sex with men', Abstract 252, Second National Conference on Human Retroviruses and Related Infections, Washington, DC, January 1995.
5. See Chapter 4; and Positively Women and Terrence Higgins Trust, *Positive Women: A Guide to Symptoms and Treatments for Women Living with HIV and AIDS*, 1994.
6. N. S. Padian *et al.*, 'Female-to-male transmission of human immunodeficiency virus', *JAMA*, 25 September 1991, 266 (12), pp. 1664–7.
7. H. Haverkos *et al.*, followed by N. S. Padian *et al.*, 'Female-to-male transmission of HIV', letters, *JAMA*, 14 October 1992, 268 (14), pp. 1855–7.
8. Padian *et al.*, *op. cit.*
9. C. Wofsy *et al.*, 'Isolation of AIDS-associated retrovirus from genital secretions of women with antibodies to the virus', *Lancet*, 1986, i (8 March), pp. 527–9; M. W. Vogt *et al.*, 'Isolation of HTLV-III/LAV from cervical secretions of women at risk for AIDS', *Lancet*, 1986, i (8 March), pp. 525–7.
10. J. A. Hill *et al.*, 'Human vaginal leukocytes and the effects of vaginal

fluid on lymphocyte and macrophage defense functions', *Am. J. Obstet. Gynecol.*, 166 (2), February 1992, pp. 720–6.

11. J. A. Hill *et al.*, 'Quantification of CD4 lymphocytes, macrophages and HIV antigen levels in vaginal secretions of HIV+ women', Fifth International Conference on AIDS, Montreal, June 4–9, 1989, p. 181, Abstract A 625.

12. D. B. A. Clemetson *et al.*, 'Detection of HIV DNA in cervical and vaginal secretions: prevalence and correlates among women in Nairobi, Kenya', *JAMA*, 9 June 1993, Vol. 269, No. 22, pp. 2860–4.

13. S. D. Holmberg *et al.*, 'AIDS commentary: biologic factors in the sexual transmission of HIV', *Journal of Infectious Diseases*, 1 July 1989, 160(1), pp. 116–25.

14. B. Voeller *et al.*, 'Heterosexual transmission of HIV', letter, *JAMA*, 8 April 1992, 267(14), pp. 1917–18, discussion, pp. 1918–19.

15. M. W. Vogt *et al.*, 'Short papers: isolation patterns of the Human Immunodeficiency Virus from cervical secretions during the menstrual cycle of women at risk for the Acquired Immunodeficiency Syndrome', *Annals of Internal Medicine*, March 1987, 106(3), pp. 380–2.

16. M. J. Blaser, 'Letters and corrections: isolation of the Human Immunodeficiency Virus from cervical secretions during menses', *Annals of Internal Medicine*, June 1987, 106(6), p. 912.

17. C. Paglia, *Sexual Personae*, Penguin, Harmondsworth, 1990, p. 11.

18. Mike Bailey, personal communication.

19. Numerous studies have consistently reported less partner change by women, whereas men report significantly more sexual partners. This is found in Wellings, *op. cit.*, p. 101, which references five other studies with the same finding; 24.4 per cent of the men reported more than ten partners in their lifetime, whereas this is reported by just 6.8 per cent of the women (Table 3.1, pp. 95–6).

20. J. A. Jacquez *et al.* suggest that in the early years of the epidemic most gay men acquired HIV from non-steady partners. Partner change was important because men ran a far higher risk of encountering a man who was seroconverting and thus highly infectious. 'Role of the primary infection in epidemics of HIV infection in gay cohorts', *J. AIDS*, 1994, 7, pp. 1169–84.

21. European Study Group on Heterosexual Transmission of HIV (ESG), 'Comparison of female to male and male to female transmission of HIV in 563 stable couples', *BMJ*, 304, pp. 809–13 (1992).

22. I. de Vincenzi *et al.*, 'A longitudinal study of HIV transmission by heterosexual partners', *NEJM*, 1994, 331:6, pp. 341–6.

23. Padian *et al.*, *op. cit.*

24. ESG, *op. cit.*

25. A. M. Downs *et al.*, 'Per-contact HIV transmission rates in hetero-

sexuals', IX International Conference on AIDS, 6–11 June 1993, Abstract PO-CII-2859.

26. C. Patton, *Sex and Germs*, South End Press, Boston, 1985, p. 9. This area is also explored in more detail in S. Watney, *Policing Desire*, Methuen, London, 1987, Chapter 3, 'Moral Panics'.

27. K. Alcorn (ed.), *AIDS Reference Manual*, NAM Publications, January 1995, p. 87.

28. H. A. M. Van Druten *et al.*, 'Homosexual role separation and the spread of HIV', VIII International Conference on AIDS, Amsterdam 1992, Abstract ThC 1518; I. Keet *et al.*, 'Orogenital sex and the transmission of HIV among homosexual men', *AIDS*, 6:2, pp. 223–6 (1992).

29. In his letter to the *Lancet*, 1992, *op. cit.*, Haverkos suggests that four studies have shown this, but it is not apparent to which studies he is referring.

30. K. Wellings *et al.*, *Sexual Behaviour in Britain: The National Survey of Sexual Attitudes and Lifestyles*, Penguin, Harmondsworth, 1994, p. 175.

31. A. Nicolosi *et al.*, 'Risk factors for woman-to-man sexual transmission of the human immunodeficiency virus', *J. AIDS*, 1994, 7 (3), pp 296–300.

32. F. S. Sion *et al.*, 'Absence of female-to-male transmission of HIV in stable couples in Rio de Janeiro, Brazil', VIII International Conference on AIDS, Amsterdam, July 1992, Abstract PoC 4169.

33. These are documented in Alcorn, *op. cit.*, pp. 94–5. [M. Quarto *et al.*; W. Rozenbaum *et al.*; M. Landor and L. L. Cregler].

34. *Women Like Us*, pp. 24–8.

35. Alcorn, *op. cit.*, p. 136. Some people doubt that female ejaculate exists; they would be well advised to see Annie Sprinkle's videos. Thanks to Dr Lucia Grun for repeated advice about this.

36. R. Raiteri *et al.*, 'No HIV-1 transmission through lesbian sex', letter, *Lancet*, 24 July 1994, 344, p. 270.

37. S. Y. Chu *et al.*, 'Update: epidemiology of reported cases of AIDS in women who report sex only with other women, United States 1980–91', *AIDS*, 6 (5), 1992, pp. 516–9.

38. P. Spitzer *et al.*, 'Transmission of HIV infection from a woman to a man by oral sex', *NEJM*, 1989, 320 (4), p. 251.

39. Amber Hollibaugh, comments during her presentation 'Lesbian and AIDS', London Lighthouse, 1 October 1993.

40. M. T. Sabatini *et al.*, 'Kaposi's sarcoma and T-cell lymphoma in an immunodeficient woman: a case report', *AIDS Res.*, 1984: 1, pp. 135–7.

41. M. Marmor *et al.*, 'Possible female-to-female transmission of human immunodeficiency virus', *Annals of Internal Medicine*, 1986, 105, p. 969.

42. See M. Fumento, *The Myth of Heterosexual Aids*, Regnery Gateway, Washington, DC, 1993, pp. 362–7.

43. I am indebted to Drs Jayne Kavanagh, Lucia Grun and Charles Farthing for explaining this point.

44. P. Greenhouse, 'Female-to-female transmission of HIV', *Lancet*, 1987, 2 (8555), pp. 401f.

45. J. D. Rich *et al.*, 'Transmission of Human Immunodeficiency Virus infection presumed to have occurred via female homosexual contact', *Clinical Infectious Diseases*, 1993, 17(6), pp. 1003–5.

46. There is one odd report in the literature of rimming-associated HIV transmission. This is another example of what King terms 'eccentricities', and describes a man who acquired HIV by being rimmed by a recently HIV-infected man. It appears that the man who was rimming had severe gum disease and may have inserted blood on his tongue into the other man's rectum. S. K. Gill *et al.*, 'Transmission of HIV-1 infection by oroanal intercourse', *Genitourinary Medicine*, 1992, 68(4), pp. 254–6.

47. See Alcorn, *op. cit.*, p. 128.

48. G. Rubin, 'Thinking sex: notes for a radical theory of the politics of sexuality', in C. S. Vance (ed.), *Pleasure and Danger: Exploring Female Sexuality*, Pandora, London, 1992, p. 299.

49. Sue Golding, statement at 'Lesbian and AIDS' meeting, 1 October 1993, *op. cit.*

50. B. Donovan *et al.*, 'Brachiopractic eroticism and transmission of retrovirus', *Genitourinary Medicine*, 1986, 62: 6, pp. 390–2.

51. Fumento, *op. cit.*, p. 80.

52. A. Carr, 'Swallowing the evidence – is oral sex (or anything else) safe?', *Outrage*, January 1991, pp. 50–3; quoted in E. King, *Safety in Numbers*, Cassell, London, 1993, p. 111.

53. For example, see: D. Gibb and S. Walters, *Guidelines for Management of Children with HIV Infection*, 2nd edition, AVERT, UK, November 1993; R. Gorna, *AIDS Treatment Update*, Issue 13/14, NAM Publications, November/December 1993; K. Alcorn (ed.), *op. cit.*, pp. 104–8; L. Sherr, *HIV and AIDS in Mothers and Babies – a Guide to Counselling*, Blackwell Scientific Publications, Oxford, 1991. Scientific reviews include: F. D. Johnstone, 'HIV and pregnancy (review)' *International Journal of STD/AIDS*, 1992, 3(2): pp. 79–86; A. E. Ades *et al.*, 'Vertically transmitted HIV infection in the British Isles', *BMJ*, 15 May 1993, 306, pp. 1296–9; M. L. Newell *et al.*, 'Risk factors for vertical transmission of HIV-1 and early markers of HIV-1 infection in children', *AIDS*, 1993, 7 (Suppl. 1): S91-7; C. S. Peckham, 'Human immunodeficiency virus infection and pregnancy', *Sexual Trans. Dis.*, 1994, 21 (2 Suppl.): S28–31.

54. S. Faludi, *Backlash*, Vintage, London, 1991, p. 463. This skewed approach to human rights is documented in Chapter 14, 'Repro-

ductive rights under the backlash: the invasion of women's bodies', pp. 436–91.

55. *Independent*, 14 May 1993, p. 6.

56. *Women Like Us*, p. 23.

57. M. L. Newell *et al.*, The European Collaborative Study, 'Risk factors for mother-to-child transmission of HIV-1', *Lancet*, 25 April 1992, 339 (8800): pp. 1007–12; D. T. Dunn *et al.*, 'Risk of human immunodeficiency virus type 1 transmission through breastfeeding', *Lancet*, 5 September 1992, 340, pp. 585–8.

58. The information presented here incorporates pieces I wrote previously for NAM (*The AIDS Reference Manual*), pp. 104–7; *AIDS Treatment Update*, Issue 13/14, *op. cit.*, pp. 8–9; and in R. Gorna, *Positive Practice: An HVA Guide to Caring for Families and Children Affected by HIV/AIDS*, Health Visitors Association, 1994, pp. 31–3. In preparing the initial pieces I was guided by Dr Diana Gibb, and I am extremely grateful to her for her patience in sharing her expertise.

59. S. Blanche, 'Update on mother-to-child HIV infection', presentation to the X International Conference on AIDS, Yokahama, reproduced in *Conference News*, 10 August 1994, p. 3.

60. Y. Brossard *et al.*, 'Frequency of early *in utero* HIV-1 infection: a blind DNA polymerase chain reaction study on 100 fetal thymuses', *AIDS*, 1995, 9, pp. 359–66; S. Sprecher *et al.*, 'Vertical transmission of HIV-1 in 15-week fetus', *Lancet*, 2 August 1986, ii, pp. 288–9; F. D. Johnstone *et al.*, 'Vertical HIV transmission in pregnancy', letter, *Lancet*, 28 September 1991, 338 (8770), p. 289.

61. Mike Bailey, personal communication.

62. R. Ryder *et al.*, 'Perinatal transmission of the Human Immunodeficiency Virus Type 1 to infants of seropositive women in Zaire', *NEJM*, 22 June 1989, 320 (25), pp. 1637–42.

63. Y. J. Bryson *et al.*, 'Correspondence: proposed definitions for in utero versus intrapartum transmission of HIV-1', *NEJM*, 22 October 1992, 237 (17), pp. 1246–7; Johnstone (1991), *op. cit.*; Newell (1993), *op. cit.*; Ryder, *op. cit.*

64. See, for example, P. Pizzo *et al.*, 'In the vertical transmission of HIV, timing may be everything', *NEJM*, 29 August 1991, 325 (9), pp. 652–3.

65. J. Goedert *et al.*, 'High risk of HIV-1 infection for first-born twins', *Lancet*, 14 December 1991, 338(8781), pp. 1471–5.

66. Newell (1992), *op. cit.*

67. ECS, 'Caesarian section and risk of vertical transmission of HIV-1 infection', *Lancet*, 1994, 343 (8911): 1464–7.

68. P. A. Tovo, 'Caesarean section and perinatal HIV transmission: what next?', *Lancet*, 11 September 1993, 342 (8872):630; also, statements by Marie-Louise Newell and Catherine Peckham to a

meeting co-ordinated by WHAN (Women's HIV/AIDS Network) regarding their intentions to conduct a controlled trial of vaginal versus Caesarian delivery, London, 23 January 1995.

69. P. Villari *et al.*, 'Caesarean section to reduce perinatal transmission of human immunodeficiency virus', *Online H. Curr. Clin. Trials*, 8 July 1993, 2:doc. no. 74.

70. Reported in Perinatal session, First National Conference on Human Retroviruses and Related Infections, Washington, DC, December 1993.

71. *Ibid.* See also, P. Boyer *et al.*, 'Factors predictive of maternal-fetal transmission of HIV-1', *JAMA*, 22/29 June 1994, 271, pp. 1925–30; D. Moodley *et al.*, 'Caesarean section and vertical transmission of HIV-1', letter, *Lancet*, 30 July 1994, 344, p. 338.

72. Newell, ECS, 1992, *op. cit.*

73. *Ibid.* B. M. de Tejada *et al.*, 'Clinical predictors of HIV perinatal transmission', VIII International Conference on AIDS, Amsterdam, 19–24 July 1992, Abstract No PoC 4235; J. J. Goedert *et al.*, 'Mother-to-infant transmission of human immunodeficiency virus type 1: association with prematurity or low anti-gp120', *Lancet*, 2 (8676), 9 December 1989, pp. 1351–4.

74. Boyer, *op. cit.*; Newell, ECS (1992), *op. cit*; Newell (1993), *op. cit*; R. Ryder *op. cit.*; M. E. St. Louis *et al.*, 'Risk for perinatal HIV-1 transmission according to maternal immunologic, virologic, and placental factors', *JAMA*, 9 June 1993, 269 (22), p. 2853; B. Weiser, 'QC-PCR Quantitation of HIV plasma RNA level during pregnancy: vertical transmission and antiviral therapy', Abstract WC3-72, 'HIV Infection in Women: Setting a New Agenda' conference, Washington, DC, 1995.

75. St Louis, *op. cit.* Ryder, *op. cit.*

76. R. D. Semba *et al.*, 'Maternal vitamin A deficiency and mother-to-child transmission of HIV-1', *Lancet*, 25 June 1994, 343, pp. 1593–7; Newell (1993), *op. cit.*

77. World Health Organisation (WHO). Special Program on AIDS statement, *Breastfeeding, Breast Milk and the Human Immunodeficiency Virus (HIV)*, Geneva: WHO, SPA/INF/87.8. This document has been followed by *Consensus Statement from the WHO/UNICEF Consultation on HIV Transmission and Breast-feeding*, Geneva, 30 April – 1 May 1992, Geneva WHO/GPA/INF/92.1.

78. A literature search (by NHPIS) selected forty-three references to breast-feeding and breast-milk in relation to HIV, but only twenty-one covering the whole area of HIV transmission rates for heterosexual sex, male-to-female transmission and female-to-male transmission.

79. Thiry *et al.*, 'Isolation of AIDS virus from cell-free breast milk of three healthy virus carriers', *Lancet*, 19 October 1985, ii, pp. 891f.

80. Editorial, 'HIV infection, breastfeeding, and human milk banking', *Lancet*, 16 July 1988, ii, pp. 143–4.

81. M. J. Oxtoby, 'Human immunodeficiency virus and other viruses in human milk: placing the issues in broader perspective', *Pediatric Infectious Disease Journal*, 1988, 7(12), pp. 825–35.

82. P. Van-de-Perre *et al.*, 'Postnatal transmission of HIV-1 associated with breast abscess', *Lancet*, 13 June 1992, 339, pp. 1490–1.

83. A. J. Ruff *et al.*, 'Prevalence of HIV-1 DNA and p24 antigen in breast milk and correlation with maternal factors', *JAIDS*, 7(1), January 1994, pp. 68–73; J. Mok, 'Commentary: breast milk and HIV-1 transmission', *Lancet*, 10 April 1993, 341, pp. 930–1.

84. For an example of this misunderstanding, see Fumento, *op. cit.*, p. 55. Requests for information on the sexual implications of HIV in breast milk have been generated by a lesbian group in London; Barbara James, personal communication.

85. See, for example, P. Palasanthiran *et al.*, 'Breast-feeding during primary maternal human immunodeficiency virus infection and risk of transmission from mother to infant', *Journal Infectious Diseases*, 1993, 167, pp. 441-4; N. de P. Rubini *et al.*, 'Transmission of human immunodeficiency virus from a newly infected mother to her two-year-old child by breast-feeding', *Paediatric Infectious Diseases Journal*, 11 (8), August 1992, pp. 682–3; A. Guerrero-Flores, 'Postnatal transmission of the human immunodeficiency virus (HIV). History of brief breast-feeding. (Presentation of a clinical case)', *Ginecol-Obstet-Mex.*, April 1991, 59, pp. 117–21; R. Colebunders *et al.*, 'Breastfeeding and transmission of HIV', *Lancet*, 24/31 December 1988, ii, p. 1487.

   The best-known case of exposure by this route is the history of the late Elizabeth Glaser, both of whose children were infected, and the first, Ariel, acquired HIV when breast-feeding. The family's story is recounted in E. Glaser, *In the Absence of Angels*, Arrow Books, London, 1992.

86. D. T. Dunn *et al.*, *op. cit.*

87. *Ibid.*

88. A baby cannot be born HIV-infected if the *father* has HIV but the mother is uninfected. The virus is transmitted to the foetus (or newborn) in the blood of an HIV-infected woman, and not by the sperm that causes conception.

89. P. Van de Perre, 2nd International Conference on Children and Mothers, Edinburgh, 1993.

90. D. Landers, 'Obstetrical Interventions', presentation at First National Conference on Human Retroviruses and Related Infections, *op. cit.*

91. Arguments for the trial are laid out in P. Van de Perre *et al.*, 'Mother-to-infant transmission of human immunodeficiency virus

by breast milk: presumed innocent or presumed guilty?' *Clin. Infect. Dis.*, 15(3), September 1992, pp. 502–7.

92. Lorraine Sherr, personal communication.

93. For more details about drug approval and trial procedures, see E. King (ed.), *HIV & AIDS Treatments Directory*, NAM Publications, London, 1995, pp. 95–6, 104–11.

94. Cited in G. Corea, *The Invisible Epidemic: The Story of Women and AIDS*, HarperPerennial, New York, 1992, p. 206.

95. E. M. Conner *et al.*, 'Reduction of maternal-infant transmission of human immunodeficiency virus type 1 with zidovudine treatment', *NEJM*, 1994, 331, pp. 1173–80.

96. The best source of information is King, *op. cit.*, updated every six months.

97. For example, E. Rubery *et al.*, *Unlinked Anonymous HIV Prevalence Monitoring Programme in England and Wales*, Department of Health, London, January 1995.

98. P. Yeni *et al.*, 'Preliminary findings of the European–Australian Delta study', Fifth European Conference on Clinical Aspects and Treatment of HIV Infection, Copenhagen, September 1995 . See also E. King, 'Combinations prolong life', *AIDS Treatment Update*, Issue 35, October 1995.

99. Dr Joep Lange, personal communication. Nevirapine is a non-nucleoside analogue – it works on the same part of the virus life cycle as AZT, but it uses a different mechanism. See King, *op. cit.*, pp. 176–7.

100. Y. Bryson, comments to the ACTG co-ordinating meeting, Washington, DC, February 1995.

101. B. Weiser *et al.*, 'QC-PCR quantitation of HIV plasma RNA level during pregnancy: relationship to mother-to-child transmission and antiviral therapy', Abstract WC3-72, 'HIV Infection in Women: Setting a New Agenda' conference.

102. R. D. Semba *et al.*, 'Vitamin A deficiency, infant mortality, and mother-to-child transmission of HIV', Abstract TF1-107, 'HIV Infection in Women: Setting a New Agenda' conference. See also R. Gorna, 'Women's treatment update', *AIDS Treatment Update*, Issue 29, May 1995, pp. 6–7.

103. B. L. Greenberg *et al.*, 'Vitamin A and hemoglobin deficiency in HIV-infected female drug users', Abstract WF1-24, 'HIV Infection in Women: Setting a New Agenda' conference.

Chapter eight

Vamps and Virgins

The tension between sexual danger and sexual pleasure is a powerful one in women's lives. Sexuality is simultaneously a domain of restriction, repression, and danger as well as a domain of exploration, pleasure, and agency. To focus only on pleasure and gratification ignores the patriarchal structure in which women act, yet to speak only of sexual violence and oppression ignores women's experience with sexual agency and choice and unwittingly increases the sexual terror and despair in which women live.

Carole Vance[1]

Although I have dwelt upon the complex details of HIV transmission, it is at heart a simple business and remarkably easy to avoid. Why, then, do at least 3000 women worldwide become infected with HIV every day?[2] How can strategies and programmes prevent more women from acquiring HIV?

The technicalities of preventing HIV infection are remarkably straightforward, it is the contexts within which risky behaviour takes place which complicate matters. Partly the technologies which prevent HIV are so simple because little research has been undertaken to develop new methods. Drug-related HIV infections can be stopped by women using clean injecting equipment, or not injecting drugs. Anything that prevents semen from contacting a woman's cervix/vagina or rectum will prevent sexual infections. At the current time, this means using male condoms with water-based lubricant, or female condoms (often known by the brand name 'Femidom') with any lubricant. Preventing HIV transmission occurs in the context of promoting health, and mechanisms for achieving this depend upon what is understood by 'health'. A simplistic definition describes health as the 'absence of disease', but there are more helpful and complete concepts, developed by WHO, which describe health as 'a resource for living' or 'physical, emotional, spiritual and sexual well-being'. Health is an active concept: something which gives opportunity, and a basis for action; it is a good thing in its own right, and is available to people irrespective of whether they have a 'disease'.[3]

The contexts for preventing HIV transmission to women and promoting women's sexual health highlight a full range of gender-related inequalities. As the editors of the US feminist magazine *Ms* point out, 'This epidemic offers terrible proof of the dire need for women's empowerment. . . . Women need prevention strategies and programs that address the social, economic, and political realities that increase our risk of infection.'[4] Calls for women's empowerment to avoid HIV must also address the *sexual* realities women face, and it is here that a woman-centred approach is complicated, since the whole arena of sex has become troubled (or invisible) in much feminist discourse.

The area which is most available to feminist thinking – and which receives increasing attention from women writing about AIDS – is the domain of sexual danger. Extraordinary levels of sexual violence and terror restrict the opportunities women have to protect their health and safety in Britain, as throughout the world. Indeed, for many women the concept of 'safer sex' may speak more to a woman's need for physical safety from aggression, or emotional safety from abuse, than to the longer-term threat of a new virus. However, equating a women's sexuality solely with the violence and terror that can surround her involves a denial of the positive components of many women's sexual experience, and submerges women in a prescriptive victimology.

In turning to women's sexual pleasure, feminist analyses become more sticky. Vance describes how, by the 1980s, for the most prominent feminists '[R]hetoric about privacy and women's health was more respectable and less risky than the language of women's sexual freedom.'[5] A fundamental component of stopping women from acquiring HIV must be to develop a language and politic of women's sexual freedom and pleasure. In the 1970s, sexuality was celebrated as a central feature of women's liberation. Soon it was shifted to the margins, becoming at best an embarrassing 'additional extra', at worst denounced as the root of women's oppression. Catharine MacKinnon claims, for example, that 'Feminism is a theory of how the erotization [*sic*] of dominance and submission creates gender, creates woman and man in the social form in which we know them'.[6] Note here that women's oppression is conceptualized as deriving from the purely sexual domain. Gayle Rubin responds to this strand of feminism asking, 'Whatever happened to the family, religion, education, child-rearing practices, the media, the state, psychiatry, job discrimination, and unequal pay?'[7]

A politics of feminism that states 'sex = women's oppression' leads to the most basic (and ineffective) form of HIV prevention: refusing sex with men. Throughout the 1980s (and in a more subtle way through the 1990s) the dominant strand of feminism disallowed sexual freedom as a proper focus for feminist energies. Rubin, writing in 1984, describes how things sexual take the flak for women's lack of freedom and power, stating that 'A good deal of current feminist literature attributes the oppression of women to graphic representations of sex, prostitution, sex education, sado-masochism, male homosexuality and transsexualism.'[8] On such an analysis, any HIV prevention which goes beyond the Nancy Reagan 'Just Say No' line will inevitably oppress women. Some feminists – notably, Sheila Jeffreys – even claim such a link. Fortunately, few are as extreme as Jeffreys, but this sex-denying approach is profoundly harmful to HIV prevention (as it is to women in general) by stigmatizing communities in need of HIV prevention, and the very mechanisms necessary to achieve it.

It is only from a place of relative freedom and power that people can make choices and develop strategies for self-protection. In the context of protection from sexual harm, including disease, WHO official Svein-Erik Ekeid states that 'Only an individual who has the strength to say "yes" to sexuality has the strength to say "no" to risky sexual behaviour – to make the choice.'[9] It is, therefore, urgent for women to acquire not only economic and social freedom and power, but crucially power and freedom in living their individual sexualities.

The economics of risk

One of the starkest illustrations of women's powerlessness is the well-known statement from the United Nations that women are more than 50 per cent of the world's population, perform two-thirds of the world's work, receive one-tenth of the world's income, and own one-hundredth of the world's property. In 1975, British women were paid 71 per cent of what a man earned for the same job; by 1993 that had risen so that women earned a stunning 79 per cent of men's pay.[10] In 1991 the pay gap between men and women stood at £42.44 billion: for a fair distribution of pay, £21.22 billion of earned income would need to be transferred from men to women. 1995 statistics showed that women earn, on average, £100 less per week than men.[11] 80 per cent of workers in personal services (like cleaning, catering and hairdressing) are women, as are 79 per cent of clerical workers, and 86 per cent of part-time workers (who earn half the hourly rate of men in full-time jobs). 10 million workers in the UK earn less than the decency threshold established by the Council of Europe, and 65 per cent of these workers are women.[12] If it were not bad enough that women have less access to a decent wage for their work, women who are not employed (or who receive low incomes) are dependent upon the wages of their husbands or male partners. A woman cannot claim means-tested benefits in her own right – if she has a male sexual partner then the law expects him to pay for her; too bad if he doesn't.

This is not the place for a litany of the continued financial hardships facing women, but these few statistics should serve to illustrate that gender-determined economic inequality is a British reality, however much it is concealed by the image of a few high-earning women. In the context of AIDS, women's economic inequality can be disastrous. A key component of power is access to resources, and this is something which women must struggle harder for, simply because of their gender. A woman's domestic decision-making may also contribute to her power,[13] and in the context of safer sex this creates both indirect and direct links. The woman who makes domestic decisions may experience a greater degree of self-confidence and agency, and she may also have bargaining power. Yet the woman who, for example, cannot find a job which will pay enough for her to buy child-care, may find herself exchanging sex with her partner for the money to feed, clothe and – even – enjoy herself. This is not to suggest all marriages are legalized prostitution, but it is beyond doubt that government-sanctioned dependencies create tensions and inequities in many a partnership. The nature of the marriage contract (and increasingly, male-female domestic partnerships) is to link financial obligations to sexual practice. So much so, that until March 1991 British legal guidance stated 'a man cannot be guilty of rape upon his wife'[14] – the marriage contract bought him the right to sex whenever he wished. Even since the change in law, there have been hardly any successful convictions, and all concern extreme cases involving men who no longer live with their wives or where divorce proceedings are under way.

Before returning to the obvious links between HIV and domestic violence, coercive sex and rape, I will consider first prostitution, then pornography – two major battlegrounds within feminist politics which have an important impact on HIV-prevention initiatives for women.

• Sex as work

'Sex is purchased through prostitution and legally acquired through marriage', states Kathleen Barry, an expert in 'female sexual slavery'.[15] Poverty and limited economic opportunities underpin many women's decision to use sex as currency. Of course, not all women do this, but there is a continuum along which many women at some time could place themselves. Sex gets used as currency within consensual situations, as survival sex, or in commercial sex. This may be as a 'marital obligation', submitting to expectations of sex after being taken out for dinner, having sex to get accommodation or other goods, receiving drugs for sex, or exchanging sex for hard cash, either casually or within the commercial sex industry. All of these activities may involve additional vulnerabilities to HIV, but it is the most organized end of the spectrum which receives the most attention. In part this attention is a way of side-stepping the complex motivations women have for sex, but it is also simply because prostitutes are such an easy (and fascinating) target for prurient observers.

The phrase 'commercial sex work' has been promoted by prostitutes as a response to the constant stigmatization of whores, especially in the context of AIDS. It seeks to highlight the economic and labour dimensions of the life of female and male prostitutes, and other workers, such as women and men who work in pornography, stripping, as brothel keepers and escorts. It is a helpful term, that puts the focus on the fact that these activities are work, and also cuts across fantasies about the moral character of people who do this work. However, by concealing the word 'prostitute', the phrase also hides the continuing moral disapproval towards women who do this work.[16]. It is so reductionist that one campaigner for prostitutes' rights fears that the complex realities of women's lives are dismissed with the glib term 'CSWs'.[17] At a programme level, of developing initiatives, it is important to include all dimensions of the industry, but in order to explore the attitudes that inhibit this work I shall rely principally on the term 'prostitute'. It is the very fact that some women trade sexual acts for cash that underpins the violent responses of feminists – like those who are 'experts in sexual slavery' – and of religious campaigners – who also seek to rescue 'fallen women'.[18] In order to understand the types of response that have been developed, it is helpful to make the stigmatization of prostitutes visible.

The symbolic meanings afforded prostitute women have created images of bad, diseased women. Lynne Segal states that, for early feminists like the Pankhursts, 'Prostitution was the ubiquitous metaphor for social disease and decay, the wretched fate of female victims of male lust and an abomination which should be eliminated.'[19] These vectors of disease are represented as reservoirs of infection, dipped into by a man who transfers the bad girls' disease and stigma to his pure wife. Throughout the world, AIDS programmes have tested prostitutes for HIV, thrown condoms at them, tested new technologies on them, all to protect the punter (and in turn the pure wife). And what of the punter? The one who pays, and so creates and sustains the industry, is apparently rather stupid and irresponsible. HIV-prevention initiatives are never directed at him, but rather at the woman, who is expected to control both her own and his HIV-exposure risk.

The shame of HIV-prevention work for prostitutes is that more initiatives have been developed to protect the punter, via the whore, than the whore herself. Although the prostitute is vulnerable to infection from the punter, he tends to be protected from blame in the same way he is protected from legal redress for engaging in commercial sex. Just as there are few initiatives, there are also few studies of prostitutes' clients. These can be hard to conduct, since the men are not easily accessed and tend not to self-define; they are also afforded low priority. In the Sexual Lifestyles survey, 6.8 per cent of the men said that they had ever paid a prostitute for sex, and 1.8 per cent said they had done so in the last five years. More interesting than the absolute numbers (which are bound to be under-reported) is the fact that men who had ever had sex with another man were 2.5 times more likely to have paid for commercial sex than men whose sexual experience was solely with women.[20] The implication of this for prostitutes' risk of exposure to HIV is self-evident. Moreover, in a study of punters in London, 36.2 per cent (of 94) said they had sex with other men, 1.9 per cent (of 105) had injected drugs and 8.7 per cent (of 92) said they themselves had been paid for sex (the base numbers vary because not all men would answer all the questions – suggesting the non-responders may well also have had risk factors). The researchers conclude that 'Men who have sex with female prostitutes cannot be assumed to be at risk of infection with HIV only by this route: homosexual contact may place them at greater risk.'[21] Surely the more important point is that these men pose a significant risk to prostitutes. Of the clients in this study, 18.2 per cent did not consistently use condoms when they paid for vaginal sex, yet the punter who wants sex without condoms is perceived as someone whom prostitutes should control and protect from HIV, irrespective of whether he offers to pay more, or he beats her. The locus of responsibility is so forceful that the client is represented as a man rendered innocent by his overwhelming lust, whereas the HIV-positive prostitute who continues to work is vilified and condemned.[22] Perhaps this is not surprising, given that it is always the workers, never the clients, who can end up in jail.

One of the remarkable features of prostitution in the UK, confounding most public perceptions, is the extremely low level of HIV infection and the extremely high level of safer-sex practice. A London study recruited 280 women who worked in a range of indoor and street settings: just two women tested HIV-positive, and both had a history of injecting drugs. They also found that 98 per cent of women used condoms for vaginal sex, 83 per cent for oral sex and 50 per cent for anal sex (just eight women offered this service).[23] This is consistent with a study of street-working prostitutes attending a clinic in Glasgow. Sixteen women said they had tested HIV-positive (all of whom used injection drugs). Of the 60 women – all the untested women, and all except one HIV-positive woman – 98 per cent said they always used condoms with their clients for vaginal and oral sex. Condom use for anal sex was not reported: 87 per cent of women said they had been asked for anal sex but 'few admitted to actually providing it'. Ninety-five per cent of the women said they had been offered more money for vaginal sex without a condom, and the women reported that the average amount they were offered for this was £45 – a 450 per cent increase on the usual cost of vaginal sex (they usually charged £10). Few of the clients carried condoms, and many women described insisting on condom use, while the client insisted on sex without a condom. Some women also reported that when a client paid for vaginal sex the woman would often hold his penis between her legs and that 'clients rarely seemed to notice'. One woman reported that a client tried to burst the condom during sex.[24]

So was that one HIV-positive woman who did not always use condoms *really* endangering her clients' life? Two members of the New Zealand Prostitutes' Collective complain of media stories 'that whipped up hysteria against prostitutes, with images of the "vengeful AIDS victim . . . a crazed hooker on revenge trip against all punters". We have yet to hear about the crazed punter hell-bent on infecting prostitutes.'[25] All the evidence suggests that, as a group, punters have scant regard for the health of the woman whose services they are purchasing; it is extraordinary that they also do not have a greater sense of self-preservation.

It is telling that prostitutes definitely do have that sense of self-preservation in their work environment. (It is likely that 'non-professional' sex workers might expose themselves to higher risk, but it is hard to conclude this from the literature, since studies tend to recruit women who identify themselves as working within the sex industry.) To the extent that they are able to secure a healthy and safe working environment, women do so. The high reports of condom use for fellatio indicate that prostitute women regularly used condoms before the AIDS crisis, and continue to do so, to avoid conditions other than HIV. One HIV-prevention project for 'men who have sex with men' at cruising grounds has taken prostitutes' high condom usage for fellatio as implying that this should be encouraged in men who are cruising.[26] However, this is a misunderstanding of why prostitutes are using condoms for oral sex. It is not that fellatio is a high risk for HIV transmission, but rather that putting a man's penis in your mouth for pleasure is entirely different from putting it in your mouth for cash.

This leads on to the final finding from studies of prostitutes' safer sex practice: 'Strangely,' say the authors of the Glasgow study, 'the women often failed to apply the same safer sex rules to their personal lives that they applied to their professional ones.'[27] The finding that only 21 per cent of prostitutes consistently used condoms for vaginal sex with a regular partner is consistent with other studies (the London study found this was the case for just 12 per cent of the women[28]). Is it really so strange? When a prostitute is at leisure, why would she use condoms any more than her sisters who have just clocked off from working in a factory, or restaurant, or bank? Prostitutes may have had sex with more men than factory workers, waitresses and bank managers, but this does not mean they are any less human in their relationships, any less subject to the pressures of desire, embarrassment, domestic violence, love, and every other factor that inhibits women from having safer sex. Prostitutes' personal lives are only more complicated than other women's because of factors that influence their sex work (such as drug use, for a few women), or because of societal attitudes to their labour – which have been generated by the 'moral' minority and also feminists.

Women's liberation was founded in a respect for the realities of women's lives, and so the mainstream feminist response to prostitution is strange. This response tends to represent every prostitute as an exploited, oppressed woman – she may be so exploited that she is unaware of the depths of her 'white slavery'. Barry claims that 'Free prostitution does not exist, whatever the means of exercising it ... prostitution of women [is] always by force ... it is a violation of human rights and an outrage to the dignity of women.'[29] Barry, and those who share her views, seem to detect false consciousness at work preventing (some) women who are unrepentant whores, porn makers and porn users from knowing and understanding the slavery of their own position. What these women need, they state, is to be rescued from their lives – like it or not. This patronizing approach to prostitutes is nothing new. 'The big sisters of the world [want the] chance to protect the little and weaker sisters, by surrounding them with the right laws for them to obey for their own good,' proclaimed one social purity feminist writing in 1913.[30]

The reality is not as simple as feminists like Barry would have it. Many women are indeed coerced into prostitution or other parts of the industry. For some this will be very direct coercion, as with the thousands of Thai and Indian girls who are sold or mortgaged by their families to unscrupulous brothel or bar owners. Yet in the UK such direct coercion is rarely documented, and where coercion exists it is more likely to be indirect, the result of patriarchy restricting women's education, legal recourse and basic human rights, and denying women options other than sex work.

There is a strand of prostitution that has no more to do with coercion than have other industries with poor working conditions, according to the women who do the work. Historian and former stripper Nickie Roberts perceives the stigmatization of whores as allowing 'middle-class commentators to focus on the "immorality" of sex workers rather than on the real issue, which is the poverty of working-class women the world over'.[31] Since the 1970s, prostitute women have been organizing in collectives, often with fabulous names like HIRE (Hooking Is Real Employment) and COYOTE (Call Off Your Old Tired Ethics). These tend to be rooted in the labour and feminist movements, with qualities combining trade unions and consciousness raising groups. For many women involved in such groups, it is vital to see prostitution in the wider context of women's work.

British prostitute Eva Rosta says this of her job:

> All work involves selling some part of your body. You might sell your brain, you might sell your back, you might sell your fingers for typewriting. Whatever it is that you do you are selling one part of your body. I choose to sell my body the way I want to and I choose to sell my vagina.[32]

Her Toronto colleague Valerie Scott goes further, and describes sex workers as making a smart career choice: 'For the amount of time they put in the money is good. It's right up there with being a lawyer.'[33] For these women, banalizing what they do to the status of just another job takes away the sting and allows an analysis to address their perceived needs: for health and safety at work, for laws which protect rather than condemn, and to be afforded the dignity of human rights. All of these are fairly classic components of any campaign for women's liberation.

Effective HIV prevention for prostitutes, and other workers in the commercial sex industry, picks up the gauntlet of the demands originating in their collectives and trade unions. After all, this is the one industry where it is easy to acquire HIV at work. One excellent example of an initiative responding to prostitutes' needs is ScotPEP, the Scottish Prostitutes Education Project, in Edinburgh. This is a prostitute-led service which offers practical support, skill-building, community services and advocacy. Organizations like ScotPEP offer practical services, some of which are HIV-related (a vast array of free condoms, Femidoms and lubricants; a doctor's surgery) and some not (showers, washing machines, breakfast), but also a radical transformatory approach. By creating opportunities for prostitutes and other commercial sex workers to talk together and organize, they can identify and advocate what is really needed to secure women's health and safety at work, part of which is ensuring prostitutes' human rights. Some of this work is immediate – training sessions to develop skills in sexual services (like fantasy games) that do not involve penetration – some is more long-term, but just as pragmatic, such as law reform. It is sadly predictable that services like ScotPEP are experiencing budget cuts – they seem to challenge the status quo too successfully, by placing the power firmly with prostitutes themselves. Often funders seem to prefer services run by ex-prostitutes, which may give condoms in the short run, but ultimately want to rescue women from the industry.[34]

The international rescue brigade are often the ones who object to the most pragmatic development that could support prostitutes in avoiding HIV. Prostitution is not illegal in the UK, but everything that surrounds the exchange is (soliciting, pimping, kerb-crawling). Policing consensual sexual behaviour inevitably creates situations of high vulnerability, both directly (how can a woman pre-negotiate condom use if she has to get in the car without discussion? Why carry condoms if the police will use them as evidence of soliciting?[35]) and indirectly (what kind of self-esteem is fostered in women who are regularly arrested, while the man who buys their services is not?). Prostitution law has been described as 'like pushing on a waterbed. Push in one place and it simply came up again in the other.'[36] The laws place great store by protecting others from nuisance and offence, but pay no attention to protecting the workers. The exact nature of law reform that would protect prostitutes is unclear, but it should incorporate 'non-discriminatory regulations that work to the benefit of sex workers and the community'.[37] Some form of decriminalization is preferable to complete legalization, which could lead to over-restrictive brothels, with the state effectively 'pimping' off sex work.

Without legal reform, prostitutes will continue to be treated as sub human, to be raped and murdered without receiving the protection of the law afforded 'good girls'.[38] Notoriously, a senior police officer responsible for the Yorkshire Ripper case told the press:

> He has made it clear that he hates prostitutes. Many people do. We, as a police force, will continue to arrest prostitutes. But the Ripper is now killing innocent girls. That indicates your mental state and that you are in urgent need of medical attention. You have made your point. Give yourself up before another innocent women dies.[39]

This sickening description of the inhumanity afforded prostitute women also highlights the final strand of panic created by whores. A feminist report states, 'prostitution victimizes women both within and outside prostitution. When prostitution is accepted and normalized, what is legitimized is the sale of body and sex of the individual prostitute and *it is the sale of any woman*'[40] (my emphasis). For centuries, women have been burdened with the role models of madonna or whore. Until Ms Ciccione started to slide one into the other, women had the choice of Mary the Mother of God or Mary Magdalene: the virgin, bearing fruit and nurturing to divine life, or the self-willed, socially outcast, sex trader. The decriminalization of sex work would remove some of that polarization, and this seems to create panic in women who need to secure their innocence as sexually safe, non-whores.

• *Representing sex*

Prostitutes are perceived as having a degrading impact on pure women who are subject to oversexed men, who have had their perceptions of women perverted by the fallen women in the sex industry. This perception also features in responses to pornography, and they too are marked by unholy alliances between mainstream feminists and the Far Right. In respect of HIV prevention, the feminist anti-porn movement is even more pervasive than the anti-whore lobby (in so far as they can be disentangled).

The prevention of sexual HIV transmission involves educating about sex and inspiring people to make low-risk choices, and as such is likely to involve representing sex – graphically and verbally. This is hard enough, given the way the tabloid press profiteer on the British fascination with all things sexual, while simultaneously expressing high indignation that anyone else should respond to this interest in sex. Health authority condom seminars and workshops on eroticizing safer sex are pounced upon as fodder for an odd mixture of salacious and prurient tabloid stories. The idea that sex might be acknowledged as joyful and recreational rather than problematic and procreational provokes reactions oscillating between the ribald and the disgusted.

On top of this comes an equally condemning, but differently

motivated, disgust from feminist quarters. The politics of desire and representing women's sexuality hinge on questions of the feminist response to sexually explicit material, and this has been characterized by outrage that these representations harm women. This is not the place to explore in detail the porn wars, but there are some key elements which have a major bearing on HIV work.[41]

The mainstream feminist response to women who work in porn is the same as that to prostitutes (they are damaged victims, so oppressed that some do not understand how misused they are). However, the analysis in respect of the pure, innocent women outside the industry goes far further, and can be summed up in the classic phrase, 'Pornography is the theory, and rape the practice.'[42] If the connection between sexual image and act was this simple mimicry, HIV prevention would be extremely straightforward (if a touch cynical). Prevention workers would only have to flood the world with safer sex pornography – men might rape a few women, but at least they would all be doing it safely and so HIV would stop. Some gay men's HIV-prevention programmes look as if they are adopting this strategy (there are no reports of massive rises in gay rape), but such strategies alone cannot work. Partly this is because the link between sexual imagery, fantasy and action is neither that linear, nor that simple. There is no doubt that much pornography is misogynist, racist and classist – as is society – but does viewing pornography lead men to rape? Alice Henry concludes that no evidence has proven such a direct link,[43] and Elizabeth Cowie, describing psychoanalytic perspectives on pornography, states that 'The pleasure of sexual fantasy and pornography is desired for itself, not as a simple means to physical sexual gratification.'[44] Fantasy functions in complex ways, and there is rarely such a direct connection to acting out the content of the fantasy.

The feminist anti-porn thesis states that the root of women's oppression is located in pornographic imagery that not only creates and feeds an aggressive male gaze, but programmes women as 'dehumanized sex objects'.[45] Yet, as Sue George identifies, '[P]ornography is not just about power, but about sexuality, and sexuality is about emotion.'[46] This is why pornography is important in the context of AIDS. In order to develop individual, and community, responses to avoiding HIV, it is necessary to explore attitudes to sex, the meaning and importance of sexual activities, links between sexuality and emotions, and ways to gain pleasure without acquiring disease. Images, writing and fantasies are often a useful spur to such exploration, yet these are restricted by a (so-called) feminist line on porn. The line between what is sexually explicit and erotic and what is pornography is a line that many have sought to draw, but no one has done so adequately (the only line that gets mass agreement is that porn tends to be bad art – a subjective interpretation if ever there was one). When pornography is prohibited, prohibitions on all things sexually explicit follow in due course, and the attack tends to begin at the margins.

It is telling that in Canada, the first prosecution under a new feminist pornography law was against material published in the lesbian magazine *Bad Attitude*. The law is designed to 'promote the equality of women with men' by eliminating 'degrading' or 'dehumanizing' materials. Becki Ross, who gave expert evidence during the case, describes the result as creating 'a sexual discourse that infantilizes women and centres victimization, trauma and violence at the same time that it renders a politics of female sexual pleasure, desire and fantasy ... not only unlikely, but almost unimaginable'.[47]

The fall-out after the *Bad Attitude* prosecution also included restrictions on the distribution of safer-sex material by the AIDS Committee of Toronto. I have written elsewhere of my experiences of attempted feminist censorship of mildly erotic safer sex material.[48] The young women who received this material found it more informative (and less erotic) than the men, yet this would have been irrelevant to the women's committee, who were shocked by the use of sexually explicit terms and a sexy photograph of a (clothed) woman. The overt censorship of erotic safer-sex resources for women is not a huge problem since so very little material of this type is produced. Rather, the principal concern must be the indirect censorship that has de-sexed women so that HIV-prevention messages tend to be extraordinarily bland and distant from women's sex lives.

Aggressive feminist anti-porn messages have created a situation where woman-centred sexual imagery is suppressed before it has a chance to flourish. Women who have sex with men have no organized community sexual expression, and consequently there are no foundations for exploring pleasure and desire which can be transformed by AIDS to explore safer pleasure and desire. That is not to say that there have been no attempts to explore women's desire, but rather that the early forays never became established, and in part this must be because the feminist agenda became so entwined with anti-porn battles. Segal charts the ways in which women who were initially notorious for their pro-sex attitudes have been subdued by the anti-porn brigade so that they are now reduced to patronizing younger women or promoting erotophobia. Erica Jong, who encouraged a generation of women to fantasize about a zipless fuck with a stranger, now welcomes AIDS for making sex 'a little more mysterious and precious again'.[49] Without wishing to be ageist, it does seem unreasonable of Ms Jong, Germaine Greer and their ilk to be pushing at young women the line 'We tried it, it wasn't worth it, and that's a good thing because your generation has to deal with AIDS.' The anti-sex line does not gain greater appeal just because it hails from a beloved aunt who was pretty raunchy in her youth.

The anti-erotica line doesn't work well for young women, because of course they want to explore sexuality. Perhaps the much vaunted decline in feminism is linked to unrealistic, humourless sexual politics. At the same time as hordes of young women are stating 'I'm not a feminist, but . . . ', so too an eroticized culture is hesitatingly finding new ways to represent women's sexuality. One of the arguments for the oppressive male horror of porn was that women never used or created it. The top shelves of high street newsagents now stock *For Women* and *Women on Top* alongside *Playgirl*, while lesbian stores have increasing numbers of magazines (if they can get through the customs restrictions). Such developments would horrify women, like 'radical feminist lesbian' Elizabeth Carola who rages at early lesbian porn saying, 'This new "woman's" porn is neither about nor for women. Like all porn it is, in a most basic sense, *against* women and *about* male fantasy – the basic male fantasy of Woman as Wholly Sexual Object whose Purpose is To Be Fucked – which feeds men's egos, fuels their violence, and keeps their wretched patriarchy rolling smoothly along.'[50] Maybe I'm missing something, but I fail to see how the work of queer sex radicals can sustain the patriarchy.

The accusations of false consciousness start to become a little wearing: why should these feminists keep women so enchained in victimhood that they can never claim and celebrate their sexualities? Doubtless this celebration will include claiming some painful, disturbing (maybe even violent) stories as well as egalitarian pleasure romps – after all, the psychology of desire and lust is a complex and glorious thing. Yet it does seem bizarre to found a movement to liberate women to explore every area of life, except their own sexuality, which may be explored only within carefully prescribed boundaries.

The materials which are making their way into WH Smith's are subject to crazy extremes of censorship – like showing no images of erections (enough to put most women off new woman's porn). One of the perverse responses to this is to turn pornography into sex education, which has fewer restrictions. Perhaps the sudden upsurge of 'educational videos' could be perceived as a good thing – after all, they link explicit sex and information about sexual disease (sometimes including HIV). The theory would be good if the erotica already existed, and the AIDS messages could be integrated into a pre-existing medium (which is the case for gay men – and could be the case for straight men, if anyone dared to do this). Instead, there is a whole series of videos peddling inadequate education and less than raunchy sex, and still outraging the anti-porn campaigners – who know full well that this isn't sex education, but just an easy way for people to access footage of other people fucking. Why shouldn't that material be available in its own right?

• Sexual choice

The relationship between prostitution, pornography and HIV remains contested territory for feminists. The relationship with coercion and rape does not cause this kind of fury. Aggleton describes safer sex as 'something to be decided by nominally free individuals in the context of broadly consensual sexual encounters',[51] and such a statement betrays the location of safer-sex discourse within a gay male model. The assumption that sexual encounters are 'broadly consensual' is one that fails to take into consideration the experiences of an enormous number of women. Although some men are raped and coerced into sex (and I certainly do not mean to minimize the pain and horror of rape for gay men, especially where it results in HIV transmission), gender power dynamics function very differently for gay men than for women. In the same way that sex work exists on a continuum, there is a continuum of sexual consent where many women can place themselves. It is invidious to try to determine what exists at the extremes of the continuum: for some women the worst non-consensual sex would be stranger rape; for others, sexual abuse by their father or a trusted family friend. Coerced sex also includes marital and relationship rape, date rape (the media's favourite) and situations where mental or physical abuse makes submitting to sex the least awful option.

Since HIV in the industrialized world began among men, inevitably HIV-prevention models are gay and male. The fundamental problem for developing safer-sex messages appropriate to women is that the qualities of this community are only comparable with (perhaps) two sub-groups of women: commercial sex workers, and lesbians. The American gay male community in the early 1980s was a community of high sexual literacy, with the ability to communicate verbally about the detail of sexual activity and a community norm supportive of sexual diversity and experimentation. This community fought (literally) for the human right for its 'free individuals' to make their own choices about engaging in 'broadly consensual sexual encounters'. No wonder they were able to invent safer sex.[52] Lesbians and commercial sex workers – for different reasons – may also have high sexual literacy, ability to communicate about sex and supportive community norms. Lesbians also invented their own community and sexual norms, and the place of HIV messages in that community is reviewed in Chapter 10. I have dwelt on some of the constraints that exist for prostitutes, yet in the context of the sexual interaction, they tend to have power and opportunities for verbal negotiation, and – except when prostitutes are raped – the sex is so consensual that it is within a contract. Scott defines her choice to work in the sex industry as reflecting a woman's control of the resources around her. 'It's not about sex,' she says. 'It's about power.'[53] This is a neat subversion of the analysis of rape – men inflict their power on women through rape; women do the same through sex work.

These two 'groups' of women are, however, exceptions to the more general rule that women tend to have less access to free decisions than gay men. Yet, traditional safer-sex messages have generally failed to adapt the HIV-prevention model to address the ways in which non-consensual sex is almost institutionalized for many women who are in sexual relationships with men.

Only 2 per cent of violent attacks on women,[54] and less than 25 per cent of rapes, are reported to the police.[55] The statistics on rape reporting vary a great deal. A survey of 1236 London women found that just 8 per cent of the women who were raped and 18 per cent of those sexually assaulted reported this to the police; less than 38 per cent of these women were glad they had reported the offence. The same survey shows that women who go to rape crisis centres were more likely to report the crime: approximately 25 per cent of those who went to the London Rape Crisis Centre reported to the police, as did 18 per cent of women who called Southampton's Rape Crisis Line. The low reporting of rape and sexual assaults conceals their prevalence, as does the media gaze (fond of rare occurrences like women's false accusations), which keeps well hidden the monotonous regularity of this crime. The trivialization of much coerced sex, and the aggressive tactics of some lawyers in rape cases, make it hard for many women to articulate their experiences of non-consensual sex. Judge Wild summed up a 1982 rape trial with the words:

> Women who say no do not always mean no. It is not just a question of saying no. It is a question of how she says it, how she shows and makes it clear. If she doesn't want it, she only has to keep her legs shut and there would be marks of force being used.[56]

The lack of shared language about coercion means that many women do not express their experiences as assault and crime. This leads to stupid statements like Katie Roiphe's comment, 'If I was really standing in the middle of an epidemic, a crisis, if 25 per-cent of my female friends were really being raped, wouldn't I know it?'[57] Well, I wouldn't tell her. In her remarkably inadequate book, Roiphe does at least highlight the way some women's experiences are side-stepped by rhetoric about sexual violence. By focusing the feminist spotlight on sexual danger, and ignoring sexual pleasure, sexual encounters have become polarized as 'rape' or 'not-rape', rather than sometimes being located in a complicated place wavering between desire and coercion. Roiphe's outburst responded to a survey by *Ms* magazine, published in October 1985, which found that 25 per cent of women students had experienced rape or attempted rape. The definition of their assault was given by the researcher, and one critic points out that 73 per cent of these women did not personally define the experience as 'rape', but rather expressed that the experience was in some way non-consensual. Roiphe seems to think this makes it all right. Yet even if none of the 73 per cent were raped, a staggering one in fifteen (6.75 per cent) of American women students were raped at university, with a further one in five having sex which was beyond their control. As Naomi Wolf points out, 'These figures show that much AIDS education has been utterly naive. If a quarter of young women have at some point had control denied them in a sexual encounter, they stand little chance of protecting themselves from the deadly disease.'[58]

Part of the strategy to enable women to be protected includes revealing the prevalence of coercive sex and finding ways for women to resist and for men to change their unacceptable behaviour. It is extremely hard to access reliable statistics about sexual violence, and American figures will not help since the political climate surrounding sexual violence is radically different. The London study described earlier was conducted in 1982, but it does report the experiences of over 1000 women. *Ask Any Woman* reports that 17 per cent of women were raped, 31 per cent had been sexually assaulted, and 20 per cent experienced attempted rape. 23 per cent of women had been raped or sexually assaulted once, and 14 per cent had experienced this repeatedly.[59] There are obvious links between rape and HIV: condoms are rarely used, and the violence of the act may create genital trauma which would increase the probability of transmission. Some cases have been reported of women acquiring HIV following a rape,[60] but official statistics have no mechanism for recording whether consent is involved in incidents of transmission.

Many women who report rape are concerned about HIV,

but there is no obvious practical response that can be offered. One clinic in London reports that concerns about HIV are a major reason why women access services, and consequently they routinely offer HIV counselling and testing.[61] Of course it is important to develop services which are responsive to women's needs, but counselling will need to be careful and sensitive and not premised on the idea that the test will necessarily give her good news. It is alarming that at the same time as struggling with the trauma of rape, women may find themselves adjusting to an HIV-positive diagnosis.

One approach to dealing with anxieties about HIV transmission subsequent to sexual assault has been to HIV-test the perpetrator (where his identity is known). In the USA several states impose mandatory testing on convicted rapists, yet it is calculated that the implementation of this policy means that only twelve out of 10,000 alleged rapists will be tested.[62] The benefit to women of this approach is low, and from a human-rights perspective it is untenable to force knowledge of HIV status almost as a part of punishment. Another suggestion is that where a rapist does not consent to testing, the test could be conducted without his being informed of the result, but the woman would be counselled to test if the result was positive.[63]

Bio-medical solutions have also been promoted. Some hospitals have given antivirals, such as AZT, to staff who have suffered needlestick injuries. The results from such policies are not impressive, and the toxicity of the compounds, and reduced efficacy of future treatments, makes it an unhelpful approach for women who have been raped – especially given that most rapists are not HIV-infected. Some doctors have suggested that Nonoxynol 9 or vinegar douches should be offered in an attempt to block transmission. Such an approach requires the woman to seek medical attention immediately after the assault. Also, when these debates appeared in the medical press, the damaging effects of Nonoxynol 9 were given more attention than its microbicidal qualities, and such an approach was rejected.[64] However, this discussion does serve to emphasize the importance of developing microbicides that can be used *post*-coitus.

The arena of rape and HIV also reopens the question of consent. Cases have now been reported of rapists who use condoms, some apparently to avoid detection from DNA tests, and to avoid acquiring HIV from the women they rape.[65] In some cases the woman has asked for a condom to be used because of her fear of HIV. The defence in one case argued that this request meant that the woman 'implied consent' to sex. The jury split ten to two in favour of the man accused of rape, and the case was declared a mistrial.[66] In another trial, the case was dropped against a man convicted of aggravated sexual assault, again because the woman he tried to rape persuaded him to wear a condom. She testified: 'I knew there wasn't much I could do to prevent what was going to happen. I thought maybe I could protect myself from dying from AIDS.' He was subsequently convicted, after the police pressed charges a second time and the jury decided that a woman's actions to protect herself did not 'reduce the attacker's culpability'.[67] Lawyers like Judge Wild have convinced women that rape accusations will have little likelihood of success unless the woman bears marks of violent struggle; juries' cynicism about condom use may take this to a yet more extreme level.

Securing a rape conviction has always depended upon the nature of the woman who has been assaulted, and her ability to persuade twelve men and women that a (usually) private exchange took place against her will. For married women this has been accentuated by the law's belief that the marriage contract gave men unlimited 'conjugal rights'. Despite the law's tardy recognition of marital rape as a crime, the prevalence of this coercion is high, and the implications for HIV extreme. A 1989 study showed that one in eight women had been raped by her husband.[68] A more recent survey of domestic violence reported that 23 per cent of women had experience of sex with their husbands or male domestic partners where they had not given consent – for 39.1 per cent of these women the rape was accompanied by physical violence, and another 56.5 per cent of them were threatened with violence.[69] The scale of domestic violence is huge, and extends well beyond the arena of non-consensual sex. In London, 100,000 women every year seek treatment for violent injuries they received at home, and 50 per cent of women have experienced actual or threatened violence from a current or ex-partner, with half of these women subject to this repeatedly.[70] Almost half of all murdered women were killed by a current or ex-partner, and one British researcher suggests the true figure is as high as 80 per cent.[71] Research that has looked at male attitudes to sexual violence is equally disturbing. A Gallup poll of 1000 British men discovered that only 32 per cent of men would report to the police a man they knew who had committed rape; 72 per cent would report someone they knew who had been shoplifting.[72] The North London study found that nearly two-thirds of men believed they would respond violently to their partner in certain situations, and 71 per cent of Scottish men said they were likely to use violence in future relationships.[73]

These shocking statistics suggest that many women experience degrees of terror within relationships, so that their sexual experiences will not always be characterized by mutual desire and control. Even where sex is mutually desired, a woman's sense of her ability to influence the type of sex and the use of condoms will be severely restricted if she has good reason to fear physical or emotional violence. The majority of women who acquire HIV do so within a stable relationship, and given the prevalence of non-consensual sex within relationships it is easily possible that some of these infections occurred as a result of sex that was not freely desired by the women. Studies of discordant couples also show relatively high levels of non-condom use, and while it is important not to lose sight of the fact that the motivations for practising unsafe sex are diverse, some of this may well be linked to coercion. Twenty-one per cent of British HIV-positive women in discordant couples stated that their partners refused, or did not understand safer sex, were cruel or left them, with one woman recounting that they have 'arguments over use of condoms. I try to assert the use of condoms, but my partner will not take me seriously'.[74] It is not difficult to imagine the scenario if it was the man who was HIV-positive: other research (Chapter 5) shows that HIV-positive men are less likely to practise safe sex consistently than women who have the virus.

The final area of non-consensual sex which I want to consider is the mid-point between 'stranger rape' and domestic violence: date rape. Roiphe became the media's post-feminist darling with her polemic that date rape is little more than the morning-after blues, and her transatlantic message was especially welcome as it landed soon after the salacious details of the Austen Donnellan and Angus Diggle date rape cases.

In the context of HIV prevention, it is interesting to see what the media excitement has to say about young women's sexuality. Although anyone who goes on a date can experience it, the discourse of date rape is located principally in a student domain. Many journalists have been sent to campuses to investigate the phenomenon, and these safariing men (as they usually are) bring back tales of drunkenness, debauchery and condom use. They also tell us that women are defining the boundaries of sexual relationships, but men are still pushing them.

After Austen Donnellan was acquitted of the rape charge bought against him, Miss X (who brought the case) told journalists, 'I have never been that drunk before. It was totally unintentional . . . I have never said I didn't kiss Austen, but a kiss is just a kiss: ask any student.' Despite harrowing press attention, defining her as a vindictive, hedonistic, wanton woman, hell-bent on deliberately besmirching the reputation of an honourable man, she stated clearly, 'I still believe I was raped.'[75] What I find intriguing about the comments of this woman, and several of the students who were interviewed at the time of the case, is their ability to articulate so clearly the limits of sexual engagement. Twenty-two-year-old Emily Barr (soon to hit the headlines in her own right because of an affair with an MP) told the *Daily Mail*: 'Even in bed if a girl doesn't want penetration she doesn't have to have it. Saying "I don't want to have sex with you" is quite common. I would use those words myself.'

Drawing the line at certain sexual activities is not just a female thing, according to fellow student, twenty-two-year-old Simon Rix, who explains:

> Faced with a dilemma in bed I've said to girls, 'Do you want to have sex?' and they have said Yes or No . . . It's often done verbally, to make sure you're not misreading the signals. If the girl knows what she wants she will often say so first or make the first move. If she wants to have sex during foreplay she will grab a condom.[76]

There is no way of knowing whether these paragons of

negotiated virtue are representative, but they do highlight that the notion of verbal communication about the scope of sexual activity is acceptable to some students.

The fall-out around the date rape cases, and what has been characterized as 'sexual correctness', tends to be commented on by people who left the heated realms of college bars twenty years ago, and who may fail to appreciate these new rules of sexual engagement (and the cases are adjudicated by men who were advanced in their careers before those involved were born). The media have pounced with glee on guidelines from Antioch College in Ohio, which require students to acquire active consent for each new stage of sexual activity. This has been roundly ridiculed: 'How silly this all seems; how sad. It criminalizes the delicious unexpectedness of sex,' says *Newsweek*'s Sarah Crichton.[77] It might seem silly, or at least uncomfortable, to many people who are not twenty-year-old college students; so too might the hankie code to anyone but gay men. What the commentators fail to consider is that perhaps, for this sub-community of young people, guesswork is no longer central to sex – rather they appear to have developed their own way (a 'post'-feminist way) of ensuring choice and desire. If within this small 'society', verbalizing consent is not only an acceptable, but also an expected, form of engagement, then women who describe date rape are indeed experiencing non-consensual sex. If women are having sex to which they have not explicitly consented, and they and their peers experience explicit verbal consent as a normal part of sexual interaction, what is this if not rape?

One argument is that date rape is not rape, it is just bad sex or, according to the editor of *Guardian Women*, 'another example of the complicated world we have created by increasing our sexual freedom'.[78] This argument suggests that women really know what they are getting into when they go on a date, so that it is not that the man misreads the signals, but that the woman signals 'yes' the minute she enters into a date where, as Camille Paglia would have it, 'sex is already hovering in the air'. It is strange to have this argument rearing its head at exactly the time when marital rape is criminalized: the formal long-term contract is no longer *carte blanche* to fuck, whereas the informal, temporal agreement has a 'no turning back' clause. In most of the troubled debates, the argument turns on whether 'rape' is the correct term for an event which could be little more than a misunderstanding.

Whether or not 'rape' is the correct term for the undesired sex that seems to occur during many 'dates', there is a clear association between rape and acquaintance. Home Office statistics (recording proven rapes) show that 85 per cent of rapists are known to the women who are raped, and 61 per cent of rapes take place in the woman's home.[79] The question of whether sex is rape does not depend on the woman's perception of violation, but turns on the issue of the man's perception of consent, according to law lecturer Aileen McColgan. She describes as consenting the situation where 'you would rather go through with the sex than make an issue of it'. Whereas, by contrast, 'If the woman is too frightened of further violence to struggle and the man *knows* she is frightened, that is not consent.'[80]

In the popular debate there are two broad critiques of the notion of date rape, which I will define crudely as male and female. The male attack is grounded in sexism and is premised on the distrust of young women who are 'sexually shameless',[81] and sympathy for victim men who complain 'women have all the power here on sexual conduct ... It's very dangerous for us'.[82] This argument is boring and transparent, but the female attack is more intriguing and troubling. Linda Grant proposes that date rape may be highlighting 'that there are significant differences in the way women experience rape and that those who seem less traumatised than others are not necessarily suffering from a form of what used to be called false consciousness'.[83] When Germaine Greer suggested a similar argument, but going further to argue for a reframing of the law on rape and sexual assault, there was a lengthy, angry postbag complaining about her trivialization of the crime. The difficulty with drawing definitions from the diversity of assault is that the rape which is most traumatic and damaging in my life, would be the least devastating sexual attack for another woman. So long as one does not attempt to define a hierarchy of rape, the approach can be helpful. It is intuitive to most women that there are differing degrees of coercive or non-consensual sex which have different outcomes and impacts – both at the time of the sexual interaction, and in the longer-term effects on the psychological and physical health of the woman.

In the context of AIDS, whether the word rape is an appropriate or adequate description for the context within which sex like this occurs, the risk for HIV is elevated. The examples which are dismissed as not being rape are still coerced or non-consensual from the woman's perspective, to the degree that she does not have control over the situation – she may not be sufficiently aroused to lubricate. She is unlikely to have her needs met, including her needs for safer sex and condom use.

The pleasures of risk

For many women, most sexual encounters do not exist at the extremes of orgiastic delights nor, mercifully, are they all coercive. But the images of women's sexuality tend to have been dominated either by traditional male fantasies of women's sluttishness, or by feminist reconstructions of oppressed victims of standard male desire, subject to onslaughts of sexual terror. One feminist, who has the audacity to write about her sexual fantasies and enjoyment of pornography, finds that people assume she 'must be a babe, a sex goddess or completely promiscuous, and I'm not any of these things. It's like sex is only available to some people.'[84]

Discussing sexual danger is important in the context of AIDS, in order to ensure that interventions acknowledge and address the power imbalances which can impede women's ability to take control in sexual situations. However, Segal highlights the fact that in addressing women's sexuality there is another vital part of the equation, which is to 'figure out how to increase the potential confidence of all people to pursue the differing comforts, pleasures and perils of the flesh, free from all intimidation and threat, if only to try to help to undermine the perpetual displacement of people's fear, envy or anxiety into rage against others' pursuit of pleasure'.[85]

It is this rage against some women's pursuit of pleasure which seems to underpin not only tabloid diatribes, but also some feminist discourse on prostitution and pornography. The pain and anguish which form part of some women's sexual experience deserve attention precisely because of 'the threat they pose to joy, infatuation, love, expression of feelings, and need for bodily contact'.[86] Feminism will fail women if the pleasures of sex, which are denied by danger and terror, remain concealed by feminist attention condemning the horrors, but making no effort to celebrate the delights.

HIV prevention for women is able to focus so often on the negative, Just Say No, because the range of female sexual realities is rarely acknowledged. The silence surrounding women's sexualities and sex lives is usually masked by the clamour of sexual images and noise which dominate society. It is a cliche to talk of billboard sex, but it has become a crucial part of Western cultures. Sex is why some people buy ice cream, it's sold in darkened rooms filled with people eating popcorn, it can't be seen before 9 p.m. and it shouts from the covers of most magazines.

In reality, sex is so much more than these meagre representations. Sex may be an expression of love, a cementing of commitment; it might also be used as a soporific, or to release the cramps of period pain. Sex may be a demonstration of affection, a feature of friendships, it might be an outpouring of lust, the challenge of exploring physical possibilities. And sometimes sex is forced, it is unwanted or violent. Sex may happen out of boredom, or frustration, or simply because it's easier than saying no; it can be an act of generosity, because the other person wants it so much; it may be an expression of joy, or infatuation. Sex can be an exploration of the limits of pain, or to play with ideas of power. It may be the sheer pleasure and warmth of being with and exploring another body; the thrill of flesh on flesh.

Sex may be several things with one partner, or have only one function with a particular person. The meaning sex has may change throughout each woman's life. Yet despite these complexities, sex is frequently represented as one absolute thing, which women should strive to achieve (in a perfect way, with one or more, preferably simultaneous, orgasms).

HIV-prevention initiatives need to bring together knowledge of the diversity of sexual meaning within women's lives, the limited range of representations of women's sexuality, and the urgency of women's vulnerabilities to HIV. In the face of such a challenge, the most common response seems to be to reaffirm that sex is bad; now not only is sex morally dirty, it's also physically dirty. In many campaigns, sex has become disease, it has become death: 'Sex = HIV = AIDS = Death'. The more enlightened may turn this around and emphasize 'sexual health', with a stress on cleanliness and health. Here, the formula 'Sex = Health' does not describe the health of an emotionally, spiritually, sexually fulfilled individual, but the health which is absence of disease. One of Michael Callen's songs ends with him screaming 'Great Sex is Healthy Sex. Let's hear it for Healthy Sex, Yeah. . . . '[87] His great whoop of joy always strikes me as pointedly ironic. Given the choice between hot sex, horny sex, loving sex, squelchy sex and healthy sex, which would you choose?

The phrase safer sex is just as problematic. The moment of sex is rarely a time which is about health and safety (except for professional sex workers, which is why they have such high rates of safer sex practice). Health and safety have always been a part of sex, and an especially important part for women, yet few will be minded to concentrate on the negative consequences in the midst of consensual sex (a key reason for the popularity of the Pill is that it is 'coitus independent'). The wild and wonderful fun, the pleasure of sex is not about the long-term (even when it is within a long-term relationship); it is not about the consequences; it is the excitement of *now*, of the irrational; the touch, smell, sight, sound and taste of another body; it's about losing control. And these things are rarely linked to serious reflection about disease, health, or safety.

Notes

1. C. S. Vance (ed.), *Pleasure and Danger: Exploring Female Sexuality*, Pandora, London, 1992, p. 1.
2. Worldwide estimates from WHO.
3. This is of critical importance in respect of health promotion for people with HIV and AIDS – if health is the absence of disease then anyone with a disease is condemned, *ipso facto*, to an unhealthy life. This is alien from the experience of many people living with HIV.
4. *Ms*, March/April 1995, p. 18.
5. C. S. Vance, 'More danger, more pleasure: a decade after the Barnard Sexuality Conference', in Vance, *op. cit.*, p. xviii.
6. C. MacKinnon, *Feminism Unmodified: Discourses on Life and Law*, Harvard University Press, Cambridge, MA, and London, 1987, p. 50; cited by L. Segal, 'Introduction', in L. Segal and M. McIntosh (eds),

Sex Exposed: Sexuality and the Pornography Debate, Virago, London, 1992, p. 312. MacKinnon is an American legal scholar and a leading anti-porn activist.

7. G. Rubin, 'Thinking sex: notes for a radical theory of the politics of sexuality', in Vance, *op. cit.*, p. 302.

8. *Ibid.*

9. S.-E. Ekeid, 'Policy perspective: a comparison of national programmes and policies in Europe', in H. Curtis (ed.), *Promoting Sexual Health: Proceedings of the Second International Workshop on Prevention of Sexual Transmission of HIV and Other Sexually Transmitted Diseases, Cambridge, 24–27 March 1991*, HEA, London, 1992, p. 17. Ekeid was then Co-ordinator for the WHO Global Programme on AIDS at the Regional Office for Europe.

10. Statistics from the Equal Opportunities Commission, cited in the *Guardian*, 3 October 1994.

11. Statistics from the Equal Opportunities Commission, cited in the *Guardian*, tabloid p. 2, 8 May 1995.

12. Statistics cited by S. Faludi, *Backlash*, Vintage, London, 1991, pp. 5, 397, based on *A New Future for Women*, Labour Party, 1991; *Putting Equality into Practice, A Shadow Ministry of Women Consultation Document*, Labour Party, 1991; Lesley Abdela, letter to Jane Hill, November 1991; Melissa Benn, 'Brace yourself for the backlash', *Cosmopolitan*, February 1992, p. 12; Joanna Foster, plenary address to the 1989 Human Rights Congress, Melbourne; *The Pay Gap Between Men and Women in 1991*, Low Pay Unit, 1991.

13. J. E. Mantell *et al.*, 'The effects of household and decision-making powers on condom use among drug users', International Conference on AIDS, Berlin, 1993, Abstract POD17-3925; cited in C. Beeker *et al.*, 'Is empowerment theory a useful framework for HIV/AIDS interventions with women in the United States?', at 'HIV Infection in Women: Setting a New Agenda' conference, Washington, DC, 1995, Abstract TP435.

This study found that women who had more power and control in the home were more likely to use condoms.

14. Archbold, *Criminal Law Practice and Proceedings* (the criminal lawyer's bible), quoted in H. Kennedy, *Eve Was Framed: Women and British Justice*, Chatto & Windus, London, 1992, p. 130.

15. K. Barry, *Female Sexual Slavery*, New York University Press, New York, 1979; quoted in N. van der Gaag, 'Soliciting for change', *New Internationalist*, no. 252, February 1994, p. 7.

16. There are some similarities between women's and men's experience of the commercial sex industry, but gender and power dynamics create key differences for men which cannot be addressed here. See B. Gibson, *Male Order: Life Stories from Boys Who Sell Sex*, Cassell, London, 1995.

17. Cheryl Overs, personal communication.

18. I always find this a rather weird religious response since Jesus seemed to be more interested in inviting prostitutes to dinner than finding them retraining schemes to quit their work.

19. L. Segal, *Straight Sex: The Politics of Desire*, Virago, London, 1994, p. 81.

20. K. Wellings *et al.*, *Sexual Behaviour in Britain: The National Survey of Sexual Attitudes and Lifestyles*, Penguin, Harmondsworth, 1994, pp. 122–3.

21. S. Day *et al.*, 'Prostitution and risk of HIV: male partners of female prostitutes', *BMJ*, 307, 1993, pp. 359–61.

22. See, for example, Trisha's story in S. Mayes and L. Stein (eds), *Positive Lives: Responses to HIV – a Photodocumentary*, Cassell, London, 1993, pp. 34–7.

23. H. Ward *et al.*, 'Prostitution and risk of HIV: female prostitutes in London', *BMJ*, 307, 7 August 1993, pp. 356–8.

24. S. T. Green *et al.*, 'Female streetworker – prostitutes in Glasgow: a descriptive study of their lifestyle', *AIDS Care*, 5(3), 1993, pp. 321–35.

25. C. Healy and A. Reed, 'The healthy hooker', p. 17, in *New Internationalist*, *op. cit.*

26. Pilot programme code of practice, 'Men who have sex with men sexual health detached project (Solihull)', Appendix III in S. George *et al.*, *Bisexuality and HIV Prevention*, HEA, London, 1993, p. 57.

27. Green *et al.*, *op. cit.*, p. 334.

28. Ward *et al.*, *op. cit.*, p. 357. See also, S. Day and H. Ward, 'The Praed Street Project: a cohort of prostitute women in London', in M. Plant (ed.), *AIDS, Drugs and Prostitution*, Routledge, London, 1990, pp. 61–75.

29. K. Barry, UNESCO/Coalition Against Trafficking in Women, *The Penn State Report on Sexual Exploitation, Violence and Prostitution*, 1991; quoted in van der Gaag, *op. cit.*, p. 6.

30. J. Young Norton, 'Women builders of civilization', *Women's Political World*, 1 September 1913, p. 5; quoted in E. C. DuBois and L. Gordon, 'Seeking ecstasy on the battlefield: danger and pleasure in nineteenth-century feminist sexual thought', in Vance, *op. cit.*, p. 38.

31. N. Roberts, 'The whore, her stigma, the punter and his wife', p. 9, *New Internationalist*, no. 252, February 1994.

32. Quoted by G. Pheterson (ed.), *A Vindication of the Rights of Whores*, Seal Press, 1989; and by van der Gaag, *op. cit.*, p. 6.

33. Van der Gaag, *op. cit.*, p. 7.

34. Based on personal communications with Ruth Morgan-Thomas, and visiting ScotPEP.

35. The English Collective of Prostitutes has campaigned vigorously against the use of condoms as evidence in court to convict prostitutes of soliciting, and the Home Office does seem to have shifted its position.

36. C. Overs, 'Unfair cop', *New Internationalist, op. cit.*, p. 26.

37. D. Langsam, 'Not on our street corner', *Guardian*, 8 September 1993.

38. On 17 May 1995 there was the first-ever conviction of a British man for raping a prostitute. S. Weale, 'Private case brings rapist to justice', *Guardian*, 18 May 1995.

39. *Manchester Evening News*, 26 October 1979, quoted in J. Smith, *Misogynies*, Faber & Faber, London, 1989, p. 175.

40. *The Penn State Report, op. cit.*, quoted in G. Corea, *The Invisible Epidemic: The Story of Women and AIDS*, HarperPerennial, New York, 1992, p. 327.

41. Useful collections of essays, which include references to most of the other key texts, are Segal and McIntosh, *op. cit.*; G. Chester and J. Dickey (eds), *Feminism and Censorship: The Current Debate*, Prism Press, Dorset, 1988. Vance, *op. cit.*, is a primer for all debates about women's sexuality, including important analyses of the porn debates.

42. R. Morgan, 'Theory and practice: pornography and rape', in L. Lederer (ed.), *Take Back the Night*, William Morrow, New York, 1980, p. 139.

43. A. Henry, 'Does viewing pornography lead men to rape?', in Chester and Dickey, *op. cit.*, pp. 96–104.

44. E. Cowie, 'Pornography and fantasy', in Segal and McIntosh, *op. cit.*, p. 137.

45. Lederer, *op. cit.*, p. 122; quoted by L. Segal, 'Introduction', in Segal and McIntosh, *op. cit.*, p. 9.

46. S. George, 'Censorship and hypocrisy: some issues surrounding pornography that feminism has ignored', in Chester and Dickey, *op. cit.*, p. 111.

47. B. Ross, 'Wunna his fantasies: the state/d indefensibility of lesbian smut', *Bad Attitude*, 8 (5), 1993, pp. 34–9. In early 1994, Eli Langer, a gay male artist, was also prosecuted in Canada, this time for alleged child pornography in paintings from his imagination (*Pink Paper*, 28 January 1994).

48. R. Gorna, 'Delightful visions: from anti-porn to eroticizing safer sex', in Segal and McIntosh, *op. cit.*, pp. 169–83.

49. E. Jong, 'AIDS: is all the hysteria a blessing in disguise?', *Good Housekeeping*, November 1986, p. 65; quoted by Segal, *op. cit.*, p. 69. Segal's book is an excellent analysis of the silencing of explorations of women's sexuality as a result of the anti-sex agendas of feminism.

50. E. Carola, 'Women, erotica, pornography – learning to play the game?', in Chester and Dickey, *op. cit.*, p. 169.

51. P. Aggleton *et al.*, 'Risking everything? Risk behavior, behavior change and AIDS', *Science*, 265, pp. 341–5. Quoted in Beeker *et al.*, *op. cit.*

52. M. Callen and R. Berkowitz, *How to Have Sex in an Epidemic: One Approach*, News from the Front Publications, New York, 1983.

There have been claims that lesbians or the feminist movement invented 'safer sex'. This is nonsense. Of course many women engaged in the sexual activities which define safer sex – in particular non-penetrative sex – before AIDS, and developed political thinking about this. Yet the codifying of these activities as safer sex – a strategy to avoid HIV – was created because of AIDS, and by the first community ravaged by the epidemic.

53. Van der Gaag, *op. cit.*, p. 7.

54. R. E. Dobash and R. Dobash, 'Women, violence and social change', 1992; cited by the ALA (Association of London Authorities) Zero Tolerance campaign.

55. R. E. Hall, *Ask Any Woman – A London Inquiry into Rape and Sexual Assault*, Falling Wall Press, London, 1985, pp. 28, 106.

56. *Sunday Times*, 12 December 1982, quoted in Smith, *op. cit.*, p. 15.

57. K. Roiphe, *The Morning After: Sex, Fear, and Feminism*, Hamish Hamilton, London, 1993, p. 52.

58. N. Wolf, *The Beauty Myth: How Images of Beauty Are Used against Women*, Vintage, London, 1990, p. 167.

59. Hall, *op. cit.*, p. 33.

60. For example, S. Murphy *et al.*, 'Rape and subsequent seroconversion to HIV', *BMJ*, 1989, 299, p. 718.

61. F. Boag *et al.*, 'Rape, STDs and HIV' (letter), *International Journal of STDs and AIDS*, 1, 1990, p. 291.

62. C. Ogu and N. Yamaguchi, *More Harm than Help: The Ramifications for Rape Survivors of Mandatory HIV Testing of Rapists*, Center for Women Policy Studies, Washington, DC, 1991; cited in M. Berer with S. Ray, *Women and HIV/AIDS: An International Resource Book*, Pandora, London, 1993, p. 235.

63. This solution was suggested by Judge Professor Johan Westenberg, in response to a complex rape case. His judgement is rendered more intriguing in light of the fact that Westenberg was Chair of the Dutch association for people with HIV. He died of AIDS-related complications on 27 February 1994.

64. I. Foster and J. G. Bartlett, 'Rape and subsequent seroconversion to HIV' (letter), *BMJ*, 1989, p. 1282; S. Murphy *et al.*, 'Rape and subsequent seroconversion to HIV' (letter), *BMJ*, 1990, p. 118.

65. C. Goodwin, 'Rape condoms beat DNA test', *Sunday Times*, 28 August 1994.

66. 'Jury remains split in condom rape trial', *Daily Telegraph*, 15 July 1993.

67. Associated Press, 'Condom dilemma in sex case', *The Times*, 13 May 1993; C. Laurence, 'Rapist who used condom is convicted', *Daily Telegraph*, 15 May 1993.

68. Painter, 1989, cited by Liz Kelly, handout for the ALA Zero Tolerance campaign.

69. J. Mooney, *The Hidden Figure: Domestic Violence in North London*, 1993, Middlesex University, Centre for Criminology.

70. *Punching Judy*, BBC Television, 22 May 1989; A. McGibbon *et al.*, *Abuse of Women in the Home*, London Borough of Hammersmith and Fulham; Mooney, *op. cit.* – all cited by ALA Zero Tolerance campaign.

71. Victim Support, *National Working Party Report on Domestic Violence*, 1992; Jalna Hanner, cited by McCollum, Hackney Women's Unit in ALA Zero Tolerance campaign briefing.

72. *GQ (Gentleman's Quarterly)*, January 1994, cited by ALA Zero Tolerance campaign

73. Mooney, *op. cit.*; Edinburgh District Council, *Adolescents' Knowledge about, and Attitudes to, Domestic Violence*, 1992.

74. *Women Like Us*, Positively Women, London, 1994, p. 25.

75. Quotes and description of Miss X's character from *Daily Mail*, 20 October 1993, pp. 1, 4–5.

76. Quoted in G. Levy, '"Witch-hunt" in a private room', *Daily Mail*, 20 October 1993, p. 6.

77. S. Crichton, 'Sexual correctness: has it gone too far?', *Newsweek*, 25 October 1993, p. 54.

78. L. Chunn, 'No still means No, doesn't it?', *Guardian*, 20 October 1993, p. 2.

79. *Concerns about Rape*, Home Office report on rape, 1989; S. Grace *et al.*, *Rape, from Recording to Conviction*, Home Office Research and Planning Unit Paper 71; cited in ALA Zero Tolerance campaign.

80. A. McColgan, quoted in L. Grant, 'Bad sex', *Guardian Weekend*, 24 September 1994, p. 34.

81. *Daily Mail*, 20 October 1993, p. 1.

82. David Danon, sophomore student, quoted in Crichton, *op. cit.*, p. 56.

83. L. Grant, 'Sex and the single student: the story of date rape', in S. Dunant (ed.), *The War of the Words: The Political Correctness Debate*, Virago, London, 1994, p. 86.

84. S. Tisdale, quoted in S. George, 'A dirty nice girl', *Diva*, no.7, April 1995, p. 49.

85. Segal, *op. cit.*, pp. 208–9.

86. S.-E. Ekeid, *op. cit.*, p. 8.

87. Michael Callen, 'How To Have Sex', from his album *Purple Heart*, Significant Other Records, 1988.

Chapter nine

Just Say No?[1]

Fourteen years into the epidemic, virtually all HIV prevention messages provided by public and private health entities
have focused on:
1) Abstinence
2) Mutual Monogamy
3) Use of a Male Condom
These messages simply aren't achievable, acceptable or
realistic for millions of women.

Anna Forbes[2]

In addressing HIV prevention to women there is a tension
between the need to focus on long-term societal change and the
need to develop short-term protective measures. For example, a
woman who is economically dependent on a man and subject to sex
against her will has limited opportunities to 'demand' that men
wear condoms, making prevention technologies which women
wear or control an urgent necessity. Anke Ehrhardt states that 'In
the short term, we need to expand our methods of protection from
only condoms to a greater repertoire that includes methods under
women's control such as a virucidal or microbicidal agent that
increases women's independence of partner negotiation and protects them against infection.'[3] Short-term approaches like these
could be said to maintain the status quo by not challenging it, and
so keep underlying oppression and inequality intact. However, the
paucity of HIV-prevention technologies is as reflective of women's
disempowerment at an environmental level, as the disempowerment of coercive sex is at a personal level.

The contexts within which sex happens are sufficiently diverse and complicated that it would be logical to expect a range of technologies to reduce the risk of HIV transmission. Not so. To date there is but one method which is proven: the latex male condom; and one which can be recommended: the polyurethane female condom. This reduction of HIV prevention to condoms is bizarre when compared with the range of contraceptive technologies available for women. It is also depressing since they rely on male control – the female condom relies on male consent, and he can avoid it if he is opposed to it. (It is possible for a man to side-slip it and insert his penis between the vaginal wall and the female condom.) This reliance on male control significantly reduces the efficacy of the approach. Studies have shown greater levels of STD reduction with methods that are female-controlled, compared with male-controlled technologies. This is not because of any technical features with the methods, but because women use them more efficiently – probably because they have greater interest and motivation to avoid the consequences.[4]

In this chapter I will review some of the concerns about proven HIV-prevention technologies (male condoms and female condoms), potential HIV-prevention technologies (diaphragms and microbicides), and other strategies to avoid infection (what Anke Ehrhardt delightfully terms 'outercourse'). I will then turn to some of the approaches used to convey messages about these different technologies. HIV prevention exists within the discipline of public health, and I will consider traditional approaches – including antenatal testing strategies – as well as risk-reduction models of health promotion that have developed to promote HIV-prevention messages. In particular, I will consider the application of an empowerment model to HIV-prevention activities for women.

HIV-prevention technologies

• Male condoms

Officially condoms (both male and female versions) can only be promoted for vaginal sex, and those which have passed government standards state that they are 'designed for vaginal intercourse only'. Although condoms have been used for anal sex for many years, and gay men's studies show that they protect against HIV being transmitted, no research has assessed their efficacy for anal sex. Consequently it is impossible to advise women and men about how reliable the latex male condom is for anal fucking, or whether different types of condom (for example, thicker ones) are preferable for this. Even so, a whole mythology has grown up that 'extra-strong' condoms are the only reliable type for anal sex, and that regular condoms are only for vaginal sex. I am not aware of any data proving this, and indeed some condoms labelled as extra-strong may be less reliable than regular condoms.[5] The theory arises from the fact that more stress may be placed on the condom during anal fucking (because the rectum tends to be tighter than the vagina), so that thicker latex will bear the friction better. However, if the intention is to reduce stress on the condom, then this is more likely to be achieved by good lubrication than thicker latex.[6]

No one is willing to undertake the trials which would establish the efficacy of different forms of condom for anal sex. Condom manufacturers refuse to conduct trials because it would be 'bad for their family image'[7] – after all, only nasty queers do that sort of thing. The other reason used against conducting research into the use of condoms for anal sex is that, since it is bound to be more risky than vaginal sex, running a trial will, in itself, place people at risk. This is an odd concern. The people who make such statements know full well that men and women will continue to have anal sex, and that condoms will continue to be (inconsistently) used, so how can it be more risky to know what level of protection they offer?

The fact that condoms are not tested for anal sex – and therefore do not carry any advice about using them for this practice – appears to be one of the reasons why women do not use them systematically for anal sex, when they *are* using condoms for vaginal sex. For example, Ehrhardt reported that condoms were never used for vaginal sex by 34 per cent of the women enrolled on the trial 'FIO', yet in the subgroup of women who had anal sex in the last three months, 55 per cent never used condoms.[8] While gay men and bisexual men are bombarded with messages telling them to use extra-strong condoms and water-based lubricant for fucking, women are just told to use condoms, in a blissfully non-specific way. The pleasure some women enjoy from anal fucking is generally denied by HIV-prevention materials, which either ignore it all together, or slip it in as an afterthought. Since women are used to considering the potential complications of vaginal sex (i.e. unplanned babies), but not of anal sex, this is quite some afterthought. Indeed, the legalization of anal sex between men and women, which took place in The Criminal Justice Bill of 1994, was ignored by British AIDS activists – despite the fact that this was a significant step forward in protecting consensual sex. While the neglect of the importance of this move is worrying, the fact that the law was changed is extremely encouraging. Not only is this important for women (and their partners) who enjoy anal sex, it also demonstrated an awareness of HIV prevention by the legislature. It would have been easy to argue that, since anal sex is a high risk for HIV, the legal status should not alter. Yet the willingness to legalize anal sex for women suggests an awareness that preventing HIV is not concerned with the practice of sexual acts *per se*, but whether they are protected by condom use.

Condoms are only effective when used properly, and a central feature of good condom technique is also often neglected in instructions to women: lubricant. While this is a necessity for anal sex (since the rectum hardly lubricates), frequently it is also important (and pleasurable) for vaginal sex. One of the main reasons that condoms fail is that the friction of fucking causes them to split or burst. This is easily remedied by using sufficient quantities of lubricant – which must be water-based when used with latex – and this is stressed in HIV-prevention information for gay men. The fact that women do not always lubricate sufficiently during vaginal sex is so frequently ignored that lubricants do not receive anywhere near the same priority in information for 'heterosexuals' and women. Lubrication (and lack thereof) is often a source of embarrassment for women – it is supposed to be natural, so it must be her fault if it does not happen. Throughout the menstrual cycle, levels of vaginal juices change – they are more copious and stickier during ovulation, for example – and they can also alter with other hormonal changes (such as using the pill, and when women are post-menopausal). Another factor is arousal. While sometimes women do not lubricate when they *are* aroused, they rarely do when they are not. There are many reasons why women have sex when they are not aroused – overt or covert force, allowing him his 'conjugal rights', ambivalence about the situation. Whatever the reason, if a condom is used but no lubricant, the likelihood of the condom splitting is far higher.

• *Female condoms*

The UK seems to have given a relatively generous welcome to the 'female condom'. In the USA, things were a little more troubled, with the FDA (Food and Drug Administration, responsible for approving new products like this) dragging their feet, and delaying approval by perhaps two years. The reason for their delay is hard to uncover. There seems to be a root anxiety about yielding the central role of the male (penile) condom. In the midst of a crisis which is so complex and changing, perhaps the certainty of a central prevention method gives reassurance and stability. The cause does not appear to be financial greed from condom manufacturers (which I would have expected), who have been remarkably restrained in the welcome they give AIDS. Perhaps this is because they don't want to queer their family-planning market. Male condoms also seem to be preferable to those with patriarchal fantasies of protecting women. One male journalist bemoaned the genesis of the female condom for depriving men of the opportunity to rescue women; men could be robbed of some of their power over women's lives.[9]

Alternatively known by its brand names, Femidom (in Europe) and Reality (a particularly weird choice for the American product), the technical term for a female condom is a 'vaginal pouch'. It is a soft, pliable polyurethane sheath which lines the vagina. It has an inner ring which is used for insertion and which holds the sheath in place beyond the pubic bone, and an outer ring which lies flat against the labia. It is pre-lubricated, odourless and tasteless and appears to be equivalent to male condoms in its efficacy as a barrier to pregnancy, HIV and other sexually transmitted infections. Trials in the United States and Britain show a pregnancy failure rate of 2.4 per cent when the femidom is used properly, and

12.2 per cent when not used properly and consistently. Kitemarked (i.e. quality-controlled) male condoms have a 2 per cent pregnancy failure rate when used properly, which rises to 15 per cent for improperly used condoms.[10]

The issue with female condoms is not, therefore, whether they work as a contraceptive, but whether they are acceptable to women (and men). Much has been made of the comic appearance of the device (one colleague claims he uses it as a handbag). It is anything but discreet – the outer ring and some of the sheath hang down beyond the labia – and some users have reported that it makes a noise (variously described as rustling and farting. Apparently this can be rectified by using more lubricant). Cunnilingus is rarely possible when wearing a female condom because the outer ring can cover the clitoris. Some women report that this means they have less sensation during intercourse; for other women, the outer ring rubs up against the clitoris and it becomes a combined prophylactic and sex toy. Some men report irritation with the inner ring, which they bang up against during penetration, and occasionally women experience discomfort because of this. This is easily resolved by ignoring the manufacturers' instructions, removing the inner ring, and wearing the female condom like a large baggy male condom. (This is also claimed to reduce the noise problem, and it is the most practical technique for anal sex.[11]) While the device is by no means perfect, neither are male condoms, and it does have some technical advantages. As it is bigger than male condoms it is less constricting, and some men report that this significantly increases sensitivity. As it is made of polyurethane (a type of plastic), the female condom is suitable for people who are allergic to latex. Polyurethane is also thermo-sensitive, so that it heats up to body temperature, making it less intrusive than latex products. It can also be used with oil-based lubricants, which do not destroy plastic in the way they do latex. Some HIV-prevention workers express anxiety about this, fearing that it will confuse the simple message promoting condoms and water-based lube.

'Acceptability and affordability have to be a major component of research,' states Dr Anne Johnson, 'We don't need lots of irritating and messy preparations.'[12] The manufacturer's own trials suggest that two-thirds of women who try a female condom find it acceptable, and slightly higher rates of male acceptance are found. Trials not sponsored by the company have tended to show a lower rate of acceptability, yet Ehrhardt reports that a graph of female acceptability of the female condom fits the classic bell curve, with 50 per cent of women displaying a neutral attitude to the product.[13] It is more popular with women who are comfortable with their bodies, who are happy to touch their own genitals, and with women in an established sexual relationship. The femidom offers a new barrier method, and it can be used as an exciting alternative to play with. Ehrhardt emphasizes that one critical factor remains under-researched: the effect of the female condom on a woman's ability to orgasm. Although it is still a long way from being a technology which is truly under women's control (and the look of the thing creates a tendency to scoff), the female condom is an exciting addition to the options women have for HIV protection.

• *Diaphragm*

Missing from all HIV-prevention campaigns is the information that, in addition to the two forms of condom, there are two existing technologies which have some effect against HIV. How much effect is unknown. Diaphragms and spermicides, and perhaps sponges containing spermicides, are routine forms of contraception and STD control, which should have some role to play in HIV prevention. The sponge is simply a vehicle for spermicide, and I will consider spermicides under the more general category of microbicides. The diaphragm (or cap) works by holding spermicide in place at the top of the vagina, and it also provides a protective physical barrier across the cervix. In the UK, the cap comes in different sizes and shapes, and has a range of names. In the USA, only three varieties are available, apparently because of trade restrictions, not efficacy concerns. The contraceptive action of the spermicide has a time limit, so that it may have to be topped up just before fucking, and if the couple fuck a second time. The cap has to stay in place for six hours after ejaculation, and so it can become quite messy and slippery. Some women like to use the cap during their periods because it covers the cervix, and so holds the blood. Another technical advantage is the fact that the cap is designed to be reused.

There is so little awareness of the potential value of the diaphragm and spermicide as HIV-prevention options, that any such role is sometimes actively denied. One women's leaflet, after recommending condoms, states: 'Remember other forms of contraception, such as the diaphragm (cap), the coil or the pill DO NOT protect you from getting infected with HIV.'[14] A simplistic 'condom lobby' appears to have emerged, that promotes (usually male) condoms at all costs. While relative risks are allowed for in the coding of different sexual *activities*, such an idea is anathema in respect of different forms of *protection* during penetration.

A woman choosing a contraceptive method can turn to booklets that will tell her that the cervical cap and diaphragm are 85 to 98 per cent effective, as are the male and female condom. The IUD (intrauterine device) is 99 per cent effective, the combined and POP (progestogen-only) pill rates 97 to 99 per cent, the sponge 80 to 87 per cent, injectable contraceptive 99 per cent, sterilization over 99 per cent, implant over 98 per cent, and natural methods 80 to 98 per cent.[15] As well as the efficacy rates, she will find information about how the method works, and the advantages and disadvantages associated with it. In the advantages, she will discover that three of these methods will help to prevent her acquiring (or transmitting) STDs, but that only one – the male or female condom – is effective for HIV. Why the difference? If barrier methods like the diaphragm and the sponge, when used with spermicide, can prevent a woman from acquiring chlamydia and gonorrhoea, why would these be ineffective for HIV? And if they are not *as* effective as a male condom and lubricant, why can she not be told that, in the way that she is told about contraceptive differences?

The usual excuse for information being restricted to the use of male condoms is that no other method has been tested for HIV prevention. And why haven't they been tested? It seems to be the same rationale used against checking whether condoms work for anal sex (it's bound to be more risky so it would be unethical to check), tied in with the US panic about female condoms – if they work, men won't be able to look after women any more. Thus far (at a group level) men have not been doing a very good job, so why should women be denied a life-enhancing device that they can use if men fail to look after women's sexual health? Anxiety about the levels of efficacy of prevention technologies is nothing new. When condoms were first mooted as effective HIV prevention, there was concern that they might not be sufficient to block transmission entirely. As late as 1988, THT debated whether condoms should be freely distributed to gay men, out of concerns that they might break and thus not be as effective as non-penetrative sex.[16] The role of condoms in anal sex was not solved by research trials, but rather by observation of community acceptability of the method (and its alternatives), as well as the gradual accumulation of data from epidemiological studies. Why shouldn't these methods apply to the diaphragm?

The first, 'gold standard' HIV-prevention technology was devised to stop HIV getting into the anus, so it is no wonder that the diaphragm was not considered. The fact that safer sex was invented by gay men means that there are inevitable restrictions with its methodology for women. By the time it was translated to vaginal sex, the concept 'safer sex = condoms' was well established, and it would (and will) take a lot to shift the orthodoxy.

The importance of exploring the potential of the diaphragm as a safer-sex technology is two-fold. There are good theoretical reasons to assume that its technical efficacy would be in a similar range to the male condom (probably just a little lower). The biology of HIV transmission during vaginal sex suggests that, in general, the virus attaches at the cervix, not the vaginal wall (see Chapter 6). This means that the diaphragm should protect the site of greatest vulnerability. If a woman is HIV-infected, she is more likely to transmit HIV from her cervical secretions or menstrual blood – not from the secretions which are exuded from the vaginal wall (see Chapter 7). In this scenario, the diaphragm should contain these fluids and thus protect the man. This seems plausible from biological experiments with HIV, and also research into the efficacy of the diaphragm and spermicide method in controlling other STDs, in particular gonorrhoea and chlamydia. Beyond the biological concerns are the psycho-social ones. Diaphragms are controlled by women, so that the efficacy rate is likely to rise due to user compliance (even enthusiasm). Although cumbersome to insert, the diaphragm can be put in place well in advance of sex, and does not have to disrupt the flow of the sexual encounter (one of the classic anti-condom gripes). As well as having control over the device, women can also conceal it. The taste and smell of the spermicide can be detected (and off-putting), and the man may find himself hitting against the outer ring of the device, but it is certainly far easier to conceal than the female condom.

- *Microbicides*[17]

A microbicide is a gel, cream or foam that would prevent the transmission of sexually transmitted diseases (including HIV) when placed in the vagina (or anus); it may or may not be combined with a contraceptive spermicide. The concept is based upon spermicides, most of which have activity against STDs as well as their principal role of deactivating sperm (and so blocking conception). Currently, no proven safe and effective microbicides are available, although one existing product (Nonoxynol-9) may be a partial option for some women. Research is underway into new products, and also to consider the best methodologies for undertaking trials into promising compounds.[18] Although WHO announced in 1993 that they would afford a high priority to the development of microbicides, even if one of the compounds currently being researched is found to be safe and effective, it will not reach the market until at least the year 2001. If the rates of transmission to women do not increase (and they probably will), worldwide another 602,250 women will acquire HIV before there is a chance of them having access to a truly female-controlled HIV-prevention method. This is the context that means it is vital to consider the existing compound, Nonoxynol-9, before turning to the promising possibilities of science.

NONOXYNOL 9

The only microbicidal compound currently approved for use in both Europe and the USA is the spermicide Nonoxynol 9 (henceforth, N9). The role of N9 in HIV prevention is characterized by muddled, wishful and gloomy thinking. The response to the chemical has wavered between over-enthusiasm (it was nearly incorporated as a mandatory element of the official European condom standard) and total rejection (with alarmist warnings that it is toxic and encourages HIV transmission). AIDS workers' popular understandings of N9 have been created from two sources: initial *in vitro* studies, which showed that N9 deactivated HIV within a few seconds; an *in vivo* study, which found more HIV seroconversions among women who used sponges containing N9 than among those who used nothing (Kreiss *et al.*[19]). When the initial laboratory tests showed that N9 destroyed HIV, people were advised to use condoms and a water-based lubricant containing N9; and many condoms were manufactured to include N9. However, the chemical N9 is a small molecule, which can be absorbed by genital mucosae, and consequently it may cause inflammation or irritation. This was seen in the Kreiss study where the women who used N9 sponges developed more genital ulcers which facilitated the acquisition of HIV. The Kreiss study created panic, and overturned the prior general advice to use N9.

The knee-jerk reaction to Kreiss was fairly predictable, and has become quite unhelpful. In part the reaction was so absolute because of a perception that the trial was unethical, as the 138 commercial sex workers (enrolled in Nairobi) were not advised about standard methods of safer sex. The outrage at the way these women's lives were endangered seems to have fed a willingness to damn the product, whatever the result. It is worth dwelling on the methodology and outcome of this trial, since it has had a major influence on thinking about N9. The ethics of the trial were clearly dubious, and such shoddy practice should never be repeated. It is inevitably difficult to test any new prevention technology (including, one day, a primary vaccine), because it will only be possible to see if the new technology works if a substantial number of people do engage in (apparently) unsafe behaviour.

However, there are methodologies that will allow comparisons to be made without either encouraging people to act in an unsafe way, or concealing important information from them. In brief, these involve counselling women to use both condoms and the microbicide, and to keep a coital log recording what they used for each act of intercourse. Women are provided with free condoms and microbicide, but half the women receive a placebo version of the microbicide. Since condom use is never 100 per cent, if this population has high rates of HIV prevalence there will be some new infections. These would have happened anyway, and should be fewer than would have happened, because of the free condoms and counselling.[20]

Returning to the Kreiss study, it emerges that there were other methodological problems apart from the ethics, and these may have confused the results. The women were given sponges which contained a very high dose of N9 (1000 mg). Because of the women's work, the sponges were changed several times a day. This increased the likelihood of causing trauma to the genitals, and exposed the women to far too much chemical (on average 3000 mg per day – whereas less than 100 mg is necessary to deactivate HIV). It is plausible that the sponges – not the N9 – caused the ulceration, since the 'placebo group' was not properly controlled; these women received a cream, instead of N9 or sponges. The women using N9 had higher levels of genital ulcers, and these all occurred on the vulva – not the vagina or cervix – which suggests that inserting the sponge could have been a significant factor.

These factors are important, because other studies confirm that N9 can cause irritation, often connected to a dose response. The manufacturers estimate that 5 to 10 per cent of the population have an immediate allergic reaction to N9 – these women and men cannot use the product safely. There are no data on anal intercourse, but anecdotal reports suggest that irritation may be greater in the rectum since the mucosae are more delicate. N9 irritation can be easily detected – within one month of starting to use it – and the chemical should be discontinued by those affected. The dose response which has been reported suggests that (if a person is not allergic) less than 150 mg N9 per day is safe and causes no epithelial disruption, but high levels of disruption to the cervix and vagina are seen where 600 mg per day (or more) is used.[21] This is important as the different products containing N9 have a range of concentrations. The sponge has 1000 mg, vaginal jelly or cream contains 350 mg, suppositories 100 to 150 mg and the contraceptive film has 75 mg.[22]

The logical conclusions – that lower doses might protect without causing epithelial disruption – appear to be borne out by other studies which followed Kreiss. Feldblum, in a study of 57 discordant couples, found no increased ulceration among the women who used 100-mg suppositories of N9. More importantly, there was 40 per cent less transmission to the woman from her HIV-positive male partner in those couples where N9 was used regularly.[23] An even more impressive rate of protection against HIV was seen in Zeking's study of 273 commercial sex workers in the Cameroon. N9 was an effective measure for preventing HIV acquisition by women who used it as a spermicide, even without condoms. The couples using N9 experienced a 90 per cent reduction in transmission; for women who only used N9, and not condoms, their risk of acquiring HIV was reduced by over 50 per cent.[24]

It is already established that N9 is lethal (*in vitro*) to gonorrhoea, trichomonas, herpes simplex, treponema and urea plasma, and it may be effective against chlamydia. Women who used a diaphragm and N9 halved their chance of developing cervical gonorrhoea, reduced by 50 per cent the risk of tubal infertility and by 60 per cent the risk of hospitalization with PID.[25] These benefits of N9 are significant in the context of HIV. It is well known that the presence of any STDs significantly increases the risk that HIV will be transmitted. The reduction of STDs is not only good of itself, but also a key feature of HIV prevention. However, N9 is also known to increase risks for urinary tract infections, candidiasis, bacterial vaginosis and toxic shock syndrome, since it disrupts the delicate vaginal ecology. Consequently – and frustratingly – the jury is still out on N9. In 1995, Stewart concluded a review of the options available to women, stating, 'This is a research emergency: we still don't know if Nonoxynol 9 is good, bad or indifferent.'[26]

POTENTIAL MICROBICIDES

In addition to the obvious need for safety, there are many requirements of microbicides. Different formulas need to be developed which are contraceptive or allow a woman to become pregnant. One of the problems with promoting the message of 100 per cent safer sex to women is that many will, at some time, wish to conceive. Microbicides also need to be assessed for interactions with other contraceptives. Ideally they will block transmission of HIV and other infections from a woman, and protect her from acquiring them. Microbicides should be capable of clandestine use, and this means that attention should be paid to their detectability (for example, Nonoxynol-9 has a distinct taste) and method of application. At what point would the product become active – and for how long? Could they, like the female condom, be applied some time before intercourse? Would they be effective if applied post-coitus (for example, if a woman was raped)? How would they be disposed? How much would they cost, and how easily available would they be? One question, which is rarely asked, is whether microbicides would work only in the vagina, or also in the anus? Most data on microbicides discusses their use for vaginal inter-course. This is principally because the vagina has the form of a 'pouch' – which can be fully lined by a product and contain it – whereas the anus is 'open-ended', so that a product may not be contained within the rectum and could leak up into the intestines. Microbicide research also appears to concentrate on the vagina because of the general prurience and neglect of the anus as a sexual organ.

In 1994, Stein identified eleven products known to have potential microbicidal activities: Nonoxynol-9, Octoxynol-9, Benzalkonium Chloride, Menfegol, Gossypol, Protectaid Sponge, Butylurea, Polyanionic Polysaccharides, Myeloperoxidase, Immuno-globulins and 'Defensins'.[27] There are a number of ways in which microbicides could work, including:

- altering the vaginal ecology – the acidity of the vagina would be maintained to create a naturally virucidal environment;
- as a physical barrier – the presence of the gel itself would prevent HIV from being transmitted (in a similar way to male and female condoms);
- as a pharmacological barrier – anti-HIV compounds would be incorporated into a gel to inhibit the virus;
- as a chemical barrier – chemical compounds, such as spermicides, would be incorporated into a gel to destroy the virus, other STDs and (perhaps) sperm.

Nonoxynol-9 is a classic example of a chemical barrier, and other compounds may be subject to similar constraints. Because the action of the microbicide is to destroy unwanted items, it will inevitably risk destroying or disrupting wanted ones (like intact epithelia, and perhaps sperm). Pharmacological barriers should strictly be described as 'virucides' as they are designed to block HIV directly. Although this may sound logical, it is also the most contested and risky route. One group of researchers has developed a gel that can incorporate and continuously release anti-HIV agents: AZT or ddC for fifty hours, ddI for twenty-five hours, and Foscarnet for twenty hours. This approach has several problems. It is only focused on one infection, whereas an individual is likely to be vulnerable to many, and it involves introducing potentially toxic drugs into the highly sensitive mucosae of people who are not infected with HIV (who would derive no personal disease-related benefits). Given the problems of toxicity, and complications (such as AZT resistance), one of the researchers developing this approach deemed it 'theoretically crazy'.[28]

The most interesting approach to microbicides develops compounds which could function as physical barriers, in particular the polysaccharides. Polysaccharides are used as food additives (dextran sulphate is perhaps the best known), and they work as microbicides by coating the lining of the vagina and cervix and blocking the virus from passing from infected lymphocytes or macrophages and becoming attached to the (uninfected) epithelium. Polysaccharides are large molecules and (unlike chemicals such as N9) they cannot be absorbed by the genital mucosae. In the laboratory, when carrageenans are added to epithelia they are very effective at blocking infection with HIV.[29] Carrageenans are food additives derived from red seaweed; they are used in ice cream and are very safe and non-toxic. This product works in a very general, non-specific way, and it is possible that, at a very low concentration, it could block nearly all sexually transmitted infections (HIV, HTLV, HSV-1 and 2, CMV, EBV, HPV, gonorrhoea, treponema pallidium, trichomonas, candida and chlamydia). However, there may be some technical problems with some of the current compounds. One researcher reports that dextran sulphate (another polysaccharide) is highly effective at inhibiting laboratory strains of HIV, but does not appear to work against real-life strains. Another prime candidate is benzalkonium chloride, yet this compound is inactivated by proteins and so it would be unable to work in the presence of high viral load.[30]

The final microbicidal approach, which has received little attention, would be to find mechanisms to manipulate the normal vaginal environment. Since the vagina is generally an acidic environment, one approach could be to maintain it at a pH of 4–5, even in the presence of (alkaline) semen. However, there is concern that permanently altering such a fundamental feature of female physiology could have unforeseen negative consequences.[31]

HIV-prevention initiatives have tended to ignore such technicalities of prevention, concentrating instead on different sexual activities, and promoting pleasure in their practice. This is vitally important for developing safer-sex work with women, but there are also key technical considerations. The fact that women do not always have control within a sexual encounter, and rarely have direct control over condom use, necessitates a broader perspective. In the long term, this entails empowering women so that they are not coerced in sexual relationships. In the medium term, this means advocating the speedy, ethical and accurate development of microbicidal products. In the short term, it entails promoting realistic strategies to women based on the few available data. Consequently, in New York, public health officials have described and promoted a 'hierarchical method of prevention'. This has a staging of effective risk-reduction approaches, from which a woman can choose, depending on her circumstances. It starts with recommending celibacy as the most effective way to avoid HIV, then mutual monogamy, and then promotes male condom use with lubricant. This is followed by the female condom, then the diaphragm with spermicide, and finally spermicide alone.[32] This has been a controversial approach, but it is also a realistic one. In the UK, HIV-prevention workers have consistently recognized the importance of assigning relative risks to different activities, and this approach is consistent. Since 1993, this has been recommended by the UK *National AIDS Manual* as a strategy for women who cannot 'demand' that their man wears a condom.[33]

• *Outercourse*

All of these discussions of technologies to prevent HIV assume that fucking is inevitable. Frequently it is. However, one of the components of safer sex much welcomed by feminists is the emphasis on what is usually called 'non-penetrative sex', and Ehrhardt upgrades to 'outercourse'. Outercourse has always been a strategy for HIV prevention, and derives from the fact that penetrative intercourse was not fundamental to all gay men's sexual repertoire with all partners. However, this led – in the early days of safer sex promotion – to a slapdash denial of the importance of fucking for gay men. For women having sex with men, there has always tended to be an assumption that fucking is the staple diet of sexual interaction and any attempts to avoid it would be dismissed. Indeed, one HIV-prevention brochure for women states, 'There are three main phases of sex: Foreplay, Intercourse, Orgasm (coming).'[34] Such a linear narrative of sexual engagement is precisely the type which many feminists have been struggling to overcome. The focus of this model appears to be male orgasm rather than mutual pleasure – is a woman allowed to have her orgasm during foreplay rather than intercourse?

The fact that, for many women, orgasm may be more frequent with outercourse than intercourse has sometimes been used by feminists to make the counter-argument that women would do better with just outercourse.[35] Doubtless some would. Yet opening up the discussion about women's desire can then create a new taboo where women cannot acknowledge their desire for fucking or penetration (one of the major points of policing in the lesbian community in the 1970s). 'There is a very fine line between talking about sex and setting norms,' suggests Vance; 'we err very easily given our ignorance of diversity, our fear of difference, and our naive expectation that all like the same sexual food as we.'[36] The potential exists for replacing the patriarchal policing of women's sexuality, with policing by a new ideological group. Despite these provisos, safer-sex discourses can affirm women's (and men's) enjoyment of sex other than fucking, and this is a key strategy to avoid HIV transmission. There can be an assumption that if condoms (or femidoms, or diaphragms or spermicides) are not available, then safer sex is impossible. Ehrhardt suggests that outercourse may be a viable option for young women, and reports that approximately one-third of a cohort of extremely vulnerable eighteen- to thirty-year-olds reported using outercourse when protected intercourse was not possible.[37]

Public health

HIV-prevention messages which are defined as appropriate and effective are conveyed by the discipline of health promotion, which in turn exists within the framework of public health. Strategies to protect the public health have been a component of British statutory activity since the nineteenth century, and focus principally on infectious diseases. This may include, for example, measures to protect hygienic sanitation or to ensure that council housing stock does not contribute to ill health. Such measures tend to be ensured by Environmental Health Officers and depend upon a broad based appreciation of the impacts upon health. However, public health has also traditionally focused on controlling infectious diseases that are sexually transmitted. The traditional methods for addressing this have been described as a policy of 'contain and control', and Patton goes as far as to describe these activities as 'classist and anti-sex' with a focus on 'protecting morally pure (middle-class) women who might contract VD from their men'.[38] It is such an approach that develops screening for certain STDs, followed by treatment of the infected person and mandatory contact tracing in order to test and treat their sexual partners. It is also the model used to control the outbreak of Ebola virus in Zaire in May 1995 where authorities sealed off the city where the first cases where detected, and aimed to identify those infected and ensure they accessed healthcare.

This classic model has been transformed into calls for mandatory HIV testing and restrictive measures for people identified as HIV-positive. A reductive understanding of public health has led some commentators to postulate a conflict between human rights and public health – suggesting that the rights of an individual to self-determination should be swayed in order to 'protect the public' from that person's ill health. This is the approach of countries like Cuba and Sweden, where the liberty of individuals is curtailed in order to prevent infections. There is no data to suggest such an approach works, although these strategies appeal to a few traditional, medically oriented public-health practitioners, as well as sections of the media which appreciate the simplicity of the approach. Unlike other STDs, there is no treatment for HIV, and restricting behaviour is impossible with a disease which has a decade-long incubation period (for Ebola it's a matter of days).

In general the 'contain and control' formula has been abandoned for HIV in favour of 'co-operation and inclusion' – a strategy that is simultaneously more liberal and more effective. Indeed, Professor Henriette Roscam Abbing explains that '[A] wise legislator steers clear of measures which restrict individual human rights and liberties, because in case of HIV/AIDS, there is no public health rationale to do so.'[39] Public-health approaches based on 'co-operation and inclusion' work with individuals and communities, enabling them to appreciate the impacts of ill health and participate in activities to overcome it. In the case of STDs, for example, this would mean implementing programmes of information, voluntary testing, counselling and treatment, and support with partner notification. It is this approach that has evolved into activities indicated by the buzzwords 'peer-led' and 'community-based'. Numerous researchers have shown that by involving people in their own health-seeking behaviours, diseases are better controlled, especially diseases that are subject to moral approbation and societal stigma.[40]

Dr Mike Merson, then Executive Director of the WHO Global Programme on AIDS, states unequivocally that '[M]andatory screening for HIV [is] a violation of human rights and an action which is at best futile and more often harmful to true prevention . . . wherever you look, it is usually the less powerful who wind up getting tested – patients more than doctors, women more than men.'[41] It is strange, therefore, that he has nothing to say about the increasingly routine violation, all over the globe, of the human rights of one sub-population: pregnant women. Public-health officials claim to have developed recommendations for the *voluntary* testing of pregnant women, but a glance through the documentation shows that, in practice, these programmes are mandatory in all but name. Most of these programmes claim to exist for the woman and her (potential) child; however, they are clearly concerned with reducing the possibilities for HIV to be transmitted to the foetus or newborn. It is important to clarify this difference (whether the programme is in the interest of the woman or the child) as this has a major impact on exploring the ethical dimensions of antenatal HIV screening.

The US Public Health service recommends that 'Health care providers should ensure that all pregnant women are *routinely* counselled and *encouraged to be tested* for HIV infection . . . for their own health and for reducing the risk of HIV transmission to their infants and others.'[42] Although a brief paragraph in the main text states that women should be monitored in order to begin prophylactic drugs and other medication as early as possible, the real emphasis of this guidance is clearly on babies. Recalcitrant women who refuse testing will not get away lightly with their decision, but will be harangued into knowing their HIV status after the child is born: 'If the mother refuses testing for herself, she should be informed of the importance of knowing her child's infection status for the child's health and encouraged to allow the child to be tested.'[43] What a lot of encouragement these women seem to need! A woman might be encouraged, by the HIV infor- mation from her routine counselling, to make the rational decision that she does not want to know her HIV status, and so she will not breast-feed (just in case she is infected), and will watch her child's health hawkishly during the early years. This will not go down well, and she is likely to find herself repeatedly 'encouraged' to reconsider.

It appears inconceivable to these doctors that a pregnant woman might, voluntarily, make some choices that do not coincide with their vision of what she needs. A rather limp paragraph in the recommendations notes that some women may be reluctant to test because of concerns about 'possible negative effects'; however, these are dismissed with a statement that 'serious adverse effects of HIV testing are infrequent' and by stressing 'benefit from the multiple health advantages of early HIV diagnosis.'[44] In part, the American vision of what pregnant women need is dominated by a general pro-testing climate – one supported by all the major AIDS service organizations[45] as well as healthcare providers. This is probably due to the fact that the USA is living an AIDS epidemic (rather than the European HIV epidemic, where far fewer people have become sick), and regular lack of access to good healthcare has a major impact upon mortality rates. They also have a somewhat over-optimistic faith in existing therapeutic interventions for people with HIV, with a tendency to begin treatment far earlier in disease than is the way in Europe (this in turn reflects the fact that, once accessed, healthcare in the USA is generally quite interventionist).

It is not only on the other side of the pond that pregnant women may be under pressure to test for HIV. British reserve results in guidelines (not recommendations) which are for offering (not encouraging) pregnant women in high HIV-prevalence areas (not everywhere) to find out if they have HIV. Although the language is far less thrusting, the implication is little different. The guidelines explain at least seven advantages of voluntary named ante-natal testing; although these are described as both for the woman and the baby, the advantages are really addressed at the well-being of the child. These are spread over two pages of the document, with just half a page given over to the disadvantages. If the woman tests HIV-negative, the disadvantages are technical: she may be seroconverting, and there have been concerns about the response of insurance companies. No thought about her ongoing needs for HIV prevention, or considerations if she is in a 'high risk' relationship. For the woman who tests HIV-positive, they highlight: 'the medical, social and psychological consequences of a positive result and the possible changes in family and other relationships'.[46] That's it. Nothing about the fact that this is a life-changing event; nothing to indicate the depth of the shock and horror most people experience with a positive result; nothing to indicate that prejudice, stigma and overt discrimination are frequent bedfellows of HIV; nothing to question whether this was the best point for this individual to know this information. The guidelines require that pregnant women receive 'appropriate private pre-test information and discussion' (note, not counselling), but will healthcare providers be equipped to offer this, based on such a scanty overview of the issues? Any 'discussion' grounded in this kind of simple understanding is unlikely to enable a woman to consider her legitimate concerns, and to decide whether this is the right time for her to know whether she has been infected with HIV.

These critiques are generated from the assumption that antenatal testing is also for the benefit of the woman. Whenever activists criticize antenatal HIV-testing programmes, they are told that this is an excellent way of identifying women who would not otherwise access HIV testing, and that this, in turn, will improve their medical opportunities. This sounds all very well, but it is bluff. These guidelines are about babies, not mothers. For example, the UK costings are all based upon 'the cost per truly infected child detected'. For each truly infected infant, there will be seven truly infected adult women detected; these do not warrant a costing. If the interest was to detect HIV-infected women, a more logical site for voluntary named HIV testing would be abortion clinics. The anonymized HIV-screening programme uncovered (and ignored) the fact that 0.49 per cent of women having terminations in London were HIV-infected, compared to just 0.18 per cent of pregnant women.[47] This is consistent with what one would assume – as a group, women who terminate a pregnancy may take fewer steps to preplan their sexual health. Other studies confirm this. A comparison of French women who took their pregnancy to term with those who aborted found that the women who aborted had double the high-risk factors: 38.9 per cent of women who terminated had engaged in activities which are risky for HIV, compared to 17.7 per cent of the women who gave birth.[48]

Antenatal HIV testing is, therefore, principally a strategy to reduce the risk of a baby acquiring HIV. How do the benefits of this risk reduction balance up against the costs of women testing at a time which they do not independently choose? While the Department of Health is fascinated by the financial costs (£18,000 if one in 200 pregnant women is HIV-infected, and £870,000 if the prevalence is one in 10,000),[49] my interest is the ethical and psychological costs of this approach.

According to one calculation, in an area where one in 500 pregnant women is HIV-infected, then it would be possible to prevent one additional child from becoming infected for every 20,000 pregnant women who were offered HIV testing.[50] This means that thousands of women might find themselves taking a test they would not otherwise consider. These women will be alerted to HIV, but are unlikely to receive adequate prevention messages to support them in remaining HIV-negative (which the overwhelming majority will be). Those few women who test HIV-positive will find one (usually cheerful) life-changing event overlaid by (usually distressing) life-changing information.

For the woman who tests HIV-positive during pregnancy there are some options. Although she has fewer options than the HIV-positive woman who wants to conceive, she will be faced with many choices. It may be particularly hard for her to make such major choices in the midst of the turmoil of pregnancy and the shock of her diagnosis. Should she terminate the pregnancy? There is also a six in seven chance of terminating an uninfected baby. A snap decision to abort, solely on the basis of HIV, could be ill advised, and there are several reports of women who abort under the pressure of this situation conceiving again after a short time. Should she have an elective Caesarean section? This may halve the risk, but the data are unclear and she may face other complications. In some areas she may experience difficulties finding a doctor willing to carry this out, if they know she is HIV-infected. Should she take AZT? While the results of 076 suggest a two-thirds reduction in risk, these were based on American rates of transmission (which tend to be higher than in Europe). The wonder drug has a tarnished image, and she may well be anxious about potential toxicities. She should also be wary of the long-term implications of this for her ability to choose the most effective therapies for her own health. Should she breast-feed? Not doing so can halve the risk of transmission, and she will be under strong pressure not to. This pressure can cause intense distress, especially for women who perceive major emotional and cultural advantages from this method of feeding.

For many pregnant women, the interests and health of the baby are of utmost priority. For some, but by no means all, these take a far higher priority than the woman's own needs. This argument has underpinned policies of 'opt-out' testing in antenatal clinics (where the pregnant woman is tested for HIV unless she objects). There are practical benefits to this: it normalizes the test, and reduces lengthy pre-test counselling, which is off-putting for many women, and inappropriate if the goal is to prepare for a positive diagnosis (which most will not have). However, many would argue that it is not necessarily a benefit to normalize a test which has so many negative, and unresolved, consequences. Standards for pre-test counselling emerged from a particular context, and it is not clear if such counselling in an antenatal clinic can ever provide an adequate HIV-prevention intervention. It is highly unlikely that for those whose result is positive, such counselling will have adequately prepared them for adjusting to the diagnosis. This too is alarming, and intensified by the fact that many of the women who test HIV-positive in this situation have specific cultural and linguistic needs.[51]

It has been suggested that antenatal HIV screening might be best compared to the screening of blood donors, where a similar proportion of people are infected. In the blood transfusion service, written consent to testing is obtained based solely upon written information. Unfortunately the comparison does not entirely stand up. The most glaring difference is that in the context of blood donation, there is a 100 per cent effective mechanism for blocking transmission: the blood is destroyed and not used. In pregnancy it is a question of reducing risk, and there is no intervention which has 100 per cent efficacy (except termination). Blood donation is normally an altruistic act (only one element of child-bearing, and not for all women) and involves potential transmission to a stranger (making testing in pregnancy more appealing). Moreover, (apart perhaps from a fear of needles) blood donation is a psychologically neutral act, whereas pregnancy involves a complex range of motivations, feelings and relationships at a time of high vulnerability for the woman and her partner or family.

It is because of the psychological complexity of learning this life-threatening diagnosis during the process of creating new life, that it is important to return to the purpose of HIV testing during pregnancy. With nearly all other conditions which can be detected during pregnancy (or pre-conception) the implication is for the health of the infant; HIV is special because it also confers a life-threatening diagnosis on the woman. Despite these differences, the test is being offered to enable women to choose interventions which are risk-reducing for the baby. This means that it is a matter of competing rights, often polarized between the positions of the feminist (rights of the woman) and the paediatrician (rights of the child). An American journalist combatively queried a bio-ethicist who took a feminist line, 'Is [the mother's] freedom that important that you might allow 15,000 babies' lives to be poured down the drain?'[52] This is the ethical crux of the matter.

For so long as the woman is pregnant, and perhaps whilst giving birth, arguments about the rights of the mother not to know her HIV status, and of the child not to be infected with HIV, parallel abortion arguments. Either one holds that a foetus is entirely dependent upon its mother, so that her rights take priority, or one takes the position of the 'pro-life' bumper sticker that says 'Unborn children are people too' – the child's rights are equally balanced with the mother's. Another component (deriving from abortion arguments) is the perspective of disability activists: how essential is it for a child to be born 'healthy'? Why should extraordinary measures be taken to prevent diseased babies from being born?

From a classic feminist position, the rights of a woman not to know her HIV status overwhelm the rights of a foetus to receive *pre-partum* AZT. It is less clear whether the woman's rights over-whelm the rights of the neonate to receive AZT *intra-partum*, or to be born by the least infectious route, but it is arguable that the balance just tips in favour of the woman (since a foetus in the process of being born is not yet as fully human as the person giving birth). However, the conflict arises once the baby is born: does one human's right not to know her HIV status overwhelm another human's right not to receive HIV-infected fluid on a regular basis? It is ironic that doctors have seized the AZT results as a basis for increased HIV screening, when it is really the breast-feeding data which are of more significance. Once a baby has been born s/he is a human being with equal rights to the woman that gave birth. There is no way of establishing before the first feed whether the child will be further endangered by receiving breast milk, with the exception of knowing whether the producer of that milk is HIV-infected. One solution to this dilemma of competing rights would be to mandate HIV testing for all pregnant women intending to breast-feed. Those who would not wish to take the test would be encouraged (?required) to bottle-feed.[53]

One of the many challenges involved in reducing HIV transmission from a woman to her child is that, whereas in sex it takes two to tango, this is not a matter of consent: a child cannot weigh up the options and decide it prefers to be born, or to be breast-fed. Moreover, preventing transmission also demands abandoning a healthy activity. Encouraging all people to use condoms for penetrative sex means that many uninfected people will be adopting unnecessary measures, but barrier methods are a healthy measure for penetrative sex, so there is no loss. A blanket campaign that encouraged *all* mothers not to breast-feed, on the other hand, would mean large numbers of uninfected people giving up a healthy practice. The other measures – elective C-sections and antiviral therapies – are invasive and costly, and unlikely to be offered to a woman who suspects she has been at high risk, but (for whatever reason) does not want to know her HIV status. At root, HIV testing is a diagnostic tool, and not a prevention mechanism. Yet in the context of maternity (and blood donation) this distinction blurs. There is a prevention rationale which is to identify HIV-infected women before they breast-feed.

In the more usual context of seeking to reduce the sexual transmission of HIV, identifying HIV-infected people is a poor strategy, since no correlation has been shown between the knowledge of HIV status and safer behaviour. The motivations for practising safer sex and avoiding HIV are far more complex – although this is rarely reflected in medicalized discourse about the disease.

Reducing the risks

Returning to the concept of 'co-operation and inclusion', one health promotion model which has received extensive attention in developing HIV-prevention activities, and is the basis of many programmes on AIDS, is the Health Belief Model. This proposes two broad types of influence on behaviour: factors which impact an individual's willingness to change (such as the knowledge, attitudes and beliefs they have about a health threat), and interactional factors which encourage or hinder change (such as peer support).[54]

Davies, using smoking as an example, explains that this model notes that some people 'go with the herd' and 'The decision not to smoke will be more difficult to put into practice if you are a herd follower and the herd is smoking.' The other main theory applied to HIV prevention is that of Risk Assessment. Davies shows how this model envisages health promotion as enabling an individual 'to make an assessment of two things: the seriousness of the outcome – in this case, HIV infection – and the probability of infection'.[55] Risk assessment requires energy to be focused on overcoming any 'denial' that HIV is a risk, and stressing to people their vulnerability to infection. A benefit of risk assessment is that it is highly individualized – each person decides how important a risk is for her. It is also founded on the idea of risk as a relative concept. This obvious, but important, point leads naturally to the importance of encouraging risk reduction rather than risk elimination. That is, enabling people to adopt strategies that locate HIV in the same realms as other potential life-threatening circumstances. A risk reduction strategy would be to use condoms and lubricant with an HIV-positive man; a risk elimination strategy would be never to have sex with an HIV-infected person (assuming it was possible to know this). These distinctions become especially important when considering HIV-prevention initiatives which dwell on 'theoretical' risks. What is described as a theoretical risk for HIV is usually far lower than the risk of crossing a road, passive smoking, etc.

Although there are some useful elements arising in both the health belief and risk assessment theories, overall they have been highly criticized. Davies, for example, states that they are 'fundamentally misguided, based on two fallacious assumptions which render them at best partial, at worst simply misleading.'[56] He terms these assumptions 'individualist' and 'romantic' fallacies, since they are based on notions of individual choice, and a romantic vision of the struggle between health-based reasoning and 'natural' sexual desire. These rationalist models base the possibilities for behaviour modification on the assumption that people will always consider the benefit of avoiding HIV to be far greater than the cost of safer sex. The other fundamental problem with both models is that they give primacy to the agency and self-efficacy of the individual, and such highly individualistic models are increasingly shown to be poor predictors of health behaviour.[57] Such models assume that people will always make the 'right', healthy choice, but the bio-medical conceptualization of the 'rational' is inevitably flawed within the context of the complex arena of sex. Nathalie, a French HIV-positive colleague of mine, initially tested negative when her lover was diagnosed HIV-positive. She complains that her friends failed to support her subsequent behaviour: 'I was in love with him,' she says, 'and I decided that we would go on without using protection. If he was going to die, I wanted to be with him.'[58]

Ingham proposes a shift away from the rational models 'to think in terms of a range of 'rationalities', depending on the identities and social worlds of the individuals concerned'.[59] Such an approach begins to move the debate towards the more complex social constructions within which women experience vulnerability to HIV. In 1986 WHO established the Ottawa Charter for Health Promotion, and this has become the cornerstone of health-promotion thinking. It defines health promotion as 'the process of enabling people to increase control over their health', and identifies five key elements to ensure this: building healthy public policy, creating supportive environments, strengthening community action, developing personal skills, and reorienting services.[60]

Lay understandings of health promotion have often equated it with the provision of information, but the Ottawa Charter shows that it is a far more sophisticated business. Several factors already need to be in place for people to respond to information which advises behavioural modification in order to avoid ill health. In order to respond to information about HIV, a woman needs the personal skills to, say, relate the information to her own drug use and acknowledge her need for clean injecting equipment. However, having these personal skills will be irrelevant if the public policy is to confiscate needles and syringes from drug users, if health services refuse to see her, if her friendship circle condemns the use of clean equipment and the general environment is one of acute stigmatization and rejection of people who inject drugs. Such a scenario is by no means theoretical, but broadly in line with the situation in Edinburgh in the early 1980s which led to massive rates of HIV infection.[61]

Understanding the political and legal contexts within which risk taking occurs should illustrate why it is wrong to claim that 'addicts are mad' if they continue to share equipment: a personal desire to use clean works may be frustrated by practical and social circumstances (such as being in prison). Van den Boom notes that 'One important element of this analysis (from an individual to a societal context) is that it shifts 'blame' for HIV acquisition and transmission away from the individual, onto the underlying structures which limit or prohibit choice and decision making.'[62] In moving from a highly individualized paradigm of risk behaviour, it is possible to begin to analyse and address the factors which create high-risk situations: from the politics which limit access to resources, to the individual's alienation from skills to make choices. Mann insists that central to the factors which create high-risk situations is a disregard for fundamental human rights. His analysis of current strategies to confront the AIDS crisis demands that health promotion be adopted in its widest possible sense, and that central to this are anti-discrimination measures and the protection of human rights. Since HIV is located in places of marginalization, it is only by rectifying inequities and promoting human rights that individuals and communities can develop the skills, strength, opportunities and resources to avoid infection.[63]

The recognition that motivations for behaviour are complex and multi-factorial leads on to an appreciation of the many levels which need to be addressed in order to effect behaviour modification and risk reduction to avoid HIV. One useful model has been described by Stiffman, which identifies five spheres of impact which require attention.

> Determinants of behavior are to be found in several domains:
>
> > the intrapersonal: self esteem, mastery, goals, AIDS knowledge, mental health;
> > the interpersonal: social support, peer behavior, social activities;
> > the familial: structure, socio-economic status, instability, child rearing, stress;

the communal: HIV/AIDS rate, unemployment rate, neighborhood deterioration; and

the cultural, political and economic domain: cultural and societal norms and beliefs, religious beliefs, sexual norms, power and gender relationships.[64]

Inevitably, the significance of a given domain differs for every woman, and may vary over time. At the programme level, HIV-prevention initiatives need to impact as many of the domains as possible. The relevance of the different domains is best illustrated by considering the relatively low prevalence of HIV among drug-using women in the UK. This is clearly linked to HIV-prevention initiatives acting beyond the intrapersonal domain, in particular the timely provision of extensive outlets for clean injecting equipment, combined with low threshold entry to a range of drugs services (including methadone programmes), and a political agreement that the harms associated with AIDS are greater than the harms associated with drugs. However, these factors alone did not curb the drug-related epidemic. Without simultaneous activity at the intrapersonal and interpersonal levels, why would people avail themselves of these practical resources?

A key (and insufficiently addressed) feature of the interpersonal level is that HIV risk and decision-making exist in the context of the interaction between two or more people. This is vital for anyone, and becomes critical in the context of women having sex with men, since gender power relationships feature strongly. Van den Boom highlights that 'AIDS does not happen in a vacuum, but in a given context. Individual behaviour is not the result of individual predispositions alone, but depends as well on interactions with others, social settings and circumstances, and power relationships.'[65] Women are often the focus of HIV-prevention efforts, but their problems often lie with the men they are having sex with – who tend not to be the focus of prevention efforts. Significantly, Magic Johnson's announcement that he is HIV-positive had a far greater impact on the behaviour and HIV-testing rates of black and Hispanic women than on black and Hispanic men.[66]

There are multiple contextual determinants of behaviour: some lie in what is perceived as culturally appropriate or culturally normal; some lie in what is perceived as morally and politically righteous. The context can be visualized as a set of concentric circles, the centre being the individual, the inner 'intrapersonal' realm of the self. The closest circle is then the interpersonal domain, the most distant one the cultural, socio-economic and political domain. Going from the centre to the periphery, the level of analysis is increasingly abstract, and the possibilities for effecting change decrease. Although the furthest domain may be the most difficult to influence, it is also the most impactful. For example, at a given time the availability of free condoms for a young man, and the cultural acceptance of his bisexuality, may be more significant to his decision to practise safer sex than, say, his drug use or ego integration.

Sadly, most research is purely behaviourist, addressing the intrapersonal domain rather than the others – an approach which tends toward the pathologizing of risk-taking behaviour. Despite these dangers, it is worth dwelling on some of the 'intrapersonal' components of behaviour, and the methods for addressing these. The papers presented at just one International AIDS Conference present an impressive catalogue of reasons given for not making behavioural changes, despite having correct knowledge. These included:

> forgetting, being unable and unwilling to postpone gratification; ridiculing and denying the risk; using drugs, such as benzodiazepines; daily alcohol and/or crack use; personality traits and mental health, such as denial, hostility, suicidal thoughts and behaviours; more general mental health characteristics such as ego integration and impulsivity, self esteem, level of mastery and self efficacy.[67]

People only act upon information when it seems worthwhile – for example, if they have a sense of self-preservation (absent in, say, someone with suicidal behaviour) and they are conscious of the need to act (less likely if, say, they are stoned).

Reducing HIV risks is of course more complex than a desire not to become infected, even at the intrapersonal level. One component that is essential for behaviour modification is the nature of the message, and it is increasingly evident that conflicting or over-stringent messages should be avoided. A study of women in Botswana found that correct knowledge about HIV was neutralized by incorrect knowledge. The women correctly identified the ways in which HIV is transmitted, but also believed that HIV could be transmitted through casual contact. They perceived that HIV was so readily transmitted that safer sex was not worthwhile.[68]

Similarly, De Vroome has demonstrated a 'learned helplessness hypothesis' among gay men who had sex with an HIV-positive man and who estimated that the risk of HIV transmission via fellatio was high. Their study of 330 men found that those who 'over-estimated the risk of orogenital sex *increased* high-risk [anal] behavior'. Seventy-five per cent of the men who thought HIV was easily transmitted by fellatio had unprotected anal sex, and this seemed to be due to a belief that they had already been exposed to HIV through fellatio and consequently exposure via anal sex was irrelevant.[69] The tragedy here is that hardly any (probably none) would have acquired HIV from fellatio, but they were now likely to be infected from their unsafe anal sex.

Another feature which is important to the nature of the message is the timescale it addresses. The HIV-prevention message which focuses on the potential fatality of sex invites us to consider an outcome which may be some ten, fifteen or more years away. Yet few people think long-term when they are having sex (unless they are aiming to conceive). Sex is generally about the present, the pleasure of the moment. The folly of stressing a 'sex = death' equation can easily be demonstrated by looking at other health messages. For example, which is the most effective message against drinking ten vodkas: 'You might develop cirrhosis and die', 'You'll have a terrible hangover in the morning', 'You'll make a fool of yourself and your friends will think you're stupid'? Or with smoking: 'You might develop lung cancer', 'You'll be out of breath in your exercise class', 'I won't kiss you – you'll taste like an ashtray'?

The appeals to long-term consequences are the most powerful, but also the least persuasive. There is no guarantee of the outcome, although there may be a high probability. The consequence is so far removed from the moment of pleasure that it doesn't bear serious attention, and it fails to challenge a sense of inviolability. Appeals to long-term consequences are often countered with a 'Just this once' argument – acceptance that the health consequences may be severe, but bargaining that the odds are favourable. This explains young women's focus on contraceptive measures, rather than prophylactics to avoid STDs. The undesired consequences of unprotected sex will become evident within weeks, or at most nine months, if she conceives, whereas few STDs will change her life that quickly.

Short-term messages address the present and the motivation for action. The (potentially) health harming behaviour is in the moment, and effective interventions respond by addressing concerns of that moment. They are also more effective when they address pleasure and peer norms. In the context of HIV, this might involve messages stating that your friends will laugh at you if you don't use a condom, or that condom use frees you from worries, to experience the joys of sex.

Such messages may be developed within the context of peer education or other community development approaches, which emphasize the involvement of communities in designing as well as disseminating appropriate messages. This goes beyond mere consultation, to the more radical imperative to strengthen communities and build supportive environments (as highlighted by the Ottawa Charter). Notably, these strategies do not rely solely on the individual's capacity to choose and make changes. Societal structures and community norms can facilitate or impede the maturing of individuals' concepts of self, identity, and agency. Yet individuals' sense of identity, self esteem, self efficacy are still powerful determinants of behaviour. Good health promotion will address the positive reasons and motivation for behaviour, rather than fixating on unpleasant outcomes and consequences. It will emphasize the values of (sexually) healthy behaviour, with messages that are positive, pertinent to the receiver and affirm health-enhancing behaviour. Messages which strengthen a sense of community or acceptance by peers are more successful than abstract intellectual arguments. Messages which reflect values which the receiver already holds, rather than suggesting alternative values, have greater success, as does promoting behaviour which is relatively easy to adopt. It is well documented that the use of doom-laden imperatives fails with all other diseases connected to lifestyle (e.g. lung cancer and smoking), and is a deeply flawed approach to encourage people to adopt and, most importantly, *sustain* sexual health strategies which many find economically, psychologically or socially problematic.

Reducing women's risks

In order to address the concerns HIV raises for women, it would be helpful to construct a framework which incorporates women's sexual danger and sexual pleasure, developing approaches to overcome the constraints some women experience without descending into a generalized victimology. Beeker *et al.*, in a literature review, propose a model of empowerment which has three strands:

> identifying situations where the 'actors are not socially equivalent',
>
> specifying the underlying factors determining the power imbalance,
>
> defining 'interventions which promote or maintain power equity at the individual level, household or couple level, and community level'.

'Empowerment approaches are uniquely distinguished from other approaches by their focus on the *contexts* of decision-making and action', they state, and they emphasize the distinction from rational models, such as the Health Belief Model.[70]

An understanding of empowerment depends upon first understanding what is meant by power, and particularly its relationship to the sexual arena of women and men. At root, empowerment calls for a reorienting of power towards the powerless – as such, it has a tendency to make men nervous. Individual power incorporates access to practical resources (including information, time, money, services and support), and also psychological and personal resources. This includes self-efficacy and self-esteem, as well as what Friere defines as 'critical consciousness', that is a recognition of the link between personal problems and social structural problems.[71] Individual power is also linked to social recognition of authority. A woman's sense of her own power is fairly meaningless unless it can be translated into her interactions with others, and her ability to influence or even control others, for example her sexual partner(s). Such control also incorporates her power to resist the control of others, to exert her autonomy, and be free from abuse or threat. Beyond the interpersonal domain, power exists at the collective level (the familial, communal, cultural, political and economic domains). This is the fundamental focus of much feminist energy, ensuring that women have the power to access and participate in the collective level of decision-making and control. Within the context of AIDS this dimension is as important as the more direct levels of individual and inter-personal power, since it is evident that the absence of women's full participation in the planning and implementing of strategies to control the epidemic have led to a very male model which does not incorporate the real needs of the 'second sex'.

Identifying the dimensions of power already hints at the many situations within which some women lack power. It is impor-tant to stress that power and powerlessness are not universals. Power is lived out in different ways – direct or indirect, formal or informal, alone or in interaction with others – and moreover the power to con-trol sexual encounters may not be a once-for-all state of being. Research by the Women Risk and AIDS Project (WRAP) found that 'Women may be empowered in some situations or with some partners, but not in others or with different partners'.[72] In the light of these provisos, Beeker *et al.* identify three components to models for empowering women: person-centred, environmental, and trans-actional approaches (the last describing the interaction between a person and her environment). Person-centred approaches are those which work directly with a woman to enable her to develop skills. These skills may be directly related to HIV (such as condom negotia-tion strategies), to sexuality (encouraging women to prioritize their pleasure), or more fundamental approaches to enable her to have self-confidence and a sense of personal worth. There are several inter-ventions which can support women in developing these skills, including one-to-one counselling, work with couples, small group sessions, support groups, self-help groups and social networks.

Moving from the personal to the environmental, empower-ment encourages women to develop their own skills in social action and community participation, to create change in health- and non-health-related environments, such as schools, churches and the workplace. It can also be mediated by classic processes of community development, encouraging the development of community groups and social networks. This is often perceived as a somewhat passive, low-level, activity, but this is a radical reorienting of power 'allow[ing] health through the transferring of authority, resources, tools, and income [to the powerless]'.[73] Whereas gay men's work may describe community mobilization in terms of men passing on safer-sex skills in the most direct way possible (i.e. having sex with each other, otherwise known as 'each one, teach one' or 'shag one, nag one'); for women, community mobilization may involve passing on more fundamental skills through building a healthier community together (and some will also do direct education). It is not just a case of learning by example, but rather the development of personal and communal power which leads to safer sex. 'When people develop action plans for their own communities, they simultaneously develop a belief that they can make a difference in their own lives and in the lives of those around them', suggests one health promoter.[74]

This approach to empowerment is not only about the action individuals take within the environment, but also the ways in which the environment acts upon individuals. Those who create environmental norms, in particular the media and popular culture, have a key role to play in creating climates within which women's sexual pleasure and assertiveness are normalized, and strategies for safer sex are popularized and affirmed.

Ultimately it is the interaction between the personal and the environmental – the transactional approaches – that bring together the levels of empowerment within a woman's life. One example of this would be the interaction between a woman's personal skills and confidence in using the female condom, and the environmental empowerment which forges her self-esteem and sense of control over her life. Female condoms are used principally by women who are at ease with touching their own genitals. Since they are cumbersome, slippery objects they may take some getting used to for a woman to feel sufficiently able to integrate them in her sex life: these are the personal components of her empowerment. The woman's desire to use this technology, her commitment to safer sex and protecting her health, and the power she has to negotiate her wishes in the sexual context, are mediated at a more environmental level of empowerment. The interaction between these environmental and personal levels is by no means an HIV-specific approach. The International Cairo Conference on Population and Development, held in Cairo in 1994, declared that 'the empowerment and autonomy of women' are 'essential for the achievement of sustainable development'.[75] The finding that 20 per cent of British women born after 1965 will not have children is proof, according to Sara Maitland, that feminism can indeed triumph over excess population growth. 'Feminism has caused this,' claims Maitland, 'by insisting there were choices, and that women could not be defined any longer solely by their reproductive competence.'[76]

The Cairo conference focused attention on the, so-called, developing world, which created a tendency to assume that inequities have dissolved elsewhere. While the horrors of gender imbalance are often starkest outside the industrialized world (for example, in Uganda, where divorce is a male prerogative and wives have no legal recourse if they are beaten for refusing sex,[77] and the Sudan, where genital mutilation is commonplace[78]) the UK still has its fair share of inequity, despite the rhetoric of 'post-feminism'.

Although feminism has always stressed global solidarity among women, I am concerned here with the elements of women's powerlessness in British society currently, and how this lack of power has a direct link to HIV. Empowerment of women has already made some strides forward, as Maitland highlights, but this is no time for complacency with the gains of freedom over fertility – there is still a long way to go. Empowering women means enabling women to have the power to be free from sexual terror and resist sexual danger where it arises; it also means enabling women to explore and enjoy the full range of their sexual pleasure.

At a structural level, women's empowerment will be secured by measures which respond to and reflect the diversity of women's sexual realities, and from this enable women to develop individual and collective strategies to control their vulnerabilities to HIV. A key reason for overcoming sexual violence must be to enable women to embrace their own sexual pleasure and gratification. The truth of sexual desires, needs, pleasures and powers have been silenced because such energies were thought 'unladylike'. In the feminist era, they have become submerged and lost beneath the horrors of sexual pain. Individually, and as communities, the transition from sexual victim to sexual victor, from survivor of sexual terror to a self-respecting sexually powerful woman is not immediate or linear, and such transitions may not be possible or desirable for some women. Yet the challenge for feminism now is to insist, and ensure, that women have choices to secure the most complete sexual health they desire.

Notes

1. Although Nancy Regan used this phrase to campaign against drugs, it relates as easily to facile and repressive attitudes towards sex, promulgated principally by the 'moral' Far Right.
2. A. Forbes, 'When women can't use condoms: woman-controlled HIV prevention options', Abstract WP 407, 'HIV Infection in Women: Setting a New Agenda' conference, Washington, DC, 1995.
3. Anke Ehrhardt, 'Sex education for young people', IX International Conference on AIDS, Berlin, 6–11 June 1993, PS-02-1.
4. Erica Gollub, 'Women-controlled prevention methods: sexual transmission', Session TB2, 'HIV Infection in Women: Setting a New Agenda' conference.
5. See K. Alcorn (ed.), *AIDS Reference Manual*, NAM Publications, London, January 1995, p. 121.
6. Personal communications, Mike Bailey and Patrick Frierl.
7. This argument was used to me by representatives of the London Rubber Company in 1988. I have no evidence to suggest that their attitude has shifted.
8. A. Ehrhardt, 'Gender specific risk and strategy for behavior change among women', Abstract TB1-91, 'HIV Infection in Women: Setting a New Agenda' conference.
9. Cited by D. Shirvington, 'Women-controlled prevention methods: sexual transmission', Session TB2, 'HIV Infection in Women: Setting a New Agenda' conference.
10. Information provided by Chartex (manufacturers of the Femidom) and Durex, cited in Alcorn, *op cit.*, pp. 24–7.

11. See Alcorn, *op. cit.*, p. 126. The attempt to insert the female condom in the anus in the same way as is recommended for the vagina (i.e. like a diaphragm) strikes me as a wholly unnecessary piece of gymnastics.

12. R. Gorna, 'The female condom leads the way to new ideas', *World AIDS News: The Newspaper of the Harvard-Amsterdam Conference*, 24 July 1992, p. 5.

13. Ehrhardt, *op. cit.*

14. Positively Women, *Prevention*, London (undated).

15. For example, L. Sussman, *The Ultimate Sex Guide: A Bedside Book for Lovers*, pp. 64–7, free with *More!* magazine.

16. Personal recollections of discussions at the Board of Directors. The decision was that condoms should be distributed, but early literature clearly reflects this ambivalence, with a strong emphasis on non-penetrative sexual activities. E. King discusses this in *Safety in Numbers*, Cassell, London, 1993, pp. 89–93.

17. The battle for women-controlled prevention mechanisms, in particular microbicides, has been tirelessly spearheaded by Anke Ehrhardt and Zena Stein of the HIV Center for Clinical and Behavioral Studies, New York State Psychiatric Institute and Columbia University. Most of this section is based upon presentations made by them, as well as presentations made at the 1995 conference 'HIV Infection in Women: Setting A New Agenda', and some of my articles, including: 'The female condom . . . ', *op. cit.*; 'HIV in women', *Journal of the International Association of Physicians in AIDS Care*, Vol. 1, No. 11, November 1994, pp. 36–7; contribution to Alcorn, *op. cit.*, pp. 24–7; 'Women's treatment update', *AIDS Treatment Update*, Issue 29, May 1995.

18. The most important paper addressing these concerns is C. J. Elias and L. L. Heise, 'Challenges for the development of female-controlled vaginal microbicides', *AIDS*, 1994, 8, pp. 1–9.

19. J. Kreiss *et al.*, 'Efficacy of nonoxynol-9 contraceptive sponge use in preventing heterosexual acquisition of HIV in Nairobi prostitutes', *JAMA*, 1992, 268, pp. 477–82.

20. Elias and Heise, *op. cit.*, pp. 4–6.

21. S. Niruthisard *et al.*, 'The effects of frequent nonoxynol-9 use on the vaginal and cervical mucosa', *Sex. Trans. Dis.*, 1991, 18, pp. 176–9; R. E. Roddy *et al.*, 'Dosing study of nonoxynol-9 and genital irritation', Abstract PoB 3783, VIII International Conference on AIDS, Amsterdam, 1992; cited in Forbes, *op. cit.*

22. Forbes, *op. cit.*

23. P. Feldblum, 'Efficacy of spermicide use and condom use by HIV-discordant couples in Zambia', Abstract WeC 1085, VIII International Conference on AIDS, Amsterdam, 1992.

24. L. Zeking *et al.*, 'Barrier contraceptive use and HIV infection among high-risk women in Cameroon', *AIDS*, 1993, 7, pp. 725–31.

25. W. Cates and K. Stone, 'Family planning: the responsibility to prevent both pregnancy and reproductive tract infections', in A. Germain *et al.*, *Reproductive Tract Infections: Global Impact and Priorities for Women's Reproductive Health*, New York, Plenum Press, 1992, pp. 93–129.
26. F. Stewart, closing speech to 'HIV Infection in Women: Setting a New Agenda' conference.
27. Z. Stein, plenary address, 'Women Helping Themselves', X International Conference on AIDS, Yokahama, 7–12 August 1994.
28. M. G. Bergeron *et al.*, 'Incorporation of microbicides into a gel formulation to prevent the sexual transmission of HIV in women', Abstract FA1-166, 'HIV Infection in Women: Setting a New Agenda' conference.
29. R. Pierce, 'Women-controlled prevention methods: sexual transmission', Session TB2, 'HIV Infection in Women: Setting a New Agenda' conference.
30. S. Lard, 'Pre-clinical developments of drug products to block sexual transmission', Session TF1-110, 'HIV Infection in Women: Setting a New Agenda' conference.
31. Stewart, *op. cit.*
32. Based on Forbes, *op.cit.*, and Ehrhardt, 'Gender specific risk'.
33. Alcorn, *op. cit.*, p. 120.
34. 'Sex: How To Do It', in *Body Talk: Everything a Girl Needs to Know*, Durex, pp. 8–9.
35. See, for example, M. Berer with S. Ray, *Women and HIV/AIDS: An International Resource Book*, Pandora, London, 1993, pp. 134–5.
36. C. S. Vance, 'Pleasure and danger: toward a politics of sexuality', in C. S. Vance (ed.), *Pleasure and Danger: Exploring Female Sexuality*, Pandora, London, 1992, p. 21.
37. Ehrhardt, 'Gender specific risk'.
38. C. Patton, *Sex and Germs: The Politics of AIDS*, South End Press, Boston, 1985, p. 59.
39. H. Roscam Abbing, in H. Curtis (ed.), *Promoting Sexual Health: Proceedings of the Second International Workshop on Prevention of Sexual Transmission of HIV and Other Sexually Transmitted Diseases, Cambridge, 24–27 March 1991*, HEA, London, 1992 p. 36.
40. See, for example, Curtis, *op. cit.* In particular, papers by S. E. Ekeid; R. Erben, pp. 27–32; H. Roscam Abbing, pp. 33–7.
41. M. Merson, Plenary presentation, Tenth International Conference on AIDS, Yokahama, *op. cit.*
42. *U.S. Public Health Service Recommendations for HIV Counselling and Testing for Pregnant Women*, draft, 23 February 1995, p. 9.
43. *Ibid.*, p. 10.
44. *Ibid.*, pp. 5–6.

45. Personal communications with workers at GMHC, AmFAR, San Francisco AIDS Foundation.

46. Department of Health, *Guidelines for Offering Voluntary Named HIV Antibody Testing to Women Receiving Ante-natal Care*, June 1994, p. 6.

47. E. Rubery *et al.*, *Unlinked Anonymous HIV Prevalence Monitoring Programme in England and Wales*, Department of Health, London, January 1995.

48. D. Rey *et al.*, 'Differences in HIV testing, knowledge and attitudes in pregnant women who deliver and those who terminate: Prevagest 1992 – France', *AIDS Care*, Vol. 7, Supplement 1, 1995, pp. S39–46.

49. Department of Health, *op. cit.*

50. The calculation assumes that 50 per cent of HIV-infected women already know their status; 70 per cent of the pregnant women accept testing; 50 per cent of unknown HIV-infected women are detected; and normally 20 per cent of pregnancies would result in infected babies, and this rate can be halved. Dr Frank Johnstone, personal communication. I am particularly indebted to Dr Johnstone for his inspiring correspondence which has expanded (but not resolved) my thinking on these complicated issues.

51. L. Sherr *et al.*, 'Psychological trauma associated with AIDS and HIV infection in women', *Counselling Psychology Quarterly*, Vol. 6, No. 2, 1993, pp. 99–108, reports that some women who did not receive adequate counselling on diagnosis attempted suicide; cf. *Women Like Us.*

52. Quoted in N. Hentoff, 'AIDS breakthroughs and AIDS politics', *Washington Post*, 22 December 1994.

53. I am grateful to Holly Ladd for her insight into the connections between human rights and the antenatal testing debates.

54. M. H. Becker (ed.), 1974, *The Health Belief Model and Personal Health Behaviour*, Charles B. Slack, Thorofare, NJ. See L. C. Leviton, 'Theoretical foundations of AIDS prevention programs', in R. O. Valdisess (ed.), *Preventing AIDS: The Design of Effective Programs*, Rutgers University Press, London, 1989, pp. 51–2; P. Davies, 'Acts, sessions and individuals: a model for analysing sexual behaviour', in M. Boulton (ed.), *Challenge and Innovation. Methodological Advances in Social Research on HIV/AIDS*, Taylor & Francis, London, 1994; R. Ingham *et al.*, 'The limitations of rational decision-making models as applied to young people's sexual behaviour', in P. Aggleton *et al.* (eds), *AIDS: Rights, Risk and Reason*, Falmer Press, London, 1992, pp. 103–73.

I am indebted to Katie Deverell for providing this source material.

55. Davies, *op. cit.*, p. 58.

56. *Ibid.*, p. 59.

57. Cited in Ingham *et al.*, *op. cit.*, p. 164.

58. Nathalie Dagron, quoted in *Colors*, no. 7, 'What is AIDS?' p. 68. Dagron was active in ACT UP Paris, co-ordinated TRT-5, the French Treatment Advocacy group, and was a Director of the European AIDS Treatment Group. She died of AIDS-related illnesses on 30 September 1995.
59. Ingham *et al.*, *op. cit.*, p. 171.
60. World Health Organisation, *Ottawa Charter for Health Promotion*, WHO, Copenhagen/Geneva, 1986.
61. See, for example, Alcorn, *op. cit.*, pp. 42, 61.
62. F. van den Boom, 'Social Impact and Response, Track D', in R. Gorna (ed.), *Conference Summary Report: VII International Conference on AIDS/III World STD Congress, Amsterdam, The Netherlands*, Harvard AIDS Institute, 1992, p. 34.
    I draw frequently on Dr van den Boom's report, which I participated in researching and drafting (as well as editing for the full final report of the Conference). In places I have re-edited the grammar and American spelling, changing it slightly from the text found in the Summary report.
63. This has been the theme of a number of speeches made by Jonathan Mann, for example, at the Second International Conference on HIV in Children and Mothers, Edinburgh, 1993; Tenth International Conference on AIDS, Yokohama, 1994.
64. van den Boom, *op. cit.*, p. 33. Based on A. R. Stiffman *et al.*, 'Communal, familial, interpersonal, and intrapersonal determinants of HIV risk behaviors', VIII International Conference on AIDS, Amsterdam, July 1992, Abstract PoD5375.
65. van den Boom, *op. cit.*, p. 34.
66. *Ibid.*, p. 36, citing Mills and Rapkin (Abstracts MoC0060 and ThD1527).
67. *Ibid.*, p. 33. This draws on findings from at least nine research groups – these are referenced in Gorna, *op. cit.*
68. K. F. Norr *et al.*, 'Knowledge about AIDS among urban Botswana women: complexities hidden by surveys', VIII International Conference on AIDS, Amsterdam, 1992, Abstract PoD5848 – cited in van den Boom, *op. cit.*, p. 33.
69. E. De Vroome *et al.*, 'Overestimating the risk of a low-risk sexual technique increases or decreases behavioral risk, depending on mediating factors', and hand-out, 'Overestimating the risk of oro-genital risk may increase unsafe anogenital sex', VIII International Conference on AIDS, Amsterdam, 1992, Abstract PoD5125. King discusses these issues in his excellent review of oral sex messages, *op. cit.*, pp. 99–114.
70. C. Beeker *et al.*, 'Is empowerment theory a useful framework for HIV/AIDS interventions with women in the United States?', 'HIV Infection in Women: Setting a New Agenda' conference. This paper is

expected to be published imminently. It incorporates an extensive list of references which demonstrate many of the following points.

71. Freire, 1983, *Education for Critical Consciousness*, Continuum Press, New York; cited in Beeker *et al.*, *op. cit.*

72. J. Holland *et al.*, 'Pressure, resistance, empowerment: young women and the negotiation of safer sex', in Aggleton *et al.*, *op. cit.*, pp. 142–62. WRAP comprises British researchers Janet Holland, Caroline Ramazanoglu, Sue Scott, Sue Sharpe and Rachel Thomson, who work together collectively.

73. W. Auslander *et al.*, 'Community organization to reduce the risk of non-insulin-dependent diabetes among low-income African American women', *Ethnicity and Disease*, 2, 1992, pp. 176–84; cited by Beeker *et al.*, *op. cit.*

74. N. Wallerstein, 1991, 'Powerlessness, empowerment, and health: implications for health promotion programs', *American Journal of Health Promotion*, Vol 6(3), 1991, pp. 197–205; cited in Beeker *et al.*, *op. cit.*

75. Quoted in Hooper, 'The spiritual vs the secular', *Guardian*, 20 August 1994, p. 10.

76. S. Maitland, 'Feminism's triumph in population control', *Guardian*, 14 April 1995.

77. Jonathan Mann, speech to the Royal Society of Medicine, London, 29 March 1995.

78. See A. Walker and P. Parmar, *Warrior Masks*, Jonathan Cape, London, 1993.

Chapter ten

Dam Those Dykes

Whether or not we as lesbians can transmit HIV through sex is not the crux of whether or not we are or should be involved in AIDS work, activism, research, or safer-sex talks.

Sue O'Sullivan and Pratibha Parmar[1]

The category 'lesbian' and the category 'don't get semen in your anus or vagina' are not mutually exclusive.

Cindy Patton[2]

Women like Gorna are 'in denial'.

Sheryl Marsh of Sisters' Health Education (SHE)[3]

Lesbians and bisexual women have been an active part of the fight against AIDS in the UK since it began. Indeed, it is the mixed Lesbian and Gay Switchboard which is credited with taking the first steps to inform gay men about the new health crisis at the start of the 1980s. By the time the specialist agency The Terrence Higgins Trust had been established, lesbians were so involved that one of the two initial staff members recruited (in 1985) was a lesbian. The involvement of lesbians began as (principally) a political act, linked to a sense of connectedness women felt for queer communities besieged by state-sanctioned prejudice and potential coercion. Indeed, Pratibha Parmar notes that 'Lesbians and feminists have been at the forefront of AIDS activism because many of us have already experienced the ways the media and the State attempt to control women's bodies and minds.'[4] Those who were already engaged in fighting for women's rights perceived that this new health threat had the potential for similar levels of political fall-out and restriction.

Since those early days of lesbian solidarity with the gay catastrophe, of lesbians supporting and caring for gay men experiencing the horrors of AIDS, the mainstream perception of the epidemic has shifted, and the role and perspective of the lesbian community has changed with it. This can be described as a shift from care to prevention (although such a neat description is inevitably crude). The thrust of 'AIDS affects everyone' campaigns has been to highlight the risks of HIV outside 'high-risk groups', and in particular among those marginalized communities traditionally addressed by equal opportunities policies. Since the late 1980s, many queer women (especially those working in the [then] expanding AIDS industry) have redirected their attention to lesbian vulnerabilities to HIV. Sometimes this has been fuelled by the fact that some lesbian and bisexual women have been diagnosed with HIV. Naturally many of these women, especially those involved in AIDS work for many years, are concerned to use their energies to prevent lesbians from acquiring HIV.

Curiously, nearly all the work which has been undertaken under the banner 'lesbians and AIDS' focuses on the fears of HIV being transmitted during sex between women, rather than addressing how HIV-positive lesbians have become infected (i.e. sex with men and sharing works). I describe these health education messages as 'latex lesbianism' – they have also been described as 'laminated sex'[5] – since they promote an approach which advocates a range of latex barriers to prevent HIV from being transmitted in circumstances which are (to say the least) fairly unlikely. Interestingly, latex lesbianism has been one of the most successful campaigns, if efficacy is measured by the degree to which a health-education message has penetrated community norms. In some sectors of the lesbian community, protected sex is normative and has become an erotic shorthand. This would be a remarkable achievement if such measures were actually necessary.

What is worrying is that the emphasis on the 'theoretical' risks of sex between women conceals and ignores the very high HIV risks encountered by some lesbians and bisexual women.

Unprotected anal or vaginal sex with a man, and sharing works for drug use, carry risks of HIV which do not figure on the same scale as the potential HIV risks of any sexual activities between women. Yet, women and men who question the latex lesbianism line risk being denounced as 'lesbian killers', and viciously attacked for endangering lesbian lives. It is established that HIV prevention which overestimates small risks can encourage people to take high risks,[6] so that latex lesbianism itself may be more accurately characterized as endangering lives.

My concern here is not to review the totality of lesbian involvement in AIDS, but rather to focus in on this single area of conflict. From the start, lesbians have been in the frontline of AIDS work, and I do not intend for this rich history of care and activism to be reduced to such a minor concern. (Interestingly, the proportion of lesbians working in AIDS organizations has decreased since the early phases of activism. It may be that the generalization of the epidemic has lessened the sense of AIDS as an issue for lesbian and gay solidarity.) The conflict about latex and lesbian sex creates far more heat and vicious disagreement than any other discussion about women and AIDS. It is easy to get drawn into, and this book is no exception. One problem is that this debate happens in a vacuum: women do not consider the lesbian issues in a holistic framework of the epidemic. It is impossible to understand how and if HIV affects lesbians without understanding the overall impact of AIDS and how, in particular, the health crisis affects women as a sex.

Since I believe that AIDS work should be driven by current and projected epidemiology, I should not devote a whole chapter of this book to lesbians. Yet it would not be true to my experience of AIDS activism, in particular the increased attention paid to women and AIDS, to ignore these issues. The debate has been a terrible distraction from my own work and my personal experience of the crisis, yet it is a distraction founded in genuine concerns and good motives which deserve some attention. It tells a great deal about the ways in which women's experiences of the epidemic have been mediated by anxieties about sexual identities. Since AIDS is universally queer, it is hardly surprising that women who acknowledge themselves to be queer should find themselves entangled with notions of sexual identity and disease.

The conflict about latex lesbianism may also shed light on broader discussions about targeting HIV-prevention work. It is an interesting, and frankly depressing, phenomenon in the context of the total response to women and AIDS, since this is the most coherent approach to the prevention needs of a group of women. Lesbians invented their own communities and these are relatively developed, well organized, with established communication structures and access points – something which is rare for women. Lesbians also created their own sexual norms, so they may have the ability to communicate verbally about the detail of sexual activity, and the lesbian community is comprised of women who possess an above average level of empowerment (earned through fighting homophobia). In these communities some women have particular vulnerabilities to HIV, as well as specific needs concerning the epidemic. Consequently this grouping of women incorporates many of the pre-conditions which may enable them to make choices and secure sexual health and pleasure.

Yet lesbians also lack some of the pre-conditions for effective sexual health and HIV prevention, notably community norms rarely support sexual diversity and experimentation, and there has been a terrible lost opportunity. Instead of targeting real vulnerabilities, losses and needs, attention has been focused on exploring theoretical and low risk sexual activities – which no other group perceives as significant risks. Why is this? In what ways can more appropriate prevention initiatives be developed for these communities? And what can be learned for other communities?

Latex lesbianism

Early on in the epidemic, when 'risk groups' were the stuff of epidemiology, lesbians were identified as the 'lowest-risk group for HIV'. Sometimes the AIDSphobic, homophobic reactions encountered by gay men were directed at lesbians too – for example, in 1986 the Nottingham Lesbian Line mounted a campaign when the local Blood Transfusion Service refused to take blood from one of their members.[7] The response was obvious: activists countered the facile linking of lesbians and gay men, and pointed out that lesbians are low risk for HIV since sexual activities between women do not facilitate HIV transmission. Soon this low risk was even institutionalized in organizations such as 'Blood Sisters' – a Californian group of lesbian blood donors who gave blood to help their gay brothers overcome AZT-induced anaemia (the attempt to organize this in London in 1987 was short-lived). Blood Sisters expressed the natural solidarity that lesbians might be expected to feel for gay men living with the AIDS crisis.

Relatively fast on the heels of Blood Sisters came the activist rejection of the concept of risk groups. Risk groups were rejected in favour of 'risk activities' and reciting the rules of transmission. For lesbians there was some clarity in talking about risk activities. Most lesbians have engaged in risky behaviour since most lesbians have had sex with men before coming out, and a significant proportion will therefore have had condom-free vaginal or anal intercourse. Moreover, some may still have sex with men for pleasure, babies, money or practical reasons. One London sexual health clinic for lesbians records that 35 per cent of the lesbians it sees had sex with a man in the last six months.[8] While the clinic may be attracting a higher than average proportion of dykes who fuck men, this does emphasize that activity is not always consistent with identity. In addition to having sex with men, some lesbians may wish to become pregnant and use artificial insemination, which might involve a risk of exposure to HIV in semen. Lesbians may have received blood transfusions prior to HIV screening in 1985. Finally, lesbians may inject drugs and may share needles and works to do so. Talking about risk activities enabled everyone, including lesbians, to reflect on the fact that they may engage or have engaged in behaviour which carries a high risk of HIV transmission if the other person is HIV-infected.

Defining risk activities for HIV transmission was only part of the story. A key component of HIV work has involved explaining 'the rules' of HIV transmission, and so lesbians began to ask whether the rules might apply to any other activities, not just the universal risk activities (fucking, needle sharing and blood transfusions before 1985). The imprecision of 'the rules' began to hinder rather than help. Information for lesbians contains vague statements such as 'Any practice which involves exchanging vaginal fluids or menstrual blood could be a possible route for the transmission of the HIV virus, whether this is on sex toys, fingers or any other part of the body.'[9] Such alarming imprecision is also expressed in detailed advice, such as the 'Guidelines for Protecting Ourselves', from New York's ACT UP shown opposite.[10] This is a fairly standard summary of lesbian HIV rules, or latex lesbianism. Although it is relatively old (1988), the same messages are contained in a current glossy brochure, created in New York in 1993.[11] Although latex lesbianism has its roots firmly in the American epidemic, it also has branches in Australia[12] and Europe, including the UK. All promote differently diluted versions of the same extraordinarily (and unnecessarily) restrictive message.

The message is often horribly muddled, for example, in the document containing the above table, ACT UP ask, 'Can lesbians get AIDS?' and reply, 'Many lesbians also sleep with men or have done in the past, or sleep with people who use IV drugs, or bi-sexual men or women.' Of course this is true, but not terribly helpful. Is sex with bisexual women really supposed to involve the same HIV risk as sex with bisexual men? And if you are one of those lesbians who sleeps with men, where are you going to get the information about HIV risk reduction? Not in any detail here.[13] There is detail about 'always using a condom and nonoxynol-9 spermicide', but what for? Masturbation? Fellatio? If they mean penetrative anal or vaginal sex, is this *really* the same HIV risk as French kissing?

Latex lesbianism insists that the use of latex barriers is essen-tial for sex between women – in summary, 'if there's an exchange of body fluids, make sure there's rubber in the way.'[14] It says that latex gloves or 'finger cots' (single glove fingers of latex) should be used for fingering the cunt or arse, and latex gloves with lube for fisting the arse or cunt, sex toys should be covered with condoms or washed if shared, and dental dams should be used for oral sex and, usually, also rimming. Dental dams (also known as oral shields, or sometimes safety squares) are squares of latex used by dentists. Some educators suggest using cling film – often referred to in the USA as Saran Wrap – or cut-up condoms or latex gloves to provide a barrier. Some suggest that these 'safer sex accessories' are only necessary when the woman being licked/fingered/fisted is

GUIDELINES FOR PROTECTING OURSELVES

HIV (the virus thought to cause AIDS) is transmitted through blood, semen (cum) and vaginal secretions. Therefore, none of these fluids should enter you or your partner through the mouth, vagina (cunt), anus (ass), or cuts in your skin. There's no evidence that HIV is transmitted through saliva. For lesbians considering pregnancy, sperm must be checked for HIV. You can use these guidelines after you and your partner discuss your sexual histories.

DEFINITELY SAFE	MOST PROBABLY SAFE	UNSAFE
Body to body rubbing	French (wet) kissing	Unprotected oral sex, especially during your period
Social (dry) kissing	Protected oral sex (use a latex barrier, *a dental dam*, between vulva & tongue). No studies have been done on dental dams, but it's what we've got. Wash after each use with 10 parts water to 1 part bleach and rinse well.	Unprotected rimming (mouth/anus [asshole] contact)
Massage, hugging		
Voyeurism, exhibitionism, fantasy, costumes		Unprotected hand and vaginal/anal contact (if you have cuts on your fingers, like hangnails)
Masturbation		
Finger penetration wearing surgical (latex) gloves or finger cots (individual finger gloves)	Using nonoxynol-9 (a spermicide) may inhibit HIV. This jelly can be your lube.	Any activity which could draw blood (like vaginal/anal fisting without lube or glove)
Individual vibrators/sex toys (if you share, wash in 10 parts water to 1 part bleach, rinse well)	S/M without exchange of body fluids or drawing blood	Urine or feces (piss or shit) in mouth or vagina or on hands with cuts
Condoms on dildos with lube	For sex with a man, always using a condom and nonoxynol-9 spermicide	Sharing sex toys that have your partner's juice on them
Creative sex that doesn't exchange body fluids	Washing drug works with 10 parts water to 1 part bleach 3 times.	Sharing needles or any part of drug works or any skin piercing needles (even for ears or tatoos)
No sharing of drug works or needles		

Dental dams and gloves can be purchased at the Community Health Project, 208 W. 13th St. (in The Center). Call them for more health information about lesbians and AIDS at 212-620-7310.

It's our love for women that motivates us to protect ourselves and each other.

menstruating, others that this is necessary at all times. As for gloves and finger cots (or, rarely, waterproof plasters), these are recommended either at all times; if there are cuts, sores and abrasions including hangnails; or when there are severe breaks in the skin, such as eczema. These are measures to prevent HIV transmission where risks are theoretical, or at most low. Most of latex lesbianism clings to a notion that 'theoretical' or low risk is risky enough. For example, Cole and Cooper state, '*Theoretically*, lesbians can be at risk for HIV transmission from a variety of sexual activities with HIV-infected female partners because of the exchange of infected blood and vaginal secretions'[15] (my emphasis).

Low risk isn't no risk

The Terrence Higgins Trust never said, 'Low risk is no risk', nor implied such a thing, but you'd never guess that from the fury which greeted their 1992 Lesbians and HIV campaign. This is the only example I know of a campaign which challenges the growing orthodoxy of latex lesbianism. It is important to clarify that latex lesbianism is *not* safer sex, but rather *safe* sex, it is risk elimination. In the USA a 'risk elimination' model is more common than elsewhere; it suggests that any possibility of transmission should be blocked 100 per cent, rather than 'risk reduction' where possibilities are reduced to the acceptable levels adopted in everyday life (like crossing a busy road, or drinking too much at a party). The motives behind adopting a risk elimination model instead of risk reduction are mixed. One of the many reasons for its prevalence in the States seems to be the extent to which litigation is used concerning medical issues. For example, one physician working in Boston noted, 'As long as the evidence is inconclusive, I have to tell HIV-positive women that they need to use dental dams for cunnilingus – I can't risk their partner's becoming infected and suing me.'[16]

So what does it mean to take a theoretical risk, the backbone of latex lesbianism? This is not really a risk in the useful sense of the word. Rather, it is code for 'something that cannot be proven to have ever happened, or ever be likely to, but which it is logical to imagine given "the rules" of HIV transmission'. 'Theoretical risks' are rarely, if ever, mentioned in connection with other conditions: 'In no other illness is there such constant displacement of attention from the real routes of transmission onto freak modes of transmission or minimal risks.'[17]

I am allowing myself the luxury of dwelling on the story of this notorious THT campaign, since it exhibits several of the underlying reasons for latex lesbianism. In February 1992, the second European Conference on Homosexuality and HIV was held in Amsterdam. Lesbians, gay men and bisexuals working at, and associated with, the Terrence Higgins Trust attended with delegates from twenty-eight other European countries. The conference was depressing. It was depressing because the urgency and horror of the AIDS crisis for gay men and bisexual men was not recognized, nor were the increasing repressive measures against gay men, which hinder effective interventions, discussed. By contrast, HIV issues for European lesbians were discussed at length.

Two extracts from the official conference report demonstrate this astonishing, unbalanced approach. Part of the report on the policy track (written by a gay man and a lesbian) reads: 'Exploring the impact HIV has on lesbians and the threats it poses to lesbian communities is very urgent' and a 'suggestion' is: 'Make people from the lesbian and gay communities with key positions in HIV work (mostly gay men) bring up and work on HIV issues for lesbians (for example by developing information materials on medical and other transmission routes).'[18]

These comments occur within the section headed 'Lesbian needs, lesbian contributions'. Yet there is no section on 'Gay men's needs, gay men's contributions' and there are no parallel comments or 'suggestions'. The report, like the event, talks constantly about 'equality'. 'Gay men' are always balanced with 'lesbians'. It is as if lesbians and gay men are experiencing this epidemic in exactly the same way.[19] In frustration at this terrible muddle, one delegate concluded that the conference was 'hopelessly unable to acknowledge, let alone confront, the catastrophe that already surrounds us'.[20]

This meeting failed to confront the epidemic because it was treating AIDS as just another lesbian and gay rights issue, requiring a traditional equal opportunities response. The conference talked more about the relationship between lesbians and gay men than the AIDS crisis. My sharpest memory of the conference is the blossoming of European latex lesbianism, to the extent that British lesbian Diane Richardson gave a speech bemoaning the lack of focus on 'woman-to-woman transmission', contrasting this with 'all the resources' focused on gay men. This at a time when 70 per cent of the British population with HIV (gay men) were receiving less than 5 per cent of government funds for HIV education. A few women were disturbed by the direction things were taking, among them Frankie Lynch, then Health Education Manager at THT and Sue O'Sullivan.

Partly as a consequence of this conference, Gay Men Fighting AIDS was launched[21] and THT began to develop a campaign to counter misinformation for lesbians. The issue here is not whether this was technically a good campaign, but rather why factually correct information was damned as 'murderous'. THT staff conducted a thorough literature review of documented cases of lesbians with HIV, and HIV risks associated with sex between women. THT had first published an information leaflet on HIV for lesbians in October 1990. Overall it was in line with THT's literature for women, although there was more discussion of dental dams and theoretical risks in, for example, oral sex. Following the literature review the leaflet was revised to stress that risks are low in different sexual activities between women, while lesbians do risk HIV from sex with men, donor insemination and sharing injecting equipment.

THT relaunched the leaflet with adverts in the lesbian and gay press, and half-page advertisements appeared at the end of June. Under the heading 'Lesbians & HIV What are the risks?' there is a large photograph of five women of different races laughing and hugging each other. It is an affirming, positive image of community, friendship and support. To the right of the image there is the following text, half the size of the heading:

- <u>very</u> low risk in oral sex
- . . . so ditch those dental dams
- don't bother with gloves unless it turns you on
- if you share sex toys, use condoms.

In smaller text, about half the size of the bullet points, running below the photograph, it reads: 'However, lesbians have been infected with HIV through sharing "works", sex with men and donor insemination.' This is followed by information on where to obtain the leaflet as well as the helpline number.

The gay press was bombarded (to the extent the gay press is ever bombarded) with protests, and THT received noisy objections and letters of complaint, especially from lesbians involved in ACT UP chapters. There were objections that lesbians living with HIV would be isolated by the adverts, that they were portrayed as 'bad lesbians', that the adverts fed into lesbian denial of HIV risk, made assumptions about lesbians' sexual practices, that the adverts were unnecessary, counter-productive and dangerous. The phrase 'Low risk isn't no risk' was used frequently.[22] THT did not withdraw the advert (as many demanded), but continued with production of a poster with the same image and text.[23]

In July, THT took the poster and leaflets with the Roadshow (a mobile health-education display) to the VIII International Conference on AIDS, also held in Amsterdam. This was attended by over 10,000 scientists and activists from all over the world. The lesbian material was only a small part of the display, but soon became the central focus. Near the end of the conference, ACT UP zapped THT. They surrounded THT's stall blowing whistles, shouting 'Shame!' and defacing posters with slogans like 'This poster is killing lesbians'. There were violent verbal exchanges of the type usually reserved for pharmaceutical companies. Two stalls away from THT, another voluntary organization was displaying a poster which encourages gay men to suck without latex; no one commented on this, let alone zapped it. Nor did they confront any of the nearby stalls, such as those from cult organizations with appalling records of human-rights abuses against people with HIV, and governments which had entirely neglected the HIV-prevention needs of gay men and bisexual men.

Whereas the ACT UP approach to pharmaceutical companies relies on correcting their information, the counter-information here was poor. ACT UP's anti-THT 'fact' sheet was predictably headed 'Low Risk isn't No Risk' and is clearly written by Americans (or

Brits who can't spell). They claim that THT use the 'CDC definition of "lesbian" in order to justify that Lesbians are a low risk category'. This is strange since the poster says nothing about risk category, merely the risks of sexual activity. And why would a British agency even know about the definition of lesbian used by an American agency (the CDC), much less use it? It seems as if an American agenda is being foisted on an English group, with scant regard for cultural specificity. I later found out that some of the Americans who zapped THT did not even know that it was an ASO – they assumed it was a charitable giving trust.[24] The 'facts' about transmission presented by ACT UP were predictable: that there are significant amounts of HIV in vaginal fluids and menstrual blood, that 'contact with menstrual blood' should be avoided and gloves worn. They claim THT assumes 'that only one method of oral sex is practised by Lesbians, i.e., cunnilingus, and does not take into consideration anilingus which has always been considered a potential mode of HIV transmission'. This last accusation proved too much for a spontaneous group calling themselves 'ASS LICKERS OF AMSTERDAM'. They distributed a sheet headed 'ZAP ACT UP!' clarifying that rimming may lead to many infectious diseases, but *not* HIV, and ending: 'ACT UP . . . GET YOUR FACTS RIGHT!'

The evening of the zap, the Gay Men's Health Crisis (GMHC) Lesbian AIDS Project (LAP) called a meeting, and during the shouting at the THT stall they demanded that THT women attend. In the small room, crammed with over sixty women, we were systematically ignored. The meeting was fascinating, with an evangelical feel. There was repeated 'testimony' from HIV-positive lesbians, all from New York, all from LAP. Early on, one of the women started to shout, 'demanding' that lesbians with HIV in the room come out, protesting that their silence was killing her by reinforcing invisibility and isolation. She insisted that she 'knew' that there were lesbians present who were HIV-positive but keeping quiet. She was insistent, angry and aggressive. What was so telling about this meeting was the way in which the women polarized into 'right-thinking' lesbians (pro-latex) and 'wrong-thinking' (THT and closeted HIV-positive lesbians). The antagonism and lack of discussion was as sharp as in the porn wars and SM debates.

Lesbian culture has a strong tendency towards prescribing what behaviour is required for membership of this 'group'. Consequently, wars rise and fall (with a certain regularity) to decide whether 'real' lesbians can ever have sex with men, to define correct dress and appearance, to (dis)approve certain sexual acts, to determine cultural representations, to formulate political allegiances. Despite a heavy rhetoric extolling the diversity of lesbianism, the practice smacks of a drive to homogeneity and fusion. The policing of this small meeting in Amsterdam is reflected in the incessant policing of the discussion about lesbians and AIDS.

Why do lesbians give a dam for AIDS?

On one level these conflicts exist because of straightforward academic disagreements about the relative HIV risks of a range of sexual practices, and the best approaches for health promotion. Yet this is presented as a violent dispute between 'lesbian killers' and their saviours. What is going on here? One key factor behind the aggression is the fact that many of the alleged 'lesbian killers' (those who venture into the public affray and say latex lesbianism is not essential) are gay men, noted for their 'key positions in HIV work'. That they should be making such statements is not entirely surprising, but is it because they are insensitive to lesbian needs; or because they know a lot about HIV and AIDS, since they've been doing this work for a long time? The rejection and antipathy towards gay men who enter this debate is expressed in a curious fashion. Could it be that a major element of the vehemence of latex lesbianism is fighting insensitive gay men? I cannot imagine the rationale for a gay man who has suffered the horrors of the AIDS crisis to mislead dykes into unsafe behaviour, but many lesbians do not seem to trust gay men to give them accurate information about HIV. Yet the fundamental concern for these health promoters is how women get 'life-saving' or, even 'life-enhancing' health information. Why would it be so awful if women found out that 'life-saving' information for women is 'Enjoy having sex with women'? What would be so awful in finding out that women can get all sticky with each other's juices and not get sick?

The latex orthodoxy says women might indeed get sick if they get all sticky with an HIV-positive woman's juices. The (1992) orthodoxy means that 'lesbians are currently subjected to the most demanding and extremist "safer sex advice" given to any group. ... It is interesting that straight men, the other group in society who have sex with women, aren't subjected to this kind of scare-mongering. Is this the latest form of discrimination against lesbians?'[25] Perhaps feminists care so little about men's lives that they are happy to 'threaten their lives' and hold back the information on dental dams, latex gloves and finger cots which is considered so essential to dykes and bi women. I can't believe that lesbians have any such wicked motive.

So what are the motives? Although the debate on lesbians and AIDS has volleyed back and forth since 1986, there have been few attempts to account for it. Why should some groups of lesbians (and bisexual women) evaluate HIV risk differently from their heterosexual sisters? There appears to be a rational disjunction between the position of the majority of AIDS activists and latex lesbians. (Incidentally, although bisexual women have been used in this discussion in a particular way, few bisexual-identified women focus so obsessively on theoretical sexual risks between women – perhaps because they are so aware of the high risks in sex with men. Whatever the issues for bisexual women, latex lesbians are a dyke thing.)

Unfortunately, it is only gay men who seem to have hypothesized about the nature of the underlying concerns. The hypothesis is, basically, that the lesbians who overemphasize the possibilities of 'woman-to-woman transmission' are suffering from 'AIDS envy'[26]. This hateful phrase has enraged many women who would otherwise have a degree of sympathy for these men's understanding of the probability of transmission between women. The phrase seems to pathologize lesbians' legitimate concerns and frame their motivations for seeking to raise the issue as some longing to suffer more, a resentment of the attention paid to their sick and dying gay brothers. If this is the motive, it is sick indeed.

I do not believe that latex lesbians necessarily suffer from

AIDS envy – although I can understand why this has become a shorthand to describe the phenomenon. It must seem very strange to men who are battling with the virus in their own bodies, whose sex lives have been radically changed, for whom hard-won sexual freedom is destroyed, to understand why lesbians are focusing on risks which gay men have struggled to explain are not there. Some gay men and bisexual men have spent the last decade patiently explaining that HIV is not transmitted easily. They have explained this to each other, and struggled to make the worst excesses of tabloid journalism understand this. Why, they legitimately ask, are lesbians seeking to overturn this? Why don't lesbians and bisexual women rejoice and celebrate the sticky safety of sexual expression with other women?

Well, why not? Partly because celebrating sexuality is not something dykes do, at least, not until very recently. Lesbianism of the 1970s, unlike gayness for men, was not a very sexy business. While gay men developed a strong, outspoken sexual vocabulary and culture, lesbians were busy with sisterhood. Lesbians were building communities opposed to mainstream culture, were affirming their connections to other women, and rejecting the conditioning that a woman's role is to service men. These were the 'man-hating' days of vigorously opposing subservience and inequities based on gender. Rejecting patriarchy was far more urgent and important than developing a language about sexual desire. Women fell into known women's arms in cosy communes, while men fucked unknown men in dark places. Male homosexual liberation was back rooms and anonymous sex. Not only this, of course, but the distinction serves a purpose.

There have been great differences in the development of lesbian and gay consciousness and pride. Among other things this has led to complex and difficult relationships for gay men and lesbians working together, and this has had an important impact on AIDS and the lesbian response. This is also important for an understanding of the relationships lesbians have with sex and sexual desire, since this would seem to be one of the critical factors behind the development of latex lesbianism. This phenomenon has come about because of the intersection of several factors, and the first I want to consider is how dykes feel about sex.

• *What's a* sexy *lesbian?*

While the big development for gay men in the 1980s and 1990s is HIV positivity, for lesbians it is sex positivity. The last decade saw the birth of lesbian 'porn', of sex clubs, of lesbian sex-radicals and overall of a more erotically charged lesbian scene. The bitter SM wars of the 1970s, the charged debates on penetration, have calmed and been replaced by an approach which says that to be a dyke is to be a sexy, horny, erotic woman. This is no mere 'community' thing, with most British soap operas as well as mainstream magazines like *Time* and *Vanity Fair* pushing the line of the lusty lesbian or the designer dyke, and lesbian chic an established style in the USA (albeit not one which most political dykes were keen on).

Some commentators have suggested that the prohibitive attitudes surrounding gay male sexuality in the light of AIDS have formed this explosion of erotica. If the boys' sex is now bound in restrictions, rules and 'don't dos', lesbians can reclaim the sex in homosexuality. Women now prove that queer is sexy.

> Some observers wondered whether lesbians were picking up where gay men had left off. . . . Lesbians, critic Cindy Patton wrote, 'have adapted the hanky code of sexual options, and the randy attitudes that go with them, from gay male culture,' and may represent the reinforcements for a sexual liberation movement badly damaged by the right wing and AIDS. 'We got off on fighting back, while gay men got off on putting out,' she wrote. 'But sex is political and sex lib theory rings false without some good, sweaty praxis.'[27]

As safer sex for gay men is eroticized, especially by community organizations, there has been a greater openness about what gay men actually do. Cabinet Ministers talk about anal sex, and State Health Authorities list information on sucking, fisting, watersports, rimming, bondage and on and on. And so lesbians want a slice of the action – after all, the boys always get more attention. 'Heterosexual sex' is the societal, cultural norm, but that norm is being challenged by a more open discussion of sex between men. What on earth can *women* be getting up to? Telling about sex, talking about what women (want to) do is all part of the positive claiming of identity, sexuality. And if gay men can educate the government in their preferred wide range of sexual acts, why shouldn't lesbians do so too? The fact that no one is asking about lesbian sex lives, isn't that just re-enforcing lesbian invisibility? Especially lesbian *sexual* invisibility?

It is frequently the producers of lesbian porn who have been in the vanguard of latex lesbianism. The British magazine 'for dykes of all sexual persuasions', *Quim* (now defunct), carried articles on AIDS and safer sex from its second issue in summer 1991; since then every issue had photographs, fantasies and comments with gloves, dams and cling-film. The same thing happens with American lesbian porn. Pat Califa and Susie Bright frequently integrate talk about HIV, safer sex and latex in their writings. The July/August 1991 edition of *On Our Backs* screams above its masthead: 'Lesbians and AIDS: Are We Really a Low Risk Group?' No way, suggests the six-page article: 'The greatest risk behaviour for contracting HIV is denial.' This fairly balanced article includes talk of sex with men, shooting drugs and pregnancy, and discusses genital herpes risks in sex between women. Yet the magazine ends with a full-page, full-colour ad for an 'On Our Backs Love Kit'. Readers are exhorted to 'Love Sex. Be Safe. Use the Kit' – for $19.95 you can buy ten condoms, dams, finger cots, gloves and five lube kits in a soft black bag. A new industry is emerging, to push a lot of unnecessary latex at lesbians (no one is pushing this stuff at straight men) – all these gullible dykes are a marketing manager's dream. One organization sells 144 dental dams for £50, and is adamant that they must not be rinsed or reused. The most extraordinary attempt at profiteering I have encountered comes from an American firm which has developed something they call a 'latex facial dam'. It retails at $7 for three dams. Like a large rubber band, the device snaps over your head. The latex then fits under the chin, covering your mouth – with a pocket to stick your tongue in – up to the base of your nose, and stretches back to cover your ears (just in case there is a risk of getting cunt juice in to those aural cavities).

Also on the market are latex knickers, harnesses and variously flavoured dental dams.

Most lesbian porn now incorporates latex accessories in erotic photos and stories with far greater frequency than in gay male porn. How many penises in gay porn mags are dressed in condoms? Nearly every lesbian strap-on sports one. When did you last see a man's hand (or even clenched fist) swathed in a latex glove? They are frequently on display in lesbian mags, sheathing hands, hanging out of jeans pockets or causing an erotic sensation – 'I hear the snap of latex gloves and look back at Andy who's lubing up her hands.'[28] This is a common theme in lesbian porn these days: the sight or sound of latex is a big turn-on. Latex has acquired a symbolism in the lesbian sex media. It says, 'I'm a dyke about town', 'I fuck around', 'I have so much sex I have to use latex'. Lesbian sex radical Susie Bright reports, 'when I recently demonstrated rubber gloves in Denver, a couple of women in the audience flushed bright red as soon as I slipped one on my hand. They obviously have had the slick, smooth, delicious experience of being fucked by a gloved hand.'[29] A latex lesbian = a lusty lesbian. Latex screams sex.

It is so ironic. Health-promotion research demonstrates that an erotic HIV-prevention campaign will be a successful campaign; that prevention will succeed when safer behaviour is accepted as a norm. Yet the community which has succeeded in establishing a visible, erotic, safer-sex peer norm is the community with the least need – at least in respect of the activities to which these norms apply. (And it is not clear whether many lesbians put these ideas into practice.) It has even reached the extreme of a series of photos showing a woman masturbating herself wearing a latex glove.[30] Just imagine how it would be if men got turned on by the sight or sound of a condom being unwrapped; if for gay men the most potent symbol for sexual possibility was a condom and a little dab of lube. The real reason for latex lesbianism is not disease avoidance – indeed, it is not clear whether many lesbians actually put these ideas into practice. Rather, it is a handy code for lesbian sexual visibility. It is symbolism which says, 'What do lesbians do in bed? We have *real* sex.' At one ACT UP demo, a woman held a placard proclaiming, 'Dykes: We Fuck Therefore We Are'.

Claiming sexual agency becomes a fundamental proof of identity – and if lesbian sex has no disease implications, does that mean it is not real sex?

• *The 'yuck!' factor*

One reason for latex lesbianism may be sex-positive, but it is also sex-negative. Few women have grown up with a very positive appreciation of female sexual organs and fluids. At school, boys were pissing in front of each other, and report wanking competitions, but I know no women who were busy comparing labia size with their friends, who checked their cervices with mirrors and specula, who discussed how stickiness changed during their cycles. I know many a woman who worried that her period would start suddenly and stain her clothes, felt shame when the boys told jokes about the blind man walking past the fishmonger (and who still rages when gay men call women 'fish'). Boys are taught pride in their growing sexuality, girls are taught shame.

Dykes and bisexual women are often at the forefront of (re-)claiming pride in women's sexuality, enjoying the variety of women's body shapes and sexual bits, and relishing the taste and smell of women's sexual juices. Learning to love sexual fluids has been treated as part of what it means to be a feminist, suggests one of the matriarchs of feminism: '[Women] still recoil at the idea of intercourse during menstruation . . . If you think you are emancipated, you might consider the idea of tasting your menstrual blood – if it makes you sick, you've a long way to go, baby.'[31]

Just because they enjoy sex with other women does not mean queer women are perfect – they grew up with the same nonsense. How many lesbians and bisexual women are really comfortable with their lovers' vaginal juices, ejaculate, menstrual blood, shit and piss? This concern is clearly present in some latex lesbianism, for example, 'How do you decide, when you wake up with her *caked menstrual blood under your chewed cuticles* (from fucking in the dark so you didn't see she'd started her period), if you've put yourself or her at risk' (her emphasis).[32] What stays with you from this vivid piece of writing? Fear about risk, or the bloody description? In a very early debate about latex lesbianism, I remember a lesbian asking how on earth I could countenance putting an ungloved hand into a menstruating woman's cunt – 'It would be like putting your hand into a bucket of blood.' Lovely sex-positive image!

It is interesting that so much latex lesbianism focuses on menstruation. Yes, there is an elevated risk if a man fucks an HIV-infected woman during her period without a condom, but it is still far from an absolute risk. There are no data confirming HIV transmission from menstrual blood entering the mouth during oral sex – nor through chewed cuticles during fingering or fisting. What would be so awful in saying, 'Yes I want to go down on you, but I don't fancy the taste of blood' or 'I hate blood under my fingernails'? Why use the disease excuse?

Another feature of latex lesbianism is that it clings to the earliest fears about HIV in piss and shit. These are not efficient body fluids for HIV transmission – bacteria yes, but not HIV. Yet even recent advice for lesbians repeats the prohibition on 'unprotected' rimming, anal fisting, watersports and scat. Susie Bright talks about dental dams with great playfulness in her book *Susie Sexpert's Lesbian Sex World*, and her latex lesbianism is calming over time, yet even she falls foul to confusing health risk and taste:

> [I]magine this: with a latex dam stretched vertically from the anus to the vagina, you can happily take one long lick from bottom to top, without flinching. It feels great! You can't believe you're getting away with it! You can't believe this is called Safe Sex![33]

There is some risk of transferring bacteria if you go back to front with a finger, fist or dildo, but the best medical advice I can get says that the risk of such transfer by tongue is no more than a very low theoretical one.[34] There is almost a collective fantasy that lesbians should not be squeamish or touched by ideas of sexual hygiene. Exaggerating health risks may help with the immediate embarrassment, but it sets up dangerous concepts of contagion. 'Combat exaggerated notions about the infectiousness of HIV', proclaims one ACT UP slogan.

Frequently latex is more a matter of taste than health risk, as in this classic example of how latex can turn the sex-positive, sex-negative. Jo Ann Loulan, like Susie Bright, is a 'lesbian sex radical', although of a more homely, therapeutic bent. This is a description of one of her performances on the lesbian lecture circuit:

> Loulan coaxed a volunteer on stage for a twenty-minute demonstration of 'safer sex', which involved the placement of a dental dam on a fully clothed woman as Loulan pointed and announced, 'That's your pussy, this is your clitoris, and here is your asshole.'[35]

Wouldn't her pussy, clitoris and asshole have been in the same (clothed) place without the dental dam? Latex gives lesbians far more safety than the mere safety of prophylaxis against HIV. It is the safety of acceptability – there's no need to be afraid of sexual fluids, or even sexual organs, latex will protect! Beyond the sex positive statement that 'latex = real lesbian sex', it can go on to suggest, 'Our sex is so real it can even be life-threatening.' In some cases it can even become an excuse for being upfront, 'Don't tell us off for talking about sex. We don't really want to, but this is life saving information.'

• *What is a sexy* lesbian?

Latex defines a lesbian as both sex-positive (my appetite is so voracious latex is essential) and sex-negative (my taste buds require latex to keep your fluids at bay). Latex lesbianism also asks the question 'what is a real lesbian?' This question is by no means new:

> Every definition has placed some lesbians in the blessed inner circle and some outside it. Is a woman who identifies herself as a dyke but who's never slept with a woman a lesbian? Is a lesbian who sleeps with men really a lesbian? What about a woman who sleeps with women, but has had a primarily heterosexual past? If she becomes involved with

a man next year, was she ever a true lesbian? Lesbian theory has often worked its way through this minefield by making a distinction between 'real' and 'false' lesbians, explaining away those women whose experiences don't fit our definitions.[36]

Notice here that the major crisis is women who have sex with both sexes. 'Natural enough', you might say, 'a lesbian is a woman who has sex with *women*, not men.' Yet, there is little comparative discussion by gay men of *their* identity. The discourse surrounding male bisexual behaviour usually frames a married man who is having sex with other men as gay. This man is either 'in transition' to his true (gay) identity or simply a married gay man – he will remain married, but still be an acceptable sex partner for out gay men. The existence of gay men who (occasionally) enjoy sex with women is either ignored or dismissed as irrelevant. Once a man has attained the dizzy heights of a gay identity, a trivial matter like fucking the other sex cannot shift his identity.

Women who 'have it both ways' are troubling indeed for the lesbian community. Women who behave bisexually can be seen in three categories: heterosexual-identified, bisexual-identified and lesbian-identified.[37] The heterosexually identified rarely concern lesbians (unless they are having relationships with them), these women tend to be perceived as 'swingers' and distant from the lesbian community. It is those with a queer identity who are of concern:

> Lesbians who sleep with men (termed 'hasbians' by the feminist publication *off our backs*) are often seen as turn-coats, betraying their lesbian sisters and unable to deal with their 'true' desires. ... Because bisexuality may call into question the notion of sexual identity as necessarily being fixed, consistent, and either homosexual or heterosexual, it makes some lesbians uneasy. In a society where hetero-sexuality is the norm and lesbianism is still stigmatized, bisexual boundary crossings often lead to hurt feelings, as when a woman is left by her female lover for a man.[38]

In both bisexual scenarios, misogyny runs riot: women are such insufficient sexual beings that sex with one or two won't change a gay man's gayness, whereas, men are such potent sexual beings that sex with just one *will* topple a woman from her lesbian pedestal. 'Like mainstream society, lesbians have often devalued bisexual women's relationships with other women, and over-valued their relationships with men', says Sue George.[39]

It is perhaps indicative of the innate weaknesses of a lesbian sense of community and identity that bisexual behaviour is perceived as such an enormous threat. Overt and covert bisexuality is the hidden threat to the purity of the Lesbian Nation. 'These women refuse or are afraid to own their own bisexual identity. They dilute and pollute the very definition and essence of lesbianism.'[40] This strikes me as a very telling comment: bisexuals are *polluters*, bringing the most fearsome pollution of the late twentieth century: HIV.

This is translated explicitly in both the UK and the USA, where writers note that 'Some [bisexuals] have even been accused of importing AIDS into lesbian communities.'[41] The bisexual woman is most definitely the worst kind of 'HIV carrier' in this discourse. She imports a dangerous substance, dirties an otherwise pure group. Yet, does a smoking lesbian bring throat or lung cancer into the lesbian community? Are dykes with breast cancer, MS, or cervical cancer importing these life-threatening conditions? The bisexual woman does indeed have a greater vulnerability to HIV than the 100 per cent pure '*echte*' dyke who never fucked a man. And yes, this very same bisexually behaving woman, even if she finds out she is HIV-positive, may want to retain her identity within the lesbian community. What is interesting, here is that, once again, the facts of HIV transmission disappear. It is no longer what this woman does, but simply the fact of her being bisexual which is a threat. And so, as the ACT UP table demonstrated, for a lesbian to 'sleep with . . . bisexual men or women' places her at risk: no explanation of the fact that unprotected sex with men is infinitely more risky than unprotected sex with women, no differentiation between bisexual men (with their particular vulner-ability to HIV) and bisexual women. In this discourse it is something magical about bisexuality which is risky; it is as if the very condition of bisexuality indicates contagion.

Could it be that the fundamental lesbian fear of bisexuality is a fear of contagion – a fear that other lesbians will 'catch' the condition? That they will abandon women for men. This magical thinking gets transferred into a 'medical' model. Once it becomes treacherous bisexual women who transport HIV, not activities with HIV-infected women, then thinking can reach such muddled extremes as this:

> *Lesbian* sex, in any form, during menstruation or not, is SAFE!! The only time when it may not be is when the partner is a bisexual woman and *may* have contracted HIV from her male partner, a possible bisexual as well, who *may* have had sexual contact with a gay guy/bisexual who *may* have the virus i.e. lesbian women should be careful/wary of having sex with bisexual women (or guys – it happens, I've heard! 'Brotherly/Sisterly love?') How do you identify a bisexual woman/man?[42]

Now all this 'biphobia' may be pretty unpleasant for bisexuals, but does it really matter in terms of HIV? For bisexuals who identify as heterosexual, probably not. Their HIV-prevention needs should be met via their heterosexual identity, at least messages will be addressed to it. If they are part of a 'swinging' scene, and their male partners are also likely to have bisexual behaviour, then some cultural specificity may be lost, but messages about using condoms should reach them. But the HIV-prevention needs of bisexual-identified bisexual women have been totally disregarded.[43] They may have an increased vulnerability to HIV, because many choose men who behave or identify as bisexuals as sexual partners; yet the story of AIDS underplays the impact HIV may have upon them.

This biphobia also has a more insidious and dangerous effect. As health-education theory demonstrates, and gay men have documented so clearly, behaviour change is linked to self-esteem, and self-esteem is linked to self-worth and pride in one's sexual identity. How is it possible to develop the self-esteem to protect bisexuals from sexual ill health when they are constantly told that their sexual identity is a joke, meaningless, traitorous, cruel, despicable; and they are repeatedly marginalized within the community with which they identify socially, politically and sexually? Bi-bashing may succeed in making bisexuals ashamed of their sexuality, but desire does not change that easily.

Shame is also central to the ways in which lesbian-identified bisexuals have been dangerously disregarded by HIV efforts. This works in subtle ways with talk of 'bad lesbians', or pretence that lesbians only ever fuck men before coming out, or for money, or by force. This intensifies invisibility, as Susie Bright notes:

> Since most human beings, and that *does* include lesbians, are neither exclusively homo or heterosexual, it's not surprising that many lesbians, who would never think of themselves as bisexual, are touched by this epidemic. But the lesbian public front is this pure-as-the-driven-snow bullshit which keeps women from being honest and unafraid with one another. We have now reached a point, because of AIDS, where we either confront our taboos and get real, or we're going to watch our own silence and secrecy kill us.[44]

The queer connection

Latex lesbianism says a lot about understandings of what it means to be a lesbian – how women define themselves and allow themselves to be sexual. Latex lesbianism proclaims sex positivity, it protects against acknowledging any sex negativism, and it is a barrier against the 'pollution' of bisexuality. But responses to the AIDS crisis and the causes of latex lesbianism can only be understood by also exploring how dykes feel about men.

The 'lesbian movement' was born of the women's movement, born to the politics of separatism and overturning the patriarchy. For some women, lesbianism was a conscious choosing of women, and for some it was a rejection of men, politically and sexually. Whatever the definition of a 'lesbian' (and that is not within the scope of this book), lesbians were distant from men, so much so that the pollution and impurity of the bisexual woman is her physical contact with men. But however individual women choose to live, on a collective level lesbians in the 1990s have become part of a mixed 'community'. The lesbian movement as a young adult lives in the queer world.

The term 'queer world'[45] expresses for me the current reality more powerfully than the usual phrase 'lesbian and gay community'. I do not use queer pejoratively, nor as an indicator of how individuals self-define, nor as an imperative description. 'World' seems preferable to 'community' since the notion of a lesbian and gay community or communities is as idealistic as talk of a 'lesbian nation'. It postulates some uniting factor which cannot be provided simply by the fact of same-sex desire and practice – just as there is no 'women's community' based purely on sex, but rather subgroups of people of the same sex who may form their own communities. The uniting factor of same-sex desire does, however, mean that there is a 'world'. A world with its own media, social venues, intelligentsia, commerce, organizations, support services, political spokespersons and structures. A world to which queers have access in addition to the 'real' world of heterosexuality. Some people choose to live outside the heterosexual world – or the queer one. However, most queers in industrialized countries have some contact with the queer world, even if it is only second- or third-hand.

The reality of the queer world in the 1990s is important for lesbians and bisexual women. Even if a woman's lesbianism is a strong emotional, sexual and political identification with other women, and an identification which leads her to desire women-only environments, it is practically impossible to live a queer life without men. In London's queer world, for example, every week I can pick up for free the *Pink Paper* ('The national newspaper for lesbians and gay men'), *Gay Gazette* (a weekly London paper for gay men), *Boyz* ('for gay adults', but really a lively, sexy, tabloid-style paper for young gay men – brother of the *Pink*), *Thud* and *QX* magazine (a weekly guide to the queer social scene). What if I want something just for queer women? I have to pay £2 for *Diva*, the (excellent) bi-monthly sister magazine of *Gay Times*. This is not to knock the press – it is an extraordinary portfolio compared, say, to New York City. The reality is, however, that as communities have matured, the political and economic benefits of organizing together have led to closening social and sexual identities for women and men. There is lesbian-and-gay everything: television and radio programmes, Pride marches, SM organizations, book lists, dance clubs, centres, helplines, you name it. Like it or not, in the 1990s queer women live alongside queer men: they inhabit the same world.

Yet isn't sex a greater divide than sexual orientation? Hetero, homo and bi are on the same sexuality continuum, but are male and female on a continuum? At the risk of distressing the transgendered reader, I doubt that they are.[46] Despite the profound differences of sex, the sexes are often considered to be just the opposite sides of a coin. If there is another factor uniting a group of people – such as race, disability or, in this case, sexuality – then that factor becomes the overriding concern: sex (or gender) simply subdivides the normative group. In this way lesbians are frequently perceived (and may perceive themselves) to be the same as gay men, just a different sex. This is a relatively new development, suggests one sociologist: 'In the 1960s, many "sex experts" abandoned the concept of inversion, adopting the idea of the "female homosexual" and popularizing the view that lesbians are attracted to women in much the same way that gay men are attracted to men.'[47]

Whether or not lesbians *are* 'female homosexuals' in this way, the fact is that queer women are closely aligned with queer men. This is critical to the lesbian response to AIDS. Why do women-identified-women care about something that started with men and still (in the industrialized world) infects more men than women? What on earth could be the motivation for expending that precious, and rare, women's energy on anything other than a women's issue? Much as it is linked to lesbian identity and sexual desire, latex lesbianism is also about who queer women are in relationship with men. If lesbians lived in a lesbian nation with absolutely no contact with men, or media which addressed men's concerns, could latex lesbianism have happened? I don't think so. Certainly some individual members of the nation might have become infected prior to entry, but then the condition would be like any other life-threatening condition – the lesbian response would have been one of care and support for these individual women. It is because AIDS is a queer disease, and lesbians live in that queer world, that lesbians care about the AIDS crisis – and that latex lesbianism could happen.

This does not mean that queer women are obliged to care for queer men who have AIDS – but many do. It does not mean that lesbian issues have to be addressed in concert with gay men's – but many are. It does not mean that lesbian concerns mirror gay men's – but it is often assumed (by queer women, queer men, and those outside our queer world) that they do. Lesbian reality has become enmeshed with gay men's reality.

• *Shared concerns*

The benefits of joint organizing in the queer world may be of particular benefit to queer women at a social, political and economic level if (as many suggest) queer men outnumber women (which, at the very least, they do on the commercial scene). It is not just pragmatism that brings women and men together. The fact of not being heterosexual entails struggles and concerns which transcend sex. The expression of homophobia may differ in respect of gay men (e.g. an assault to masculinity), lesbians (e.g. invisibility) or bisexuals (e.g. being dismissed), but the root fear engendered by queers' rejection of the societal norm of hetero-sexuality unites women and men. This is the most fundamental, but not the only, concern that is shared.

A consequence of joint organizing has been cleaning up the queer equal opportunities act: lesbians and gay men are all exhorted to look at race and disability politics, and gay men (especially) at sexism. The result may not be profound in terms of real change, but lip service is getting a lot better. Perhaps it is not really the right lip service: anything gay and male gets equated with something gay and female. There are lesbian sex clubs and saunas (often held in the same venues as gay men's clubs), gender-fuck and daddy-boy dykes – but gay men rarely follow a lesbian lead.

In AIDS work, a crass equal opportunities approach often takes hold. The result is: dental dam = condom. Even if the low, theoretical risk of woman-to-woman transmission is perceived as a risk, a dental dam (or other latex accessory) will never have the same life-saving value as a condom and lube. OutRage! (the direct action group) handed out both to schoolchildren in an AIDS-awareness zap to show that not all schoolchildren are heterosexual.[48] Many of the (too few) mixed lesbian and gay venues or social events which make condoms available now offer women dental dams or other bits of latex; stalls at Lesbian and Gay Pride are awash with the things. When some dykes even want to call them 'Condams',[49] how much more closely aligned with gay male sexuality can it become?

The reality is that 'All gay men face the epidemic head-on every time we have sex. We have mostly learnt to live with this, though God knows the personal costs are high for very many of us. This is not how lesbians live.'[50] But the dental dam has taken on a key role as symbol of lesbian sexual visibility.[51]

It is as if women's need for economic and social equality translates in the queer movement into a need to be equal in all things. It is as if equal opportunities has become perverted into 'equal experiences'. The one thing women *do not* need is equality with queer men's suffering as a result of this health crisis, and most would deny seeking equal importance around AIDS. Equality is, however, the form of discourse often used when discussing 'Lesbian and AIDS'.

One of the main ways in which this push for equality makes itself visible is the current positioning of health as the principal queer rallying point. It has achieved a symbolic value in the mixed community, as representative of queer needs. But as a group of (predominantly) young, childless women, lesbians are a GP's dream, since they have very few physical health problems. Why, then, should inequities in health become a priority issue and more symbolic of lesbian oppression than inequities in (say) education, employment or parental rights? Precisely because for queer *men* it is threatened on a daily basis. Health had no (or little) symbolic value or political position for them before the AIDS crisis. The importance of health, and the expertise in healthcare, research, policy and health education, have since been hard-won in the face of extreme adversity. AIDS has made health the priority political issue it now is for the queer world simply because so many gay men and bisexual men have discovered that they, their lovers and their friends have a complex, political, life-threatening health condition.

Access to these areas, and to sympathetic healthcare providers, are all now highlighted as critical areas of queer concern for both sexes. Sexual health promotion is actively pursued, and the UK has three lesbian sexual health clinics (the Bernhard, Audre Lorde and Vita clinics), and the sexual health video *Well Sexy Women* is in many lesbian video collections. Yet, sexual health is not a lesbian issue for the same reasons as AIDS is one for queer men. Research is demanded into lesbian sexual health not because the 'community' or lesbian doctors are aware of high levels of sexual disease, but because no one knows whether there is a connection. This does not mean that the research is irrelevant, but it does mean that it comes from a different level of urgency. What will lesbians do if dyke doctors discover that there is no connection? Or if the connection is that lesbians have fewer STDs? Will there be rejoicing? Or fights to keep the clinics open?

The lesbian health priority goes beyond sexual health – which is such a close mirror of gay men's experience of sexual disease. On a fairly regular basis (at least in the American queer press) diseases are described as 'lesbian AIDS': breast cancer, Epstein Barr Virus/M.E./CFIDS. Breast cancer, in particular, is presented as a health complaint which disproportionately affects queer women, and is in some way linked to sexuality. Any doubts that lesbian health is a priority issue are dismissed by reference to breast cancer which (at least in the USA) attracts the same kind of visible philanthropic support as AIDS does for gay men. So, the conclusion runs, health is a priority queer issue because AIDS is the priority political issue for gay men, and breast cancer is the priority political issue for lesbians.

However, the breast cancer analogy simply does not work. Significant numbers of lesbians and bisexual women do get breast cancer and die from it every year. This happens because lesbians have breasts. Lesbians also get cervical cancer (and need to be encouraged to have cervical smears) because they have cervices. Some say lesbians have an elevated risk for breast cancer since the additional risk factors for breast cancer include not giving birth to children, not breast-feeding, late (or no) first sexual intercourse with men, smoking and drinking. A disproportionate number of lesbians have these risk factors. Yet they are not exclusive to dykes, but are shared with bi and straight women. Not all dykes (by any means) refrain from giving birth/ breast-feeding/ fucking men, or enjoy smoking and drinking. Breast cancer is *not* lesbian AIDS. It is not a lesbian disease. It is a *woman's* disease, and except for being a life-threatening condition, the comparison with AIDS is lousy. Watney points out:

> If breast cancer were proved to be caused by an infectious agent, and if demonstrably effective prevention measures were subjected to the same horrifying levels of harassment, prejudice, discrimination, and actual violence as apply routinely to people living with HIV/AIDS, and if effective treatment drugs available and in use overseas were denied to women with breast cancer, then, perhaps, there might be a meaningful analogy.[52]

Breast cancer *is* a serious and important health concern for many queer women. However, as a community of queer women, breast cancer does not exact the same daily toll of grief and suffering that AIDS exacts on my life, the life of many gay men, and the queer world as a whole.

• *Simultaneous concerns*

The search for lesbian AIDS does not arise from AIDS envy, necessarily, but from living in a combined community. Queer women and men do share some concerns, but there are many differences. What are the current needs of queer women? What is the political agenda? When women see what AIDS is doing to queer men, how can they even begin to imagine their own agenda?

The horror and destruction of the AIDS crisis, the intrinsic links with gay sex, the homophobia which fuels discrimination, and the failure to develop imaginative solutions because of hatred of gay lifestyles, make it inevitable that AIDS is the priority of queer men's agenda. For queer women it is almost as if the agenda has been hijacked. Women have nothing so utterly devastating, so thoroughly linked to lesbianism, so how can they dare to raise their own concerns? The most courageous description of being a lesbian, in a queer world that is living with AIDS, came from Natasha Gray in New York City. She had the guts to state,

> I am bored with gay men. . . . And most of all I feel a nauseating boredom with AIDS, the virus that won't go away, the fight that I can't abandon, the spectacle of gay death that makes lesbian life seem so insignificant. Or maybe I'm not bored, maybe I am just tired of envy. . . . It is not a clean, honest envy but a guilty one, like the resentment a healthy child feels for a sick sibling who is getting all the attention.[53]

For many queer women, AIDS reinforces the trauma of being raised as little girls who should not have needs, who should let the boys speak first. Just as women learn to acknowledge their own needs and desires, to speak up for themselves, to feel worthy and know that they matter, just at that moment the boys get something really awful. And so women are silenced again, letting go of their needs and feeling churlish for even daring to mind. Health has arisen as such a defining lesbian issue, because it seems like the only decent thing to do. How could queer women say that what really matters is being out as a mother, being out in the workplace, finding housing? These are all concerns which may be high priorities for queer women in their twenties and thirties – but it is hard to compare these with the high priority which queer men have in their twenties and thirties.

This sense of the worthlessness of lesbian concerns may lead towards an extreme identification with queer men in their struggle. For many queer women there is a natural solidarity with friends and members of extended queer 'families' and 'communities' in times of adversity. Many queer women are profoundly affected by the AIDS epidemic raging through queer men, and have devoted immense parts of their life to caring for them. One of women's traditional skills is the ability to empathize. How many carers (for whatever condition) find themselves imagining what it would be like to face the reality of the person we care for? They may well not want that condition, but will be better carers if they make the imaginative leap of understanding; and sometimes it offers a precocious opportunity to check out our own reality:

[When] thirty-five-year-old Lisa Heft, an AIDS hotline and speakers bureau volunteer, mused aloud about what she'd want for her memorial service, or whether her lover would hold her hand if she were in a coma, her lover was horrified – and accused her of being morbid. '"Why do you think about death all the time?" she asked. She didn't understand that death had become such a daily part of my life.'[54]

The imaginative leaps which are important for lesbian AIDS workers to empathize with their clients, and understand the epidemic, can sometimes take things too far. This may be the case with the lesbian who, perhaps, muses thus on her gay male friends' lives: 'How can it be to have to restrict your sexual practice, to introduce measures that decrease the pleasure, to always be aware that sex can be a life threatening event?' She then ends up practising 'restrictive sex', covering up with latex to prove her solidarity. This is no fantasy. I have met more than one woman who knows she and her lover are HIV-negative, but they practise safer sex as 'solidarity'. Does this really support queer men through the AIDS crisis? It can easily slip from solidarity to competition, and one lesbian in San Francisco muses, 'I think safe sex is just one more way of competing with the boys ... you know, if *they* have to have safe sex, then we do too.'[55]

The most disturbing example of misplaced solidarity and over-identification is the phenomenon I call 'Munchausen AIDS', where a woman or man claims to have HIV but is not in fact infected. This is something which at a mild level has been seen in a range of people – often women or men who perceive the AIDS industry as an easy touch for money. However, there is a more severe version of the syndrome, which goes beyond the need for money, to a need for status, attention and more generalized care. Here an individual also accesses a range of services, including invasive medical services, and develops an identity and visible profile as a person living with HIV. This is a complex psychological condition, and one which American doctors have linked to a prolonged history of sexual or physical abuse.[56]

The first case of this, documented in the scientific press,

occurred in a young lesbian to whom I provided services at THT in 1988.[57] She hospitalized herself on at least two occasions, received extensive practical, financial and emotional support, and became the public face of an organization of people with AIDS for a number of months. When she was confronted with the fact that she had recently twice tested HIV-negative, she disappeared to other AIDS agencies complaining that THT didn't believe lesbians could get AIDS. Eventually the other agencies discovered that she was not HIV-infected and also had to withdraw services. In 1994 she reappeared at a number of AIDS organizations – a smart move since most staff had changed in the six years.

Clearly this woman has serious psychological problems, which may or may not have a link to her sexuality. My reason for describing the case is that it is not unique. One of the founders of Positively Women has met a number of lesbians and bisexual women living with HIV, and she has also encountered at least ten lesbians with Munchausen AIDS. I have had dealings with four, including Kate Birch who, in 1994, created 'Positive Strength', an organization for HIV-positive lesbians. This folded within months, when Birch was unable to provide a letter proving her HIV diagnosis. She had gathered massive media profile in the queer press, claiming that hundreds of HIV-positive lesbians had written to her (in fact, three had). The publicity surrounding this case has a terrible impact upon truly HIV-infected lesbians, not only in snatching services from them, but also many may now feel a sense of having a higher burden of proof (although it is now standard for all people with HIV to be asked for proof of diagnosis before receiving services).

I have been strongly advised not to discuss this element of the lesbians and AIDS discourse, because it will enhance the alienation of HIV-positive lesbians, and it will be misused to condemn all lesbian concerns about AIDS. The same argument has been used to dissuade discussion about over-latexing. Yet every community (not just the lesbian one) has inappropriate responses to AIDS, simply because it is a condition which heightens funda-mental fears and emotions. 'Silence = Death', and not addressing these problems, even when they are as deeply uncomfortable as lesbian Munchausen AIDS, will not help to develop responses for lesbians in general, nor for these troubled women. My concern in raising this issue is not to condemn, but to ask how lesbians who develop such extraordinary emotional health problems can get their valid needs met, in a context which responds to their own needs, not at the expense of someone else's health crisis.

There are women in the UK living with HIV and AIDS who are lesbian, bisexual or enjoy sex with women. Yet there have been a number of women making life increasingly difficult for them by pretending that they are HIV-positive lesbians when they are not. Since the phenomenon of Munchausen AIDS is rarely reported, it is impossible to know if this is more prevalent among lesbians than other women and men – it may just be that I am in a position where I am more likely to encounter them than I am, say, straight male drug users with Munchausen AIDS. However, there does appear to be a lesbian dimension to this condition, and that is the fact of being so enmeshed with gay men, and their experience of the epidemic. It is perhaps the failure of the lesbian community to articulate clearly separate and vital agendas which leads some lesbians to such unfortunate positions as needing to use a fake HIV diagnosis to have their needs met. Perhaps to a confused young woman, struggling with the daily pain of homophobia, the easiest way to get some care and attention is to follow the same route as her gay brothers. It is unlikely that she notices (or cares) how disastrous her behaviour is for lesbians, and other women and men, who are struggling with the daily pain of an HIV diagnosis. Munchausen AIDS among lesbians is a tiny, extreme element of lesbian response to AIDS. It is easy to leap on it and use these rare occurrences to pathologize all of lesbian concerns around AIDS. There are many genuine concerns which lesbians have about AIDS, and the shame is that they can so easily become concealed under sensationalist reports and mounds of latex. This displacement can conceal the extraordinary, often self-sacrificing, energy and commitment displayed to AIDS by thousands of dykes around the world.

• *The carers*

Many, many queer women have been, and continue to be, carers of people with AIDS. This is hardly surprising given the queer world, and given that women of all sexualities so often find themselves in caring roles. This care may be for best friends, acquaintances, friendship circles or on a voluntary or professional basis. Many queer women already work in the caring professions (like social work, medicine, counselling, nursing) and may be drawn to specialize in AIDS. Others seek to work, or volunteer, for ASOs. The motivations for becoming involved in such work are diverse, and will range from direct personal involvement (close friends who are sick) through political idealism (to fight the oppression and stigma of AIDS) to employment benefits (to work in a homophobia-free zone). The initial motivations will undoubtedly affect queer women's experiences of involvement, paid or unpaid, with AIDS organizing. The vast majority will encounter some of the difficulties surrounding men and women working together which have been so fundamental and divisive to lesbian and gay politics. These fundamental difficulties tend to be intensified by the personal pain of AIDS and the inequality of the impact of AIDS. Whereas general organizing around lesbian and gay issues demands equal opportunities, in AIDS equal opportunities has an entirely different meaning. A fundamental problem for many ASOs is maintaining a focus which responds to the reality of the epidemic whilst ensuring respect for all people providing this response. This has to include countering sexism, something which (in my experience) is not easily achieved and remains a problem for nearly all ASOs. Perhaps some latex lesbianism arises as a response to unrelenting sexism: there is a genuine and realistic sense that women's needs are ignored, women's sexuality rendered invisible, making it plausible that there is some conspiracy theory from the boys to keep information from women.

Some latex lesbianism undoubtedly responds to the highly sexualized environments of most ASOs where gay sex can be an unrelenting feature of conversation – professional and personal. American AIDS educator Carol Camlin describes her delight at discovering an erotic poster of two women in a steamy bath (produced by THT) which she could pin on her office wall. 'This environment, brimming with gay male erotic safer-sex posters, would make any healthy lesbian long for images of nude women.'[58] If they can have sex on the walls, why can't we? In some ways this reflects the confusion of personal and professional boundaries which is a common, and inevitable, feature of AIDS work. Are the gay men's posters displayed to highlight a recent campaign? Or because the workers fancy the models? This too may lead lesbians towards latex lesbianism. There are two sides to the AIDS equation: sex and death. And as carers, queer women want their sexuality to be recognized, as much as they expect to be confronted by their own mortality as a result of their engagement in the epidemic.

AIDS creates fear. For lesbians who are bombarded with information that the AIDS crisis is a daily thing, but for whom it is not a part of their friendship circles and daily reality, perhaps fear is a logical response. By sharing the queer world with men, they may know more about AIDS than most. For some queer women the response may well be to raise the barricades higher still to keep the lesbian nation pure. The porn debates have been a notorious cause of unholy alliances – perhaps AIDS is also now creating them: lesbian feminists and the Far Right become united against 'libertarians'. They become united to police the walls of their safe space and keep the plague out.

Curiously with AIDS (unlike the alliances against pornography and prostitution), these lesbian feminists include sex radicals. One 'lesbian erotic fiction' magazine[59] carries a letter from a woman who wants to know if she can 'contract AIDS from french kissing' her new girlfriend who has just told her she has AIDS, and that's 'as far as we have gone'. The magazine replies:

> It's a good thing the woman told you she had AIDS before you got sexually involved. A person with AIDS who has sex with someone should always tell their partner before sex occurs. If they don't they are committing a senseless crime – murder! It is your choice whether or not you wish to pursue a sexual relationship with the woman.

The writer then goes on to describe classic latex lesbianism, saying that the jury is still out on HIV transmission and french kissing (this is 1991!) advising, 'I would avoid french kissing an AIDS person. . . . I doubt that you contracted AIDS from french kissing. However, it is best to be safe than sorry, so don't french kiss.' After telling her enquirer about testing procedures she ends: 'Keep in mind, people with AIDS are just like us – they need lots of love.' Well it doesn't sound like dykes with HIV are going to get much sexual loving from the readers of *Bad Attitude*. The magazine got that name because 'that's what women who take their sexuality into their own hands (so to speak) are told they have'. It also seems to refer to their approach to people living with HIV.

Such a commentary usually comes from people who are distant from the realities of the epidemic. No gay agony uncle could state, 'If people with HIV don't reveal their HIV status before having sex, they are committing a senseless crime – murder!' I'd love to see the letters page if he tried. People with HIV have fought hard for their rights to remain sex-positive, and this is now denounced in a magazine which fights hard for lesbians to be sex-positive – as rabid as any *Sun* editorial. I doubt that *Bad Attitude*'s motive was hatred of people with HIV, but rather an ignorance fuelled by fear – and it is not only queer women who are distant from the realities of AIDS who fear it. Queer women who have supported friends through illness and lost people they love to the epidemic are likely to have an above-average motivation to avoid HIV infection. For queer women most profoundly affected by AIDS, this may translate into an urgent desire to survive the crisis, even a sense of duty to ensure the survival of the queer world. Indeed, the leaders of all American lesbian and gay (non-AIDS) organizations are now women, and there is a sense that lesbians are taking responsibility for pursuing gay liberation, while gay men's energies are focused on the daily urgencies of fighting HIV and AIDS within their bodies and communities.[60]

So why do lesbians give a dam?

The sub-community of lesbians which promotes latex does not have 'AIDS envy'. Latex lesbianism can be traced to two basic questions: the 'What do lesbians actually do?' of nosy heterosexuals, and the 'Why do you waste your energy on men?' of radical feminists. It is driven by lesbians' relationships to sex and to men.

On an individual level, lesbians will be motivated by different degrees of each factor, maybe even by a touch of envy too. But these are about individual psyches. The issue is not each individual's motives, but rather the collective impact of this phenomenon. Although its roots are clearly American, why has it taken hold in so many different industrialized countries?[61] This is not a pure academic concern. Some say, 'Who cares? If lesbians want to make their sex lives sterile for no reason, that's their business.' It's not so simple. Lesbians do not live in a hermetically sealed society. As latex takes off for lesbians, how will HIV-positive women understand that they are not highly infectious? Why should the general public believe that HIV is hard to transmit except through penetrative sex? Who will believe that HIV-positive doctors don't infect their patients?

The impact of latex lesbianism on the lives of HIV-positive women of all sexualities is immense. Many people diagnosed with HIV experience a period of adjusting to the condition where their identity becomes entwined with the virus in their white cells. They may perceive of themselves as a 'walking virus' or 'germ'. This is usually a phase which shifts as the woman or man adjusts to the diagnosis, and panics less about implausible modes of transmission. One lesbian with AIDS describes how latex reintensifies these anxieties, and forces back on herself the sense of being no more than a virus, so much so that she restricts her sex life to little more than dry kissing. 'I cannot deal with [dental dams and finger cots]. They just emphasize the fact of my disease, and even though I may want to be touched in certain areas, I can't deal with that emphasis of feeling like some *freak*!'[62] Another woman with HIV complained, 'Lesbians have ruined my sex life. I've read all the scientific literature. I know lots of HIV-positive women who've been fucking unsafe with men for years and the men haven't become infected. I'm convinced that I won't infect a man or a woman who goes down on me. But my lovers are now terrified of oral sex, so I don't get the sex I want.'[63] After watching a series of lesbian 'safer sex' videos, a third woman responded, 'I just wish I didn't have any sexual urges. I'd like to stop my juices flowing, because if that's all there is I don't want to bother. If you'd just been diagnosed it would totally freak you out.'[64]

When people overestimate and muddle the so-called risks of

'low', 'theoretical' or 'no' risk activities, they tend to develop a fatalistic approach to truly high-risk activities, and consequently practise them.[65] It is my contention that latex lesbianism *increases* the risk to lesbian and bisexual women's lives. Some queer women will be *less* likely to use condoms on the (perhaps rare) occasions they have penetrative sex with men, if they have developed an excessive estimation of risk. Women who believe that HIV is so readily transmitted that it is necessary to go through elaborate rituals with alcohol swabs,[66] finger cots and latex gloves, may conclude that condom use for fucking is not worthwhile. There may even be anecdotal evidence of this, with suggestions that latex lesbian educators do not practise what they preach.[67]

Everyone's motives for taking risks and making behavioural change are complex, in whatever area of their lives. In respect of HIV, like other health-related decisions, risk-taking (or not) is rarely rational or based on 'the facts'. Yet the facts do matter, and if they are misrepresented, or plain wrong, people have little chance of understanding their choices. A person who believes, say, that HIV is transmitted in drinking water, or that AIDS is caused by pharmaceutical products, is in no position to adopt risk-reducing strategies. In order for people to make individual choices about the behaviours and levels of risk they are content with, there is a responsibility to make the true facts known. A recent vogue (to slip around the argument of 'to dam or not to dam') is to talk of 'enabling lesbians to make a choice' about whether to practise safer sex. This is laudable, yet it still depends on AIDS educators and activists understanding and presenting the facts which will truly enable lesbians to make choices. This means presenting all reliable information – not only that which backs up the educator's position.[68] There is a responsibility not only for ensuring the information is available, but also for not exaggerating minimal risks.

Preaching at lesbians that dental dams, latex gloves and other bits of rubber are essential at all times when they have sex with each other is not only pointless, but potentially harmful. Some lesbians have been scared into unnecessarily restricting their sex lives, because of a remote risk of HIV in sexual activities between women. Such excessive, and often irrational, fear has

sometimes been translated into a rejection of HIV-positive
lesbians. Frequently it has been used to exclude, and to reject from
the lesbian community, those women who acknowledge having
sex with men or using drugs. Irrespective of their HIV status,
these women are stigmatized as 'bringing AIDS into the lesbian
community' (the lesbian community being a construct that needs
to be vigorously policed). These men-fucking, drug-shooting
women are excluded for not being 'real' lesbians.

Although such rejection is disconcertingly common, there
are also thousands of lesbians who have given of their time and
energies to fight the real epidemic. Many have been key players
in the work to support the communities which experience the
greatest vulnerability and impact of the epidemic: in particular,
supporting gay men and drug users. Living in the midst of the
horror and pain of AIDS, lesbians can at least celebrate the fact
that sex between women is remarkably free of disease – and open
up dialogue and support about the risky practices of having sex
with men and injecting drugs, from a lesbian perspective. Whatever
the reasons for the extreme, and bizarre, reactions of some
lesbians, the majority of lesbians who have engaged with the AIDS
crisis have done so to support people with HIV and AIDS. Many
lesbians have tirelessly and (inevitably) thanklessly devoted huge
chunks of their lives to the epidemic. This is especially remarkable
because they have chosen to do this out of their dedication to
fighting a disease of 'others'. It is precisely because it is not a
matter of self-interest, that the lesbian contribution to fighting
AIDS is so remarkable. Watney points out that, 'Many, many
women have proved true friends to gay men throughout this
epidemic. It's a great shame that [this group of lesbians] can apparently only reduce all that care, and intelligence, and love, to
latex.'[69] And if a few women do want to do just that, it is vital that
the marginal politics of latex lesbianism do not conceal the love,
the intelligence and the care of the overwhelming majority of
lesbian responses.

Notes

1. S. O'Sullivan and P. Parmar, *Lesbians Talk (Safer Sex)*, Scarlet Press, London, 1992, p. 16.
2. Cited by M. L. Adams, *Rites*, April 1989, pp. 10–12.
3. S. March, quoted by J. Goodwin, 'A marriage made in hell', *Guardian*, 17 December 1994.
4. P. Parmar, 'On reframing AIDS', in A. Klusaček and K. Morrison (eds), *A Leap in the Dark: AIDS, Art and Contemporary Cultures*, Véhicule Press, Montreal, 1992.
5. Barbara James, personal communication.
6. See E. King, *Safety in Numbers*, Cassell, London, 1993, pp. 113–14; and Chapter 9.
7. Such silliness started earlier in the USA – from 1982 to 1983 the American Red Cross advised lesbians not to give blood.
8. Audre Lorde clinic, statistical breakdown, May 1995.
9. Adams, *op. cit.*
10. Women's Committee of ACT UP New York, *AIDS: A Lesbian Issue? Yes! And We Can Do Something about It*, distributed at Lesbian and Gay Pride march, 26 June 1988.
11. *Safer Sex Handbook for Lesbians*, GMHC, Lesbian AIDS Project, New York, 1993. This is an extremely erotic, elegantly designed twenty-page pamphlet with gorgeous photographs. There is no comparable material from Gay Men's Health Crisis for women having sex with men.
12. A 56-page booklet, *Lesbian Sex*, was produced by ACON (AIDS Council of New South Wales) in 1994. I am not aware of any parallel material for non-lesbian women.
13. In the 1993 GMHC pamphlet the only mention of sex with men comes in tiny type hidden at the end of the glossary; it states, 'For lesbians having sex with men, use a condom every time. Call the GMHC hotline for more information about protecting yourself and your partners.'
14. Jackie Dutton of London ACT UP, quoted by S. George, 'Oral examination', *Guardian*, 19 February 1992.
15. R. Cole and S. Cooper, 'Lesbian exclusion from HIV/AIDS education', *SIECUS Report*, December 1990/January 1991, p. 19.
16. Karin Galil, MD, quoted in R. Gorna, 'Everything you ever wanted to know about oral sex . . . but you won't find it here', *World AIDS News – The Newspaper of the Harvard-Amsterdam Conference*, 20 July 1992, p. 4.
17. K. Alcorn (ed.), *National AIDS Manual*, B2-10, NAM Publications, spring edition 1993.
18. N. Tamsma and A. Hendriks, 'Report on the policy track', *Report of the Second European Conference on Homosexuality and HIV*, Amsterdam 14–16 February 1992, pp. 15–16.

19. I had assumed that this was a mistaken artefact of the early European epidemic. However, on a visit to New York's Gay Men's Health Crisis in early 1995 I discovered that the same linkage is common there – to the extent that in the organization's statistical monitoring they classify the clients they see as 'lesbians or gay men' and do not distinguish between the genders. The USA has immense problems with developing HIV-prevention work, and one of these problems is the fantasy that AIDS is as much a lesbian as a gay issue.

20. S. Watney, 'The killing fields of Europe', *Outrage*, July 1992, p. 45.

21. See King, *op. cit.*, pp. 262–3.

22. See, for example, letters, *Capital Gay*, 10 July 1992, p. 2.

23. There was one change: the reference to donor insemination was removed, as evidence of transmission by this route (especially to lesbians) was weak at that time.

24. Joyce Hunter, personal communication.

25. E. King, *Pink Paper*, 7 June 1992.

26. There are plenty of conspiracy theories about where this phrase originated, but despite extensive searches I am unable to trace the source.

27. A. Stein, 'The year of the lustful lesbian', citing C. Patton, 'Brave new lesbians,' *Village Voice*, 2 July 1985, in A. Stein (ed.), *Sisters, Sexperts, Queers: Beyond the Lesbian Nation*, Plume, USA, 1993, p. 31.

28. T. Thomas, 'Straight people call me Sir', *Quim*, issue 3, winter 1991, p. 25.

29. S. Bright, 'Dam it, Janet!', in *Susie Sexpert's Lesbian Sex World*, Cleis Press, Pittsburgh and San Francisco, 1990, p.76.

30. Photos by China, *Bad Attitude*, Vol. 8, No. 4, pp. 21, 27.

31. G. Greer, *The Female Eunuch*, Flamingo, London, 1993, p. 57 (first published 1970).

32. Sophie, 'Vent', *Quim*, issue 4, 1992.

33. Bright, *op. cit.*, p. 77.

34. Dr Jayne Kavanagh, personal communication.

35. In Stein, *op. cit.*, p. 24.

36. V. Whisman, 'Identity crises: who is a lesbian, anyway?', in Stein, *op. cit.*, p. 53.

37. This is by no means a complete categorization. In Sue George's book, *Women and Bisexuality* (Scarlet Press, London, 1993, p. 159), of 142 bisexually behaving women, 108 identified as bisexual, the others identified as 'lesbian', 'heterosexual', 'heterosexual and lesbian', 'heterosexual/bisexual', 'bisexual/lesbian' and the rest stated that they did not use 'a label', or made statements such as 'confused', 'not sure', 'my sexuality is fluid'.

38. Stein, *op. cit.*, p. 29.

39. George, *op. cit.*, p. 80.

40. L. Conforti, *Out/Look*, no. 9, 1990, p. 7, quoted in Stein, *op. cit.*, p. 54.

41. Stein, *op. cit.*, p. 29. The same phrase is used by George, *op. cit.*, p. 118.

42. ERIKA, 'Don't alarm lesbian readers' (letter), *Capital Gay*, 13 June 1986.

43. At the time of writing a new project, BASH – Bisexual Action on Sexual Health – has just employed its first part-time worker, and it is possible that she will make steps to redress the situation. Although many workers identify their role as with 'gay men and bisexual men', their practice is usually to address the homosexual component of a man's behaviour. Research presented as this book went to press suggests that bisexually behaving women who could be classified as 'swingers' may in fact have an additional vulnerability. Ten per cent of bisexually behaving men have unprotected anal sex with both their male and female partners – and these women often have sex with other women. P. Weatherburn *et al.*, *Behaviourally Bisexual Men in the UK*, Sigma Research, London, 1995.

44. Bright, 'Over the Dam', in *Susie Sexpert*, pp. 134–5.

45. The genesis of these thoughts was Penny Arcade, in her inspiring show *Bitch! Dyke! FagHag! Whore!*, at the ICA, London, 30 September 1993.

46. However, see K. Bornstein, *Gender Outlaw: On Men, Women, and the Rest of Us*, Routledge, New York and London, 1994.

47. V. Whisman, in Stein, *op. cit.*, p. 51.

48. World AIDS Day 1993. Individual members of OutRage! agreed that condoms are not equivalent to dental dams – and that the latter might not even be necessary – but apparently could not find another way to make lesbian sex visible.

49. This is suggested by Jean Carlomusto in ACT UP NY Women & AIDS Book Group, *Women, AIDS & Activism*, South End Press, Boston, 1990, p. 217.

50. Simon Watney, letter, *Outrage*, July 1992.

51. See, for example, B. James, 'Lesbians and HIV: automatic immunity or pressing concern?', *Reproductive Health Matters*, No. 5, May 1995, pp. 117–20.

52. Simon Watney, letter, *Outlines*, July 1992.

53. N. Gray, *NYQ*, 26 April 1992.

54. R. L. Schwartz, 'New alliances, strange bedfellows', in Stein, *op. cit.*, p. 234.

55. Gina, quoted by G. Rodgerson, 'Dykes and the condom culture', *Gay Times*, April 1988.

56. M. D. Mileno *et al.*, 'Munchausen's HIV syndrome in young women', Abstract WP-313, 'HIV Infection in Women: Setting a New Agenda' conference, Washington, DC, 1995.

57. F. C. Kavalier, 'Munchausen syndrome', *Lancet*, 15 April 1989, 1, p. 852.

58. C. Camlin, 'Dams be damned!' *QW*, 20 September 1992, p. 44.
59. *Bad Attitude*, Vol. 7, no. 4, p. 5.
60. See S. Schulman, *My American History: Lesbian and Gay Life During the Reagan/Bush Years*, Cassell, London, 1995; and R. Gorna, 'Think Tank Girl', *Diva*, February/March 1995, pp. 14–15.
61. At the IX International Conference on AIDS (Berlin, June 6–11 1993) a 'Meet the Experts' session was held on women. Experts came from Madras, Cuba, Calabar, Rio de Janeiro, Casablanca and New York. The third question to their broad-ranging presentations was, 'What is done in your country to educate lesbians about HIV?' The woman from New York talked about dental dams. Other women explained that they had terrible trouble persuading people in their country that male homo/bisexuality exists, that the epidemic was developing out of control, and that the luxury of considering potential routes of transmission was not theirs. 'Lesbian AIDS' is a western, urban phenomenon, whereas 'gay AIDS' is universal.
62. Anonymous, 'Having AIDS and being loved', in the ACT UP NY Women & AIDS Book Group, *op. cit.*, p. 157.
63. Privileged communication.
64. Bea, quoted in R. Gorna, 'Sticky moments: do we need latex sex?', *Diva*, issue 3, pp. 10–14.
65. This is discussed in Chapter 9.
66. This is documented in James, *op. cit.* Some latex lesbianism suggests using these swabs to detect whether skin on the hand is broken. If they cause a stinging sensation then (they claim) gloves or finger cots should be used.
67. See, for example, Nancy Solomon's excellent article 'Risky business. Should lesbians practice safer sex?' in *OUT/LOOK*, Spring 1992.
68. This should be an obvious approach, yet a glance through reading lists presented by latex lesbians usually reveals that they have 'forgotten' to include any of the articles proposing that dams are unnecessary.
69. Watney, *Outlines*.

Epilogue

Fight Back

A feminist approach to AIDS is long overdue. AIDS activists and feminists need to join together to articulate an agenda which places women and our diverse needs at the centre of the way this crisis is imagined and fought. This should be articulated for women who are living with HIV, for women profoundly affected by AIDS and for all the women who are vulnerable to infection, and whose (sex) lives are affected by the epidemic. The existing generic research can be used to extract what is useful for women, and it is essential that women identify the areas where research has not been developed, or where protocols and analyses should be adjusted to answer women's questions. Awareness must be intensified into the ways in which women are misused in policies which purport to be in our name – how can we shift the emphasis to bring these back into line with women's real needs? An effective feminist agenda will forge alliances and stand in solidarity with other communities who are affected and devastated by AIDS, discovering the common ground and the battles which can be waged together. As feminist thinking about AIDS deepens, and as the impact of the AIDS crisis on women achieves greater visibility, so too should the feminist agenda mature and develop. What follows are some of the initial steps women can take to fight AIDS:

- *Misrepresentation*
- Resist notions of heterosexual AIDS – explain why they are facile, politically motivated, and obscure the unequal impacts of AIDS on women.
- Reject the promotion of monogamy as an HIV-prevention

strategy. It is a simplistic and dangerous strategy which ignores the fact that women cannot control the most crucial component: the monogamous behaviour of their male partners.

- Fight homophobia and biphobia – hatreds and prejudices which fuel the AIDS crisis and enhance women's vulnerabilities to infection, by concealing the diversity of desire and sexual experience.

- Prevent commentators from pitting women against gay men, in an AIDS competition for attention and resources.

- Refuse the normalization of AIDS – promote the concept of AIDS as a queer disease which affects others.

- Avoid notions of heterosexuality which define the 'normal' – question the use of 'heterosexual' as an adjective. Is it a descriptor? Does it define something more clearly? Does it obscure gender differences?

- Reject simplistic messages about HIV as an equal opportunities virus – explain how generic equal opportunity policies are inappropriate and harmful to understanding the inequities and marginalization of AIDS.

- Confront facile messages about a generalized spread of HIV – reorient discussion to where the epidemic is. Explain that infectious diseases cluster in core groups, and then spread beyond, through adjacent groups.

- Struggle for the realities of women's lives to emerge in popular representations of women and AIDS – avoid women's lives slipping into symbols and AIDS exceptionalism.

- Demonstrate how HIV in women matters because of the effect it has on the woman, not merely on her potential for child-bearing.

- Resist the infantilization of women, which strips them of their adulthood, sexuality and integrity.

- Reject fantasies of the evil rampant whore gleefully spreading HIV with psychopathic revenge sex. Don't allow men's fear of the *vagina dentata* to transform a woman living with a life-threatening disease into a monster.

- Question stories of HIV-positive virgins – what exactly are they afraid of? are they protecting their mothers?

- Resist the use of HIV-positive women to make the issue of AIDS safe.

- Confront popular perceptions which assume that bisexual men never reveal their sexuality to their women partners – encourage a sophisticated understanding of the spectrum of human desire.

- *Data*

- Query statistics: how were they gathered? Were the right questions asked in the right way?
- When statistics are promoted, question the agendas that are being pushed. Do they present information that is relevant to real-life concerns?
- When someone presents a statistic based on the rates of increasing infection, or the proportions of cases of AIDS or HIV, always ask for the absolute number of reports.
- Ask what is known about the lives and needs of the women reported as HIV-positive or living with AIDS: does anyone know how they were infected? What are their ethnic or national origins? What are their sexual orientations?
- Ask what is known about the lives of the men reported as HIV-positive or living with AIDS, in particular their sexual lifestyles. How many of the men infected by sex between men also have sex with women? Do they identify as gay, bisexual, heterosexual, nothing?
- Demand more attention for women who terminate pregnancies – why is all the focus on pregnant women who give birth, when those who terminate have higher rates of infection?
- Demand information about the natural history of HIV disease in women. Does the virus have an impact on the endocrine system, on gynaecological conditions, on the menstrual cycle, and on pregnancy? Is the pattern of opportunistic infections and cancers different from HIV disease in men? Why?
- Do HIV-positive women have different life expectancies from men? Are the reasons biological, social, or economic?
- Do women get diagnosed with AIDS earlier or later than most men? Why? What impact does this have on their survival?
- Don't let an American agenda be foisted unquestioningly on the UK. Check whether it serves the real needs of British women.

- *Treatment*

- Review the treatments HIV-positive women get: are they under-treated? over-treated? How do women get pertinent information about their treatment options?
- Insist that HIV-positive women receive complete health care. Do all clinics offer a full gynaecological service? Are pelvic examinations a regular feature of monitoring?
- Demand government guidance on standards for cervical screening and monitoring of HIV-positive women. Educate GUM doctors, GPs and other primary care providers about HIV in women – what symptoms should they watch out for?
- Ensure that effective treatments for gynaecological conditions, especially invasive cervical cancers, are developed as a matter of urgency.
- Resist unnecessarily invasive screening for HIV-positive women – encourage research which will predict genital cancer disease progression.
- Demand that all new clinical trials monitor the gynaecological implications of their new compounds, as well as the haemotological ones. Ensure the methodologies are adequate to the task.
- Request gender breakdowns of all clinical trial results. Does efficacy vary by gender? Demand that data on pharmacokinetics, safety and tolerability are also gender analysed.
- Demand that new compounds are evaluated for interactions with other medications, including hormonal therapies (the oral contraceptive pill, hormone replacement therapy, etc.).
- Intensify research into the complementary therapies and 'natural' remedies which women are using.
- Promote screening and treatment for sexually transmitted diseases to all women (and men). Raise awareness about the silent nature of many STDs in women.

- *Empowerment*

- Fight discrimination and stigmatization of women living with HIV and AIDS, and campaign for full human rights. Smash through the invisibility, and break down the isolation of HIV-positive women.

- Reject descriptions of HIV-positive women which trivialize or victimize; promote the empowerment of women living with HIV and AIDS.
- Resist all attempts to 'encourage' women to take HIV tests, unless it is clearly for their personal health benefit. Campaign against any service that coerces women, tests them without fully informed consent, or avoids post-test support.
- Demand thorough research to understand the complexity of HIV-positive women's psychosocial needs, not only in respect of reproductive rights, but also sexual fulfilment, empowerment and social and practical needs.
- Encourage HIV-positive women – and the female lovers of HIV-positive men – to live powerful, sexual lives, and generate initiatives and information to support them.
- Create opportunities to hear the realities of women who love and care for people with HIV. Research their needs, and the long-term impact on them.
- Resist the de-sexing of carers – ensure that women are constantly educated about their sexual vulnerabilities to HIV.
- Devise ways to support women suffering from multiple grief, and for women who do not belong to a community which affirms their caring role.
- Reduce homophobia amongst straight men, and find ways to share the load of care for gay men.
- Confront gay men's misogyny. Support women working in the firing line of their prejudices.
- Record the histories of the invisible women who strive to end the AIDS crisis.

- ## Risk

- Demand proper gender analyses in any research describing the 'heterosexual transmission' of HIV.
- Emphasize the differences of the giver-receiver relationship, and fight simple messages of body fluids 'mingling'.
- Require more sophisticated research into the real HIV risks faced by women. Are there times when women can safely have un-protected sex with HIV-infected men (for example, to conceive)?

- What are the real risks from fellatio? How sophisticated are the sexual histories behind case-studies of infection by this route?
- Re-establish discordant couple cohorts to monitor the effectiveness of protected penetrative sex and whether other activities transmit HIV.
- Demand biological attention is paid to the question of whether HIV infects the cervix or the vagina.
- Demand biological attention is paid to the question of whether HIV is found in the seminal fluid or the spermatozoa, or both.
- Fight the invisibility of anal sex as a pleasurable activity for women. How risky is it? For women? For men? Educate women about the risks, and how to avoid them.
- Research the variability of infectivity of HIV in women. What are the links with the menstrual cycle? What are the real-life implications of this information? How significant is the acidity/alkalinity of vaginal fluids? How much more infectious are menstrual fluids?
- Overturn taboos about sex during menstruation. Resist attempts to use any HIV risks to detract from women's sexual pleasure.
- Fight the simplicity of public messages explaining women's lower infectivity and encouraging men to abandon their responsibilities.
- Fight the simplicity of public messages which heighten HIV-positive women's fear about their sexual infectivity.
- *Are* there any risks from cunnilingus?
- What are the real risks from sharing sex toys?
- Insist that sexual history taking becomes more sophisticated.
- Require research attention to focus as fully on sexual risks of transmission as on the risks maternity poses to babies.
- How does HIV infect men in anal or vaginal sex?
- Demand proper training and the protection of effective guidelines for women healthcare workers. Ensure that occupational risks of HIV are prevented.

- *Maternity*

- Demand unlinked anonymous serosurveillance of women in settings beyond the antenatal sector. Explore opportunities for greater HIV advice (and perhaps testing) in other sites.
- Demand honest information about the rationale for testing at antenatal clinics and appropriate support for women who test HIV-positive; question why these policies are in place and who stands to gain from the test results.
- Ensure that ethical research methodologies underpin any new studies on transmission from women to babies. Ask whether planned research is to meet women's needs, or scientific needs for ever more precise statistics.
- Demand that any trials of compounds to reduce transmission to babies are assessed for their impacts upon the woman's health and quality of life, as well as the immediate and long-term effects on the child. Question whether there are equally effective, cheaper, simpler and less toxic ways to achieve the same results.
- Demand that viral load testing is made available for HIV-positive women to plan when to conceive most safely.
- Intensify research into how uninfected women can safely conceive from an HIV-infected man.
- Challenge attempts to impose Caesarean sections on HIV-positive women. Ask about the adverse events associated with these interventions.
- Analyse carefully the balance of information for HIV-infected women who want a child. What is prioritized? The most effective approaches, or those with the highest degree of medical intervention?
- Ensure balanced information about breast-feeding to promote it as a generally healthy activity, while being realistic about the significant risks for the infants of HIV-infected women.

- *Sexuality*

- Promote the wide diversity of women's sexual desire. Reject attempts to swamp this with talk of the sexual violence against women. Reject attempts to silence the realities of the sexual terror many women experience.

- Campaign for women's economic equality with men, and resist all forms of sexism which undermine women's fundamental human rights.
- Decriminalize prostitution and all forms of consensual sex. Support women working in the sex industries, and let their agendas lead the responses. Condemn patronizing responses to prostitutes' rights and needs.
- Shift blame away from women prostitutes, and make visible the role of men in commercial sexual exchange. Develop initiatives to educate punters about their health, and the health of the women and men they have sex with.
- Reject simplistic campaigns against pornography which silence women's sexuality and erotic enjoyment, and which threaten the promotion of safer-sex material. Question the linear linking of fantasy and reality.
- Support women promoting women's sexual pleasure through erotica and sex shops, and encourage them to integrate safer sex in their work.
- Fight for proper recognition of coercive sex, abuse and rape, support for women who experience this, and legal recourse. Make visible the links with HIV, and women's lack of power to protect themselves.
- Resist the trivialization of date rape and marital rape. Emphasize the importance of equalizing power dynamics in sex between men and women.
- Develop sophisticated messages which explore the scope of sexual desire, which recognize that sex is frequently irrational, and which promote safer sex.

- *Prevention*

- As a matter of urgency, test the diaphragm as an HIV-prevention mechanism.
- Accelerate the research priority to develop and trial a range of microbicides to offer women independent control over their sexual health.

- Question simplistic rejections of Nonoxynol-9, and demand that researchers answer the basic questions about its current potential to protect women. Provide women with accurate information to make their own choices.
- Promote the delights of female condoms as well as their problems! Campaign for the development of a wide range of protection mechanisms (e.g. polyurethane condoms), and ensure they are tested for anal sex as well as vaginal sex.
- Question the single-minded fascination with condoms as the sole answer to HIV transmission. Remind people that women don't wear them. Emphasize the importance of using lubricants.
- Promote the hierarchical method of prevention, to enable women to make their own choices about the most feasible methods for their personal situations.
- Promote the pleasures of outercourse – without trivializing the pleasure many women derive from intercourse.
- Resist appeals for coercive public-health messages which restrict individual human rights and liberties, and are not effective ways of preventing diseases.
- Promote the development of a broad range of community-based, peer-led, health promotion initiatives, to educate and support women in avoiding HIV. Reject simplistic approaches which lump all women together.
- Ensure that information about HIV clearly differentiates between the risks of different activities, to empower women to make informed choices.
- Empower women in all domains of their lives, to make sexual decision-making possible in the context of their whole lives.
- Demand effective sex education for girls, and resist the pressures of the Right to determine what they are allowed to learn about such a fundamental element of their lives.
- Promote women's self-esteem and skills to avoid infection, and ensure the representation of a diverse range of women in educational initiatives.

- *Queer women*

- Honour the work of all women involved in the fight against AIDS, and the long history of lesbians' and bisexual women's work.
- Reject latex lesbianism, which denies lesbians a positive appreciation of their sexuality, and promotes the message that HIV is far more infectious than it is, causing confusion and distress.
- Refuse cynical attempts to exploit lesbians and bisexual women financially by promoting unnecessary 'safer-sex accessories'.
- Emphasize the risks lesbians and bisexual women face, especially in having sex with gay and bisexual men. Develop targeted education to meet these needs, and resist the displacement from these real risks onto the theoretical risks of (for instance) fingering.
- Ensure that lesbian messages are understood in a full context of the impact of HIV on women. Support lesbians and bisexual women in relishing the safety of sex between women.
- Resist biphobia – it endangers lesbians' and bisexual women's lives, by silencing the complexity of desire. Remind people that identity doesn't always equal behaviour.
- Reject the facile linking of lesbians with gay men. Support lesbians in having their own priorities recognized, and not being subsumed in the HIV agenda of gay and bisexual men.

- *Remember . . .*

- Support all women living with HIV and AIDS.
- Stay safe!

Whatever you can do, or believe you can do, begin it. Boldness has genius and power and magic in it. Begin it now!

ACT UP – Fight Back – Fight AIDS

Index